*'til the river
runs dry*

JFA Press

Minneapolis • Galena • Riga

*'til the river
runs dry*

'Til the River Runs Dry
Copyright © 2013 by John Freivalds
All rights reserved. No part of this book may be reproduced
by any means without prior written permission, except for the
inclusion of a brief quotation in a review.
For information address
JFA, Inc. International Communications,
3640 Black Oaks Lane,
Minneapolis, Minnesota 55446

ISBN: 978-0-615-72410-2

Manufactured in the United States of America

To the Mogush clan for giving
Margo the values and love to keep her going

To my daughters who have given
me much love and have watched
my back as I learn to stand on my own

Prologue

*A*s I sit and write this book I have always felt Margo's presence. And as I came to terms with the "absence of her presence," I had to deal with the neediness I experienced. Someone had always been with me—my family, my first wife, then Margo. So now I have this void. However, I am dealing with it the best way I can. I have made many mistakes and probably hurt a lot of people. But there are no rules for grief and what follows.

It was pure joy to write of Margo's life adventures and to now be an evangelist for people going out and exploring what the world has to offer.

I have a different belief system now than when I first met Margo and I am less judgmental than I used to be. And although I am making and will make new relationships, there will always be that empty feeling of loss. Not morbid or obsessive but more like what a famous public figure once said after talking about the loss of his wife. "Trust me. There will come a day when your memory of what you lost will bring a smile to your face and not a tear to your eye."

Contents

Part I

culebra: no straitjacket for margo	9
why write?	14
muddling through	25
the slow boat to china	37
innocence abroad (but was she?)	48
aquatic australia september 1986	76
annie's soapy massage and the bus ride from hell	85
来自中国的慢船来于抵达了 translation: the slow boat to china has arrived (finally!)	117

Part II

dream job	133
take a chance on me (and my considerable baggage)	157
almost heaven	187
bad assed rocks and cliffs / people / events	202

Part III

the blessed mess	224
the hip parade	264
mississippi and the mayo	288
2008 was great and 2009 was just fine	301
dislocation nation	329
labyrinth	337
end of the line	347
Epilogue	352
Many Thanks	355
Appendix: The Legend of Thelma and Louise	358

1

culebra: no straitjacket for margo

Travel changes, challenges and stretches us. We discover that we are more than we thought; we can do more than we imagined... As we travel, we reclaim our sense of self and strength. Travel takes us to the core of ourselves and changes us.

– Mary Beth Bond, *Gutsy Women*

*M*argo looked back at me with a devilish smile, one I had never seen before. We were kayaking across the treacherous windswept mile-wide strait between the Puerto Rican island of Culebra and Luis Peña, a cay adjoining it. The tide was bringing more water and winds through the straits and we had to paddle vigorously to keep moving in a straight line. The sun was hot and the glare of the water intense and beautiful. The water was very warm and quite choppy, and, stupidly, we didn't even have life vests. For a while, huge sea turtles swam alongside my kayak.

Although this was five years after we had gotten married, it was actually the first time I had experienced firsthand the sense of danger and adventure that Margo enjoyed. I now had a much better understanding of how she had taken her Asian adventures, many years earlier, in such stride.

Margo's long legs barely fit into the kayak and her six-foot frame gave her plenty of leverage to keep her kayak moving. She was wearing a two-piece bathing suit and though not buxom, she was all woman. Her arms were toned and tanned and her blue eyes matched the blue of the current.

She had salt-and-pepper hair in a "puffy hairstyle" and a thirty-six-inch inseam. She was always a size twelve.

She had an irrational relationship with danger. One friend of mine said she was "intellectually reckless" while another put it this way: "I don't know about intellectually reckless. I think she did have a real spirit of adventure which might have left her reacting rather than thinking things out if there was some excitement to be had."

Margo and I belonged to an elite group which writer Daniel Kalder calls anti-tourists. He defines us thusly: "The anti-tourist seeks out the lost zones of our planet, eschewing comfort, embracing hunger and hallucinations and always traveling the wrong time of year…they love these places because no one else does because everyone passes them by."

When Margo was twenty-seven years old, she wrote that she didn't need a Hilton Hotel to go traveling. *I'm quite relaxed in woods—working hard, getting and being dirty, bugs, cold weather, rain don't really bother me—feel at home and quite secure.* Her anti-tourist sentiment would last her lifetime.

In her kayak, Margo was paddling faster than I. The muscles in my arms were burning but I dared not ease up, as the current would have carried me out into the Atlantic.

"Come on you can do it!" Margo implored me, and I did.

When we finally reached Culebra after an arduous hour of paddling, my muscles were burning and my arms hung like limp noodles from my shoulders. I don't think I could've lifted a fork, but I was able to down more than a few beers at a beach bar. As the two of us looked out over the strait, we happily talked about the day's adventures. Margo looked ever so contented with my accomplishment. She would cherish that memory, and whenever she thought I was weakening in some future physical endeavor, she would say, *"You conquered Culebra; you can do this."*

Culebra, while in the nearby Caribbean, nonetheless had all the elements of adventure that Margo held dear: a little-known, out-of-the-way island; no easy way to get there; do-it-yourself activities, and funky people all about. We ended up going to Culebra three times over a ten-year period; the real-life sharing of an adventurous place with her made it easier for me to understand what had gone on in Asia when, at the age of forty-two, she had "dropped out" to explore ten countries in a single year.

Although her solo Asian trip lasted many months, Margo never wanted to go back to Thailand or any other place she visited on that trip, except for New Zealand. Because we didn't have time to go to the

South Pacific that 1998 winter, we wanted something closer to home. She and I had been to many of the tamed islands in the Caribbean, and she wondered whether there were any rugged places left. She found Culebra just as she had found Ko Samui in Thailand in 1986: a place that hadn't been "discovered" yet.

Culebra is a twelve-square-mile island seventeen miles east of the Puerto Rican mainland. It and a companion island, Vieques, are together known as the Spanish Virgin Islands. During and after World War II, the U.S. Navy used part of Vieques for target practice and weapons tests until the locals protested and in 1971 forced the Navy off the island. But unexploded ordnance still dots the island, and cleared hiking trails run through bomb fields—signs warn one not to wander off the trail. Probably for this reason, Vieques has been spared the ravages of volcanic tourism that have engulfed Ko Samui in Thailand and other beautiful places around the globe.

When we went on one of our many hikes through the island Margo exclaimed, *"I love it!"*

The islands are semiarid and water must be brought in, as it rarely rains except when a hurricane hits the island or brushes by in the fall. There is grass, but all the pastures have been overrun by sharp-needled acacia trees. There are some horses and goats but no crops of any kind, not even the coconuts that flourished in Ko Samui. There are no fishermen and the tropical fish are merely to look at. Huge sea turtles—some as large as Volkswagens—can be seen from the shore.

A grand total of some six-hundred people live on the island: locals who serve the tourist trade and work at a government-subsidized pharmaceutical plant, and all kinds of funky, sun-bleached, beachcomber dropouts of the type that Margo found so intriguing in Asia.

One blogger wrote, "The residents can be divided into four groups: intellectual Americans who dropped out of the rat race and set up tourist businesses (night-time walks to look at sea turtles, glass-bottom reef boats); they run restaurants with names like Mamacita's and Dinghy Dock; dropouts, spaced-out losers from the U.S. who are high ALL THE TIME; waiters and waitresses who come to work for a couple of years, and the local Puerto Ricans."

There are no golf courses, tennis courts, water parks, crocodile farms or wax museums, but there are beautiful beaches and coral reefs—our kind of place.

Of course, there was a small artists' colony and Margo became good friends with Dana Moses. Dana was living on Culebra when it was devastated by Hurricane Hugo. In the aftermath, pieces of roofing tin were everywhere. Dana started to create art from pieces of tin. Her website says: "Dana Moses Tin Fish Art; whimsical art fashioned from recycled tin." So when people ask Dana what medium she works in she doesn't say watercolors or pencil or paint, but rather "tin" that she shapes with a blowtorch and then paints. (I now have Dana's work throughout my house.) Dana was Margo's type of person—the nonlinear type whom she actively sought out in her earlier travels.

Culebra was a quintessential third world environment. The airline that was supposed to fly us to Culebra for our first visit had its FAA certification pulled two weeks before we got there. But of course, nobody told us, so when we transferred to Isla Grande Airport from San Juan International Airport, there was no connecting flight to Culebra. I called the innkeeper at Tamarindo Estates where we would be staying and told him of our plight. A fellow standing nearby overheard my end of the conversation and said, "I deliver mail and merchandise to Culebra—I'll take you. You'll be the only passengers." We negotiated a fare.

So there we were, surrounded by bunches of burlap sacks heading to Culebra, which was less than thirty minutes away, and we had hitchhiked a ride on a small plane. She loved it! Suddenly, Margo saw one of the sacks move, then another. The pilot looked back and saw us fidgeting. "Don't worry," he said, "those are just roosters." Not only were we on the mail run, we were also on the rooster run. Turns out there were five fighting cocks in those big bags. They were on their way to Vieques, the larger island next to Culebra.

But the fun was just beginning, for the tiny plane had to land on a minuscule runway nestled between two cliffs. A blogger writing for mercifulgrace.com put it this way: "The descent was the landing. Straight through two cliffs—straight down to the runway. It was one of those moments that seemed to last forever—where you actually do think about those end-of-life things ... your will, your children, whether you really believe 'Once saved always saved'."

Margo was in traveler's heaven. I must admit, this was certainly different than flying Delta to Kansas City.

We rented a small jeep and then had to travel four miles over a very bumpy dirt road to get to our lodgings. The owner of the Tamarindo didn't want to pave it because that would have made it too easy for robbers to get in. (Turns out robbers don't like to walk much.)

When we finally got to the Tamarindo, we thought the same as Margo had thought at Lucky Mother's years earlier in Ko Samui, Thailand: *"We'll get a better place in the morning."* We both agreed that Tamarindo was a good place to start our adventure.

The next days were lots of fun as we hit all the beaches, swam and snorkeled. And in the evening drank rum. It didn't rain half the time as it had for Margo in Ko Samui. Flamenco Beach was the prettiest; it gently curved around the shoreline. At one end was the rusting hulk of a tank the Navy had used for target practice. Margo had on a smashing yellow bikini, and though she had gained a few pounds, she still looked great. The sun was blazing hot, but the tank created a nice cool shadow on the ocean side. Margo saw this before I did. She yanked my hand, pulled me behind the rusted-out tank and we made love on the cool, shaded sand.

You don't get to do this on Miami Beach, not in broad daylight anyway.

The next day we did our kayak paddling to Luis Peña accompanied by Margo's devilish smile. The same smile everyone she met on her earlier Asian adventures remembered.

2

why write?

Steamer chest: A large cuboid container for holding clothes and other personal belongings typically around four feet wide and two feet deep. Used for extended periods away from home.

– Universal College Dictionary

*P*eople ask why I am writing this memoir about Margo Mogush Freivalds (1944-2010), my wife of many years. The chief reason is her battered brown steamer chest that accompanied her throughout her life. If not for the contents of that trunk—filled to the brim with marvelous stuff written in her beautiful cursive hand—I wouldn't have had an insight into her soul, nor a clue about all the things she had done before we first met on April 22, 1988. And I had a feeling that these diaries had much more to tell me about Margo. But what could those things be?

My editor asked me other questions:

- Are you writing it as catharsis?
- Are you writing it to help other bereaved people?
- Are you writing it as therapy?
- Are you writing it for Margo's family and friends?
- Are you writing to inspire people?

Yes to the first and the last questions. I am a writer and now I have the time and the resources to write about things that are dear to me. The other book project I was working on had to do with a boring, fabulously wealthy Texas cattleman who sued Oprah Winfrey over disparaging remarks she made about beef. Margo hated that book and what it was doing to me; she disliked the man who didn't want her in his ninety-two-foot yacht because she was wearing a hip brace.

But Sweetie, did you have to die at the age of sixty-five (the new forty) to have me quit that book?

This battered steamer trunk and its contents are my most cherished mementos of Margo, whom I knew for twenty-four years and who was my wife for nineteen of those years. If Margo had not filled her trunk with two-hundred-page diaries (twenty-seven of them), as well as hundreds of postcards and letters, never-before-seen-by-me photos, assorted memorabilia and countless scraps of paper covered with fine, readable jottings, this book would not have been written. It took me a couple of months to organize and lovingly catalog the items. In fact, Lory Strom, my secretary and confidante of many years, and I continue the process, and stuff is still flowing in the door.

All that writing done during Margo's remarkable Asian trip (1986-7) helped her later.

> *Whenever I sit down to write I experience a feeling of foreboding and gloom and dreariness. It comes from dissatisfaction with my writing skills both in terms of verb usage and grammar. It's a huge effort for me to write anything but letters and even then I sometimes have trouble. During my year in Asia I wrote regularly in my journal and heaps and heaps of letters and postcards. My goal is to keep that up; improve on my business writing skills; and take a try at a book on my travels. I want to enjoy writing.*

As I organized this mass of "content," as it's now known, her spirit seemed to waft out of the trunk and ask me to tell her story. So actually, Margo is, in effect, the coauthor of this book.

For most people who knew and even loved tall, angular, sensuous if not nonlinear Margo, the interest in her life ended with the eulogies offered at the celebration of her spirit in September of 2010. Those people found the closure they needed and then moved on with their lives. I have moved on as well, but when I started going through the contents of Margo's trunk, a whole new relationship with her began for me—a relationship with her spirit, or what some might call her essence and others might call her soul.

Several things stand out about Margo:

- At age forty-two, trying to be forever young, seeing Asia from the ground up on her own, either unconcerned with or oblivious of how it might, could or would impact her business career.

- Returning from Asia to secure her dream job, dream husband and dream house on top of a mountain on the rim of the Shenandoah Valley of Virginia—all because of her travels to Asia.
- Developing compensating mechanisms to deal with her medical problems that led to many, many surgeries and giving up a lot of dreams.

Although I had moved the steamer trunk many times (it still carries Mayflower tag #159 from our last move), I had never looked inside. It's not that Margo forbade me; we were just too busy living our life to its fullest to spend time reminiscing. So when people tell me, "I'm sorry you lost your wife," it's difficult for them to grasp when I respond, "I really just *found* her."

Although Margo had told me of her Midwest childhood and her disappointing first marriage, I knew very little about her graduate studies and the convoluted business career she'd had before we met, or about the many fruitless and exploitative personal relationships she'd been victimized by. A subchapter—"Looking for Love in All the Wrong Places"—covers that period in her life.

I knew next to nothing about the details of her Asia trip where this story really begins. In 1986 she decided to drop out of the corporate rat race and see Asia on her own. I have tried to contact people she met on her trip, but since it was twenty-five years ago, apart from David Cranna in Australia and Gray Packer in New Zealand, those people just didn't want to talk; they either hung up on me or were too "busy" to reminisce. One even said I shouldn't write the book because Margo's thoughts were private and they didn't want anyone to change the image of Margo they had in their minds.

What was she thinking—going off with a backpack and climbing the Fox Glacier, windsurfing for the first time in the Whitsundays, snorkeling the Great Barrier Reef, climbing and camping throughout Australia, experiencing every sort of pleasure in Bangkok and Ko Samui, taking nine-hour rural bus rides through the scorching heat and unimaginable filth of India and then organizing a seven-day mountain trek through Nepal—not to mention the calmer activities in Hong Kong and China? One perceptive woman in Australia asked Margo, "What are you running from?"

During Margo's travels, she wrote:

I have been struck multiple times by how my spirit surges as I'm traveling. I generally feel higher than a kite when I'm on the go, be it roaming a city, traveling on a train or bus, hiking the countryside, but on entering a new overnight spot and on the arrival of the evening I swing into a slump of blahs, feeling out of sorts and alone. What's important I guess is to know when it happens probably because it's an unknown situation for the new town because p.m.'s are quiet with little happening. So I'm really just with myself and dependent upon myself at that point.

As she pushed on, she noticed big changes in her mental state.

I trust me more than ever... respect me—know that I can make friends and survive anywhere—I'm strong, brave, independent and OK with me alone but know friends and family are important.

Not surprisingly, this followed:

I've spent a fair amount of time thinking about relationships—I'm feeling strongly that I do want an ongoing one. There are always men around if you want them, for temporary liaisons, but there is something definitely missing when that's all there is. I'd like a lovable man to come home to, to cuddle, to love and love me on an ongoing basis. That will be a goal when I return to the States.

In that year she wrote down everything she did—which made me wonder how she had time to see and do all this stuff. She listed every postcard and letter she sent to everyone and on what date; she later recorded how many cards and letters were sent to each person. She was constantly buying presents and she noted what she bought, how much she paid and who received them. She assiduously itemized every penny she spent every day on this year-long trip. Amazing— the mental discipline that took. She listed everything she saw, every person she met, particularly the men with whom she had short-term "liaisons." I particularly enjoyed the dichotomy between what she wrote to friends and family in contrast to what she wrote in her diaries.

People knew Margo through the many things she listed. Her steamer trunk was full of lists on scraps of paper. On one of those scraps, she recorded what she liked most about herself:

- *My height*
- *My laugh*
- *My smile—when it's genuine*
- *My acceptance of people*
- *My friendliness towards people and animals*
- *My joie de vivre*
- *My willingness to take personal risks*
- *My friends and willingness to work with them*
- *My sense of adventure*
- *My willingness to work on personal growth*
- *My interest in a wide range of things*
- *My ability to take care of myself*
- *My increasing ability to reach out for help from friends*
- *My sense of taste and style*

Careful: Fragile

These are the attributes she took with her to Asia. Although Margo did write down some of her many accomplishments on those scraps of paper—for example, Young Dietitian of the Year (1974) in Minnesota—she had no ego and was happy to have her two diplomas, one from the University of Minnesota and the other (her master's) from Emory, stuck away in a corner closet.

I am the opposite; my walls are lined with diplomas, book covers, awards, and the like.

Margo indulged me in my ego wall—actually walls—extending along both sides of a hallway leading towards my office. It was fine with her as long as all that stuff wasn't visible to anyone standing in the middle of the other room.

She wrote down her life's accomplishments, as well as things I did, in one of her many notebooks and diaries. Her first impression of me, documented (April 24, 1988) a couple of days after our first meeting, was: *"He's egotistical but also seemingly somewhat sensitive and caring. Last night, our first 'date,' he said he was smitten with me because I was so nice, honest, fun, sensible and had good moral judgment."*

Also deposited in that steamer trunk were armloads of medical records from her eighteen major surgeries (2000-2010), as well as many reports from psychiatrists. Margo was sometimes clinically depressed, and while she outwardly and genuinely exhibited all those things she liked about herself, there was a darker, more insecure side she didn't let anybody—including me—see. One psychiatrist who examined her wrote:

"History of Present Illness
Patient is a married woman referred for an on-call evaluation of depression. She has basically had a low-level depression all her life and she has always had some problems with concentration and feeling disorganized...Her mood is blah, detached, anxious and apathetic. She was recently in Caribbean but she really couldn't enjoy herself very much and her interests and enjoyment in general are overwhelmed."

So the smiling mask of Margo one often saw was as thin and fragile as an eggshell. And, Mamma Mia, did we buy drugs—not only for her depression but for the many medical issues brought on by her surgeries. In 2009 at the neighborhood Walgreens in Dubuque, Iowa, we were the largest single customer for prescription drugs.

All this did affect Margo's mental state but not her outward attitudes, particularly toward me. She figured I had enough to do as her caregiver so she rarely let me know what was going on in her brain. To our benefit, the University of Virginia New Psychology Assessment Laboratory told her that to further reinforce and remember "the benefits of a cognitive behavioral strategy," she should maintain a written journal to document each day's mood, personal difficulties and the outcome of her "redirective activities." These journals all made their way into that huge steamer trunk, and provided unique glimpses into her thoughts and reflections.

But we all should be as fragile as Margo was: taking the risks that she did and, in spite of all the medical issues, developing compensating mechanisms to deal with those issues. The hardest part of my research effort was to read through pages and pages she had written about things that had upset her, as I dealt with the recurring wish to have her materialize and hear me say, "I didn't know where you were coming from."

One of the opening chapters of this book, "Muddling Through," briefly describes Margo's upbringing in Hopkins, Minnesota, a suburb of Minneapolis. Hopkins is home to the annual Raspberry Festival and is well known for having a "genuine" main street. In short, it's the Midwest.

Maybe Margo, a professional dietitian in corporate America, wasn't cut out for the high-level, back-biting corporate world. Maybe that world was in some way incongruous with her Midwest upbringing. After all, she did take off on a ten-country Asian jaunt for a whole year. Before the trip, she had been in a total muddle on what to do with the men in her life and her business career: should she stay a professional in the corporate dietetics field, or start or buy a business? In the steamer trunk were reams of scraps of paper containing addresses and phone numbers for franchises and stores that sold music, art, books, bread, balloons, bathroom accessories, a hat/belt accessory shop, bicycles, catering services, cheese, lingerie, exercise equipment, kitchenware, and gourmet items.

Margo's mother was a woman of her era who would dress herself, Margo and Margo's brother for dinner each day, in anticipation of the arrival of the head of the household, who worked at Cargill, the world's largest agribusiness firm, as a commodities trader. Margo's father was never able to understand her crazy-quilt business career—or mine for that matter—as we both muddled through various jobs. She had a love/hate relationship with her father, whom she blamed—unfairly, I think—for her lack of self-worth. (My own father was a "cold fish" and an alcoholic to boot.)

As part of Margo's therapy, she was directed to write—but not mail—letters spelling out her frustrations. Here is an excerpt from one such unmailed letter to her dad:

All you gave me is the belief I should be something other than what I am and a lot of pain over what I think in my head could be but no knowledge or confidence to make myself right. I'm so tired of feeling all the sadness and blah feelings I have to contend with—shit. Why didn't you help me take what I had and feel good about that to build on my abilities and talents; I learned no systems approaches from you.

Margo foresaw many years ago the changes in American lifestyles—the old paradigms of marriage: get a house with a thirty-year mortgage, be a lifetime employee someplace and get a pension, send kids to college, then spend your Golden Years (what the heck are those?) in Florida, and travel on a package tour to Cancun. Instead, Margo's idea was to do it now: follow your dreams, exert yourself and go the limit while your knees and hips work, and do it on your own terms.

Regardless of how she got tossed around by life, she was always kind—even though some people didn't deserve it. I was surprised to discover my own obituary in that trunk, written by Margo as our relationship started out on rocky terms. But as the old song by Gene Pitney says, "True love never runs smooth."

Men were responsible for much of Margo's muddle before she went off to Asia. Combine her lack of self-worth, the raging hormones of her late twenties and thirties, and a couple of unscrupulous men, and you have someone who was ready for a major change of pace. She got tired of "looking for love in all the wrong places" as the Waylon Jennings song goes.

While it took me some time to organize the trunk's contents, Margo did us a favor by writing a fifteen-page, single-spaced autobiography titled simply My Life. Full of such exciting events as getting her tonsils out, her biography describes in great detail working for a start-up medical company where she did well, even though it eventually folded:

> ...For two years I handled crisis after crisis...and managed to help the sales group hold on to our initial business in spite of horrible product failures and having to call some customers numerous times to apologize for the latest one. It was one of my strongest emotional times. Our sales and marketing team drank a lot those years but never out of control. I went out a lot but I never found anyone with whom I had a real relationship.

Clearing Her Head

Looking at a failing company, no lasting male relationship, and a stoic family, she decided to clear her head and travel to Asia:

> My decision to quit was made after I was brought to the realization that I was in a position that I could travel for a year.
>
> So I bought a 'round the pacific' airline ticket. I traveled alone for that year to the Pacific Rim, India, Nepal and China. I met many wonderful people, walked, swam, drank, saw lots and loved every moment of it. Every now and then I would get really lonely—mostly when I had been on the go for a period of time. I would then realize it was time for a day of laundry, reading, writing and going/doing nothing. It was thrilling to stop at American Express in the big cities to find mail from friends and family. Always made me cry. I was a rarity in the travel world at the time being a forty-two-year-old woman traveling alone for such a long time. Everyone else was in their twenties so I got to be young."

21

She wanted to escape too because of thoughts like these:

September 16, 1988 I'm feeling reflective… anxious to try to capture my feelings to try and make sense of them as I feel I'm right on the edge of figuring out what my life is to be.

May 21, 1978 My past putdowns of myself have become an extremely comfortable place for me to be in all these years. It's an easy out for a lot of things—relationships, work. If I'd focus all that negative energy to positive tasks, I'd be a different person.

And then this…

December 8, 1985 What's going on with me? I'm letting others direct my life—letting it float.

She realized during her graduate studies at Emory University that she functioned best when she had focus. And her trip to Asia gave her such a focus and led to a more focused life:

Am feeling like withdrawing from society. When I'm with people I don't feel like I really want to be there. Just want to be by myself—nobody can keep me with them. I feel the men are only interested in their own pleasures and not mine. I can't give as much as I used to in a lovemaking scene.

What I Learned From Her

Margo is gone. And oh, does it hurt! We all did what we could. Medical "science," even at the Mayo Clinic where she was diagnosed with terminal cancer and then died twelve days later, is as much a mystery as ever. On our go-see list, we had: dermatologists, acupuncturists, surgical oncologists, endocrinologists, gynecologists, gastroenterologists, neurologists, orthopedists, radiation oncologists, internal medicine generalists, lymphoedema specialists, psychologists, not to mention faith healers, pain and meditation specialists, and physical therapists—you name it, we saw them all. And every piece of medical equipment and drugs—we had them all.

Good Grief

Even as I mourned, my column "Good Grief" appeared in a number of papers and blogs around the country (see www.TheRiverRunsDry.com) and pretty much cleansed my soul.

22

I get helpful, empathetic letters from grieving people all the time. Donald Galleher in the English Department of George Mason University wrote: "I lost my wife when I was fifty-seven yet I wanted to live the rest of my life looking forward, not backward. So for a few months after she died, I jotted down all the things we shared together but I found in the process I was gradually letting go of her."

For me also, what helped the most was to write things down, so that by the end of the second year I was finished grieving. My editor, who lost a husband, has a different take: "People tell you it gets better with time: that's a lie. What happens is that you get accustomed to living with grief—the way one gets accustomed to blindness or deafness or a missing leg. But there is always what Anna Quindlen called the 'presence of an absence'."

So what do we learn from Margo's life and how do we celebrate her? There will be no tombstone in some lonely, forgotten cemetery, but rather little quips of simple wisdom she left us in that steamer trunk and a plaque honoring her work in putting in a handicapped ramp at a church in Dubuque, Iowa. The plaque reads:

OPEN TO ALL
This walkway celebrates
the vision of
Margo Freivalds
with the support
of the fellowship
in making our church
accessible to all.

– 2011

She taught me:
- Less is more
- Patience
- There is always another side to whatever story
- Most people (but not all) have some virtue
- As the Nike commercial says: "Do it"

- Make alone time for yourself
- Be positive

That last one was very hard for Margo. She never looked at the underside of people to understand that too many friends are merely acquaintances and good-time Charlies; they are friends when it's convenient, when you don't have any problems, when you're willing and able to have lunch or play a round of golf. It hurt Margo a great deal after writing or phoning these fair-weather friends, to discover that they would not respond. Perhaps they thought of Margo as their Camelot and my extracting facts from her diaries would damage the myths they created about her—and yes, themselves. She found some solace in keeping female friends who were much older than she: they always responded. Thus, she once wrote, *"John is the only person who cares about me."* And after we first met, she wondered how I would be around her "friends" who now have disappeared, moved on, and are just names I found in her steamer trunk.

3

muddling through

"Margo is an egg; men are rocks.

If a rock falls on an egg, it's too bad for the egg. If an egg falls on the rock, it's too bad for the egg."

– Adapted from an old saying

*I*n this "Muddling Through" period right before Margo's Asia trip, a whole series of men entered and left her life. Since there were no lasting relationships, there was no one waiting for her to return. It was a wake-up call for me to discover from her journals the depth of the personal and emotional torture she had gone through. A great deal of anger surfaced in me as I discovered how she had been used by these men. But, at the time, she rationalized it all by writing, *"I'm only interested in a classy, lean man; only a few available, I'm sure, so until then I will settle for fun."*

While she lived in New Jersey, right before leaving for Asia, she even developed a personal ad—never published—for the type of man she was looking for:

5'11" SWF seeks trim 6'1" SWM who is exhilarated by a day of hiking, biking, canoeing, followed by an evening at Carnegie Hall, fine wine, cheese in a romantic NY café.

Some of the words of Waylon Jennings' song "Lookin' for Love in All the Wrong Places" are particularly telling, as Margo tried everything to meet Mr. Right.

"I was looking for love in all the wrong places
 Looking for love in too many faces
 Searching your eyes, looking for traces
 Of what I'm dreaming of…"

And goodness, she looked everywhere. North Dakota, Minnesota, New Jersey, Illinois, Indiana, New Jersey, Vermont, St. Croix, the U.S. Virgin Islands, Martinique, Norway and Sweden—and we haven't yet gotten to Asia.

Looking back, I don't think any of the men Margo went through to finally get to me (and she wrote down every one) ever told her, "I love you." This was sad to write about, particularly when it came to the actions of two men who should have known better than to take advantage of Margo's naïveté. Interestingly, in the fifteen-page epistle she wrote on her life, she never mentions these two by name. It was painful to look back. She was reluctant to tell me about these "escapades," for she realized just before we finally started living together that *"I am too willing to accept my old feelings and attitudes re myself and my life rather than to view them as unacceptable and to push them away and get rid of them."*

Since she was extremely tall and grew up in an era before tall supermodels were the rage, Margo always felt like the ugly duckling and had a poor physical self-image. Kimberly Johnson, herself 5'11", summed it up in an article, "How I Loved Being Tall." "My height was an unavoidable reminder that I was different, and being different isn't cool often when you are a teenager who wants to fit in—or simply shop for pants that fit!"

In high school and college Margo didn't develop any real social skills when it came to men. Her first "lover," later her husband, was Brownie, whom she married at age twenty-four. Patsy, her sister-in-law (Margo's brother's wife), later said that given Margo's social immaturity at the time, "this was way too young."

Brownie, however, was an experienced social person and Margo thought she might never get another offer of marriage:

> *I met Brownie through a friend of a girlfriend's boyfriend. He was a very social fellow who had just spent four months on an iron boat on Lake Superior, which he had done to earn a hunk of money to pay off a previous girlfriend whom he had gotten pregnant and who turned out to be one of my high school classmates. He was fun-loving, made everyone laugh, had no interest in education, but seemed to like me. He was the first male to really pay any attention to me.*

Since Brownie didn't have a college education, Margo's liberal guilt came into play and she actually thought she was "helping the underprivileged"—a novel reason to marry someone. They were married for seven years (1968-1975), but his impact on her psyche would, unfortunately, last all her life.

Margo's marriage to Brownie got off to a bad start: on their honeymoon he stayed up watching TV and munching popcorn. He almost immediately became suspicious and jealous of her professional career and constantly berated her. He did not like her working at a neighborhood health center where she started her professional career because "those liberals were influencing your thoughts and actions."

Eventually Margo's athleticism and sense of adventure began to outpace their marriage. She bought a fancy French Motobecane racing bike (today everyone seems to own a Trek) and rode it all the time, mostly alone. Immediately after their divorce, she really got into it. One of her proudest possessions was a certificate from the Minnesota Ironman Century. On April 25, 1976, she bicycled sixty-four miles in six hours and fifteen minutes.

Eventually she left Brownie and hoped to find someone.

Her thoughts on men in the wake of her divorce are captured in the following:

> *I fall into it easily, hoping to find intimacy—but can't seem to establish the other…it's like I am selling my soul to get companionship. I must stop being a doormat and start being more respectful of myself."*

The next chart, drawn by Margo, illustrates it all.

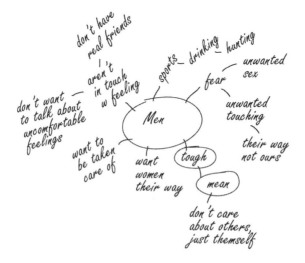

I was vaguely aware of most of this history, but I wish I had known more so I could have been more insightful. But Margo kept it all bottled up inside her and in the steamer trunk and only slowly released it to me.

Her best friend, Laurel Sandberg, had another take on Margo's relationships at the time:

"Laurel affirmed that I've talked of men as objects." And then she concluded after this merry-go-round of men: *"In fact I have no desire for any man—they're fading into the sunset after my recent experience with each of them. Maybe this is my problem but I feel I don't get enough in return for the energy I put out... My energy is once again geared to me and my career."*

So what of Margo's career before she went off to Asia?

Jobs

"Think you are indispensable? Put your hand in a bucket of water. When you take it out the hole that's left is how much you will be missed if you leave."

– Pete Brennan, Coolsmart.com

We can all remember how hard it was and how anxious we were to get our first professional job and then how disappointed we were when we finally realized it didn't immediately lead us to where we wanted to go. The Rolling Stones expressed it best with their lyrics:

No, you can't always get what you want
You can't always get what you want
You can't always get what you want
And if you try sometime you just might find
What you need

In other words, you have to pay some unpleasant dues to finally get what you want. For me it was having to go live in the blazing hot Iranian desert with an economic development firm and endure working with a lot of burnt out and alcoholic expatriates in Iran for two years right after leaving the Peace Corps. For Margo it was groping for some sort of nutrition spot in the public sector. Margo said this upon entering the job market:

I can feel myself waiting for magic to happen; someone to guide me. I must make something happen. I have refused to develop fervor for anything. The times I have been most motivated and active were when I was getting some love/support from someone.

The irony in her life was probably she had to leave the best job she ever had because she thought the company was about to implode. Biosearch was the last company she was with before she took off for Asia in 1986. One of the employees there remembers Margo as "wanting to go off and see the world."

She tried to make a go of it as a nutritionist for the Pilot City Health Center in a poor part of Minneapolis, then as a nutrition educator with the Minneapolis city schools. She took a position as a nutrition program director with the—this is a mouthful—Laboratory of Physiological Medicine at the University of Minnesota; then became co-owner with a friend (married to a very groping husband) of Nutrition Educator Inc., which sold, or at least *tried* to sell, wellness programs before their time. She spent a couple of years at Emory University in Atlanta getting her master's degree before finally landing a good corporate job as associate product manager of the nutritional division of Mead Johnson. But none of these career stops gave her the focus and professional fulfillment she was looking for. The total elapsed time for these five jobs/interludes/dreams was fourteen years. (For you calendar-watchers, it was from 1968 to 1982.)

Kim Carpenter remembers those days:

"Margo and I met in May, 1981. She was Margo Brown then. I had just moved to Evansville, Indiana, to begin work at Mead Johnson Nutritionals (then part of Bristol-Myers) in marketing, and was eager to meet an entirely new set of friends and colleagues. Marketing was the perfect place to mingle. Our offices were all arranged around a central hall filled with cubicles for admin assistants (of course, we called them secretaries back then). Margo was responsible for adult nutritionals and I worked on the pediatric side, but we were all together in the same space.

"I remember that Margo and I hit it off immediately. Her warm but mischievous smile often erupted into her fabulous laugh. I've always liked a good laugh myself, and hers worked very well for me. I won't ever forget her laugh. Through the years, it brought joy and exuberance to every interaction we had.

"Yes, she was tall. Our longtime friend Lance Stalker reminded me not long ago that Win Hamilton, our intrepid Marketing VP, used to call her 'Too-Tall Brown' after the then-popular Dallas Cowboys' defensive end Ed 'Too-Tall' Jones. The nickname was endearing, not at all derogative. In fact, we all looked up to Margo and her talents, least of all because she happened to be tall.

"Margo had a very special knack of bringing people together. That August of 1981, Margo had a party at her townhouse one Saturday afternoon, and she invited me. I arrived, and it was mobbed. Everyone was having a great time, but no one more so than Margo. In the fall, Margo and I decided that we would hold a Halloween party. We held it at her townhouse and invited a lot of people. We spiced it up by actually renting a casket and filling it with a 'body' made from a Quasimodo mask, stuffed shirt, and jeans—complete with a rubber snake slithering out from an indiscreet place. Margo really stood out as Dracula's bride, dressed all in white with her mouth covered in blood. That party was goofy and crazy, and everybody remembered it for a very long time. Time passed. In 1984, I had a wonderful opportunity to shift to Bristol-Myers International and Margo left the company in 1986 to seek her own adventures."

Margo's parents did not understand her career path. They thought she was a drifter, for her dad spent his entire thirty-five-year working career at the agribusiness giant Cargill and only understood lifetime employment. With my job history, I was more than suspect as well. I did earn some points with her dad as we were both mentioned in the same book about Cargill (*Cargill: Trading The World's Grain*) where "… John Mogush was one of a group of dedicated managers in the oil division" and where my first book *Grain Trade* was mentioned as "one of the books on the grain trade in the period 1960-1990 but none can be considered comprehensive."

Regardless, this is, however, the most comprehensive book on Margo Mogush Freivalds you will ever read!

Although Margo's parents may have found her career path at odds with their beliefs about employment, her ride through the job market is about average for these days. Current job counselors say someone will have ten jobs in their lifetime and two separate careers—a far cry from the one job for a lifetime belief of previous generations. The job world is full of surprises and during those years Margo wrote about one unexpected development in her life history:

I was given the opportunity to do a segment on the local CBS evening news called 'Marketing with Margo,' a sixty-second bit on getting the most nutritious food for your money (there was a beef shortage at the time). It was great fun but after my screen test I became so nervous that the pieces were not as good as I hoped—nervousness showed on the screen. However it was a fun month and very fun to see myself on the screen. Made for sleepless nights from the excitement.

Alas, there were no comments, either bad or good, from TV viewers and the experiment was canceled. Since I too flunked my screen test for a local TV program on money, there was another communal bond Margo and I shared—and would talk about in later years.

But back to Mead Johnson where she hit a brick wall (in today's parlance, a glass ceiling) professionally as the first woman in the marketing group and with her old boss moving and a new one on the way: *"…The message to me however—I'd better move on."*

Margo thought: *"What next? MBA? Find a business to get into? Fine American crafts, Haagen Das Ice Cream, a little restaurant."*

She had actually made a more exhaustive list, which is fun to go over. In all cases, the job she liked didn't involve pushing paper as she did now, but had more interaction with people. Yet the reality of our world is that you make more money by pushing paper around as the Wall Street bandits have shown.

What kinds of jobs do I equate a zest for living with where I could fit?

Toys	Fashion Model?
Comedies	Musician
Bicycling	TV Personality
Outdoor Stuff	Playground Director
Sales	Public Relations
Bartending	Travel Bureau Manager
Jewelry/Belt Store	Fitness Center
Acting	Camp Counselor
Teacher	Interact with people as opposed to paperwork

The businesses she selected weren't all that frivolous. One reason she took off for Asia was to explore Australia in some depth with the thought of eventually setting up a travel agency whose task it would be to sell tours to that huge island continent. But whatever the case, she was done with Mead Johnson and her nutritional sales job for the moment. So she pondered her exit strategy.

She had written about ten drafts of a resignation letter to Mead Johnson before sending off this one:

> *This letter is to serve as formal notice of my resignation as of December 17, 1982. I have accepted a position with another company. My 3½ years at Mead Johnson has been a positive experience. I want to thank you and all the other people who have helped me in my success at Mead Johnson.*

She never realized how important that letter was to be, not only because she went on to get what she thought would be a better job, but also because it allowed her to get the dream job she wanted ten years later with the same company. Goodness, how tight those six degrees of separation circles really are in life. Or as they say in rural Virginia where we lived, "Better not piss in your own bed!"

In all her job "leavings" Margo was really a closet Zen Buddhist. Charlotte Jok Beck, author of *Everyday Zen,* captured Margo's attitude towards the corporate world when she wrote: "Since anger, and its subsets, depression, resentment, jealousy, backbiting, gossip and so on—dominate our lives, we need to investigate the whole problem with care…In spiritual maturity the opposite of injustice is not justice but compassion, not me straightening out the present ill, fighting to gain a just result for myself and others, but compassion, a life that goes against nothing and fulfills everything."

She never left a company saying, "You can take this job and shove it" like a lot of people, especially as some unshaven truck drivers in Appalachia do, but just moved on, didn't look back, and always left a good impression so that she could, and sometimes did, come back if she wanted to. She learned and understood the truth found in the phrase never burn your bridges. There was only one angry letter (unsent) in her steamer trunk and that was to her *"despicable"* boss who back-stabbed her many times. But Margo didn't mail the letter and retired instead. I won't mail the letter either but you can find excerpts in this book.

In modern human resource parlance, companies are actively seeking "boomerang employees." *The Wall Street Journal* in a headline story on

October of 2010 exclaimed: "Boomerang Employees: More companies tap into alumni networks to re-recruit best of former employees." Smart companies are not mad when good employees leave; they want them back because they are proven performers. One management consultant in the article was quoted, "You can check out but you can never leave."

But having left Mead Johnson in folksy and slower-paced Evansville, Indiana, hard upon the wide Ohio River, she finally found the focus she needed with a company called Biosearch, in the busy if not manic suburb of Somerville, New Jersey. Imagine that, a Midwestern-born-and-bred woman in New Joysey? The best thing said today about Somerville is that it is "the center of commerce where U.S. 22, U.S. Route 202, U.S. Route 206, and Route 28 meet and is within five miles of Interstates 287 and 78."

Margo packed herself up and left for the bright lights of this congested and busy New York suburb. I know how congested and fast-paced this whole area is, as Margo asked me to visit certain places from her past when I was courting her. So when I was in the general area on business, I wanted to see where she lived—a little peculiar, since few people go to Somerville on vacation!

Margo told me very little about Biosearch so what I am writing now is based on original research. Although the company is still around, now a subsidiary of Hydrometer, it prides itself on being the industry leader in the coating of monitors and feeding tubes in a very specialized area. It was a very small company headquartered in one of those faceless, one-story, low-slung industrial parks when Margo joined, but headed up the introduction of a revolutionary product.

She wrote this in her Life Story:

> *I gave my heart and soul to that product until the company started to run out of money. It was a small company with grand ideas. It allowed me the opportunity to see the inner workings of corporate America and to begin to distrust that segment of the world. The most significant part of the experience was for two years I handled crisis after crisis with the product and managed to help the sales group hold on to our initial business in spite of horrible product failures and having to call customers numerous times to apologize for the latest one. It was one of my strongest emotional times.*

Although Margo didn't consider herself a technical geek, she was frequently called for information by geeks who wrote for geeky technical journals. Thus she ended up being in such well-known journals as the *American Journal of Clinical Nutrition* and the *American Journal of Infection Control,* which ran an article by two scientists on "Microbial Growth in Clinically used Enteral Delivery Systems" in which her work was cited. And since you asked, the greatest microbial growth in all cases was at the distal tubing hub.

The "troops," the people who were clerical workers there, are still there and recall a number of details.

- Margo wore and showed off a necklace one day which was melted down jewelry and rings that Brownie, her first husband, had given her.
- Another time everyone in the office was invited to a wedding of a co-worker but only a select few were invited to the reception. So after the wedding, Margo invited all the unaccepted to her neat Victorian-style house in Morristown and they had a party of the "uninvited."
- And after a business trip to St. Croix a bunch of them stayed out late and were surprised to find the hotel chain gates locked when they got back. They found the hotel—fearful of robbers and bad people—had locked them out. They couldn't rouse anybody (before the age of cell phones) so they all took off their dresses, threw them over the fence, climbed over the fence in their underwear and then put their dresses back on. Margo kept a detailed diary of this trip to St. Croix but this incident she didn't write about—getting away from a groping bar patron. Oh, those groping men are everywhere.

She considered staying at Biosearch and wrote out the pluses and minuses of her job on some notebook page I found floating around in the steamer trunk.

Staying at Biosearch

Pluses

Can definitely impact business and company

Easily recognized when you've accomplished something

Potential strong for advancement

Could be a star more easily in management if I plan and implement and bring in some new things

Have been given the vote of confidence from New Jersey Health

Opportunity to be involved in more/learn more due to the negatives

Flexible hours/rules

Love sales force

Love most of dealers

Can stay in my townhouse that I like

Not far from work

My friendships are beginning to blossom

Great bicycling here—non-structured

Close to Philly, NY, DC; not far from New England

Minuses

Status of company?

Frustrations of no system

People who are difficult to direct

Weak management throughout company

Limited resources to fix production problems to implement various programs, i.e., pkg., technical

Distance between home office and plants

Difficult to know who's responsible for what

Low pay

Problems with distribution

Have to develop systems

I always wondered why Margo had so few diaries covering this time in her life, though I suppose she simply didn't have much time for introspection, focused as she was on getting all of the above done.

One of her last entries about working at Biosearch with all her defense mechanisms gone was: *"Work is awful! People are uncooperative, tense and I look like shit. I MUST LEAVE!"* She had made her decision to leave and set a tight budget of US$100 a day for her upcoming Asian jaunt. She was tightfisted *"so much that I do experience the place instead of staying in an international hotel."* She was as frugal on her Asian journey as she was in her product marketing job.

Her friend Margaret Pyles recalls this time.

"I visited Margo at her home in New Jersey when she was with the marketing company and she was so down. Everything she related about the job was negative. Budgets were cut from her position but money was being spent on expensive decorating for the office, managers were negative and gave no positive feedback and she didn't care much about some of her co-workers. We talked all evening and I told her it was time for her to get out and do something else. What a shock I had when only a few weeks later she called me to tell me she had quit her job, leased her house and had bought an open one-year airline ticket and was leaving the country. I laughed and said that when I counseled her to make a move I didn't expect anything so drastic. But that was Margo, open for anything and needing to find herself, which I believe she did on that trip. What a wonderful example she set for all of us."

When it came to her career, she seemed to follow the advice that management consultant Sherry Sandberg gives today, which is now conventional business wisdom but was a no-no before Margo's trip.

"Careers they're not a ladder but a jungle gym…Look for opportunities, look for growth, look for mission. Move sideways, move down, move on, move off…Build your skills, not your resume…Don't plan too much and don't expect a direct climb."

With her job a Biosearch having come to an end, Margo began her Asian trip. The first entry in her trip diary was from a woman named Katie who wrote:

"To reach your goal must be a passion,
Your goal must be part of your life,
One of the things that makes you happy,
That makes you the person you are.
Have a wonderful trip, I will think of you often."

4

the slow boat to china

> *If you do not change course, you might end up where you are heading.*
>
> – Chinese Proverb, Lao Tzu,
> *Book of the Way*, 500 BC

*A*s I was fumbling around on how to start this book in June 2011, the *Today Show* started a series on "How Women Can Jump-Start Their Lives." Without ever having seen this series, Margo Brown, as she was known in 1986, cast caution to the wind, interrupted her career, said, *"Why not?"* and gave a new life and a new career a jump-start by heading out for a yearlong trip through Asia. Margo did this some twenty-five years before this series aired, at the age of forty-two—a woman who in many ways was ahead of her time.

Pondering this trip, Margo came to the realization that other people had controlled her life—but once she embarked on this adventure, she would be in complete control and without restraints. Margo thought that her desire to travel alone, to be totally independent, had begun in Minneapolis when she was three:

> *I ran away from home on my tricycle and the police found me along a busy street. Guess that was the first sign of my independent streak that has served me well over the years.*

She always felt strange talking to her parents because they made her feel like a kid even when she was an adult. She also felt this way at age forty-two when she eventually revealed her Asian travel plan to them. They asked, "Does this mean you'll be gone a year?" Margo asked herself: *What difference does it make to them? They miss me—but they only miss talking to me once a week—how different can it be to them?*

In *A Woman Alone: Travel Tales From Around the Globe*, Susan Spanos eloquently echoed Margo's thoughts in Spanos' context: "A therapist might say I have control issues. Just so…Travel intensifies the elements of a woman's nature—both fine and toxic—making them stand out more starkly than they ever do in the safe, regulated environment of home. When I travel alone, I can give the whole mixed bag full rein without monitoring myself, making compromises, negotiating or even talking. I am somehow better able to tap my thoughts and feelings… At night I dream more vividly…Alone we can afford to be wholly whatever we are and to feel whatever we feel absolutely."

With Margo's job at Biosearch in New Jersey coming to an end, her desire to travel alone, independently, reached a point of no return. She would go to Asia because she realized, *"I have to quit acting and talk professionally."* She started thinking about going to Hawaii and then the list expanded to Fiji, New Zealand, and Australia. She had been studying Yoga, reading about Buddhism and about driving through exotic locales, so her itinerary was quickly expanded to also include Thailand, Singapore, India, Nepal, Hong Kong, China, and Japan.

The Minutes of Margo

After we were married, Margo took it upon herself to deal with the bills. She would happily and thoroughly go over the minutiae of each credit card charge and interrogate me as to the value of that purchase. But only after poring through the four trip diaries of her Asia jaunt did I see why—she wrote down everything and to such a degree I am amazed she found time to see every site. I documented some five hundred discrete places she went to over her ten-country Asia jaunt. I don't know if she had this financial thoroughness before she went or if it became an acquired talent. She wrote down every expense from the moment she left Newark Airport to fly to Hawaii (her first stop) to her flight back to L.A. from Tokyo.

Here's a sample from her little book written during her month in Australia.

38

1986

SEPTEMBER

MONDAY	TUESDAY	WEDNESDAY	THURSDAY	FRIDAY	SAT./SUN.
1 room 16.00 Labor Day	2 bus to Katherine 25.00 1.95 liquor 6.35 postage 3.60 beer 1.05 bread 11.50 boat	3 Kath. tour 47.00 bus to A.S. 85.00 food 3.50	4 Alice Springs post boxes 2.15 food 11.15 room 16.00	5 Palm tour 30.00 room 12.00 treats 7.00 dinner 4.80 food 6.80	6 W. McDonald 35.00 postcds 3.00 room 12.00 7 Room 12.00 Olive Pink Park
8 24.20 postage 12.00 room 10.56 food 2.00 lunch 3.00 museums 1.80 postcards 4.00 tent & bag Mailed Mom's BD	9 59.00 to Purs Rock tent spot 5.00 beer ____	10 $5.00 tent Call health ins. beer 7.55 dinner 7.40 postcards .75 brkfst 3.50	11 coffee .85 + .85 beer 6.00 dinner 8.00 cards & book 8.70 room 9.00 tour & bus 50.00	12 brkfst 5.00	13 Kings Canyon room 12.00 food 5.20 14 95.00 bus to Adel. postcards & drinks 5.90 Cooper Peedy
15 brkfst 7.00 lunch 5.60 beer 1.20 tea 3.50 Cooper Peedy	16 Adelaide campsite 6.50 fruit 3.20 shower 1.50 brkfst 2.50 wine 8.90 port 2.40	17 meal 4.90 coffee .77 renew health ins. for 6 mo. Option 1 Called M&D 10 a.m. 8 p.m. Yorke Peninsula	18 dinner 15.00 beer 2.10 room 12.00	19 Adelaide brfst 2.40 tour 6.00 entry fees 6.50 camera repair 14.00 room 12.00 Tampax & dental 7.77 lunch 2.22 ballet 22.00 dinner 2.37	20 room 12.00 21 2.40 beer lunch 4.70 stuff for Anne 16.00

Perhaps as revealing as her tenacious bookkeeping skills is this note to self—which she must have taken out and read often—that was slipped in the back flap of the expense book:

You are OK. You are intelligent and fun to be with, you are willing to take risks and play hard. You have many bright and interesting friends who like you and respect you. You are bright and interesting.

You are a good worker and are capable of doing whatever it is you decide to do. You will find, take and do an excellent job when you return to the U.S. You will be organized and follow through.

You will find a male with whom you will have a healthy and loving relationship as well as happy/fun.

You can do anything you want and be anything you want.

And to not be undone, the front flap had this little note:

Affirmation:
I believe in Margo
I am taking good care of her
I deserve all the good things I ask for and
I don't owe anybody anything.
I have nothing to hide, prove, defend and
Nothing to feel guilty about.
DO NOT ARGUE WITH THIS.
DO NOT ASK IF YOU BELIEVE IT OR NOT.
REPEAT IT TO YOURSELF FREQUENTLY.

In addition to recording in detail the state of her finances while on her Asian trip, she wrote hundreds—yes, hundreds—of postcards and letters to friends and family. Not only that, each day she listed how many postcards and letters she had sent and to whom. Then she kept a running tally of how many postcards and letters the key players in her life received.

I can't help but think the intent behind her detailed record-keeping was grounded in motives similar to those expressed by Marybeth Bond in her book *Gutsy Women*:

"I began a tradition of my first trip overseas that I still practice today. I write as though I am penning a letter to my mother, complete with all the silly details I knew she loves (like what kind of pastries I've devoured). Rereading my journals is like taking a trip back in time—one much more owed than memory can alone inspire. And for a solo traveler, it gives you something to do while waiting for food in restaurants."

I went through hundreds of cards and letters Margo wrote to friends and family who saved them and then gave them back to her. I particularly liked this one sent to her parents on January 18, 1986, from Hong Kong.

The impact/significance of these last two months of travel has come together since I've been in Hong Kong. I am extremely lucky to have been able to visit in the different countries I have as the differences in the Asian countries are quite striking when seen one after another.

Hong Kong is one sophisticated place as opposed to the dirt paths of India and Nepal. In fact I'm treating myself at the moment to High Tea (4 p.m.) at the Peninsula Hotel. It's a beautiful old English place with marble floors, gold scrolled ceilings—very posh—considered one of the elegant great hotels of the world. It would be wonderful if Prince Charming would come strolling over—like the tall handsome Swede I met in Nepal last Sunday. That would add a bit more class and fun to the tea. If I had a reasonably wealthy man in my life, I'd have him bring me to Hong Kong. My, oh my, could I spend a fine fortune here. The shopping could be nonstop here and in Bangkok. Around every corner there's a bargain to be had. I am having an Ultra suede suit tailored for myself for $230. They travel well—so I decided it was a good step towards returning to the work world!

Then in Bangkok while boarding at Annie's Soapy Massage (yep!) I had the surprise of my life. Tuesday when I went to check for mail in Bangkok—there was a telegram from Sandoz Nutrition (Minneapolis) and a former Bristol-Myers colleague of mine saying he'd like to talk to me about a job! It was a great pat on the back and opens the door for other areas...sorry, but I've run out of letter-writing inspiration. Want to put this in mail before I leave for China.

So the fear—not Margo's—that the Asia jaunt would somehow imperil her job chances was for naught.

Margo's friends and family *"knew I was a little different and an adventurer";* they felt this was Margo being Margo. She made an itinerary, got the info on the major tour operators in the places she wanted to go to,

41

and bought a huge hiker's backpack and a fanny pack.

What Margo really did was "reclaim travel" as Ilan Stavans wrote in the *New York Times* (July 8, 2012). "The returns can only be as good as what we offer of ourselves in the process... When we travel we are asking of hospitality. There's great vulnerability in this. It also requires considerable strength. To be a good guest one needs to be sure in one's own skin: Where you stand, who you are. This means we tend to romanticize travel as a lonely pursuit... Travel is a search for meaning not only in our lives, but also in the lives of others. The humility required for genuine travel is exactly what is missing from its opposite extreme—tourism."

Packing the Pack

In our years of living together and traveling the world together, I always let Margo pack my bags—she did it much more efficiently than I. Instead of folding clothes to fit, she learned to roll them up and then pack them so when you unrolled them there was not a wrinkle to be found.

Margo did not really travel alone for her year in Asia; she had a buddy, which was her backpack. When we first met, she told me a little about what went into the backpack and I was able to get a copy of what it looked like from Gray Packer, her traveling companion in New Zealand. Remember, this gal was a Girl Scout, and looking back, her expertise in packing came from those years going to Girl Scout camps in Upper Michigan. I still have her Girl Scout pocket knife!

Margo's backpack was forest green and composed of three large compartments surrounded by all sorts of little pockets of mesh and nylon. It was able to stand on its own. For her Asia trip, she strategically packed fleece pants, a thermal shirt, a sleeping bag, compass, first-aid kit, "dress" shoes, bag of toiletries including a toothbrush, hairbrush, little diaries, green nylon bag with a tent, a full-sized camera, playing cards, a knife, fork, and a bowl and plate, candle and matches, eight pairs of undies, three cotton bras (one black), green velvet stretch pants, a down jacket, a swimsuit, and two pairs of jeans.

Margo said her hands got strong from all the wedging and cramming she did every day to dig something out. On her first stop, she bought a little New Zealand flag that she attached to her backpack. Carrying the green backpack that weighed more than fifty pounds also made Margo's legs stronger and turned her calves and legs into well-defined muscles.

Finally, before departing she made mailing arrangements with

American Express, paid off all her credit cards, and away she went.

It seemed that from a practical point of view the trip was unfolding without a hitch, and it did. There was a hitch, however, but she didn't discover it until she was months into her trip. Margo had bought the 'round-the-Pacific airline ticket good for what she thought was a year—only to discover in the eleventh month that it was a six-month ticket: "Lucky me, it wasn't discovered until long after the expiration date."

Throughout the yearlong adventure, she found it was easy to leave the sights but very hard to leave some of the people, even though she knew she had to.

Gray Packer, a New Zealander totally different from most of the men she had known, was one such person:

> *Upon leaving Gray, I feel amazingly at loose ends without him. It had gotten very comfortable having him around and we were getting closer... I'm feeling the most alone and homesick of any time on this trip.*

On her last days in New Zealand, Margo phoned Gray.

> *It is strange but he sounded cold and distant... There are lots of differences between us and maybe it's better left as a New Zealand holiday romance and correspondent relationship.*

What happens in New Zealand stays in New Zealand.

Gray told me: "Spent time with Margo on several occasions...All very memorable; we enjoyed being companions very much—the sort of quiet understanding as people become friends and work out what to do there with the time they have (short in our case)."

Gray's mother was even more philosophical. She told Gray: "People come into your life for a reason when you need it most and will then depart again."

Gray went on, "In my case that was very true. I'd been in a bad auto accident, and was an emotional mess when Margo found me. But by the time she left I had become a much stronger person for having been with her."

Margo bought art and presents for everyone at every stop on this trip and how she got it all back amazes me. We can argue that Margo was good at selling things but what she really needed to sell was art. She flipped out when she stayed in a little town, Russell, New Zealand, and visited a gallery run by Eva Braun. She had accomplished it all. She started an art gallery, sold it and now works one day a week and writes the rest of the time. Of her Margo said: *"She's the friendliest gallery person I met."* As a result, she spent US$300 buying various prints—one of which, of a cat, I still have in my bathroom.

Eva suggested Margo should open a gallery:

> *Now that's an idea I like. It could mean living in a wonderful location (another reason she fell in love with Lexington, Virginia); learning more about a topic I've always been interested in; traveling to New York to visit galleries; meeting the public and art community and using my marketing skills. And dressing arty like which I've been dreaming on this trip—long skirts, wonderful jewelry, maybe long hair.*

"Those who suffer seem to grow!"

All the mishaps and good "haps" taught Margo something about her next trip to New Zealand: *"Bring gear to do treks—good boots, good rain gear, sleeping bag, strong sand fly repellent 100% DEET."* The frequent rains confirmed the correctness of her decision to leave New Zealand and head to new and drier adventures.

After New Zealand and its seemingly endless rain, Margo arrived in Sydney and was met by David Cranna, someone she had previously met professionally in the United States. The two spent some time together as Margo was getting lonely and tired of being the odd person out: *"I felt so good but also very alone. I am very tired of being alone with no male companions."*

Wherever Margo went, including New Zealand, she used her dietitian training to its utmost, remembering every meal in detail. I got hungry reading her journals. She recalls one meal at David Cranna's in Sydney:

> *He did little racks of lamb/four chops still together—stood up on end and interlocked with each other, crushed garlic over top (first oil), then mixed herbs and thyme, white wine, hunks of butter over tops of each, then a potato casserole, thinly layered shad potatoes layered—garlic and butter on bottom of pan, cream poured over layer of grated cheese on top—lovely!*

Margo took sightseeing seriously and was driven to report everything she saw. The introduction to *A Woman Alone: Travel Tales From Around the Globe* captured Margo's (and any solo traveler's) mind-set perfectly: "Every obstacle overcome is all the more exhilarating, each happy surprise—the meal you ordered actually appears on your table—more gratifying. With each misadventure and triumph, we learn...without the filter of someone else's viewpoint. Perhaps this is why we experience our solitary trips with such intensity and remember them in remarkable detail."

The details Margo remembered and documented bear proof of this. Here is one such instance:

> *Tuesday, July 15, 1986: An exhausting day of sightseeing beginning with a hydrofoil ride...Then off to the Botanical Gardens... opera house...Governor General's castle-like house...art gallery... Hyde Park Barracks.*

In spite of her vigorous sightseeing schedule and detailed recording of each and every one of her excursions, crash days were regularly noted in her journals. On July 17 in Sydney, she wrote:

> *Crash day, washed out clothes, got my locks shorn and feel more like myself. Sat on Manley Beach to sun and write to Gray. Cooked chicken cacciatore for Annette and David—it was OK but not spectacular. Quiet evening at home. It's really nice to be having a low-key home life for a bit. Learned to enjoy baked beans on toast—an Australian tradition.*

It was in Australia where two ongoing patterns of behavior began to appear. First, Margo had a lot to prove to herself as well as to others on this trip. She wanted to be perceived as self-reliant and capable of keeping up with anybody. One night at a bar after sailing on the Whitsunday Islands, she asked an entire contingent of young men to dance. Imagine that, a forty-two-year-old woman surrounded by twenty-year-old men and pretty much out-dancing them.

> *Do believe I've shown up these young ones with my level of energy. Although I'm fit but aware I'm the oldest on the boat my level of activity would never give it away... I've actually shied away from young folks' activities (like windsurfing) but finally doing them.*

Second, Margo was drawn to "the pub" as a meeting place for men. Margo mused: "*Perhaps I also need to hang around some nice bars to meet*

Mr. Traveler with $ and nice personality." This changed, however, on August 8 in Airlie Beach, Australia, when she concluded: "*It saddens me a bit but the easiest place to meet people is in the pub. It happens over and over again.*" She quickly realized that pubs often attracted certain types of Australian men—*"lost souls"* she called them. She was amazed there were so many of these *"dropouts."* She reflected, "*I admire them on one hand but not sure I could do it as I sense I'd miss the stimulation of minds working in the business and academic worlds.*"

Then while sailing and surfing in Whitsunday Bay, a fellow named Peter shocked Margo by saying that he could see her as a drifter: "You'd do OK," he told her. This advice shocked her because days earlier a South African traveler told Margo she should get a traveling companion for the remainder of her Asia trip. Being the independent and adventurous type, it is hard not to guess which way Margo leaned. Thailand and Annie's Soapy Massage, India, Nepal, China, Hong Kong, Macau would await her and she, for the most part, would explore each of these destinations on her own.

Finally, after completing her Asian adventure and returning to the U.S., she wrote this in Los Angeles on February 7, 1986:

> *Three benefits of year of travel:*
> **Belief in myself and ability to survive in any environment—self reliance*
> **Understanding of my value system—importance of friends, comfort and nice things*
> **Non-interest in living in third world country.*

And she summed up:

> *I traveled to see parts of the world I'd never seen before; to increase my understanding of different people; cultures, politics, lifestyles; to give myself a break from the rat race I was in—to take care of myself.*

Although she came across as naïve in her younger years, and certain men would and did exploit her, when she set off for Asia she knew exactly how to behave and—with one exception in India—it worked. In 2006, when her body started to break down and she relied more on me, she reflected on her approach to men:

> *As I drove yesterday, I remembered how I used to act when a single man was in my presence—always trying to flirt and the immature*

trying to find ways to see this man—run into him and fantasizing about a relationship with him. I have been with John, I have hidden that part of me—I keep saying I can/could live on my own again and be perfectly happy, yet that may not be so true after all. Yes I liked the idea of doing what and when I liked, but having a real partner is what I wanted all along.

But part of "The Slow Boat to China" was to see if such a partner did exist out there. I was lucky enough to be that partner.

5

innocence abroad (but was she?)

> *Most travel, and certainly the rewarding kind, involves depending on the kindness of strangers, putting yourself into the hands of people you don't know and trusting them with your life.*
>
> –Paul Theroux, *Ghost Train of the Evening Star*

*M*argo Brown was a beyond trusting soul when she left for Asia. She was always oblivious to potential dangers, whether climbing glaciers in New Zealand, scampering up Angel's Landing in Utah, navigating the tricky currents of the Atlantic Ocean near Puerto Rico in a kayak, or trying to find someone at Annie's Soapy Massage in congested Bangkok. This is a character trait that would get her into deep trouble, but nevertheless, she did not fear people in any situation. I often tell people who didn't know her that she was not a naïve Midwestern American Lutheran, but rather a closet Asian Buddhist. She was kind, nonjudgmental, trusting, and exuded confidence. She had an inner strength that those in her presence could often feel.

She had matured quite a bit since her first overseas trip to Europe at age twenty-two. She was struck by the behavior of all the European men she encountered on that twelve-country tour, which took sixty-six days. They groped and pinched and followed her everywhere—*"Haven't they ever seen a woman before?"*

In a journal entry recorded in Brindisi, Italy, on August 14, 1966, a young Margo noted the following:

> *Received many honks, comments, and invitations during the day— can't understand what big thrill these Italian men get out of picking*

up girls on the street or just being obnoxious. Even when they're with their girlfriends or wife they are obnoxiously intimate and loving in public. With themselves they have no concern whether they scratch themselves or masturbate. Even go potty on the street.

She took a similar trip some sixteen years later in 1982 when she was thirty-eight years old with a professor friend named Donna from Emory. In reading the accounts of this trip, I think the two women received more attention and were given more hassles as a pair than Margo did traveling by herself.

She and her pal Donna stopped in a little village called Rab in Croatia on August 23, 1982. I'll let Margo describe the rest:

Little village nestled in cove of sea. Walked from the town to the beach—one mile. Plop ourselves on a rocky ledge—more looks than we ever got before—not sure why" (you are both tall and nude! ed. note).

Sailing in the nude with a German guy—neat guy, fat wife. Absolutely out of sight—great waves—almost fall off. Another German invites me to play water volleyball—yes—don't understand much of anything—what a stitch! Fantastic!

These experiences and many others turned Margo into a well-experienced international traveler by the time she went to Asia. The major differences were she was going to a part of the world she had never before visited and she was going alone. However, she was well versed in developing complicated international logistics. In fact, she got so good at it that I respectfully called her the "logisticator."

Although Margo was unique in many ways, let's not forget she was a vibrant, tall, young woman attracted to vibrant, tall men. She was open to new experiences—this is why she went to Asia in the first place and not Topeka, Kansas. Being tall and drop-dead gorgeous would hinder the travel of some females, but not Margo. During her travels in Asia, she met many people, including many men, some of who became her traveling chums. These were not pickups, for Margo was a traveling oddity. In many instances she would be introduced to the families of these men. Thus I have separated the Asian adventures by whether she had them with a traveling chum, or whether she went off alone or with a group. Without doubt, she had more fun with the chums.

I had a number of people review the manuscripts of this memoir and many of them found it hard to keep track of all the people Margo encountered. Consequently, I will provide a little introductory scorecard to help navigate her many social encounters while in Asia. Some of the men she encountered I was able to contact and gain additional information from regarding their first impressions of Margo and what they came across together. Others could not be found. Margo had an Asian travel address book and I wrote to many of the people whose names I found in the book—some still living at the same address some twenty-five years later. That says something about how mobile Americans are as we seem to move every other week.

Hawaii

Margo's Asia jaunt began with a stop in sunny, clean, and organized Hawaii where she stayed with her friends Joel and Susan Barker. There is not much to say here except that Hawaii was Hawaii. Her trip here portended our future, as Hawaii was our honeymoon destination. She guided me around the state like an experienced hand.

What does Susan Barker remember about the launch of Margo's Asian trip? Margo arrived in Hawaii at just about the same time as Haley's Comet on March 28, 1986. Soon thereafter she cruised down Haleakala volcano about thirty-eight miles on her bike. Just one of the crazy rides Margo was to take.

Fiji

I once thought I could live in a tropical country like Fiji but now I don't think so. It's too poor and has too many uncontrollable problems like the weather...How can people get ahead when floods, mudslides continue to wipe them out and there's little industry?

Enough said.

New Zealand

This country is drop-dead beautiful and Margo was able to travel through a great portion of it with Gray Packer, a tall, bearded, rail-thin Kiwi who provided me with the only photograph I have of Margo with a backpack. (How I got that picture is a story for another book.) With Gray there was a lot of travel to different parts of New Zealand, but with pretty civilized surroundings. They got along very well.

Australia

This is a U.S.-sized island continent and Margo ran across three people of note. David Cranna was a professional in the pharmaceutical business that Margo had befriended prior to her trip and with whom she ended up spending a couple of weeks. David and his wife, Annette, lived a suburban existence. No crazy bike rides down a volcano or strenuous mountain climbing here.

Ayers Rock is the signature physical landmark of Australia and Margo ran into an eclectic Swiss accountant by the name of Titus who she termed a *"gem of a man."* I would like to be called that one day. She had a total backpacking experience throughout the Australian outback and along the shoreline with Titus.

The Zen of Australia came out in Margo when she met Bruce Burrow, *"a hunk of a man,"* in New Zealand. While visiting him, she also met his girlfriend, family and half the town where he lived in Australia. Margo even stayed for a while with his seventy-nine-year-old mother. Through Bruce, she learned what living in small town in Australia was really like. She just loved it.

Thailand

I didn't think anyone could top Margo's adventures in Bangkok and Ko Samui where she met a nonlinear fellow from Gulfport, Mississippi, by the name of Mitch David. Her experiences are very notable and I felt I just had to find this guy. I hired a private investigator and placed ads in the *Sun Herald*, the main newspaper in southern Mississippi. Would you believe it, I found him! I also found couples who were in Thailand at the same time who met Margo briefly and who shared their impressions of her with me. If you can top Margo's Thai travel adventure, please let me know because I would love to hear about it.

India

Although she traveled through India mostly by herself, she did have one bad experience—her only really bad experience of the whole trip—with an Indian military guy whom she trusted. The experience was a wakeup call of sorts for Margo and she approached the remainder of the trip with eyes that were a little wider open. Interestingly, this close call was the one Margo mentioned the most publicly, and not the apparent dangers that emerged while she was in Thailand.

The Rest

But the other parts of her trip to Fiji, Nepal, China, Hong Kong, Macau, and Singapore she handled in group settings where no male chum appeared (not that she didn't want one to) and she stuck with a group to see the sites. OK, Nepal she did take a solo trek, but that was with an army of porters and wasn't as far-fetched as it sounded. But it wasn't a Grey Line tour of Staten Island either.

Shall we begin?

"gray's anatomy" new zealand

april-june 1986

Slow morning. Stayed in to cuddle—God it's so nice to be with a man who wants to do that and not have any pressure to go off to a meeting, job or chores. The last time I had anything close to this was Skip when we went up to the condo when we were in Colorado. In fact, Gray reminds me a bit of Skip (her first boyfriend after her marriage)—*at least his body (bony and skinny). Gray is different from anyone I've spent time with lately and probably the most time I've spent with a man in years—he's young (28), educated through high school; not into a career at all. And I'm not so sure he's all that interested in who I am or what I want in life—but in any case this interlude has been quite nice.*

So ended one of Margo's diaries wherein we learn something about Gray Packer and his anatomy.

The one man Margo spent the most time with on her Asian trip was Gray. Not a rugged lumberjack, Pendleton shirt-wearing guy from the woods of northern Minnesota, but a very low-key, unassuming individual, almost childlike. He was dark-haired with gray eyes, bearded. But apart from being a little taller than Margo, he would not stand out in a crowd of New Yorkers.

Margo told me after much wine drinking one night—the only time she would reveal a little bit about her past (that was then, this is now)—that Gray was a stereotypical New Zealand male. He was a *"pioneer type,"* rural- and nature-minded, nonintellectual, unemotional, and he had little interest in anything approaching high culture. However, Margo hadn't gone to New Zealand to seek culture, but rather mountains and glaciers. Almost every day, Margo would write: *"The day was especially memorable—praise the Lord and thank Him for the opportunity to be experiencing this."*

It's hard to appreciate the limitless beauty of a place like New Zealand by yourself. You immediately want to share it with someone. Margo shared it passionately with Gray Packer. The same thing happened to me when I went to Guadalajara, Mexico (then a really pleasant place), for the first time. Its beauty overwhelmed me and I projected it onto a beautiful woman I met. My sister Ilze even called me while I was in Mexico and said, "You're not going to do something stupid like get married, are you?" (I was twenty at the time). But after I left Mexico the ardor quickly subsided if it didn't disappear altogether. So too for Margo with Gray.

Margo arrived in New Zealand on April 22 and in less than a month she had had it:

> *Today I was definitely in scenery overload and tour overload. I've been part of some tour group gazing at the scenery for five days now and that's too much for me. I could raise minimal enthusiasm today and again not be too interested in the folks around me.*

She ruminated quite a bit during tours:

> *Spent a fair amount of time thinking about relationships. I'm feeling strongly that I do want one ongoing. There are always men around if you want them for temporary liaisons but there is something missing when that's all there is. I'd like a lovable man to come home to, to cuddle and love and love me on an ongoing basis. That will be a goal when I return to the states. This ends my eighth week of travel. I am horny for some affection and need some non-tour stuff and maybe a city as a change of pace.*

After just over two weeks in New Zealand, she perked up when she got to climb and helicopter over the Fox Glacier; the photo on the jacket of this book has Margo standing in front of the glacier. She met Gray after exploring the Fox Glacier every way possible, but let Margo tell you.

Fox Glacier

It was a lovely a.m. I made it to the info office @ 8:30 a.m. to check on helicopters vs. planes, etc. to fly over the glacier. They set me up with the helicopter—I thought it was set that I'd go for a landing on the glacier at about 9:15. Well—for a few moments this a.m. I hit a low—I was about to cry, feeling sorry for myself that in reality there was no one to go up with me (three are needed)—I watched two groups of four go up and come back awed. I was CRUSHED!! and PISSED that's I'd been misled and wasted my a.m.

Mark, the assistant, was kindly, understood (his boss, the pilot, was originally surly to me) but Mark took me through the little wild game park. I watched the feeding of the wild pigs. We made arrangements to check with each other later—in early p.m. Mark drove me to the beginning of the Cone and Chalet walks on the right (south) side of the glacier.

Well—that walk was one of the most incredible of my life! It was <u>STEEP</u> and rocky. Then there was this amazing net bridge—a board down the middle of a wire net. Ye gads—and up and up I went to the most wonderful view of the glacier—Cone Mountain! From there it was another hour to the Chalet lookout (I'd already walked 40 minutes)—ooh, my thighs were feeling it, but I was exhilarated. I'd have moments of thinking it was crazy to be climbing in the woods alone. What would happen if I fell and hurt myself? On the other hand I'm not going to sit around waiting to find someone to hike with me. And besides I sort of like the aloneness.

The lush subtropical foliage alongside this glacier seems contradictory, but it's also what adds to spectacularness.

I was warned by Paul, the hotel waiter whom I ran into after leaving Cone Mountain, that I was going the "wrong way on the trail" because I was going to encounter a spot that was 'very steep' and had a chain to 'pull oneself up the incline.' Well, I almost turned around, as all I could envision was a sheer rock cliff and myself swinging from this chain straight down. I was freaked out, but decided if it was too bad I'd turn around even if I really didn't want to walk down the same trail going back. Once I found the chain it was nothing—the chain was there as there were no trees or rocks to grab onto, so it was just a major help and no steeper than any other part of the trail.

The view of the Fox River (formed by the melting glacier) is a wonderful picture—the majority of the river is milky colored due to the quantity of pulverized rock or moraine it contains. The aqua blue puddles are 'kettle lakes' formed by the glacier receding and having dug a hole—these blue lakes being those holes with the ice melted and the sludge settled.

I finally got my helicopter ride also! Wow, it was even more spectacular than the walk. I mean WOW! There aren't words to describe adequately the experience and sights. I know my pictures will never do the glacier justice. But it's humongous ridges of ice, with enormous crevasses a hundred feet deep, waterfalls appearing everywhere out of the sides of the mountains. It was a significant event. Awesome, Awesome! The magnitude is mind-blowing.

My final glacial experience was to actually climb up onto it. NEVER have I been so scared and exhilarated at the same time. The guide carved stairs out of the ice for us to walk up about three levels. Going up was spooky, but coming down was 10X worse as you could see where you could fall. I decided if I slipped, I'd smile all the way down as it was the most awesome, exhilarating experience of my life. I'd much rather die that way than waste away from cancer.

The day was especially memorable—Praise the Lord and thank Him for the beauty and opportunity to be here experiencing this.

Fox Glacier is actually eight miles long and is fed by four alpine glaciers. What makes it really neat is that it falls 8,500 feet on a seven-mile journey; it is one of the few glaciers to end among lush rain forests, only 980 feet above sea level. In the face of global warming, Fox Glacier has been advancing since 1985 at a rate of three feet a week.

Here's how Margo described her climb up the Fox Glacier, which is located in Westland Tai Poutini National Park on the west coast of New Zealand's South Island:

Well, this Saturday (May 9) was another Star ✳ Day! I walked the Fox Glacier this a.m. and oh, my, I mean to say I was almost speechless. To stand below the glacier and then begin to climb it, is—well, amazing. The magnitude of the ice is breathtaking. Ray, our guide, chopped steps into the ice so we could climb up three levels. Crevasses everywhere. Melted ice making H_2O falls everywhere. I mean it was MAGNIFICENT!!!! I loved every minute, though I was scared *shitless climbing up this mass of ice and straight down it. One could easily slip and be gone. Somewhere over the last 42 years and I've finally learned to take risks for at least some adventures and ooh, do they pay off! My legs are dying (thighs that is—feels like I've been on a 60-mile ride with inadequate training). Staying these two extra days in Fox is well worth it even if it does rain tomorrow.*

Then I walked the Minnehaha and Ngai Tahu Track—again amazing rain forest—lush subtropical bush. It was like being in a jungle. Lots of birds singing, though I couldn't find them.

Then it was back to the lodge.

Dinner turned out to be a magnificent event. I went to TeKano's, a natural foods café; it looks like a little cabin in the woods. I was the only guest and I chose a seat on pillows on the floor in front of the fireplace. With a candle, dried flowers and a live green plant on my 'coffee table,' I felt like I was at home. Absolutely the most delightful dinner I've had—tasty. I enjoyed sesame spread on crackers with wine as I wrote letters and then curried cauliflower on rice. The owners are a young Kiwi couple—quiet, but warmly friendly.

The sunset was outstanding—I walked along the beach along a lake fed by the glacier.

About the only thing that Margo didn't do in, around and above the Fox Glacier was to go skydiving. Lonely Planet put it this way: "With Fox Glacier's backdrop of the Southern Alps, rain forest and ocean, it's hard to imagine a better place to jump out of a plane."

After this adventure she had to share it with somebody and went back to The Hot Nail, the local pub, to exchange "war stories" about the glacier. All the people she had met the past couple of days were there.

She met Gray at a pub near the Fox Glacier and they discussed Keri Hulme, the author of *The Bone People*, a book dealing with the displacement of the native Maori culture that Margo had read. (It won the New Zealand Book of the Year Award in 1986.) Most everyone in New Zealand is aware of it. Gray said a friend of his said that Keri "has strange ideas." Margo wrote in her diary:

I think it's really that she has a different sensitivity to events. And perhaps a different culture. I find her intriguing. I guess I identify a bit with her—as I feel myself a different spirit often—that I don't

quite fit—and really have felt that way most of my life. Also, my inde-
pendence is rather strong in many ways. I haven't quite fully accepted
that [the fact that] I don't need to fit in the mainstream is okay.

The next day was a low-key day, as she described it. She went back to
The Hot Nail for some cauliflower, cheese, and hot chocolate. She read
quietly for a while and then *"Gray showed up."*

> *We ended up going down to Lake Matheson near the Fox Glacier*
> *despite the rain and the clouds. It was eerie and beautiful—so peace-*
> *ful; not another soul around. The trees, planes, birds were all reflected*
> *in the lake. We/I could imagine what it must be like on a clear day*
> *when Mt. Tasman and Cook reflect in the lake. It was nice to share*
> *the experience with Gray; that's really the second time this trip that*
> *I've shared with a friend—I mean someone before. The other was*
> *with a fellow I met on the beach in Fiji. It was a somewhat sensual*
> *experience for me—I get in those quiet far-away places and I want*
> *to hug and kiss the man I'm with. I was tempted to approach him*
> *but I passed. We did have a few nice kisses in the hotel lobby back at*
> *Fox Glacier. We spent 2½ hours taking in the walk and the lake. It*
> *was wonderfully relaxing.*

Gray invited Margo to visit his parents. Margo mused: *"Would be interesting to know what Gray said about me."* She got a goodnight kiss and
wondered, *"What is this man's attraction to me?"*

The air was chilly, the stars shone brightly, and it seemed like an oth-
erworldly experience to Margo; she slept some ten hours that night. The
next day, she was headed out to visit and stay at a sheep farm among
other stops, but she promised to call Gray when she got to Christchurch where he and his family lived.

Along the way she did two tours at Skippers Canyon and TeAnau.
The geography, spectacular as it was, wasn't that important, but the humanity was, as she met Bruce Burrow, whom she would later "liaison"
with in Australia.

But first she had to get to Christchurch. It's the largest city on the
South Island of New Zealand and resembles Denver in that it lies on a
flat plain with mountains in the background. She could see the mountains clearly on that sunny day and unlike Denver, Christchurch did not
have an ugly smog haze hanging over it.

Upon arriving, she called Gray:

*He actually sounded like he'd been anxiously awaiting my ar-
rival—thought I'd arrive for the weekend. He came over to the hotel
where I was staying. I got us a bottle of wine. He brought me a poster
of Lake Matheson—it's great and very thoughtful of him. We chatted
for a couple of hours sitting on my bed. Made tentative plans to visit
a bunch of tourist spots.*

She describes her adventures with Gray in a letter to her family this
way:

*One of the friendly New Zealanders I've met is a fellow Gray who
lives in Christchurch. We met over at my favorite spot of all in New
Zealand—the Fox Glacier. I called him on my arrival in Christchurch.
He was eagerly awaiting my arrival much to my surprise. We ended
up spending lots of time together for the two weeks I used Christchurch
as my base. He took me touring plus we went up to Hanmer Springs,
a natural hot springs resort area about three hours west of C.C. It was
fun having someone to hike with, ride the bus, eat and drink with.
So—he's decided to see some of his country by traveling with me for a
week. That will be an interesting experience for an independent me.*

The next day they were off to the Banks Peninsula. Christchurch is by
the sea so it wasn't a long drive. After wandering through little towns
and stopping at countless overlooks, they made it to Westport. Westport's current web page says: "Welcome to the Northern West Coast—
the ultimate getaway experience where you can discover the real New
Zealand. Switch off your cell phone and leave your watch at home—life
on the 'Coast' runs at its own pace."

The Banks Peninsula and its many hills were formed by two giant
volcanic eruptions. The little one of Akaroa was a highlight of their
touring as was the spectacularly beautiful drive along one of the craters,
and the sun would not stop shining. Again Margo projected the love
she had of the out-of-this-world scenery onto Gray. What a lucky man
he was!

I got in touch with Gray to get some photos and memoirs of Margo.
The issue of who was taller came up and Gray told me this. "All very
memorable, we enjoyed being companions very much…That quiet understanding as people become friends and work out what to do together

58

with the time they have (short in our case)… height was a joke between us… and eventually there had to be a 'measure up.' This duly happened in Napier at 'The Old Bank' then converted to a hotel. We got the old manager's office complete with the very thick vault door for a couple nights' stay. Well those doors got a couple of small pencil marks and I was the taller by only ½ inch (but of course with heels Margo would be taller)."

Dietitian and food expert that she was, she was proud of herself because in Akaroa she mastered the art of eating fish-and-chips:

> Learned how the Kiwis eat this stuff when it's all rolled up in its traditional newspaper wrap. You poke a hole in the end and use it like a sack! I'd been unrolling mine.

They then explored a cemetery and had fun guessing family stories: "It was peaceful and fun to be with Gray + there was a bit of intimacy—of butting heads; walking arm in arm."

They took a room for the night, played pool at a pub and then back to the room for lovely, gentle lovemaking:

> Gray treated me like I try to treat men with gentle caresses. It was very nice but I wasn't very communicative about how nice it was. I'm being very much to myself making few commitments about anything.

They then drove back to Christchurch with never-ending ocean views from the hilltops: "I could have sat on that oceanfront forever."

When they got back, Gray went to do his own thing and Margo took in some classical music at the Town Hall—a performance of Mozart's Mass in C Minor and The Magic Flute. Margo was in heaven—music, mountains, and a man. Gray did not care for classical music so Margo went by herself.

Over the next couple of days, Margo and Gray, at Gray's insistence, went off to explore various sites and locales. These included hiking various forest trails in and around Mount Cook and a trip to a thermal resort on the South Island:

> It was a day of walking to a forest trail, a glorious half hour in a private spout bath—wonderful gentle caressing in warm water— heavenly and very relaxing. That's a scene I've always dreamed of— in reality I would have been happier with Ted or Skip—but it was very fine with Gray. The evening ended with four hours of dancing.

After some alone time in which Margo took a bumpy ride by herself to Mount Cook and explored its beauty on *"a glorious day,"* she readied herself for her inevitable departure. She celebrated the end of three months of travel and on June 21 Margo and Gray separated:

> *Parting was so quick and unreal. I feel amazingly at loose ends without him. It had gotten very comfortable having him around and we are getting closer. I think it's good that we didn't get closer. All that time with Gray did something to me. I got pretty comfortable with him and having someone to share all of this. I'd have liked to have shared more of me—but I never felt he was open to that. He'd change the subject if the topic got too intimate.*

Then Margo ended her time in New Zealand and Gray with these words sent to her family:

> *As for traveling alone so far it's great. I've met so many terrific people. Think I'll have to stay abroad since my social life has picked up. The unfortunate part is that it's all very temporary although I may be able to meet a few of them in other countries. That could be fun—particularly in the identified spots of Thailand, India and Japan.*

"david is quite (and quiet) a goliath"
sydney, australia

July 1986

I know I am but summer in your heart
And not the four seasons of the year.

— Edna St. Vincent Millay

David was waiting for me right outside the door. Oh—did he look good—better than I remembered. Partially because he was in his suit from work as opposed to arriving scruffy from travel. Only a light peck on the cheek did I receive. But he took me on a little tour of the city—it looks lovely. The plane in fact circled around across Manley Beach to the north with the Harbor Bridge and Opera House. We stopped at the

Oakes Bar for a couple of beers and a little chat before going home to Annette. And then to his club in Fairlight for another beer. We both are expressing regret at the timing of my visit in terms of personal events. Seeing him intensifies my desire to have him.

Margo had last seen David three years before in New York City when she was still working for Biosearch and she was overwhelmed to see a professional man again. David Cranna was not a big man but he created a confident presence when he entered a room. He was then wearing a neatly trimmed beard, had brown hair and eyes, and looked exceptionally neat and fit. That he was a professional in Margo's own field of expertise was doubly attractive, plus, he had an infectious all-knowing smile which melted Margo on the spot.

He had neither of the two character traits which the website Move and Stay says typifies Australian men. "In general Australians are not pretentious by nature. They have a casual drop in approach when socializing and working…there are two common stereotypes…the first is the naïve and Neanderthal male great for beer and a laugh." Margo called these types *"funny looking." "The other is a tough, adventurous male who conceals his strength."* David was certainly this latter type of male as was Bruce Burrows whom we shall meet later.

Unfortunately, Margo was to be temporarily disappointed by David. Her first four weeks in Australia were a whirlwind of tourist stops and she hoped David would choose to be her personal guide much like Gray had done in New Zealand. She was disappointed that he chose not to. Nevertheless, in her first two short weeks in Sydney she took the ferry across Sydney Harbor, went to *Aida* at the opera house with Zdenck Macal conducting (*"he looked like he was having an orgasm several times—very passionate"*); botanical gardens; Governor General's castle; art gallery; Hyde Park Barracks; David Jones Department Store (where a clerk told her it was crazy for Americans to travel outside the U.S. when we had the most wonderful country in the world); the zoo; Katoomba (beautiful valley); museum; Jenolan caves; the town of Dubbs and more. So, in all this sightseeing, what did Margo notice? That the Aussies weren't as friendly as the Kiwis and that the Aussies had different food habits such as eating baked beans on toast.

David had a dinner for Margo her second night in Sydney and he invited a couple over who were his pharmaceutical pals.

It was fun but as usual I was the odd person out. I avoided looking at David until the end of the evening, then I felt I was getting deep penetrating looks which pierced my heart. I can't stand that as I have to rid myself of my great turn on for him. Is it again that he is unobtainable that I'm so desirous? Shit.

But at the end of the first two weeks her ardor for David had subsided. *"Feel better—not so obsessed by David and not having him now that I've had some days out of my own..."*
She added,

I feel like David and I talk alone and Annette sits back. But haven't I done the same? Can I get a three-way conversation going? Does it matter? My desire for David is dwindling but could surely rekindle if there wasn't Annette. It was cool, crisp but brilliant sunlight those two weeks. It all felt so good and I felt so good but also very desirous of David and certainly desirous of a relationship. I am very tired of being alone with no male companion.

David was a big deal and the only person Margo kept in touch with after her Asian journey. In many ways, Margo saw David as a bit of a Renaissance man and that fact helps explain why Margo was so smitten with him.

One day, near the end of her first stay, Margo put on some snazzy black pants she had purchased.

I felt good in them. Think David thought I looked good, but he's keeping silent since I was so open in my feelings a week ago, so I have hardly a clue what he's thinking since then. If we were spending time alone, I'd try to get into him more as I finally was with Gray. But at this point David is as private as Gray was for the first one and a half weeks. Are they typical of down under men?

She then started thinking about the rest of her Asia travels.

I'm feeling pretty strongly. I want to move fairly rapidly around Australia and get to SE Asia in early fall. That means eliminating time with Gray but I can't dilly-dally around for that.

So there!
Then on Monday, July 28, Margo left to see the rest of Australia but not before getting *"the nicest real kiss I've had from David on this visit."*

So here we are on October 23, four months later after much touring through Australia, and we shall hear of later…to see David waiting for her as she arrives from Canberra by train.

In those intervening months she had been to Brisbane, Fraser Island, the Whitsundays, the Great Barrier Reef, Cairns, Darwin, Alice Springs, Ayers Rock, Adelaide, the Yorke Peninsula, Melbourne, the Grampians, the Great Ocean Road and the Twelve Apostles, Laval Bank and Canberra. She had two romantic affairs—with Titus camping and Bruce Burrow and his entourage. She was to spend two more weeks with David and Annette before going on to Perth and then Thailand. My head swims when I simply recount all that I read from her diaries and the fact she was carrying a backpack with her across an entire continent.

Margo was *"very pleased"* to be greeted alone by David.

It was good to see him again but I'd certainly recovered from my crush on him.

Her big thrill in coming back to Sydney was *"lots of mail waiting for me—great fun!"* She was particularly delighted to get a letter from Pete McVay, a colleague of her dad's and a former president of Cargill, inviting her to his twenty-thousand-acre ranch in Western Australia. After so much time in the outback Margo noticed something about herself which would affect her in the future.

I noticed most times when I go into the city I get very lethargic—think it's intimidating to me—the city with its beautifully dressed people, shops and restaurants enticing you to spend dollars. Really makes me wonder what I should do when I return to the U.S.

Margo noticed that Annette was becoming more tense during her last two weeks; clearly it was time to move on again. Then, on the day before heading off to Perth to visit the McVay ranch, she had a day alone with David; Annette chose not to come along.

A very pleasant picnic with David in the Royal National Bank; saw Botany Bay, sat by a lake; chatted, walked, hugged slightly—warmly… Strange to realize this is the end of this long awaited trip to Sydney. As there has always been with David, I feel there's much left unsaid. It would be interesting to know what he's really thinking and feeling but I never feel he's really open or ready to talk about his

63

feelings for me. So I let it go. If he had real burning feelings for me I'd hope he'd say so. So I assume he just enjoys me which is fine. (Margo always writes this stuff and it isn't fine!)... Again I am a bit sad about moving on but is definitely time to.

Then on Friday, November 7, 1986, Margo said goodbye and was driven to the airport by Annette.

"the rock star"
the outback in australia
september 1986

> Study how water flows in a valley stream, smoothly and freely between the rocks. Also learn from holy books and wise people. Everything—even mountains, rivers, plants and trees—should be your teacher.
>
> – Anonymous

Uluru (a.k.a. Ayers Rock)

Backpacker, hiker, and world traveler Margo was beyond thrilled when Ayers Rock and the smaller formations of the Olgas began to raise their heads above the dead flat horizon as the tour bus neared those monoliths in Australia's Northern Territories. They're a three-hundred-mile bus ride from Alice Springs, which itself is in the middle of nowhere—a twenty-hour bus ride from Adelaide.

OK, for your geologically challenged, nothing in Australia is more identifiable (the Sydney Opera House notwithstanding) than Ayers Rock. It's a solitary, one-of-a-kind, color-changing, desert monolith two-and-a-half miles long rising a thousand feet above the surrounding scrubland. It's a lonely desert iceberg in that two-thirds of the Rock lies beneath the land. It is a sacred sight to the local Aborigine people—the Anangu.

The Rock's attraction, besides its mass, is its changing colors. If you first see it in the afternoon, it's ochre-brown; then, as the sun sets, it becomes a burnished orange followed by a series of darker reds and finally a deep, rich charcoal. Margo and I once experienced something similar in the Big Horn Mountains of Wyoming near the town of Ten Sleep at dusk.

Margo arrived at the Rock early September on a deluxe bus with a video showing movies, but she soon set about to find a campsite near the Rock. It was US$4 for the campsite and the same amount to rent a tent. *"I'm pleased with myself in deciding to camp."* She tried to go swimming at the campsite pool but the water was way too frigid. However, *"much to my surprise, Titus* (the Swiss whom she had met earlier) *was there."* The two began to converse and so began another traveling relationship on her Asian journey.

Titus was slight in stature, not as tall as Margo, spoke with a charming Swiss accent and had a sense of presence like David. He had brown-blondish, tussled hair and bright blue eyes. In terms of education, he was going to get an MBA in accounting in Switzerland.

Margo did muse a bit.

> *Too bad all those nice men and I must pass each other. Again with Titus the pattern is the same—a nice friendship developed over a number of encounters and then some intimacy.*

I think a lot of the physical attraction had to again do with the beauty of the surroundings and the need to share it with someone. She wrote of the outback:

> *The outback has grown on me and I'll be sad to leave. It has a special quality. I feel grimy and full of sand but I don't care... Oh, am I pleased with myself! It's lovely out here and I'm camping alone. The flowers are both new and old to me. New ones include egg face—white paper petals with yellow button centers, desert rose (purple poppy looking), little lavender and white flowers. The lands are blanketed with white and yellow flowers. Beautiful! Saw wild camels! Wow!*
>
> *September 10. Today I climbed Ayers Rock—started at 7:20 a.m. and arrived on top at 8:15. Steep. Steep. Incredible vistas and a sense of the isolation of the countryside from on top...I really did the climb alone though Titus passed me...My legs felt like jelly and my knees were aching but I made the trip. All I can say is Stunning! Breathtaking! Unbelievable!*

And then she added, *"Ecstatic!"*

65

After her climb, ever-moving Margo went off in a tour bus to get a closer look at the Olgas (Kuta Tjita in Aborigine): "Thirty-six soft domes on that range of conglomerate of three minerals—granite, feldspar and sand in between—that was formed six-hundred-million years ago. The tallest rock, Mt. Olga, is actually some six-hundred feet higher than Ayers Rock," said a travel book. After touring the Olgas, she came back to Alice Springs and met up with Titus once again.

They agreed to try and meet in Adelaide, a larger southern city of some 120,000 people, in a couple of days. *In fact, we talked about getting some good French bread, cheese and wine. He's twenty-nine—a year older than Gray"* (whom she'd met in New Zealand).

Once she left Alice Springs she took a Greyhound bus to Adelaide and arrived at 6:30 a.m.. After a good night's sleep on the bus, she showered at the bus depot and then, lugging her backpack, walked to the YMCA looking for a room.

Lonely Planet describes Adelaide thusly: "Sophisticated, cultured, neat, casual—this is the image that Adelaide projects, a nod to the free colonization without benefit of convict immigration." But Margo loved Adelaide because it was flat as a pancake and thus easy to walk around.

As often happened on this Asian jaunt, she ran into the same people, and as one would have it, Titus appeared once again. He was getting ready to go to the Yorke Peninsula, a favorite camping area, in a couple of days. She was elated when Titus and his male companion, Nicholas, invited her to join them on their camping adventure.

Margo said she would very much like to join them but she had no sleeping bag and all her clothes were dirty. Wow, Margo flipped out, for they waited for her to buy a bag and wash her laundry at the Y.

What a kick. Me in this beat-up station wagon packed to the gills, driven by this scruffy-looking blond Kiwi whose hair looked like an Aborigine's—totally uncombed and long at that. And the cute Titus but also with semi-messy hair and unshaven. But we had fun—totally relaxed with each other it seemed.

She commented on how green the landscape was as they headed out on the peninsula. She wrote, "*I mean green, green; green… it felt like the north isle of New Zealand or better yet Scotland or England.*" Titus was equally impressed by the bush scenery.

Finally they got to a little town—Edithburgh. It's described in *About*

Australia as a "delightful holiday destination just 120 miles from Adelaide with a population of 450…why not have a picnic or BBQ on the seashore and enjoy one of the walks ranging from historical scene and coastal." And that's exactly what they did. Margo described the scene as they set up camp while dealing with a strong wind (in 1955 wind turbines were erected) and periodically it was rainy.

> *We put up Titus' tent—all three of us slept in his two-person tent. Cozy it was to be. Nicholas began cooking tea right away—potatoes, carrots, onions and parsnips in tomato sauce seasoned with curry, ginger and garlic. It was great!*

It was still light when they finished dinner and tent clean-up and headed to the pub.

Titus was immediately taken with Margo, just as Gray had been in New Zealand, for Kiwi and Swiss women had the same dour characteristics. A blogger wrote, "Swiss men prefer foreign women because Swiss women are so backward and introverted" and no one could make that statement of Margo in her present state of mind. Likewise, Margo was equally taken with Titus.

Margo caught his enthusiasm and curiosity right away. She was much taller than Titus but he carried that confident European air and was as precise as a Swiss army knife when it came to making campfires and benches. Titus, like Margo, was enthralled with Australia's "wide open spaces."

> *We went for a couple of hours of port, billiards—I did very poorly—and darts. I held the port better than the group. Oh, yes, we'd bought wine and drank half prior to the tea. We laughed a lot over superb billiards and darts. About 8:30 p.m. we strolled back to camp arm in arm and very happy. I called him a rock star for his agility but being Swiss he didn't get the joke. I crawled into bed first. Titus crawled in to unroll his sleeping bag and we ended up in wonderful kisses. Once both he and Nicholas were in, Titus and I were locked in hugs and kisses for a half hour. It was sensuous. What a treat and somewhat of a surprise. I'm so happy to have been invited along on this trip.*

The wind was howling when they woke up. Nicholas cooked up some porridge and they were on the road by nine thirty. Although they were all hung-over, they stalwartly made their way to Innes National Park.

Innes National Park is on the tip of the Yorke Peninsula and is often considered the Miami Beach of SW Australia. It has the largest area of remaining vegetation on the peninsula and is home to 115 species. *Wikipedia* notes: "The Park contains a spectacular rugged coastline which contains the site of several shipwrecks including the Ethel, which ran aground in 1904 and is well preserved." They set up camp at Casvarina which "is a quiet campground… it has eight sites located behind a locked gate. It has access to the beach."

Once there, they all frolicked like kids. Margo marveled at the thousands of fuzzy caterpillars as she climbed over sand dunes and the guys explored the shipwrecks.

Titus then built us barracks by pounding stumps into the soft dirt; I prepared evening tea—put sliced onions into the slices of salmon I bought; cut up garlic and ginger and a little margarine—wrapped it up in foil; put potatoes in the coals; boiled carrots and parsnips. We were in heaven and plus we had an outstanding fire. Titus and I finished the day with gentle and too-short lovemaking, very sensuous only to be interrupted by Nicholas—who had given us ½ hour alone— bless him. It's no fun being the third person… The next day Nicholas woke us with a cup of tea and we drove back to Adelaide.

They went back to the YMCA where they'd first met. Titus used Margo's room to take a shower and then they were off to a last meal together at the Jerusalem restaurant in Adelaide. It seemed an appropriate venue for this trio.

The Jerusalem restaurant was still the same when I wrote this in September 2011 as they were there exactly on the same date in 1986— twenty-five years ago. One review said, "So I stumbled across this gem when my parents told me I had my first dates there. That was twenty-five years ago so the place hasn't changed one bit, the toilets are down the back of the alley, but mama is still in the kitchen and the boys are still sending out the most wonderful food. Expect no less than the best Lebanese food in Adelaide! There are no frills about this place and there is a high turnover of people, the laughter, the students, all sorts!" Boy, the network that Margo and Titus must have accessed to know where to go.

The next day it was goodbye and Margo walked with Titus to the bus.

Too bad all these nice men and I must pass each other... He's very low key happy—enjoys himself and he too doesn't mind being alone or doing things alone. I really did enjoy him. What a gem of a man.

And what a gem of a story. I would have liked to meet the resourceful Titus and I guess I did when I found him buried away in one of Margo's diaries.

"a hunk of a man"
down home australia

october 1986

I'm just a ship passing in the night.

– Margo Brown

While in New Zealand she went on a tour in a four-wheel-drive van with five other tourists in Skipper's Canyon on the South Island.

The road was a one and two lane dirt mud track with sheer drop-offs of more than 1,000 feet on each side. I've gotten lots better over the years about relaxing when others are driving. I'll let destiny do its work.

The road that Margo was taking was one of only two roads in all of New Zealand where rental car insurance is not honored. Once a bustling gold-mining area, Skipper's Canyon is today one of New Zealand's better known scenic roads. When Margo and I drove scary roads in Montana and Wyoming, I often wondered why she wasn't scared. It is quite obvious now that her absence of fear was probably a consequence of driving and surviving Skipper's Canyon Road.

Wikipedia put it this way: "It has been said that more money has been spent on its account than all the gold that had been taken out because of it. The local rock is so soft that under traffic it quickly turns to dust in dry weather and greasy mud in wet." It was more of the latter as they finished the tour with the sun glistening on the rocks. Here again the rugged scenery started to play a role in Margo's attraction to certain men.

There were five people in that rugged jeep as it gingerly wound its way along Skipper's Canyon Road (five tourists: a couple, Steve and JJ,

69

whom she'd met earlier; two others; and Bruce. She described him as *"an Aussie hunk who I thought was not divorced but found out he was."*

The next day, she went on the glow worm wave tour (yep, you got that right). They are scientifically called "Arachnocampa luminosa" and these creatures, unique to New Zealand—you can't find them in Kansas— radiate luminescent light and attach themselves to cave walls. Really, Margo, I don't know about all these stops; I don't know if I would want to see worms glowing in the dark.

Margo, with her keen eye, learned that Bruce from the Skipper's Canyon tour was also on the cave tour before her and discovered he was traveling with his "mum" (mom). The next day she went to Te Anau, a small town on the border of Fiorland National Park "famed for trekking and spectacular scenery." Lonely Planet described it this way: "Fiorland is NZ's rawest wilderness area, a jagged mountainous, forested zone sliced with numerous deeply recessed sounds (which are technically fiords) reaching inland like crooked fingers from the Tasman Sea."

Once there she took a boat ride to Milford Sound on one of the nearby lakes.

> *Bruce Burrow (Skipper's Canyon) was on the boat. I felt like we played approach avoidance but somehow there's an attraction (mutual). We spent the last half of the ride talking and sharing the experience. The neatest part was when he handed me his address and invited me to come visit him in Stowell, Victoria. Turns out he's the health officer. I'm thrilled. Every time we've come physically close it seems we touch—it's strange but nice and maybe I'm imagining. We'll see what it's like when I meet up with him again.*

So some four months later she did. He told her to call him when she got to Australia. Bruce was by far the most mystical and metaphysical of the men she met on this Asia journey. Margo had been in complicated relationships before (with a guy named Ted and later with me), but this relationship involved Bruce, his son, ex-wife, girlfriend, and even his mother Myrtle, his brother Jim, and all their friends. With this group you needed a scorecard to see who showed up.

Bruce Burrow was very unusual for an Australian man, not brash and loud and crude, but mellow and sensitive. He was thirty-two when he met Margo, and while not as tall as her, he had a toned body and brown hair and eyes; he made an immediate impression on her. While

70

not a weight lifter, she could see by his arms he had done a lot of physical work and she later learned he was renovating an old home called Stonehouse.

He did fit the Australian and New Zealand manner of not being pretentious and Margo was always attracted to men of this sort. Unlike most Australian men, he was not one to go off to a pub to socialize. She called Bruce Burrow, who lived in Stowell, ninety miles from Adelaide, a *"hunk."*

> *He dryly and matter of factly said come tomorrow. He rang back three times so he must be a bit interested in me but you certainly wouldn't know it by his voice or words...typical Aussie man in that manner.*

Then the next morning she was off by bus to Stowell, which prides itself on being "the closest large town to the Grampian National Park." The Grampians are mountain ranges—a lower-scale version of the Colorado Rockies—with spectacular wild flowers, Aboriginal wall art, and home to Australia's biggest gold mine. For you geologists reading this, the Grampians are a series of uplifted, tilted, and eroded ridges. Even I could understand a German website, "Der Grampians ist ein wirkliches highlight von Victoria."

As the bus approached Stowell, Margo wrote:

> *The land is green and filled with sheep, looks a bit like New Zealand. The bus pulled into the station. Bruce was waiting for me. Looked good. Dressed up with white shirt, tie, sweater, wool pants. Had expected a beat-up car. But no, it was a nice clean, relatively new little sedan. He drove me around Stowell a bit and up to the town lookout so I could get my bearings.*

Margo was fascinated to know they were mining gold under the town. Bruce was building out a big stone house. *"It sits with views of the Grampians to the northeast. There will be lots of windows and it'll be wonderful when it's been done but he's been working on it since his divorce."* His hands were calloused from handling saws and hammers.

His mom Myrtle (then seventy-nine) and his brother Jim were staying with him for the week to help him out. Margo was relieved by this because *"it takes the pressure off anything between Bruce and I plus it's fun to see the family interaction."*

After a fairly good night's rest it was off to Stonehouse for a day of work.

> I sanded 1½-inch ceiling boards and then after lunch took a walk over to the top of the hill. It's a magical setting and to top it off we found the mama koala and her baby in one of his trees! Wonderful!!
>
> Bruce is obviously a lover of nature, in tune with his environment, and cried when a koala died in his yard—so sensitive. I'm impressed with his gentleness.

More work filled the day as well as an opportunity to look at pictures of New Zealand. Margo noted:

> Nice day; feels good to be here. Am getting penetrating looks from Bruce and some more of the drawing together of bodies that I felt when we first met in New Zealand. If there's anything there I may never know though. I think his mom and Jim will leave soon…?

On day two in Stowell, Margo took a trip into the Grampians.

> September 27: I've had a great day of hiking and rock climbing. Saw wildflowers—purple coral-common heath, cat's claws, prickly Grevillea. Saw a cockatoo. And walked six miles up and down mountain. I was happy to be in the mountains.

Then on the fourth day at Bruce's:

> And then the surprise—a woman named Angela appeared on the scene and is apparently Bruce's woman. I was taken aback initially and had to fight off jealousy as they walked arm in arm. But so be it. I thought and just as well as then there'd be no sexual question…So then I was surprised again when evening came. We were alone for the first time and he wanted to massage my feet; then my back and face, then hugs and kisses. Nothing is too clear again.

On the fifth day, Bruce went off to work and Margo got to meet his assistant Denise. She listened to Bruce and Denise chatter about his work. As a health officer, "he oversees five shires (counties) which means he checks all septic tanks being put in, does hotel, restaurant, boarding home inspections, some immigration clinics, etc. Curious our work (my past) is so closely related." Later that evening, when everything was quiet and still, "We did walk up Mt. Dryden (his hill). The sheep were noisy. Otherwise it was still and so pretty. Then when we got back, more cuddling."

Margo arrived on a Thursday. The next day they were off for more exploration of the Grampians including Mt. Arapile, which is a favorite of rock climbers from around the world because of the hard rock and the multiple climbing spots. They then went to MacKenzie Falls which is billed by one guidebook as "hands down the star attraction of the Grampians National Park. It is a rare Australian year-round waterfall." Margo noted that the falls (some two hundred feet high) have pink and white terraces. A portion of the falls have shrubs (called kangaroo tails) growing in the middle. Margo could just sigh: *"And it's such fun to be with a man who enjoys the falls as much as I do and who would talk about incredible beauty. Bruce does—love it! Could have spent hours there."*

She adds, *"For me it couldn't be more wonderful looking at sensuous scenery during the day and sensuous cuddling at night..."*

When they got back, Bruce's mom Myrtle invited Margo to stay with her for a couple of days at a little town, Creswick. But they had one more night at Bruce's alone.

I'm sorry to be leaving him—it's quite nice being with him. He's quite caring and sensitive. I'm not good at telling him that somehow I must leave.

She was expecting to take a bus to Creswick, but instead Bruce appeared and took her on an even more intense drive than she had before. They stopped at a gold mine where she could go inside and see the gold seams, three sister rocks, a winery, drove by his old house, stopped by Angela's home and then to an art gallery. Whew!

Angela seems to view me with skepticism and interest but then why should it be any other way... I'm sorry in some ways I left his place but then I must move on. And I'm sure he was spending the night with Angela—but that's really not any of my business and I'm just a ship passing in the night.

OK, Margo's been with Bruce and his family for a week, and now will spend five more days with Myrtle, his seventy-nine-year-old mum whom she likes. Whoever heard of or has been to Creswick, Australia? It's a former gold rush town (25,000 pop. in the 1850s—today around 3,000) and it is as picturesque as a small New England town today.

After her stay with Myrtle ended, she took a quick tour of the gold mine in Stowell. She made her way back to Creswick in a big horse truck driven by a fellow she met at the gold mine in Sovereign Hill.

Once she got back to Creswick, the gang wanted to know about Margo's adventures. *"What fun it was relaying the story."* Bruce and his son appeared around nine p.m. as she was finishing her dinner.

It was great to see Bruce again. He seemed just as pleased as I was. He squeezed my shoulders when he saw me—that's the most affection he dared in front of everyone—much more than I expected! He played footsy and kneezies under the table and we did manage some real hugs, kisses in the kitchen. Oh I'd have loved more.

Margo had the urge to move on and left for Melbourne, ninety miles away, but not before calling Bruce to see if he could come in a couple of days to visit Appell Bay. She went sightseeing for a couple of days—we'd run out of space if I tried to write all the stops down from Botanical Gardens, St. Peter's Cathedral, art galleries. She even called Gray in New Zealand and realized he had moved on. As had she.

Sunday, October 12, 1986, Great Ocean Road

Great Ocean Road is rated as one of the top five coastal roads in the world and Margo was happy to be there. Incidentally, it is also the name of a favorite Australian cheese that I buy in Minnesota.

A glorious day filled with swings of emotion—elation with the magnificent scenery along the road to Appell Bay to eager anticipation and fantasizing about my upcoming time with Bruce to almost heartbroken feelings when I saw Angela in his car. Ugh! Pooh! I thought. I could hardly be joyous but then I thought—what does it matter. I live in the U.S., he has his life to live and I'm still getting to see this coast and the twelve apostles (rock formations on the coast). So I smiled, said nothing and tried to relax.

We were there close to sunset—absolutely mind boggling was the site. The ocean felt so powerful I felt myself being pulled to it—then an overwhelming sadness hit me—tears—I felt drawn to jump in and be swept away. Part of it had to do with Bruce bringing Angela but also I suddenly felt I'd been deluding myself all these months of travel about my happiness. I was feeling like I'd never find my answers—such a hopeless feeling. This all happened as I sat out on the point. Bruce sat by himself on the mainland. He told me later that he was afraid I'd fall in. I was amazed he was concerned about my safety.

Then they drove back and spent the night together.

> *Last P.M. with Bruce was very special—very tender and loving. I again feel it would be wonderful to stay and explore a longer, more intimate relationship. We said farewell and he had big tears in his eyes. How rare it is to find a man who shows his feelings.*

Once back in Melbourne she visited and stayed with some of the older women she had met earlier at Laurel Bank. This was not the backpacking and camping crowd she usually mixed with. She stayed in a comfortable house with an indoor pool and ate at the Lyceum Club—an exclusive woman's club.

> *Then out of nowhere one of them said she didn't think I was really happy—that I was running. What are you running from?*

Bruce was one of the few men she met on this trip who kept writing to her when she got back to the States, but distance put an end to that and other relationships. The last letter came ten months after her return to the States. She wrote this in one of her many steamer trunk diaries:

> *Bruce Burrow wrote. It was very matter of fact. No real closing—felt unfinished, sounds like he is more in tune with Angela than ever before. He as did Gray commented on how different Americans are than Aussies. Strange how I'm not aware of the cultural differences.*
>
> *In any case either doesn't seem to be any magical connection with me for Bruce. Guess he and all the others will just be fun memories of a stupendous year—not enough time spent with anyone but David and Annette.*

Margo got that right. For in the twenty-two years I knew her, not once did she allude to or mention Burrow or anything about the places she went with him. So if not for the diaries and the steamer trunk that held it, this memory would have just evaporated into thin air.

75

6

aquatic australia september 1986

Either you decide to stay in the shallow end of the pool or you go out into the ocean.

-Anonymous

*A*ustralia is the world's largest island, totally surrounded by water and protected on the eastern side by the Great Barrier Reef, which is slowly disappearing. While Margo met people to go around seeing the interior, she took on "aquatic Australia" on her own.

Eighty-five percent of Australians live within a strip just thirty miles wide along the country's coastlines. And half the nation's homes, many of which Margo stayed in, are eight miles or less from the ocean. Charles Fishman, writing in his book *The Big Thirst*, notes: "Riversides, bays, waterfronts and beachfronts are so present in the daily life of Australia's major cities—in Perth, in Adelaide, in Melbourne, Sydney and Brisbane that it can be easy to forget how precariously dry Australia is."

But Margo had none of that in mind in 1986 when she took off for water sports in the Whitsunday Islands, the Great Barrier Reef, and Darwin, the wettest city in Australia, where they are thinking of building a big canal to bring water south.

Water, Water, Everywhere

As earth's largest island, Australia's eastern shores, centered on Queensland, is the place for all water sports action. It was here that forty-two-year-old Margo played and cavorted like a twenty-year-old until her body ached. Her goal was to sail and snorkel at the Whitsundays, a collection of islands of various sizes off the central coast of Queensland. They are very popular, as they encompass the Great Barrier

Reef. Particularly appealing to our adventurer was the Ngaro Sea Trail Great Walk.

As with any beautiful spot, real estate developers appeared and the place changed. They showed up in the Whitsundays in 1925 and gave the whole area the name of the Gold Coast. The name has stuck; there's even a town called Gold Coast City. There is actually a fifty-mile stretch of white sand beaches, but Margo passed through this "tangle tangle," as my mother called it, to get to the good stuff.

A Saturday: Sailing the Whitsundays

George, the owner of the Coral Waters, is Croatian! (Margo was half Croatian.) Been here for 28 years. He greeted me with Dobra Ute (good morning). He was lovely to me—took me and my bags to meet the sailing bus, gave me a hug when he dropped me off: 'Who knows, we may be related'.

I did my laundry, got tanning lotion, a new rain/wind jacket (threw out the aqua one I've had for 20 years), then off to meet my new sailing mates.

So my boat, the Libra, had the three guys, myself and a young geologist, Janelle, who is bright, fairly quiet, a bit pensive and only 21, plus Peter the captain and his mate Gabriella—a gorgeous, delightful, bright woman of Uruguayan descent.

As we pulled up to the dock in the bus I was overwhelmed at the beautiful setting and water—it was the richest aqua-colored water I've seen. Oh, how fortunate I am to be off to sail for seven days!

Once on Libra we picked our berths, got oriented to the boat and off we went—motoring off to Hook Island and Nara Inlet. It was great being on the water, in the sun surrounded by beauty. Nara Inlet was quite long—there were about 10 boats anchored.

Dinner was fish Mornay and a nice salad and pudding cake. Low-key evening with fairly early bedtime. This is the first time I've been sailing and waited on. Gabriella is so easygoing and happy to please. It is a lovely experience.

Sunday: Whitsunday Island

A brisk jump into the sea for a before breakfast swim—ooh, ooh, a bit chilly but totally refreshing. And after breakfast off to shore to oyster. What a kick. We'd find the oysters stuck to the rocks, take the screwdriver to pry open the shells by pounding the driver with a rock, then pull out the oysters. Great fun!

Then we motored around the inlet out past Hayman Island where a new resort is being built to fit into the environment and onto Butterfly Bay. It was and still is fairly unruly with big swells. I've concentrated all day on not getting sick. Gabe made Oysters Kilpatrick (oysters, bacon and soy sauce—all cooked and quite nice).

Chunky Peter and I snorkeled a fair bit—oh, some beautiful coral and I know the reef is really going to be spectacular! It was rough because of the waves and no fins—but it was still fun. Peter and I swam back to the boat. What a day of exercise as I had climbed the rocks on shore for about 30-45 minutes! They were quite impressed with my energy level. But I know I have to keep moving to keep in good spirits and to not get obese.

Monday Through Friday: Sailing, More Sailing and Even More Sailing

Although Margo's steamer chest is chock-full of journal entries that describe in detail her first week's sailing activities, they, as a whole, highlight her incredible energy and zeal, love of water activities, and her admiration of the natural world. They also tell of a woman who remained on the lookout for her dream man. *"Perhaps I also need to hang around some nicer bars to meet Mr. Traveler with $ and nice personality."*

During her week cruising on the boat Libra, Margo experienced the joys of sailing, snorkeling, topless sunbathing and swimming, roaming the shores, living outdoors, windsurfing, oyster diving, the beauty of many exotic ports, dancing and drinking to the wee hours of the night, exquisite cuisine cooked by the Captain's mate, Gabriella, a failed attempt to connect with a man named Dusty and so much more. Alas, let's not forget the joy of sandflies. As she noted, *"My legs are covered with sandfly bites. There are moments when I feel like they're going to consume me."*

Great Barrier Reef: Into the Next Week

Oof-da, can I really get up and make it OK to the Reef or not? That was the question at 8 a.m. after four hours of sleep. Then came the weather question. Decided yes to both—managed to get out to bread store and back to eat it and felt amazingly OK.

Anyway—to the Reef. The weather looked questionable but Air Whitsunday assured us all it was sunny at the Reef. The flight out over the islands was great. Such fun to pick out our sailing route and mooring spots. The water was aqua blue; Whitehaven Beach glowed off in the distance. Once beyond the isles we experienced the thrill of seeing a whale and her calf gliding through the water. As we approached the Reef we could see it go for miles. It looks like brown rocks at the surface—this was low tide. Our pilot pointed out waterfalls—gushing water through crevices in the coral. The water landing was smooth and soon we were walking on the Reef. For me it was exciting to finally touch the Reef and experience the hardness of the calcium shell. The pilot picked up pieces to have us touch them—some oozed sticky liquid, some closed up when he picked them up—in the end I got much more comfortable touching pieces; one I touched I think was an anemone and it closed right up—it was like a mushroom (or the underside of one until it closed). Stunned me when it closed up so fast. I discovered a beautiful gigantic clam with brilliant blue insides—must have been three feet long. Ooh-la-la—had never known what the wavy, beautiful-colored, worm-like things were—turns out they're the insides of clams!

We were given little tubes—about five inches in diameter with glass or Plexiglas about three inches from the end. It functioned like a snorkel mask to bring the coral on the reef into clear view. Lovely! The snorkeling was good as always but I was disappointed that the coral and fish were not as spectacular as others I've seen. At this point one has to be impressed with the massiveness of the Great Barrier Reef. But—that's it for the moment. I hope it gets better off Cairns.

What Do I Do Now?

After exhausting herself on the Whitsundays and the Great Barrier Reef, Margo pondered what she should do next:

I'm quite ready to get on to Darwin to see this Northern Territory which is amongst the most intriguing to Aussies. And to the Far East—I'm feeling eager to experience new cultures and maybe to challenge myself more. Definitely need to lighten my load before I hit those hot Asian countries. And after chatting with Wendy, the South

79

African, I think I should work at finding a traveling companion for Asia—Darwin & Perth should be the places. Am also going to check on excursions to Papua, New Guinea and Malaysia from Darwin. Currently feel that'd be a kick to add on at the spur of the moment.

Crocodile Dundee

I'm excited; this is rugged territory. Darwin (pop. 73,000) was the starting point. It's much smaller than I imagined, kind of like Evansville, Indiana, (where Margo had once lived and would live again*).*

She hung around Darwin for a couple of days and then headed for Kakadu, Australia's largest national park—7,800 square miles, just a little smaller than New Jersey.

Margo flipped out when she learned about it, as it is full of crocodiles, birdlife, waterfalls, and 25,000-year-old rock paintings. And it's hot and steamy, with an average annual temperature of ninety-four degrees. Naturally, she found time to go swimming:

We (she and a friend, ed. note) *stayed for three hours on the beach. I went topless and felt heavenly. I think I have a bit of exhibitionist in me since I basically like my forty-two-year-old body. It looks pretty damn good for my age. A sense of freedom comes over me when I expose my body in public like that.*

Kakadu National Park

Finally I'm there! We passed the point on the South Alligator River where Crocodile Dundee and the lady were dropped off from the boat. Most of the day we drove through flat lands. Lots of young gums (they <u>are</u> the same as eucalyptus). We actually saw a couple pairs of beautiful cranes with long red legs—they danced for us—spread their wings; rainbow bee-eaters (when their wings are spread they look like butterflies); water buffaloes; magpie geese (all those small magpies are called Mary Magpies); three kangaroos hopping across the road; wild horses; scrub bulls and wild boars. Excellent!

Today the terrain we drove on was flat with thin forest of gums and scrub ferns (my term). The road most of the way was dirt/gravel—bumpy and rugged. We set up camp at noon. It was great as each of us had to set up our own tent. I ended up sharing with Theresa, a

55-year-old small lady traveling on her own. Lunch at the campsite and then off for a glorious afternoon of swimming at the Barramundi Gorge and waterfalls. Heavenly water and scenery. Sheer rock cliffs. We swam across a pond to climb the cliffs to get to the higher pools and falls. There are 11 of us plus our guide/driver, Steve. Andrew Mack, entertainment union organizer, is the best-looking and intriguing, but he's with his mate, Ashley, the botanist who I really like. In addition to Theresa, there's English Ellie; Jennie, a teacher from Melbourne; Alvina, a geography teacher from Sydney; Uras, the Swiss fellow, and two fun Pommies who never gave me their names. Coedzi, the Japanese gal. Good group.

A flat tire greeted us on our return to the vehicle. Took the guys 45 minutes to pump up the spare. In the meantime the rangers came by with five-month-old Joey, the wallaby, in their pack. Since it was about dusk on the return to camp, we saw heaps of wildlife.

Dinner, a great bonfire, too much wine and good conversation topped the day. For a change I was an active participant in the fireside conversation. Steve was a cracker with digs in good fun at us all.

Wow—I slept like a baby even though I was on the ground in a tent. Wonderful to wake up to hear the birds in the wilderness. A big breakfast—even offered us lamb chops, which I resisted. Breaking up of camp, checking out of birds and a slow start. Then off to the Yellow River for an excellent cruise through the waterways to view the wide variety of bird life—rainbow bee-eaters, pygmy geese, lotus birds with their red plumage, large pink lotus lilies, white-bellied eagle, snake-necked darter, one of whom was drying her scraggly wings, jaberus—crane-like birds with long red legs that bend [in the opposite direction from ours]; red-tailed black cockatoos with glorious big red areas on their black tails; pretty [water lilies in] a buffalo hole in the bog. Outstanding viewing. I really love learning about the birds and being able to identify them. No crocs unfortunately.

Next we were off to the breathtaking Ubbir Rocks where we saw Aboriginal rock paintings that were terrific—some up to 20,000 years old. The Abos have been in Australia for 40,000 years. The cliffs/rock formations are of the oldest sandstone in the world—2½ billion years old—and border on the Arnhem Plateau, a sacred

Abos area. The story goes that a rainbow serpent pushed the earth up to form the rocks and then a giant cockatoo split the one apart into three pieces. The paintings took my breath away—guess I've known of them for years but seeing them was something else. I could have spent the whole day roaming, sitting and contemplating this Ubbir area. And then when we climbed the rocks to the 360-degree lookout, it knocked my socks off to view the vast land and rock formations around us. The pictures will never do it justice—what a remarkable contrast to NYC or even Minneapolis. The thing I really don't like about tours is that one can't sit in a spot like that and just enjoy—I should have eaten my lunch quickly and gone exploring on my own rather than hanging around with the group. Ah—the great hindsight.

From Ubbir it was an ice cream stop and the beginning of the trip back to Darwin. We stopped at a termite mound—these eight-foot ones are at least 100 years old. When the wet season comes, they add on to get away from the water. One queen is in charge of one mound. She produces several thousand eggs/day. These are plant termites—don't eat into cement/bricks. Our last stop was a refreshing leap into a pool at Ambarrara. Then separation from the group but an excellent value excursion with new friends in Adelaide and Melbourne.

Nitmiluk National Park and the Katherine Gorges are inside under this park; Nitmiluk means "place of the cicada dreaming" in Jawoyn, the language of the local Aborigines. The deep gorges (thirteen, carved through the sandstone by the Katherine River) and the surrounding landscape have great ceremonial significance to the Jawoyn people.

Here it's OK to swim in the summer when harmless freshwater crocodiles are in the water. The winter season is different because saltwater crocodiles that do eat people inhabit the water. The lesson is to know your crocodiles. Margo was aware of this as the group entered the gorges; she exhausted herself, got some great advice, and learned the limits of her strength.

Katherine Gorges: September 1986

Today I did one of the best tours of my trip to date—the all-day Katherine Gorge trip with about twenty-four others. The sandstone walls of the cliffs were stunning in their reds, peaches, beiges and pinks.

My first major problem occurred today. My camera is jammed and will not work. Damn, but decided there was no point in getting excited as there's nothing I can do at the moment. Much to my amazement, an Adelaide couple offered me the use for the day of their second camera and a roll of film. That was terrific. I'll have a second set of prints made for them.

My legs haven't worked so hard since I left NZ. I'm sure tomorrow they'll feel like they did after my first two days at the Fox. I can feel the jelly in them.

We boated across or down the length of each gorge, then walked the rapids—doing this six times and finally climbed up on the rocks over gorge 7 to have a look about. It was breathtaking. We were the only people up there and we were a quiet group. Outstanding! Then we swam in all but the last or first gorge on the way back.

Terrific combination of hot sunshine, stunning scenery, exhilarating exercise in the form of hiking and swimming. Also it was a good group—a young female English physician who has been working and traveling in Australia for two years; a female architect from Sydney, a nurse who has been working for the Flying Doctor Service for the past 12 months out of Tennant Creek, the Adelaide couple who lent me their camera—just to name the ones I talked with the most.

We returned to Katherine at 6:10 and I left on the Greyhound at 6:25 for Alice Springs.

I sat with a funny lady who's been living in Darwin the past seven years. She traveled Thailand, Burma and Nepal alone last year. Says she'd never do it again—too many hassles and tight situations. It's making me think harder about finding someone with whom to travel. I don't seem to find traveling partners very easily.

Thought I felt pretty good when I arrived here. Had a seat to myself from midnight on and did sleep. But goodness I was whipped by noon. First I had to walk about five blocks to where I took a room. Oof-da, the pack is heavy—made sure I bought some shipping containers today so I can get rid of some weight before the next move. Took a room for $12 at Left Bank Guest House. Had to rent bedding for $4 for my stay. Room is fine but as in Katherine there's absolutely no soundproofing between units. These are like metal shells with just

83

plywood between them. Plus it's cold again—boo. It was nice to not worry about the cold. But—here we go again. Sure it's due to tiredness. I tried too hard to be 20 yesterday.

So what do you do when you are physically exhausted by aquatic Australia—you go off to Thailand, of course.

7

annie's soapy massage and the bus ride from hell

december 1986—january 1987

> *Suddenly, I realized I had the luxury of the unobserved life to me when, at an age, I was coming to regret how much of my life I had wasted worrying about what other people thought. It was a revelation.*
>
> *– Joan Chatfield Taylor, The Pleasures of the Unobserved Life*

*L*et's face it—there was a lot of western culture in New Zealand and Australia which Margo could immediately identify with, maybe with the exception of eating baked beans on toast. But when she got to Thailand and India all that disappeared. Margo refused to stay in five-star hotels (she couldn't afford them in any case) so she plunged head first into those cultures, free of all restraints. Some of her friends looked at those plunges as "adventures" and "Margo being Margo," while total strangers I showed the manuscript to said she was downright reckless. I'll let you decide.

But whatever the case, she survived and lived through it and enjoyed telling about it, usually while waving a glass of wine. Margo was a strange duck in that she spoke other languages poorly, yet always seemed to adeptly survive whatever culture she encountered. The "real" Asia was a no-brainer for her, as she was a closet Buddhist and Zen master, but she didn't know that when she left for Asia. In a religion like Buddhism, you need the traits of kindness and mindfulness, and her Midwestern upbringing gave her that.

This made me wonder why the heck she was living in New Jersey, which in many ways is the antithesis of that sort of thinking. Go ahead, think of what the words "New Jersey" conjure up. Time's up. I'm sure it wasn't kindness and mindfulness.

It's a shame most Westerners only experience Buddhist culture in the little strips of paper in fortune cookies they get when they buy Chinese food. So rather than add to my weight problem by eating through thousands of fortune cookies, I joined a unique club outside of Minneapolis called The Marsh (a center of balance and fitness). It offers classes in every kind of yoga—I like Yoga Nidra where you basically fall asleep—and many courses about Buddhism. I took a course given by Bhante Sathi (whose name means mindfulness in the ancient Buddhist language, Pali). Boy, would I now like to share my recent understandings of Buddhism with what Margo learned in traveling through those two countries.

The amazing automobile traffic Margo saw in Bangkok and India can be attributed to those kinds of religions, I think. For if New Yorkers were out in that milieu, there would be fistfights at every intersection. Yet somehow Buddhist drivers seem to get along. Fasten your seatbelt for these are two of Margo's journeys you won't soon forget.

thailand

> *Life is about risk and rewards and it requires you to jump. Don't be a person who has to look back and wonder what they could have or could have had. No one lives forever.*
>
> – Anonymous

Margo read the above when we lived in the sensuous green mountains of southwestern Virginia. Although she was hobbling about because of the toll multiple surgeries had taken on her body, she was still actively involved in many art classes.

However, if ever there was a time where Margo walked on the wild side and experienced life to its fullest, it was in Thailand. I would be hard-pressed to find anyone who has matched her adventures, and no one who met this mild-mannered former Girl Scout from beyond rural

Minnesota could have imagined her involvement in such escapades. Most of those adventures were due to her meeting one fellow from Gulfport, Mississippi. Unbeknownst to me, our paths would later cross in one of Margo's diaries.

As I have said, this book has been so fascinating for me to write because during the years we spent together, I did not know much of the wilder side of Margo's previous life. Those times remained hidden away in the steamer trunk and I was too busy enjoying my wife—and making plans for what we were going to do during our coming years together—to go rummaging about in her history. Boy, would I love to ask her about all those experiences now! That's why when asked: "Don't you miss your wife?" I respond, "No, I'm really just getting to know her."

It began innocently enough on November 24, 1986, as the Thai Airways flight took off from Perth, the capital of Western Australia, with its brilliant sunshine, cool climate, cleanliness, order and superb organization. Margo had gone to Perth after Darvin to see a family friend who ran a 20,000-acre ranch nearby. Perth is known as the most remote capital city in the world—1,300 miles from the nearest city of 500,000. One website notes: "Perth's remoteness makes it the perfect laid-back city where travelers can enjoy the good life without the crowds." Margo was leaving the city that ranked eighth in the *Economist's* lovability index and taking a seven-hour flight to the city ranked 132. Still, on leaving Perth, Margo admitted:

> *The city has some lovely spots but I'm tired of Aussie cities, and I'm toured-out in Australia. On boarding the colorfully painted plane we all received a pretty purple orchid. A new adventure has begun. I'm calm and ready for new stimuli.*

And did she get it!

After arriving in Bangkok, she checked into a modern Western hotel, the nicest one she had stayed in during eight months of travel: *"The lobby is spacious and filled with upper-middle-class people from all over the world."* She enjoyed a real swimming pool, Western breakfasts, a minibar, and clean toilets.

The next morning, she went for a walk.

In total contrast to Perth with its cool, crisp, clear air, Bangkok had near-stupefying heat, and air so thick with soot you could almost cut it with a knife. Margo carried a hotel washcloth to repeatedly wipe her continually sweaty brow and the back of her neck. She was always amazed to see how dirty it was after each wipe. She wondered what this dirt was doing to her lungs.

Wow. I'm really here. The sky is polluted; the streets are packed. The visual is incredible. I feel like I'm in a movie set with nothing around being real. Traffic is bumper to bumper, cars, buses, taxis, scooters with sometimes as many as three people aboard, tuk-tuks [three-wheeled motorcycle cabs]. NOISE. Noises of motor scooters whizzing down the street, noise of cars, horns, buses. SMELLS. Smells of peppers, ginger, fat, sweets, pungent, sour garbage, sewage. PEOPLE. Masses of people squatting, food stalls everywhere, sidewalk shoe and car repairs. I'm overwhelmed.

Bangkok was still pretty much of an urban village. "Where else does 90 percent of the population wear thongs and ride to work on river buses?" a website asks.

Reality and perspective crept in about Bangkok and her life in general: *"I'm sensing Bangkok is giving some real answers where to live when I go back to the States. New York City has a lot of similarity on a smaller scale. Yes, it's exciting, but I believe I'm more into quietness and smaller places."*

She mused about home and people: *"Although the traveling bums are interesting, I'm not one of them nor do I really want to be. I do want a professional man."*

After one fairly expensive night in a very nice hotel, she moved to a cheaper one, the Muangphol Mansion, which was located in the center of things in Bangkok, but had "the rudest staff in town" according to one guidebook of the era. In fact, the hotel manager came up to Margo's room and knocked on the door at 3:00 a.m. to make sure she was sleeping alone, for she had paid only for a single room.

But here she was in Bangkok, and traveling and touring was a lot like work: One had to wake up and do it. She asked at the desk that next morning whether it was safe for a woman to walk about town alone. The clerk, who spoke surprisingly good English, said, "The principal dangers to tourists in Bangkok is not crime but crossing the street and ingesting river water getting in and out of river buses."

A fragment of her convoluted Thailand schedule appears on the chart below:

MARGO'S TRAVEL & EXPENSES IN THAILAND
AND NEPAL, DECEMBER 1986

Monday	Tuesday	Wednesday	Thursday	Friday	Sat/Sun
1 Brkft. 63B Train 684B Pills	2 Koh Samui Room 90B Food on 125B Cab 20B	3 90B – Rm.	4 90B – Rm.	5 90B – Rm.	6 90B – Rm. 7 90B – Rm. Train to Bangkok
8 Return to Bangkok Bus 240B Lunch 25B Transp. 37B Room 280B Pills	9 Train to Chang Mai 385B Dinner 48B Drinks 77B Lunch 45B Brkft. 53B Bus 8B	10 Brkft. 20B Taxi 10B Rm. 60B	11 Brkft. 20B Tour 450B Fees 40B Drinks 13B Goods 1550B Room 60B Post Cds. 15B Dinner 15B Drinks 136B	12 Nancy Long's BD Brkft. 32B Rm. 60B Bus 30B Food 37B Beer 42B Phone 5B Laundry 29B	13 8:30 Taxi 15B Tour 500B Milk 17B Train 355B 4:50 14 Whiskey 360B Taxi 80R Tips 15R Plane to New Delhi Room 600R
5 Mary Jo's BD Rm. 600R Brkft. 39R Dinner 55R Pills (Wed.) P	16 Brkft. 40R Lunch 25R Tip 2R Taxi 5R Rm. 600R	17 Taxi 65R Room 600R	18 Dinner 60R Telegram 126R Brkft. 30R Taxi 10R Room 600R	19 5:50 train to Udaipur Tips 25R Frt. 5R Hotel Bill 3070R	20 Lunch 34R Fees 12R Drinks 515R Dinner 70R (Tip 10) 21 Sook 5R pd. Beer 75R Dinner 60R Tip guide 20R

NOTES: B = Thailand Baht about 20 to US$1; R = India Rupee about 12 to US$1

Taxis were unmetered when Margo was there, so every trip required a long negotiation as to price. It was fun and different at first but got to be old and tiresome rather quickly, always wondering whether one was being ripped off.

Today Bangkok is full of skyscrapers, but in those days only one was visible—the Baiyoke Hotel, forty-three stories and as yet unfinished, but already visible from many parts of the city. Margo used it as her compass needle, helping her to figure out where she was. Few of the streets in Bangkok ran straight and true; they were more likely to twist and turn much like the streets in London, where she had traveled almost twenty years earlier. Margo also noted that an odd-looking French car, the Citroën CX, was much in evidence.

As was her custom the day after arriving in an unfamiliar city, she set out to explore via a tour, seeing, among other sites, the Royal Palace and a Buddhist museum. On the tour bus she met Tim and Sally from Nantucket, Massachusetts. They were a calm, deep-thinking, almost metaphysical couple, who seemed to always finish each other's sentences. They were touring Buddhist Asia for several months of meditation study and had just been in India, so they gave Margo lots of hints about what she would be facing.

She had her first Mekong Whiskey with them that night at their hotel, and Tim gave her some very powerful sleeping pills. The "whiskey" is really a kind of spiced rum; it's made from 95 percent sugar cane molasses and 5 percent rice, with indigenous herbs and spices added. It mixes well as an ingredient in cocktails, the most famous of which is the *sabai sabai,* the Thai welcome drink. Margo enjoying this drink often as she became immersed in the culture in Thailand. The one thing she seemed to relate to me most often about her Thai travels was her frequent and pleasant run-ins with Mekong Whiskey. It must still be popular, as every time I've tried to order some online it's sold out.

Margo spent several days with Tim and Sally, her new-found and constant companions. Bangkok didn't yet have its elevated Skytrain, so one of the easiest ways to get around was via river bus, which Margo, Tim, and Sally traveled on many times. Bangkok is crisscrossed with canals, and the long, skinny, powerful river buses roar along the banks. You went to a dock to catch one. There were no ramps or wheelchair access—one just jumped on and off. Margo wondered if anyone ever didn't make the jump. She worried about getting splashed with that dark gray river water. She quickly learned to look both ways down ALL streets in Bangkok, for few traffic rules are observed.

One day they took the river bus to one of Bangkok's famous floating markets, where small, flat-bottomed boats, filled to the brim with every conceivable fruit and vegetable and trinket, were crowded into a very small space at the riverbank. The boats were expertly paddled by mature ladies in colorful dress.

Following her Asia trip, Margo visited Tim and Sally at their Nantucket home. After some extensive searching, I found Tim and Sally in the United States and asked them about meeting Margo and their impressions of her. Sally responded: "I indeed remember Margo well. Margo, Timothy, and I went to a marketplace in search of a Buddha for our collection. Margo simply called it Buddha shopping. Tim and I were headed to Burma to study meditation and Margo was headed to Ko Samui. Tim bargained for a perfect statue while Margo and I watched. When done, we left to have a cup of tea (sitting Buddha statue in hand). When we placed the Buddha on the table to get a closer look, it tipped right over. The statue had been leaning against a wall to hide its deformity. We chuckled at our ignorance. Margo was brave to take this backpacking trip; it's not easy for women to travel alone through Thailand."

Tim was quick to dispense adroit philosophical if not metaphysical advice and offered up a bunch to Margo one evening in Bangkok. After one of her *"tour around town expeditions"* in Bangkok, she called Tim and Sally for dinner:

> *We sure had a good talk—nice sharing. He suggested perhaps I was brighter than most and thus get bored easily and turn people off. He commended me for my guts to do this trip and encouraged me to apply the same principles when I look for a job.*

That evening Tim dispensed some other wisdom about the word *farang* (pronounced fa-long) which Margo would hear over and over again. *Farang* means foreigner, especially white-skinned foreigner. Not necessarily a pejorative, but a word directed at Westerners and something every traveler to Thailand should know. *Farang* was probably brought to Thailand by Persian traders, who to this day use the term *faranghi,* which I became familiar with when I lived in Iran. I talked a lot about being a *faranghi* in Iran to Margo, but she never mentioned how it was to be a *farang* in Thailand. In any event, *farang* or *faranghi* goes back to the Germanic name for a tribe, the Franks, that once roamed Europe and who gave France its name.

Tim explained to Margo that there are all sorts of *farangs.* According to Tim, thumbing through his well-worn *Fielding's Thailand,* the most frequent *farang* is "the older and not so good-looking man with a beer belly that buys women at night and sleeps during the day." So when faranghi pass by a Thai merchant, he immediately calculates their worth.

To get a sense of how *farangs* are regarded by Thais, go to YouTube and type in "Farang: A Nature Mockumentary" and you will get a visual idea of what Margo was up against.

Tim told Margo: "You probably mystify the Thais—a tall, good-looking woman traveling alone: what is she looking for?"

Margo wished she knew.

They ate Thai that night and had Pad Thai at a nearby restaurant. According to *Fielding's Guide*: "This consists of a dish of stir-fried (rice) noodles with eggs, fish sauce, tamarind juice, red chili pepper plus any combination of bean sprouts, shrimp, chicken or tofu, garnished with peanuts, coriander and lime." Margo's tongue could identify and savor the ingredients—quite a feat.

The Bridge Over Once-troubled Water

After what Margo described as a *"WONDERFUL!!!"* night with Tim and Sally, she got up at 5:00 a.m. to be able to catch the 6:30 a.m. train for a 2½-hour ride with them to the River Kwai. *The Bridge Over the River Kwai* is a 1957 film that won seven Oscars and created a huge tourist attraction for Thailand. The plot of the film, largely fictional, details how a British officer cooperated with the Japanese commandant of a World War II prisoner of war camp housing thousands of Allied soldiers. The officer oversaw the construction of a bridge over the River Kwai while oblivious of an Allied plan to destroy it.

According to a travel guide, there was one slight technical problem that the Thais discovered in making this the huge tourist attraction that it now is: the bridge that the tourists were flocking to see did cross a river, but not the River Kwai. Pierre Boulle, who wrote the original book on which the film is based, had never been to the bridge. He knew that the Japanese had built a "death railway," the construction of which had cost the lives of thousands of prisoners of war. It ran parallel to the River Kwai and Boulle assumed the bridge actually crossed the Kwai. It didn't; it crossed the Mae Khlung River. This gave the Thais a bit of a problem when the film became wildly successful. So with admirable lateral thinking, the Mae Khlung was renamed the Kwai (think back to Sally and Tim's problem with the leaning Buddha). After all this, where was the movie really filmed? In Sri Lanka.

Wikitravel described the River Kwai as follows: "Thais know it as one of the most beautiful areas in the country with its easily accessible waterfalls." Once Margo and her new friends got to the river, whichever its name, they were crammed into a minibus. There she met Mitch David of Gulfport, Mississippi. He had something to do with the military then. Bizarre, as I hired a private investigator in Newton, Mississippi, to find Mitch David. In any event, once they reached the river, Margo sat next to David on the minibus, as the driver wanted the *farangs* sitting up front.

> *David hung out with me for the day. He's tall* (in Margo's lexicon this is someone 6' 1" or better), *laid-back and unfortunately a heavy smoker. We ate sticky rice up in an abandoned house overlooking the Thais picnicking among the falls—this way we had a bit of solitude. The sound of the waterfall was WONDERFUL after the noise of Bangkok. Also it was wonderful to see green trees, tapioca bushes, rice paddies. The River Kwai Bridge wasn't spectacular but it was fun to see all the tourists pushing to walk across.*

Margo summed it all up as a *"nice excursion out of the city."*

When she first saw Mitch David at the River Kwai, she noticed a gentle swagger about him. Thus far she had been attracted to a Kiwi (Gray Packer), two Australians (David Cranna and Bruce Burrow) and one Swiss (Titus). So on this trip it was unusual to find an American, particularly from the Deep South, to whom she was attracted. Besides, most other Americans she had seen in Bangkok thus far were middle-aged and potbellied.

David's sunglasses were atop his brown hair, which was semi-bleached by the sun. His face was tanned; he had been in Thailand awhile. Margo was a sucker for tall men and noted David was around 6'3", which attracted her; she was willing to accept him as a heavy smoker. He was, she thought, in his late twenties or very early thirties. His body was quite toned; he must have been lifting weights to develop such muscular arms. A tattoo was peeking out from under the short sleeve of his T-shirt. His exceptionally large feet sported red thongs; he had gone native. He spoke with a slight southern drawl and she could tell that he was educated (no double negatives). But what's a guy like that doing on a stuffy tour to the River Kwai?

On the way back to Bangkok, David sat with Margo with her 36-inch pant leg inseam:

We ended up holding each other's legs across our laps. The physical contact felt mighty good and I could feel David growing beneath my legs. We rode a tuk-tuk home—he dropped me off at the hotel and promised to call.

He told her that he too was going to the still largely undiscovered resort island of Ko Samui (ko means island in Thai) way south of Bangkok the day after next.

The following day she got up late, had lunch with Tim and Sally, and went shopping at the now famous Jim Thompson's. Known worldwide for its silks, it's named after an American businessman who started it. In fact, many of the tourist businesses one sees around Bangkok were started by Americans after the Vietnam War.

Jim Thompson's was already an institution in Bangkok in 1986 and now is a worldwide conglomerate selling silks, design services, and Asian fine goods. The Jim Thompson who started it (after World War II) had been station chief for the CIA (then called OSS) in Bangkok. As the war was ending, Thompson knew that tourists would eventually come to Thailand. Thus he went about refurbishing the only good hotel in town (The Oriental). Then he opened a Western-style restaurant and then more hotels. Then he started selling all kinds of silk goods. His stores—as well as his house—have been tourist stops for decades. A plaque at the Jim Thompson house, which Margo visited that day, reads:

"Bangkok's Leading Farang Host. He had built a major industry in a remote and little known country whose language he could not speak; he had become an authority on art that previously he scarcely knew existed...he had built a home that was a work of art in itself and one of the landmarks of Bangkok; and in the process of doing all this, he had become a sort of landmark himself, a personality so widely known in his adopted homeland that a letter addressed simply 'Jim Thompson, Bangkok' found its way to him in a city of millions."

The next morning Margo went off to try to find David in the city, but was unsuccessful. She ended up looking in countless sauna and massage places—David had said he was staying in one—including the infamous Annie's Soapy Massage Parlor. Margo then felt he was just a sham and went back to see Sally and Tim one more time. They were staying at a better place than Margo and had a bathtub, which she took advantage of: *"It felt great and helped the trip."*

When Margo clumsily clambered onto the overnight train to Ko Samui, she had no idea that this trip would be one of the last of its kind. The travel writer, Pico Iyer, summed it up rather neatly in an article in *Time* magazine:

"As soon as a new last paradise has been found, so many people hurry to make claims on it that it becomes, almost instantly, a lost paradise. With crowds of strangers flocking together to escape the crowds, last year's lotus land becomes this year's tourist trap."

Ko Samui in 1986 was already changing. That year, in addition to Margo's arrival, electricity came to the island—previously, everything had come from the noisy portable generators—and Bangkok Airlines began direct flights from Bangkok. One could now reach Ko Samui in an hour rather than the twenty-four hours that Margo was about to spend by bus, boat, and train. And that odiferous backpacking subculture that Margo semi-represented would be replaced by monied travelers flying in on tours from Europe—mostly from Germany. Instead of chilling out as Margo came to do, this new breed of traveler would, according to a recent brochure, come to "enjoy an elephant trek on the beach, see baby elephant shows, do a tour of Ko Samui, visit Big Buddha temple, go to Lad Koh View Point, marvel at the penis-shaped Grandfather and Grandmother Rocks, see the Na Muang Waterfall Number 1 (just sightseeing, not swimming!), and finally stop at the Nathon Town for souvenirs."

Later, at the train station, Margo thought about Paul Theroux's comment that "a train journey is travel—everything else, especially planes, is transfer; your journey beginning when you arrive."

Margo decided to look for David one last time on the train. She saw his long legs and red thongs on his size 13-D feet sticking out from a berth in second class. She found out she'd had the wrong address while looking for him in the city. They ended up sharing a lower berth with just a drawn curtain separating them from the busy aisle.

Margo recalled that a veritable parade of edibles was offered by hawkers who walked up and down the cars with huge platters of food or prepared delicacies, shouting unintelligible sales pitches. Cold drinks, including our friend Mekong Whiskey, were also available. They were carried in enormous woven baskets lined with plastic and filled with ice. "Preety lady, you want," she heard again and again on that trip whenever she emerged from behind the curtain of their berth.

> *On the train David introduced me to a Roberta from New York City who worked with him. Didn't explain the relationship nor did I ask. I didn't care. He seemed pleased that I'd shown up—so that's all I care about. She probably was not pleased. We did not sleep much as David and I caressed most of the night.*

Ko Samui and Funky Fungi

In 1986 when Margo got on the train with David to go to Ko Samui, it was still a backpacker's paradise, not the Miami Beach that it looks like today. It was one of the original islands that started the backpacker migration to Thailand. Margo and her backpack did not look out of place there. At that time, one backpacker complained "there were a hundred people on the beach." Now it would be ten thousand, and it looks like Daytona Beach at spring break.

Chaweng Beach, where they were headed, was four curvaceous miles long. It was lined mostly with straw huts and primitive bungalows that were rented out by the restaurants they were attached to. When Margo went to Chaweng, it was still referred to as a "traveler's secret."

In "Ko Samui Adventure 1986" (on the *Ezine Article's* website), travel writer Dinah Johnson said: "Ko Samui is ruined now...but a very real part of who I thought I was happened when I arrived to Ko Samui in 1986. It was amazing; a round mountain jutting out of a turquoise sea surrounded by powdery white sand and blanketed from shore to shore with beautiful royal coconut palms."

Margo met a couple from Seattle at that time, the Deforests, and I found their names in her travel address book. I asked them to tell me what they saw in Ko Samui when Margo was there.

"It certainly was not built up—the lodging ranged from primitive to medium. There were no big hotels or fancy resorts. At that time the only access to the island was by boat. It definitely was oriented to the low-budget traveler. The boat to the island was, if I recall correctly, only once a day and was crowded. I would estimate there were 80-100 passengers, almost all young people of various nationalities—very few Thais. All had backpacking-type luggage; nothing hard-sided. We spent four nights at the Lipa Lodge, which consisted of a number of rustic thatched bungalows, and turned out to be quite basic: mats for siding, linoleum-type oil paper on the floor, a noisy fan, cold water only, and fluorescent lights (the one over the bed did not work). The last two nights we upgraded to a much better motel-type accommodation. Transportation around the island was by public minibus, taxi (benches on the back of an open pickup truck), motorcycle, and motorbike rentals. One could stay very cheaply—open-air thatched shelters, no windows, shared plumbing, and surf, lie on the beach, hang out at bars, etc."

But the major attraction that brought backpackers to Ko Samui then was drugs. You name it and it was sold and used openly—still is. The most popular drug then and the one most *farangs* like to talk about was psychoactive fungi—magic mushrooms. Magic mushrooms contain psilocybin alkaloids—in beachcomber talk this means you can get high on them. The beachfront "restaurants" would serve all kinds of food with magic mushrooms—omelets were a big favorite. They gave a three-to-six-hour high. But it got dangerous when some places would sneak in LSD, which could give one a really bad trip.

The Bangkok Post wrote of magic mushrooms and that era this way: "*He keequi*, mushroom growing on buffalo dung, is common throughout Southeast Asia. It has been identified as psilocybin cubensis and is known in English as 'magic mushrooms.' *He keequi* is popular among foreign tourists and is served in omelets on the resort island of Ko Samui…Once the fungus is consumed, hallucinations would appear and the effects confuse the spirit similar to smoking ganja."

A drug from dung!

Margo knew little of this as she chugged south on the train and then took the one-hour bus trip to Surat Thani Province, to the port where one caught the ferry. After that, a one-hour ride in the dark in a pickup truck with bench seats in the back and a driver with suicidal tendencies at the wheel. It was not all that bad, Margo recalled, for *"we were touching all the time."*

> We decided to stay at Chaweng Beach and stopped at the first group of bungalows we came to. We got a bungalow for $3.50 a night at Lucky Mother's.

The desk clerk gave them two candles and pointed them to their bungalow, which was really a grass-roofed shack with a doorway and open windows but no actual door. The sultry breezes just came flowing in. She could hear the ocean and distant music from a noisy bar. There was no electricity or running water and the toilet was out back.

> *Once we saw it was more than a little shabby in the daylight, we were going to look for a different place the next day but decided it was easier to stay put.*

The smell of frying coconut oil permeated everything, as that was the substance to cook with. Coconut palms were everywhere and the coconut trade was still the island's main earner; tourism had not yet taken off.

The next morning they ate omelets containing the magic mushrooms at the little restaurant facing the ocean. The omelets tasted good. Margo surveyed the beachfront, which had other restaurants, including the Bongo Bar and the Pearl. Eventually, they would stop at each of them and have a banana milkshake prepared by a wizened old Brit with dreadlocks. Besides the Brit, Margo was probably the oldest person on the beach, which was populated by Thais in thonged bikinis.

Travelfish.org noted about the Chaweng Beach scene: "If you're not fussed about creature comforts, Lucky Mother has old-style wooden huts running down to their beachfront restaurant. You're talking seriously no frills here, with basic bathrooms and super-soft mattresses, but for the money, in this part of Chaweng, these huts are a steal."

Another reviewer on the Travelfish.org site wasn't as kind about Lucky Mother's: "I travelled Thailand and Southeast Asia for six months, spending three months alone in Thailand. Lucky Mother is the worst accommodation I have EVER seen. It was absolutely disgusting. Bathroom door hanging on by a hinge, it was filthy and stank. You could also see in from outside—nice for the builders working a few feet away. The bed was uncomfortable and absolutely filthy. The walls seemed to have been used instead of toilet paper, in the bathroom and room! The staff were rude and unhelpful, the rudest I have met in Thailand... DO NOT STAY HERE. We left early and lost our money, but were pleased to leave."

But really, one doesn't get a lot for US$3.50 a night.

Margo Freivalds Expenses in Thailand November/December 1986
$1 = 20 Baht

NOVEMBER 1986

Nov 7 - Perth
21-28 to Bangkok

24	25	26	27	28	29
Take pills	10 postcards 20B	brkft 63B	50B - phone	tour 150B	train 75 B
tip - 30 B	taxi 50B	lunch 70B	40B brkft	transp. 25B	paper & milk 15B
2 tours 520 B	room 280B	drinks 30B	bus 5B=orges	dinner 300B	beer 90B
Taxi 45B	tip 10B	bus 4B	175B post(10 cards=90	lunch 22B	banana & orge 8B
3 sodas 87B	Dinner 40B	admissions 30B	5 film=85	massage 120B	
	Beer 50B	dinner 90B	room 280B	soda 5B	**30** bus 2B
	map 35B	room 285B	7.30 Bakers	entry 10B	brkft 60B
	#35 drink 10B	cards 20B		room 280B	lunch 150B
					drink 16B
					clothes 250B
					sunglasses 100B
					room 280B

DECEMBER 1986

Lent David 2500B in 12/8
Borrowed 4000B from Haripal

```
      46
   13) 600
      52
      80
```

1	2 Koh Samui	3	4	5	6→	7 →
brkft 63B	room 9B	90B	90B rm	90B rm	90B rm	90B rm
train 684B	food 125B	90B rm				
Pills	ab 20B					Train to Bangkok

360B
aqt whiskey

8 return to Bangkok	9 Train to Chiang mar	10	11	12	13	14
Bus 240B	385B	Brkft 20B	Brkft 32B	Brkft 32B	8:30	Brkft 79B
lunch 25B	dinner 48B	taxi 10B	Tour 450B	Nancy Long's BD	brkft 500B	taxi 80R
transp. 37B	drinks 77B	rm 60B	fees 40B	rm 60B	brkft 26B	tips 15R
room 280B	lunch 45B		drinks 13B	bus 30B	milk 17B	plane to New Delhi
Pills	brkft 53B		goods 1550B	food 37B	train 355B 4:50 pmbus	room 600R
	bus 8B		rm 60B	beer 42B	15B taxi	
			postcards 15B	phone 5B		
			dinner 15B	laundry 29B		

99

Margo financed the whole trip, which was a "major" expense. Each night at the candlelit bungalow cost ninety baht (US$3.50) and she lent David two thousand baht (US$100). She must have been eating somewhere else, for nowhere in her expense diary did she list anything for breakfast, lunch or dinner.

So what did Margo pen in her diary upon staying in Ko Samui?

Pretty wild week in many respects. I really experienced a bit of the other side of life—that which I've always avoided—from Tim's sleeping pills for two nights to smoking dope multiple times a day, getting very horny from it—acting out on that multiple times a day—to eating funny mushroom omelets and marijuana cookies. I'm pleased to have finally experienced it all—I obviously trusted David—but that's enough. I wouldn't smoke dope again with sex. I know people say that's good—but really enough is enough.

Margo later intellectualized this week as *"freedom from restraints."* She later felt confident enough in telling my daughter she spent the week in Ko Samui *"just screwing."* OK, she did use an expletive to describe what she did, but you get the point. And she told me that many male and female friends (including Roberta, whom she met on the train) would just come and go in and out of their bungalow while they were engaged.

Amazingly, I found the online weather records for Ko Samui for the week Margo was there and it verifies what she wrote. In trying to write up the tenor of the times to further the understanding of the diaries, I felt like Colombo, the TV detective.

She was there from December 2-9, 1986. It was sunny the first two days that Margo and David were really into it inside the bungalow, with a daytime high of ninety and an evening low of eighty. It was 80 percent humidity and the air was thick with moisture and whatever else they were doing. On the next four days, it rained, 3/100 of an inch; 2/10 of an inch; 2.9 inches; and 3.3 inches, before slowing down. She wrote a friend:

The first two days we spent lots of time indoors when we should have been on the beach for then it rained for two days. David and I just cooled down together—very low key and relaxing and fairly sensuous—it all felt good.

This contrasts to a sanitized letter she wrote to her parents, which I found in her trunk. Margo merely wrote:

> *With two weeks of Thailand under my belt, a week of which I sat on the island of Samui in the Gulf of Thailand, I am much more at ease with the scene than those first few days. Anyway it was a wonderful rest.*

Just six weeks earlier, Margo was sitting in the posh Lyceum Club in Melbourne having a dainty lunch and making fun of the rich ladies, and now here she was, eating magic mushrooms and smoking dope with a bunch of basically nude and certainly sweaty backpackers in a grass shack—uh, bungalow.

It didn't take long for Samui to permeate and consume Margo and David—in fact, it appeared it was already in David's bloodstream long before he met Margo. One truth about travel is that the journey one takes to get to a destination can often be demanding and hard on the traveler. Strangely, though, the more difficult the journey, the more one appreciates its beauty—sometimes even more than the destination itself. That's why, after Margo and I married, we enjoyed Culebra (a tiny island municipality of Puerto Rico), which was then hard to reach, as well as Panama, where I had served in the Peace Corps. Florida's Marco Island was just not our kind of place.

Margo said earlier she didn't want to become a "traveling bum" and lie on the beach forever. So her Protestant ethic crept in, and she felt she had to keep up her travel schedule, heading from the beach to the northernmost part of Thailand, 300 miles from Bangkok, to see the mountain city of Chiang Mai.

Northern Thailand (capital, Chiang Mai) is one of the world's happiest places, according to travel writer Paul Theroux, who wrote: "My recurring fantasy is dropping out and spending the rest of my days in a rural village in Northern Thailand." (Theroux's other choices: Bali, Costa Rica, the Orkney Islands, Egypt, the Trobriand Islands, Malawi, Maine, and Hawaii.)

Margo was surprised when David said he would take her to the ferry the next day at 6:00 a.m. so she could make the arduous twenty-four-hour journey back to Bangkok and then continue by train to Chiang Mai. She had David's coordinates and they would meet again in Bangkok upon her return from Chiang Mai.

Once back in Bangkok she wrote:

Bangkok was manageable today. I took a sleeping pill last night and so slept despite the noise. I moved slowly and peacefully today undisturbed by the noise and pollution—Ko Samui was good for me.

She went shopping at a number of places and then visited Annie's Soapy Massage Parlor to be repaid the 2,000 baht (US$100) she had lent David in Ko Samui:

Annie's an old looking, young lady—soft-spoken; repaid me David's loan and offered me a room when I come back thru—why not another new experience!

So she went off to Chiang Mai to see native markets, et al., on a Wednesday and then back to Bangkok on Sunday, arriving at 6:30 a.m.. She felt that she should have stayed in Chiang Mai for another week as she was getting tired: *"Ko Samui only helped me for one week. Yikes—will I make it?"*

Back in Bangkok, she visited her travel agency, and once they finished getting the visas required for entry into India and Nepal, she was taken to Annie's Soapy Massage Parlor where David was actually waiting for her:

Seemed pleased to see me and disappointed I'd taken so long in getting there. We talked over multiple coffees, snuggled, sat at a pool, went to the Sheraton to watch the finals of the 32- and 50-person rowing races. Then a nap and dinner with Annie [owner of Annie's Soapy Massage Parlor] *and Moe* [the manager/bouncer], *walk, more loving and sadly separation.*

The next day:

He sent me off to catch my plane to India—in a prepaid cab—very nice. He continues to surprise me with his thoughtfulness. A bit strange and uncomfortable aside was being at the massage parlor but everything was cool with them.

In fact, Margo arranged to stay at Annie's the following month, when she would come through Bangkok one more time on her way back from India and Nepal to China. David, though, would not be in Bangkok then. Nevertheless, more adventures were to come her way because of Mitch David's introductions.

I got in touch with Mitch David after hiring a private investigator and running an ad in the Gulfport, Mississippi, *Herald*. I wanted to know why he had Margo come back to Annie's Soapy Massage:

"John, I am the person you are trying to contact—I met Margo on the train heading for Ko Samui—and gave her a safe/free place (ANNIE'S) to stay while in Bangkok—will contact you this week—NO names please—rgds, md"

At right is the ad I ran to find him.

When no one responded, I sent my private eye, Gladys Brierley, to Gulfport to track him down. And she did. Here's what she wrote me.

"Mitch David born in February 1954 asked me what this was about. I said I would rather talk to him in person so he felt comfortable with me and my intentions. He pressed and I said Thailand. There was a pause and he made reference to that author…and said he felt you made him look like I forgot the word but like a slacker or something he wasn't. I assured him that you had felt from Margo's writings he had an interesting life and some purpose there. He said, 'What does he want from me? I met Margo on a trip to River Kwai or on the River Kwai.' He was fairly intense and concerned I had found his house. So I told him that we wanted him to feel comfortable and that we respected that his background may be why he is guarded and concerned about being 'hunted down' as he put it. I assured him we had the best intentions and would not pry into anything personal that could not be discussed. He re-

laxed and admitted yes he was in the military and was still in the military and I inferred from that he still has reasons to be protective. Anyway, he said he should have never got on Facebook. He never does that type of stuff but did admit he responded to you by saying NO NAMES. I felt that he was more relaxed when I told him that you would respect the no names. Then we talked about where he was recommending we eat, on the beach at Steve's. It turns out we had been there before, nice place.

103

"I secretly wondered after he asked where I was from if he was going to show up at Steve's after watching us drive into the parking lot and asking where we were staying. You know the hunter being hunted. Not a problem for me. Whatever makes him feel comfortable."

Annie's Soapy Message

Although I got some idea of Mitch David's motivation, I was and am still curious what he was doing in Thailand. Margo had some inkling of what her other companions were doing on her trip and she shared that with me, either directly or indirectly, through her diaries; but all I know about Mitch David is that he was "some kind of soldier" according to what Margo verbally told me—her diaries were mum about the topic.

I love my private eye, Gladys Brierley, who found a fifty-eight-year-old Mitch David in Gulfport—he would have been thirty-two when he met Margo at the River Kwai. Gladys looked up his data on the net and then wrote: "…look at how far back his history goes to San Francisco which could have been his APO area. Was his military, CIA or both? If both, it is no wonder why there is little on him; the government usually keeps most of their people in the CIA or Special Forces protected from finding out much. I need to try to find a picture of him or I may need to just go and see him, he may not admit to anything over the phone, these guys believe in denial no matter what plus sometimes they cannot even say there [sic] were at a location for thirty-five years until the event is declassified. What I would do is go and see him, get his picture first covertly and then just bring the diary portion to him and watch his reaction. Who knows why he might not want to admit he was there or with your wife, smile. Maybe he was married at the time and still is?"

Annie's Soapy Massage Parlor

What a pleasant event to step onto clean, nice Thai Airways after the filth of the past month and Indian air. After visiting rather primitive India and even more primitive Nepal, it was a pleasure stepping into clean, neat Thai airport. I was struck by how modern and western Bangkok looks this time—I mean real roads—highways and side streets, real buildings that don't look like they are going to crumble tomorrow—cars and nice ones too. It was really good I started Asia in Bangkok as opposed to India and Nepal.

She was to stop in Bangkok for three days before continuing on to China, Hong Kong, and Japan. Not once did she ever mention this layover to me.

So once again into a cab, but at least now she could give directions and not have to negotiate. Margo noted that she was a bit apprehensive pulling into Annie's Soapy Massage Parlor *"so left my pack downstairs and went up to see if they would still give me a room."*

Annie's (www.anniesbangkok.com) first opened in 1972 and is the longest-running soapy massage parlor in the main tourist district of Bangkok. According to the website, "With customers from all around the world including expatriates, Annie's special service is renowned for its 'well, you know what'."

In researching Annie's and Bangkok's go-go bars, I came across a research document I must mention, as it proves what a risk-taker Margo was in hanging out in this section of Bangkok: Research in Economic Anthropology—(Volume 25: Economic Anthropology of Bangkok Go-Go Bars: Risk and Opportunity in a Bazaar Market for Interpersonally Embedded Services). The following is an excerpt from the abstract: "Presented in this chapter is a model of uncertain market conditions. In a bazaar-type market of interpersonal service the individuals are likely to be both chance-seekers as well as risk averters. Transactions of commodified services (termed here 'interpersonally embedded services') among chance-seekers in Bangkok go-go bars often result in disequilibration, rather than equilibration of the seller-buyer relationship." Huh?

I think this says: Buyer, beware of the environment.

What constitutes a soapy massage? It's basically a bath followed by a unique massage where the girl puts you on an air mattress and throws water on you and treats you like a slip-and-slide and massages you with her body and hands. Then you are dried off for more intimate action.

Annie's home page stated that Annie's gives you "a choice of over 100 girls and you can select online; open attitude; competitive prices; and fully-stocked bar with Mekong Whiskey our specialty."

On giving directions to a cab driver, Annie's sage advice was: "If you come by taxi, you must not say the name of the place nor talk about sex as the cab driver will take you around Bangkok for three or four hours visiting every massage parlor."

The rooms at Annie's—presumably one like Margo got—"have bath tub area for soapy massage for one customer and one lady" as the sign said. As Margo described it:

> *The welcome was polite but hardly effusive but then I don't know why it should have been. Moe was helpful, but Annie barely acknowledged me but warmed up over time. Moe had my pack brought up and gave me a soapy massage room. After getting settled I sat in the lounge drinking Mekong Whiskey with Moe and some of the many men hanging around. It is a strange scene watching mostly mid- to older-age Caucasian men come in to buy female companionship and sex. A German, 'Mr. Paul,' started chatting with me and bought me a couple of drinks. And he was drinking a lot himself. These guys' approach to the women or should I say girls—they're like 15-19 years old—yikes—is to grab their breasts, feel their crotch and the girls grab the guys similarly. Paul liked to brag about all the women he's slept with but then he's probably bought most of those. He's German but grew up in Australia—served in the Vietnam War and is the only man I've met who would talk about it fairly freely. He says he's been a mercenary ever since and killing doesn't bother him. Finally I got tired of hearing this and turned in to my freezing cold room.*

Margo picked up the well-used copy of *Fielding's Bangkok* and dove into its description of what Bangkok's sex trade is all about. For starters, Thailand gets about seven million tourists a year, about 80 percent of whom are men who come here for sex and not to look at waterfalls. Thus, meeting with David at the River Kwai was all the more unusual.

The next day, January 13, 1986, was errand day. Margo went to the post office, phoned her parents, went to Jim Thompson's and bought ties for her father and her brother. Then she went to see her travel agent where a package from David with a note had arrived—but she doesn't mention what was in it.

Surprises awaited her at the American Express office. She received some Christmas cards and a short note from Bruce Burrow: "Enjoy to the limit your experiences and don't think about the mundane Australian experiences."

"Good advice which I am living!" Margo noted in her diary. The real surprise, by far, was a telex (the email of the day) asking her to visit Sandoz, a multinational drug company, upon her return. In the offing was

a position as an executive in the company. It shocked her—not exactly what she wanted to think about that day, but nice to get that pat on the back: *"Would you believe it here in Bangkok they tracked me down."*

When she got back to Annie's, Margo encountered the German, Mr. Paul, again, and for some reason—curiosity?—accepted his invitation to visit Patpong, the notorious bar-girl/red light district in Bangkok.

> *So off we went. Turns out he's a cocaine user and big boozer as well and owns a bar with girls in Patpong. Here's another man I really don't like. He kept putting his hand on my legs, handling the girls everywhere, but kept saying, "I really like you"—but couldn't remember my name. "I'm so bored with these young girls, can't get interested in them—I can tell you." Hogwash—jerk. We went to two bars where girls in bathing suits danced, and then to a show with nude girls— Thai girls have little pubic hair and certainly aren't shy displaying and having their bodies touched. Would have had more fun with a good friend. I've seen this type of man with big dollars, drugs and women—a side of Bangkok I don't like.*

But on thingsasian.com, a writer addressed the disgust that Margo felt when she saw all those G-girls. "*Farang* women urge Thai women to stand up for themselves only to bemoan their own loneliness and insecurity and the counselor ends up being the counseled. At once strong and sick, this more generally may be said to represent the *farangs* through Thai eyes."

> *Paul obviously got the message I was uninterested in him and sent me off by myself to Soi Cowboy, another red light district, on my own.*

Wikipedia states that Soi Cowboy is a 400-meter-long street with some forty bars: "The go-go bars follow the pattern common in Thailand: Alcoholic drinks are served and women in bikinis dance on a stage. Topless or even nude dancing occasionally occurs in some bars but remains technically illegal. Most of the dancers are also prostitutes and will join a customer if he pays a 'bar fine' to the bar and a separate 'fee' to the woman... The area is named after T.G. 'Cowboy' Edwards, a retired American airman who opened the first bars there in 1977. A tall African-American, he got his nickname because he often wore a cowboy hat."

It's so funky you can even go for an elephant ride down a crowded street.

"Anonymous" writes in *Stickman's Guide to Bangkok:* "I first came here Soi Cowboy in 1986 and the girls were young and pretty... really, the sight of old *farangs* groping young teenagers was unpleasant to say the least."

Even more pathos comes out in a book of poems by Peter Blair, a former Peace Corps volunteer in Thailand. The collection is titled *Farang* (Autumn House Press, 2010). The following excerpt is from a poem called "With Yigna at the Hotel Coffee Shop":

> *She says her father sold her, 10000 baht (US$500)*
> *To a Bangkok Bar. She says she accepts her karma; to be poor*
> > *and lovely,*
> *Proud of her skin, orange cream, smooth as Burmese women.*
> *She says most girls wash down valiums with cold tea each night to*
> > *make love*
> *With the Australians, Americans,*
> *Japanese men from all over the planet*

On her last bar stop, Margo met yet another German who was the Asian sales manager for some company in Bangkok. He too owned a restaurant here—many people had side businesses. There are definitely wealthy folks in Bangkok.

When she got back to Annie's that night, she had yet another chat with another German man: *"My, she does attract that group,"* Margo wrote to herself. She thus stayed up later than she'd planned and got up at 5:30 a.m. to catch a taxi to the airport and continue her Asian journey.

Whew! Did you get all that?

So, what have we learned about Margo in Thailand? Here is this six-foot tall, forty-two-year-old woman with a backpack, coming off the gentle confines of New Zealand and Australia. She lands in Bangkok and after a couple of days goes off to see the Bridge Over the River Kwai, only that is not really the real bridge or the real River Kwai. She meets Mitch David, who is laid-back and tall, but a chain-smoker. No matter, they spend the day together out in the countryside. They both are going to go to Ko Samui, a beautiful and, as yet, undiscovered resort island which is a day's journey away.

Margo wants to meet David in Bangkok and goes looking for him in Bangkok's red-light district but can't find him. The next day while on the train south she spots David, who is very happy to see her and invites her to share his berth. He is traveling with a woman named Roberta who is sidelined.

After twenty-four hours of travel, they reach Chaweng Beach on Ko Samui where they stay in a bungalow—a shack really—facing the beach, for US$3.50 a night. The days are glorious outside, but for a week they smoke pot, drink Mekong Whiskey, and eat magic mushrooms. This makes them extremely horny and they spend two whole days doing nothing but hanging out. Since the bungalow has a doorway but no door, a number of people walk in and out, including Roberta, with whom David was initially traveling. Margo writes her parents that she had a wonderful rest on Ko Samui.

Being anal-retentive about her travel schedule, Margo leaves Ko Samui to spend three days in the mountains at Chiang Mai. Upon returning to Bangkok, she stays at Annie's Soapy Massage Parlor, Bangkok's leading massage parlor. She spends a night with David snuggling in one of the rooms reserved for customers. She and David have dinner with the owner of Annie's and the manager/bouncer.

Margo then leaves Bangkok to visit India and Nepal for a month. She is happy to leave those places and come back and see how advanced Thailand is by comparison. She spends a couple of nights by herself at Annie's. I related all this to Carla Ferrell, a friend of mine and an experienced traveler who noted, "Well, having been to Bangkok and done the massage thing a couple of times plus experienced the culture, Annie's sounds pretty typical to me."

One night she meets a German in the lounge where customers come in and pick out their girls. He owns several bars, claims to have been a mercenary and didn't mind killing people. She runs into him again the next day and he asks if Margo would like to visit the red-light district to see girlie shows and drink Mekong Whiskey. She goes with him but when he starts to put his hands on her, she backs out and leaves. She discovers that she has received a job offer from a multinational drug company that has an executive position for her.

Also she receives a note from a former friend in Australia, advising her to have a good time and to excuse the mundane people in Bangkok.

I realized that Margo and Mitch David crossed paths in her diaries for a year and a half. Later, she said I turned her on sexually as much as Mitch did. In trying to get some insight on what happened between them, I hired a private investigator in Newton, Mississippi, to find Mitch—who Margo thought was from Gulfport, Mississippi.

She never had contact with Mitch David again. What happens at Annie's Soapy Massage stays at Annie's Soapy Massage.

india

India happens to be a very rich country inhabited by very poor people.

–Manmohan Singh

The Bus Ride from Hell

"Goodness what have I gotten myself into?" Margo thought when she got on a train from Delhi to Udaipur, Rajasthan. She had left the relative safety of Annie's Soapy Massage to explore India by taking an eleven-day trip around the Maharaja Circuit from Delhi to Udaipur, Jaipur, and Agra. Of this fabled route the Lonely Planet guide notes, "Though certainly feasible in a couple of weeks you'll be tempted to linger and lap up the luxury."

Here is how the Lonely Planet guide describes Rajasthan: "Here is India at its high definition best. Prowling tigers, swaying elephants, hot and spicy bazaars, fabulous festivals, stunning saris, and twisted turbans; all a pageant of color and curiosity set against a backdrop of desert sands, secluded jungles, marble palaces and impenetrable stone forts…"

This, however, is what Margo wrote in her diary on December 19:

> *The countryside was arid and the train got dirtier and dirtier, dust/dirt covered everything. The porter actually wiped down the seats several times during the journey. It really is another world. Life here is very basic indeed. Men urinate on the street—just their back to the traffic. Saw children squatting on the side of the tracks doing their toileting. Women at the town pump—it's like the stories of Jesus' time—the town gathers there to wash clothes and get their cooking water. Camels pulling wagons. Rajasthan is a desert and thus camels!*

If you saw the movie *Slum Dog Millionaire,* you saw the real India—but that was in 2010. Imagine how much worse off it was twenty-five years ago. You can get a further peak at Jaipur, where Margo ended up, by seeing the movie *The Best Exotic Marigold Hotel* which has hot bus rides and the urban-congested chaos of Jaipur itself.

She later summed up her trip to India by saying:

In the urban west we think of structures but here in India you see nothing but people. Humans everywhere. The noise is constant and dulling and everyone seems to shout even in conversation like they are mad at each other. But worst of all is the stink. Stinks everywhere. Odors of human excrement, urine, sweat, mold, dung from cows and pigs and goats even in the cities. And everywhere excrement and urine flow in the streets.

When I once asked Margo what impressed her most about India she answered: *"Nothing."*

After arriving in Delhi, she boarded the train and arrived in Udaipur at 10 p.m. Upon arrival, she went straight to bed—but only after putting her filthy clothes to soak first. During the next two days, she visited one palace after another. Udaipur has four. She described her experiences over those days as *"rather mundane."* Her instincts told her not to accept any offerings of tea, regardless of where she went. She was fearful that it would be laced with drugs.

Then she was off to Jaipur for the experience of her life.

Oh wow—have I been experiencing the India I've heard about today—I'm feeling like I'd like to hop on the next plane out to America ... the day has been filled with harassments and it's really wearing poorly on me. I feel like I should hold my breath and just hang on until I can escape. There's tension that everyone is trying to rip me off.

First there was the nine-and-a-half hour bus ride—*"absolutely one of the most incredible rides I've ever had and surely would not like to repeat it."* This is as angry as Margo gets about these things. But I asked: "Why did she do this?"

All the buses looked dirty and uncomfortable—how deluxe was the deluxe going to be (she booked the deluxe)*? Well, not very—though certainly better than the regular. The seats were vinyl padded but no* more than six inches between seats. I don't know what I would have done if I'd had to share the seat—there was absolutely <u>no</u> space for my legs. Even with the whole seat to myself I could hardly move my legs. Then for the first three hours a row of red and white lights flashed down the aisle and the squeaky Indian music blared.

I kept thinking this can't really be—it just can't be so bizarre and awful. There was only one other woman on the bus and she was Indian and with a man. That made me uneasy. And then at one stage I realized the man across the aisle from me had his hand on my leg. Ugh!!! I quickly moved my leg and made sure I didn't make eye contact.

Oh and then the windows wouldn't stay closed and there was a horrible breeze all night. Thank goodness I had my sleeping bag—it definitely saved me. Whatever I did I couldn't find a reasonable position—finally for the last three hours of the nine and a half hour voyage I moved to the back seat where I could stretch out a bit—but the bumps were worse there—oh yes the ride was <u>the</u> bumpiest ever as well. What a nightmare it was.

Next came three more horrible hours when Rajasthan Tours wasn't there to pick me up. They never did and I had no phone number to call them—no phone books—no one would help me. As I debussed I was besieged by at least five rickshaw drivers who wouldn't leave me alone—harass, harass, harass. 'Where you go? You want hotel—you want tourist bungalow.' I wanted to SCREAM!

Finally I took a motorized rickshaw to the Meru Palace where they did give me a room—it looked like they didn't have my reservation though. Took a bath and a short nap and then began another journey into hassles!

I walked to the old museum—again the rickshaw drivers were too much—one accompanied me most of the way 'where you from madam? Where you go? Go on city tour?' The sidewalks were full of defecations—perhaps one should take rickshaws but I like to walk.

The museum was dirty like everything and even the exhibits were dirty. I did see this plaque on the wall in Hindi and English on a filthy wall. Le na dekhyo Jaipario to ral main akar kai kario—if one has not seen Jaipur what is the purpose of having been born? I then decided to go to Rajasthan Tours.

They were at the beautiful Rambaugh Palace Hotel. They insisted *that they met my bus but couldn't find me. That seems incredible to me as I was the only white face there! (And six feet tall to boot.) No apologies either.*

The Near Rape of Rajasthan

Finally Margo found a quiet, clean, and luxurious place, if not a refuge, to sit. This is how the Rambaugh Palace Hotel advertises itself in a brochure Margo had in her steamer trunk.

"Rambaugh Palace exudes an unmistakable sense of history. It's an architectural masterpiece that transcends time. Request the legendary Peacock Suite which overlooks Mughal Terrace and the garden where the Maharaja used to celebrate 'Holi,' the festival of color and lights. Stage an event of high romance in a private tent, illuminated only by torchlight. Indulge in stately dining at the gilded Suvarna Mahal, formerly the palace ballroom. Enjoy a royal feast and lounging under a star-speckled sky. Play polo as the kings played it or at a more leisurely pace elephant back. Rambaugh Palace allows guests to partake a wealth of experiences that resound with memories of a bygone era that luckily has not disappeared."

Margo notes in her journal:

I made an almost fatal mistake of sitting down on the terrace at the palace as I was greeted by a 46-year-old Indian colonel who appeared friendly and concerned. He bought me tea and cakes (I was famished), showed me the beautiful pool and grounds, and invited me to dinner. I thought why not?"

Having survived drunken Aussies in pubs, obnoxious American male travelers at every stop on this Asian trip, cocaine-snorting German mercenaries at girlie bars in Bangkok who don't mind killing people, and scores of unwanted approaches by men in Greece, Italy, and throughout the United States, Margo was feeling pretty fearless.

There was little to attract Margo to this stumpy soldier except she had such a hard time getting here and it was nice to have someone be kind to her. He had a super-pressed greenish uniform and shiny jet black hair as if he'd just used shoe polish on it. Given what would later happen, it is not surprising to have read this March 7, 2001, story from the *Times of India* with the headline reading:

113

Indian men lead in sexual violence

"Nearly one in four Indian men has committed sexual violence at some point in their lives and one in four has admittedly force his partner to have sex. The findings of a recent International Men and Gender Equality Survey reflect a new low for Indian men. By contrast, only two percent of Brazilian men and less than 1 percent in Chile, Croatia and Mexico was found to have engaged in sexual violence."

Of course, Margo hadn't read up on any of this, and she relied on her fearless instincts to navigate any encounters she had with Indian men. Nor was she aware that violence against women by Indian men could be motivated by just about anything, not just sex. Margo did not know the danger all around her.

In 2012, twenty-five years after Margo visited Jaipur, an AP headline blurted, "Indian man beheads daughter in rage over her lifestyle and parades her head through village." The story concludes with "rapidly modernizing India faces increasing social classes as women resist tradition like arranged marriages or limits on women venturing outside their parents' or husband's homes."

Well our colonel turned out to be an obnoxious, near rapist—I escaped only because people came to his house at 11:30 p.m.. I ran down the street when the door opened.

All night he had been telling me what a nice, considerate man he was—I was getting suspicious with dancing, massage 'relax I'm not going to hurt you.'

But I was getting bored as I wasn't really interested in him. We had two or three heavy drinks at his shabby little house—the books were dirty, his records scratchy—sounded like the 1930s in the U.S. He wouldn't take me home after dinner. Then the attack—'you will not leave—I've locked all the doors and no one will respond to your screams'—we struggled and I looked him in the eye—don't remember what I said but I was sure I was about to be raped and I am sure I would have been if those people would not have arrived.

I dashed out of the house and ran down the dark street—I wasn't sure how I would get back to the hotel but somehow I would. Then a rickshaw appeared and I got in. Although with all the alcohol I'd had I probably didn't need a sleeping pill but I took it anyway. The day was absolutely too much.

After this incident, everything in India seemed a hassle, and while Christmas was usually a time of joy for Margo, in India it was a time of exasperation. But this is why Margo backpacked across India: so she would see the real India and not the view from air-conditioned tour buses and five-star hotels. Given Margo's kind and mindful Buddhist-like personality and tolerance, a place has to be really bad to get the following condemnation:

> *I really find the filth and aggressiveness disgusting. I feel that I'm holding my breath to avoid getting sick from all I am seeing. I think I am much more steeped in Western values and ways than I've ever realized or wanted to admit. This week has been jinxed. Rajasthan Tours came and picked me up but then put me on the wrong train car—one that was detached and I sat there for a half hour before a train man discovered and told me I was on a train to nowhere. What else can happen?*

The end to Margo's misadventures in India involved two places that were dedicated to death. She went to Agra to see the Taj Mahal, which is really a mausoleum built by Mighal Emperor Shak Jahan in memory of his third wife, Mumtz Mahal; and then to the "Benares" where the dead are cremated alongside the Ganges. People forget that the "Taj" is not just the name of a Donald Trump casino, but a magnificent structure built in the 1600s and now a major tourist destination. Some heavy-duty words are attributed to the Emperor who built it. Margo noted those words.

> *Should guilty seek asylum here,*
> *Like one pardoned, he becomes free from sin.*
> *Should a sinner make his way to this mansion,*
> *All his past sins are to be washed away.*
> *The sight of this mansion creates sorrowing sighs;*
> *And the sun and the moon shed tears from their eyes.*
> *In this world this edifice has been made;*
> *To display thereby the creator's glory.*

Although not on the same scale of grandeur as the Taj Mahal, this memoir is written by me to honor my second wife. Even though I don't think it will ever become as world renowned as the Taj Mahal, nor do I believe the plaque at our church in Dubuque, Iowa, that recognizes

Margo's efforts to get a handicapped ramp will become a tourist destination either, to me they are both just as significant.

To end her travels in India, Margo took a boat trip up and down the Ganges at Benares. *"The air is full of cooking and warming fires and candles, saw bodies in various stages of cremation—one actually beginning to burn, one just smoldering ashes and one just being prepared to burn."*

This journal entry gave me more than a little pause as Margo's body was cremated as well and the ashes scattered in the north woods of Minnesota.

She was glad to leave India and never wanted to come back. One evening she told me: *"India is the world's most populated democracy and also the filthiest."*

Surprisingly, of all of her Asian adventures, this near rape is the one she most frequently told me about. Although she was shocked by the India she encountered, she was happy to have gone, and when people asked her about the accuracy of the depictions of Indian life in *Slum Dog Millionaire*, she could say with absolute certainty, *"Yep, that's it!"*

8

来自中国的慢船来于抵达了

translation: the slow boat to china has arrived (finally!)

december 1986 – january 1987

> *Man who waits for roast duck to fly into mouth must wait a very, very long time.*
> – Ancient Chinese proverb

*W*hen Margo finally found herself on the doorstep to China on December 28, 1986, she had experienced just over nine months of journeying through Asia. Her Asian adventure began on March 26, 1986, and was drawing to an end. She was tired but more confident in her abilities to really get into different cultures. With her other dealings and experiences in Ko Samui and Rajasthan behind her, Margo found herself in Katmandu, Nepal.

> *My sense of identity no longer requires me to have a job—or that a job identifies me and makes me OK or not—I am OK just as a person. Work now can be a means to an end—not the end itself. I trust me more than ever, respect me—know I can survive and make friends anywhere—I'm strong, brave, independent and OK with me alone— but know friends and family are important.*

Margo also hoped that upon her return it would mark the end of empty relationships she had had with me. *"I want a new start."*

Not only had Margo's body gotten a workout thus far on her Asian journey, she also developed a new resolve within herself. Katmandu does awaken the Zen in one, and this is what Margo felt as she started to wander the Himalayas. She came to Asia looking for adventure and also to find truth.

Since most people have not trekked to Nepal and probably never will, here's a quick primer to help you orientate yourself. Nepal is a landlocked Hindu/Buddhist country twice the size of California that lies between India and China. In the mountainous north, it has eight of the world's ten tallest mountains, including Mt. Everest, and 240 peaks over 20,000 feet. Margo and I owned a cottage near Galena, Illinois, the Himalayas of Illinois, where the elevation rose to a whopping 1,260 feet!

There are three geographic zones, yes, the mountains, the hills, and the tropical savannah on the border with India. Margo started her adventure from Katmandu, the capital, which is in a valley in the hill region. The Lonely Planet has a list of the top five adventure countries on the planet—Zambia, Peru, New Zealand, Fiji, and, yes, Nepal. On this Asian jaunt Margo did three of the five. Although Fiji did not impress her, that's a good batting average.

When Margo landed in Katmandu, she must have wondered to herself, "Now what do I do?" Her answer undoubtedly was, "Walk. Get out and walk!" Now in her tenth month of traveling, Margo's penchant for walking echoed that period in Forest Gump's life where he decided to run, run, and then run some more. It was time to get lost in Katmandu and walk until she found her way again, or as Margo put it: *"I've spent my walking time thinking about possible jobs, the men who've been in my life, and where and how I want to live when I return."*

And remember she arrived in Katmandu from the filthy and crowded soon-to-be call center of the world—India. Her words to her family were:

> *I can't tell you how wonderful it is to be here in Nepal—it's such a pleasant surprise from the harassments of India…It's significantly quieter…When I stepped off the plane, I was ecstatic. The people in Nepal are smiling, very nice, it seems so much neater and cleaner plus of course I love the mountains. I'll stay at the Chitwan National Park—south of Katmandu—for three nights and four days where I'll be trekking out to see tigers, rhinos, leopards, exotic birds, crocodiles,*

etc. I've definitely had enough of cities for a couple of weeks so this is a great change of pace.

Most people associate Nepal with just the Himalayas but nothing could be further from the truth. It's a huge country and it has subtropical regions. A botanist would call it "Himalayan subtropical broadleaf forests." Chitwan National Park, established in 1973, was the first national park in Nepal. It covers about four hundred square miles and contains forty-three species of mammals. Lots of animals I never knew existed: marbled cat, sloth bears, Bengal foxes, smooth-coated otters, yellow-throated martins and yes tigers and rhinos. *Wikipedia* notes: "From time to time elephant bulls find their way into the park apparently in search of elephant cows willing to be seduced." How romantic. But that's not why Margo signed up for the jungle safaris—it was to see rhinos, tigers, and elephants, oh my.

After giving herself a HAPPY BIRTHDAY! in her diary, she headed off to the safari park, which took four hours. Here is Margo's description of how it began.

> *The first scheduled activity was to walk through the government land—my jeans got wet but it was fun. Then we began to search for rhinos. When we finally heard one—all of us climbed into a tree but he never appeared—how funny we looked! But finally off in the distance I spotted one and then our guards came running back—just in front of him was a great big rhino! I was very glad I was in the tree—for a moment I thought he was going to charge us. What a sight they are up close! Ugly! These are one-horned rhinos. When this one moved into the grass and then laid down, we found two more! Lov-erly. Elephants were roaring on the way back.*

After all those passionate and intimate moments we had together, Margo never once told me she was charged by a one-horned rhino. Nor that she had ridden an elephant. On New Year's Day, December 31, 1986, Margo said this:

> *It was just me and the trainer sitting straddle on one and then two guys on the other they were training—through the villages hunting rhinos—we heard several—saw the brush rustle but never saw one. I'd about given up when there was one smack in front of us. On the elephant we could not get too close as it intimidates the rhino. Terrific.*

After we found our partners, we went back and chased the rhino—trying to get the new elephant to be calm. What a kick! On the way home we found another plus two fox, a mongoose, a jungle cock and with mustard blooming against foothills and snow-capped Annapura range peeping through. It's like heaven.

Not only was she awed by her encounters with these massive mammals, she was equally captivated by the ornithological wonders that inhabited the skies. Margo got up and took a walk at seven a.m. the next day and saw: *"...common and pied minor birds; pied bush chat; red-vented bul bul; paddy field pit; king fisher woody shelter duck; black-headed shrike; Indian true pied (long tail); spotted dove; Iora (sun yellow); brown-leafed warbler; green shank pond heron; open-billed stork; black drongo; scarlet breasted sunbird—brilliant red!"*

Sunday, January 4—First Day of Trek to Shivapuri Hill

Day was slow to start as the guides, Manesh and Sherpas, Osmo were a half hour late. In meantime I chatted with an Indian fellow from Benares who is working as tour guide in Katmandu. He was surprised I knew he was Indian—but they do have distinct sharpness to their speech and very English as well. And then began the longest uphill climb of my life—to Shivapuri Hill—it was straight up and lots of it through thick bush. We lost the trail so had to blaze our own. Towards the end I wasn't sure I'd make it—my legs hurt so much! I was surprised to find hardly a bird, but there was the odd flower here and there. We started from the Vishnu Temple at 10:20—stopped for lunch one hour later—they put in the path away from them (two porters, Sherpa cook and Sherpa guide) that waited on me—first hot lemon; then hand washing and H_2O. Then lunch—H_2O, omelet, tuna, toast and orge!...When we reached Shivapuri summit the view on the backside was spectacular—snow-capped mountains with sunset reflecting on them. Made the climb worthwhile. So at end of my first day of trekking—I'm still sorry I'm not in a group—my legs are aching. It's exhilarating—the stars are bright, Katmandu lights below—and I'm glad to be up in these hills. Osmo says elevation is 6M ft. but the map says at least 7M but it's also over 8M ft! So pretty."

Monday, January 5—Day 2

Little sleep last night—don't know if it's the tea or what; felt anxious; couldn't relax—was warm after putting on booties and vest. At 7 a.m. tea was brought; then warm washing H_2O. By 8:10 we were on the trail. The mountains were spectacular this a.m. and all day as well—we've had a view a good share of the day. Everest was pointed out to me but I'm not really sure which one it is! The day was mostly downhill or flat—very muddy—wish I had boots after all. Osmo got so he snaps his fingers when he thinks he needs to hold my hand through mud—it is true I slipped a few times. At one point I slipped in front of group of villagers and let out a scream—ooh did they laugh at me! I want boots and yet they're either barefoot or wearing thongs through all this—up and down into jungle, over snow and ice, mud! What softies we westerners are. We walked through a few little clusters of huts, through some beautiful terraced farms—the terracing continues to amaze me.

Lunch stop was 10 a.m.! We ate at 11 on a hillside—no view. I almost fell asleep! More birds today and more people. Night stop was at 3 p.m. on a cleared hillside with the mountains in front of us. I can hear villagers singing—plus these guys sing a lot also—lovely voices. It is quite heavenly.

Tuesday, January 6—Day 3

Last night the local villagers passed by singing away as they returned from the 'jungle' each carrying heaps of wood on their backs. These were the same people we'd passed earlier as they went up and we came down. Such melodic sounds and happy for such hardworking souls. Delightful. Again I woke up to spectacular views of the mountains. It seems early a.m. and late afternoon when the mountains are cleared.

Today we walked four hours before stopping for lunch. We did lots of ups and down—can sure feel it in my legs. We were on heavily-traveled trails most of the day passing through many villages and small communities of a few houses—much what Grandma-Grandpa Mogush came from in Yugoslavia. One house we passed had four straw cradles with little ones in it—should have snatched a picture!

At lunch time we stopped in another little village where I was definitely the center of attention—made me feel very weird and uncomfortable to be plopped down on the only bench in town—right out front of everyone and served my tea, hot lemon and lunch. Two little boys came running over—one with no pants on as most toddlers do here—all smiles—'allo' 'allo'—then they were joined by little sister; dad had a wee one with him; mom seemed to run the shop. Palden cooked in their kitchen—I guess for a fee. I asked to take picture of three kids—he said okay and when I brought out my camera—little girl started crying—oh I didn't want to upset her and I did want her picture. Later she finally smiled at me again. Dad and another fellow sat down by me to play cards—betting. Mom breast fed two babies—I swear; then washed her hair with the water pipe there in front of us all and some clothes. An old lady all in red—necklace, bangles—in fact I noticed today all the women wearing necklaces and of course nose rings—sure don't know how they blow their noses.

The kids mostly have swollen bellies, messy hair, snotty noses, no shoes—one had keratosis I think and plays in the dirt. The chickens and roosters ran in and out of the shop; a cow went after the grain drying in field below us. It was amazing how many people stopped in front of me to stare—oh yah, the old lady was intrigued by my red watch—think she fancied it.

All day I was amazed at how the guys scamper up and down the hills—so nimble. How weak I am. For the last couple of hours we walked with an old bow-legged man with one tooth on upper plate. He led us to our evening stop—Katikat Point—on one of the terraces—a village behind us; the terraced valley right below us and lots of sounds of locals as well as young goats neighing or whatever they do. We're just below Narago where the tour buses go to see sunset over Everest. Most of the day today we could see the tip of Everest in the distance. Hard to believe from this vista that it's 8.8M meters high!

Wednesday, January 7—Day 4

We've just made camp and my spirits are low. Camp tonight is in a field in the valley—on the mud—just on the edge of villages—no bush for toileting in—no mountain view and truly out in open for all to see. Also most of today was thru villages that from afar are delightful looking but up close are quite disgusting I think—flies are thick due to human and animal excrement, animals all over, men sitting around playing cards or drinking tea—waste all about—even though the women sweep their dirt floor huts—it's far from clean. Also I'm tired of being alone with these Nepalese. Osmo speaks questionable English and is a bit centered on himself so when I don't understand he gets very impatient. He snaps his fingers when he thinks I must hold his hand to climb up or down. Honestly I hate the snapping fingers and also most times I do better on my own as then I can see where I'm going. Chockrabadu washed his clothes and shoes at noon so he walked all afternoon in bare feet over rocks!

The bright spots—every now and then I spot a flower—all very little—but it brings some color. The people and kids are attractive— the women still intrigue me with their pretty necklaces. Saw three kids pulling a little one in a two-wheeled wagon around last village we passed through. Also I took the time to watch the shop people chase a chicken for us to cook tonight—took about 10 min.

I'm much happier in the hills with mountain views than here in village—also am disappointed that tomorrow sounds much the same. First three days definitely the best! Am also feeling like a fool and thus angry at self for the prices I paid for my Katmandu experience—too much. Why oh why did I allow my Indian anxiety to transfer to Nepal as well! Live and learn! I must pay more attention when I buy travel packages the next time—like China!!

I've chosen to sit in my tent for the moment to be really alone—no villagers to stare at me and I can really ignore the guys. I can tell I'm getting ready to return to U.S. and its standards as I'm not 'into experiences' as much as I have been and I'm counting the days for each phase to be over.

And as she trekked, Margo reflected:

Also, I know more every day that I want a Christian community to become involved with. I'm tired of my search for happiness—it's got to be the spiritual part that's missing. And I want a stimulating, fun and romantic relationship with a man. And I want to be part of a family again—to have them to my house and be part of their activities. I want to find a job that's working with people to make their lives better—be it in travel, scouts, wildlife—I want good pay and stimulation but I don't need a title. I want to read books on the places and cultures I've been traveling; to take some courses related to my work and anthropology.

Once I emerged from my tent tonight I found at least 20 children surrounding us! When I sat down they clustered about me starring. I tried to talk with them. One fellow could speak a little English. I sang a song hoping they'd sing for me but it didn't work. I took a group picture. Finally when it got dark they left. Osmo dislikes the people more than I do—I at least smile and try. He could talk with them as well.

When it was dinner time he insisted I sit at the door of my tent—I tried to say no—by the fire. Finally gave up and decided to read and not try to be sociable. Screw them.

Thursday, January 8—Day 5

Breakfast was cheese omelet and chapattis—enjoyed it, but now it's 10 a.m. and we've stopped for lunch at another village on the road to Katmandu. When asked if place was okay, I said sure but it's a bit early. They contemplated but of course we stayed. Ugh! The walk this a.m. has been on road—first dirt and not sealed. So hardly the wilderness. It's finally cleared and I can now see some snow-capped mountains and green foothills instead of fog—at least that's better and I've been given my hot lemon juice—very nice. The villages were very quiet as we passed through them this a.m. I lost my H$_2$O bottle down a ravine as I prepared to toilet—damn! Almost lost me as well as I squatted on the slippery hillside. As we climbed out of the fields this a.m. we passed potatoes, rice, garlic growing and the dairy where everyone was coming to get their jugs filled. I continue to 'knock on wood' and be amazed I've had no diarrhea to date as I see living conditions and think of the excrement, etc. that must seep into water supply and watch food preparation. From a distance I feel like I could be in the Switzerland Alps—thatch roofed homes— lovely terraces. Obviously when you get up close, one knows by looking at the village you could not be in Switzerland—too dirty! But across the hills and valleys it's idyllic.

I've spent my walking time thinking about possible jobs, the men who've been in my life and where and how I want to live when I return. The job issue is still a difficult one for me. I know I'm not detail oriented or perfection minded and I really don't have the fire to have my own business though I know I have to be careful about a job. Now, however, I know the job doesn't and won't be the end of all; be all for me—that my joys will come from outside. I just need to accept Margo the worker!!

Couldn't believe it, we finally left the lunch spot at 12:30—Palden left us—we walked 15 minutes and rested, walked again 15 minutes and rested and before I knew it we had walked into another field and we were stopping for the night! I was most unhappy with stopping after so little walking, the spot—no view and again in a mud field and this time above a stagnant water hole and then to hear that we'd meet the car at that spot in a.m.! Urr—ugh. I was asked if this spot was OK—but Osmo really doesn't want to know my opinion. It's just what he's supposed to do. At least we were away from the village and only had a couple of visitors. I read Tai Pen *for afternoon—I'm glad it's so good. Dinner was tasteless macaroni, tomato sauce and cabbage and carrots. Anti-climatic end to trek.*

Friday, January 9—End of Trek

Huge breakfast—rice porridge, omelet, tuna fish toast—not quite sure if they're not trying to kill me by stuffing me. We packed up and walked 10 minutes uphill where we sat from 8:30 until 10:30 waiting for 'cart.' We all piled into car—the view returning to Katmandu was terrific as we had climbed very high. The sky was clear. It was glorious.

Apparently I trekked a lot faster than the average trekker so we finished a day early. I was most disappointed to be done walking. I didn't find out the reason until the travel agent told me.

Then sitting in the comfort of the Everest Sheraton Hotel, *"I washed my hair and soaked in hot tub—felt so good!"* Margo then penned a note to her family on the letterhead of the hotel:

I'm off to Bangkok for two days of tying up loose ends (shopping—shipping a big package off, attending the classical dance performance; this kills me—while staying at Annie's Soapy Massage) and then off to Hong Kong. I'm ready to move on and most curious to see how Hong Kong and China compare to Thailand, India and Nepal. I'm hoping they are cleaner! I've really had enough of filth, grungy streets and housing. I thought earlier in my travels and prior to then I'd consider joining Peace Corps—well I've concluded I really wouldn't enjoy living in an underdeveloped country. I'm more into our Western standards than I realized.

Needless to say, when she met me, she got the Peace Corps experience vicariously as we traveled to Panama where I served.

The Slow Boat to China Finally Arrived

On January 21, 1987, Margo arrived in China. Nine months had gone by since she'd begun her travels, and Margo was like the Timex watch, "She just keeps on ticking."

When Margo got on the plane to go to Hong Kong and China in 1986, you could say, in musician's terms, the country was between gigs. Mao Tse-tung (a.k.a. Chairman Mao—remember him?) had been dead ten years, but his obligatory portrait could still be seen everywhere. Student protests had started and would culminate in the Tiananmen Square massacre in three years. The U.S. had restarted diplomatic relations with China just seven years earlier and no one imagined that China would become the world's manufacturing center in a few short years.

On September 28, 1986, the Chinese government passed "Resolution on the Principles for Building a Socialist Society with Advanced Culture and Ideology" which became the blueprint and master plan that guided China to its current world status.

Margo roamed every nook and cranny of Hong Kong by herself, and although there were people everywhere, she was as lonely as could be.

> *I mean the cars are BMWs, Mercedes, Porsches—people are dressed to the nines and the stores up market... I'm struck by the cleanliness, quietness, the fact that no one's eating as they walk down the street, the shopping malls have no place to sit down, there aren't street vendors like the other Asian places I've been—not even people selling food. The differences between Bangkok, India, Nepal, and Hong Kong are hitting me strongly. How fortunate I am to have been so many places— one after the other to be able to see and experience the differences.*
>
> *Sunday afternoon I treated myself to High Tea at the Peninsula— put on make up and my new heels—thought there might be someone interesting but no luck.*

For those who know little about Hong Kong, the Peninsula is not just a hotel; it's an institution and has been voted the world's best hotel on several occasions. It opened in 1928 with the idea that it would be the "finest hotel east of Suez." *Wikipedia* notes, "From the moment that the

126

hotel opened its doors to the first guest the Peninsula has been synonymous with welcoming the rich, the famous, the titled and the titans of industry to a place of unsurpassed luxury and service. The hotel is also distinguished by its fleet of signature Rolls Royces which can be hired by guests. These cars are painted in a distinctive shade of green known as 'Peninsula Green'."

Had tea sandwiches, scones with cream and raspberry jam and cake roll. Quite nice—of course it would have been more fun with someone. I've not met a soul these days to bum around with—maybe on the tour to China there'll be someone—at least I'll be with people on those days.

I know exactly how Margo felt that day sitting in the Peninsula. Years later (eight in fact) I went off to Moscow and Almaty Kazakhstan. I did my thing but was so shell-shocked by where I stayed—the filth, chaos, and the fear for my life—that I had to stop to decompress before coming home to Margo. I chose the grand old hotel of Brussels—the Metropole. I stayed for two days and would sit in big wicker chairs and drink espresso and cognac at ten a.m.!

Just think, a few short days ago Margo was squatting to go poop on a hillside in Nepal with a whole village watching her; and, a few weeks ago, she was riding a filthy rural bus in India for 9½ hours; and, a few months ago, she was the third person sleeping in a two-person tent at arid Ayers Rock in Australia. Now she was sitting in the lap of luxury sipping tea and admiring the Ultra suede clothes she had just purchased.

Well, this is it—the beginning of China and so far it's a bit disappointing in that it doesn't look much different from India and Nepal in terms of farms and lifestyle.

In Guangzhou, China, Margo finally got sick for the first time on the trip. Also known as Canton, Guangzhou is the capital of Guangdong Province and one of the most prosperous cities in China. As Lonely Planet says, "There may not be much in the way of sights, but wandering the streets of Guangzhou is an interesting lesson in what China is transforming itself into—a place of Dickinson extremes of poverty and wealth."

She went to a bunch of tourist stops, the jade factory, past a store that sold "snake bile wine" and in her mountaineering spirit decided to climb to the top of the "Temple of the Six Banyan Trees with the Flower Pagoda." The Six Banyan Trees of the temple's name (which incidentally I have replicated on my O scale train layout) no longer exists. The Pagoda was built in 1097 and at 55 meters (170 ft.) it is the tallest in the city.

The Lonely Planet warns, "It's worth climbing up, although if you are tall (e.g. Margo!), you might end up with a collection of bruises as the doorways on the way up are very low. As you come down go anticlockwise for the quickest descent. Otherwise things can get a bit chaotic."

No wonder Margo wrote this:

> *I climbed almost to top but started to feel nauseous so came back down—don't know what it was—incense? food? the climb? tiredness? or all of the above but I actually vomited on the street—oh—I felt miserable. I did it again outside Sun Yat Sen's memorial. I managed to survive the museum.*

To round off her time in China, Margo joined a tour group to see the Great Wall, Terra Cota soldiers, markets, temples and everything else in Beijing, Xian, and Guangzhou.

Five different aspects of her journey through China stuck out and are worth noting. These include the best meal, fresh foods of China, her weariness of groups, the worst toilet, and the abrupt end to her travels.

Beijing Duck

January 26, 1987, Beijing, Margo partook in what she considered to be her best meal. This happened at the P.D. Restaurant in downtown Beijing and it was Beijing duck—the capital's most famous invention.

The preparation and history of Beijing duck is worth noting. The duck starts out at one of the many farms around Beijing where it's pumped full of grain and soybean meal to fatten it up. When ready for eating, the duck is slaughtered and plucked. Then it is lacquered with molasses, pumped with air, filled with boiling water and then roasted over a fire. This is definitely not fast food.

Beijing duck does carry more history than fried chicken to be sure. It was first mentioned in a cookbook *Complete Recipes for Dishes and Beverages* written by an inspector of the imperial kitchen. Moving right along, by the mid-twentieth century, Beijing duck had become a national symbol of China. To wit: when Henry Kissinger, the Secretary of State of the United States, met Zhou En Lai during his first visit in China in 1972 (fourteen years before Margo started munching on the duck), it became Kissinger's favorite. And the talks which had become bogged down started to move again. Beijing duck was hence considered one of the factors behind the rapprochement of the United States to China in the 1970s.

Margo describes the meal in a culinary fashion:

> *We started with boned, webbed feet of the duck which were covered in hot mustard. I decided I must try and was pleasantly surprised that they were quite eatable. Then was the liver and gizzard deep-fat fried which we dipped in pepper and ate with shrimp chips—it was OK—in the meantime we had some sweet pork, chicken and vegetables; the next duck dish was the skin and meat with sesame flat bread type buns and tortilla type bread, plum sauce and spring onions. It was lovely. Finally very rich duck soup. They also brought out the duck's tail and head cut up on a plate covered with two slices of the equivalent of a filet mignon—dessert was hot candied apple slices—the apples were cooked and the candy part not too sweet. A small glass of uninteresting wine preceded the meal.*

Qingping Market

Margo's trip to Qingping Market was unlike going to Whole Foods, although all the food being offered was fresh. This market came into existence in 1979 (just eight years before Margo's arrival) as part of the liberalization policies of Deng Xiaoping. Farmers could come and sell what they wanted at whatever price they could get. Fidel Castro could never grasp that concept.

The Lonely Plant refers to it as a "take away zoo." Margo describes it thusly:

> *In Guangzhou we went to the Qing market—what a sight! I saw pigs being skinned; chickens being de-feathered; a cat being de-furred; snakes being slit down the length of them and skins pulled off—snakes still moving; dead dogs cut up to be sold for meat; a dog head sitting on a counter; turtles and crabs tied up with string to carry home for fresh soup. I was amazed I didn't get sick but later in afternoon I did vomit again. Don't know—must be something at that Guangzhou restaurant even though the food seemed the nicest of any of the places we ate in China.*

129

The Lonely Planet adds: "There are bundles of frogs, giant salamanders, anteaters, raccoons—alive or contorted by recent violent death—which may just swear you off meat. This market will definitely upset the more sensitive traveler." And it did get to Margo.

The Group

Margo as a general rule loved groups. She had many therapy sessions using a group technique. In fact, she would later be in group therapy to discuss my future with her. The group in Evansville, Indiana, said John must go. He can't be trusted and he has strung you along too much. Luckily Margo said, *"I give him another chance."*

This Beijing tour group Margo was with was too "dysfunctional" for words and she began to yearn for the alone time she had when she roamed Hong Kong by herself. After seven days (twenty-five tourist sites) of touring with the same group, Margo, with her infinite patience, had had it.

> *I've found today to be very difficult. 'I'm grouped out.' Very tired of obnoxious, pushy Paul from Florida who is so demanding of his wife Gloria—wants/insists she be at his side all of the time and constant chatter Gil who is very nice but my goodness he can't ever be quiet—neither of these men seem to be very interested in listening to others—my biggest complaint about men.*
>
> *Guess maybe my intolerance for that not listening goes back to my childhood when I felt no one wanted to listen to me and this reinforced itself by my time with my first husband Brownie. In any case I'm dying to roam the streets, alone, alone. I managed to get a tiny bit in today.*

The Worst Toilet

The "award" goes to Lap Nan, the Port of New Territories:

> *I felt like I was back in India as it was poor and grungy, hard to believe it's H.K. The toilet was THE WORST I've experienced except for the bush in Nepal. It was an Asian-style latrine—not a very deep one at that. The village had all community toilets—no private ones; a village water faucet; trash everywhere; signs warning about poisonous rat bait and stagnant water breeds mosquitoes; many abandoned—half knocked down; signs warning to boil water.*

Biggest Surprise: February 2, 1987—Hong Kong

Errand day and big surprise day! Discovered that my great ticket isn't too great after all. Japan Airlines informed me that it's valid for six months—so it's invalid at this point—which of course means I've been traveling across Australia and to Bangkok and Hong Kong on an invalid ticket.

After the Beijing jaunts, Margo flew back to Hong Kong to learn her trip was essentially over, "immediately." After receiving the news, she checked into the YMCA and then went to the Regent Hotel, which was built in 1980. While at the hotel which is on the Peninsula of Hong Kong, she enjoyed a refreshing and much-needed drink. This place was classy as Rolls Royce had opened a showroom in its lobby. Margo described her day this way:

Decided to get dressed up and go have a drink at Regent on the harbor. When I walked into the lobby I was startled by the magnificent sweeping view it has over the harbor and Hong Kong Central. Even at US$20 a drink I decided I must sit down and enjoy it.

As I did, I was offered a drink by a North Carolinian, Bill Brunette, who I then joined. He's worked Asia all his life—was president of Reynolds Tobacco. Now has own business—buys items in Asia that he gets exclusives on—some are promotional items, others quality items to sell to Neiman Marcus, Abercrombie and Fitch, etc. Offered me possibility of a partnership. Keep in touch. Interesting but he confused the issue with invitation to sleep in his room at Regent. 'I'll leave you alone—you can watch TV or whatever.' Ha! Last time I believed that line I really got zapped. But conversation was good fun and stimulating and returned to YMCA at 1:30 a.m.

Coming Home

So as the plane was coming in for its final approach to Los Angeles on February 4, 1987, some 300+ days after leaving for Asia, Margo wrote this:

Thoughts on her stops on the trip:

- *Hawaii—a pleasant surprise—lovely, surprise, surprise—influx of Japanese*
- *Fiji—the biggest disappointment (weather)*

- *NZ—my favorite—the most beautiful totally—most diverse*
- *India—most interesting culturally, historically, dirtiest*

And finally as the plane touched down:

I have met many interesting men this past year and I'm going to have that trend continue! Somewhere there's also someone for me.

9

dream job

*If you are facing in the right direction,
all you need to do is keep walking.*

– Buddhist saying

When she got back to the United States from Asia on February 9, 1987, Margo wrote:

Today I feel like my travels changed me not one tenth—I still have the same questions re job; I'm not any clearer on what I want to do than when I left. But maybe it really doesn't matter to me what I do except I need to be stimulated—feel like I'm making a difference; have variety in my job and the people I work with, make a good enough salary that I have the freedom to do what I want to do.

Margo would eventually land her dream job. It would take four years but it would happen. She would land her dream job on July 16, 1990, and then get THE promotion a year later. Finding that dream job was not easy. It took a lot of soul and job searching to get there.

When a somewhat perplexed Margo got back to the United States, she did a thorough inventory of her year in Asia and what she'd gotten out of it which gave her a sense of confidence as she started to beat the streets looking for her dream job which she had not yet found.

She made a list where she outlined the benefits:

- Belief in myself and ability to survive in any environment
- Understanding of my value system—importance of friends, comfort of nice things; not living in third world countries
- Understanding of world; attitudes towards America
- Lots of walking and moving about
- Lots of exploring of new places

Official Notice

Bristol-Myers Squibb Company
Bristol-Myers Squibb U.S. Pharmaceutical
and Mead Johnson Nutritional Group

Subject: **PROMOTION**   From: Human Resources Department
Date: August 27, 1991

Margo — Ability is always recognized — congratulations — Don Harris

MARGO A. BROWN has been promoted to Senior Manager, International Business Development. She will report to Rida A. Ali, Vice President, Business and Technical Development, International.

Ms. Brown joined the Company in July, 1988, as an Institutional Sales Territory Manager. In August, 1990, she was promoted to Manager, Nutritional Business Development, International, the position she held until her present promotion.

- Lots of learning of different cultures of doing things
- Lots of new adventures all of the time
- Meeting new people from all walks of life
- Deciding/figuring out how to get from here to the*re* economically

She first went back to very urban New Jersey where she had a house and a network of colleagues.

Long-term jobs don't come easy, so Margo took a number of short-term jobs, one with an advertising agency that did work for her old firm Biosearch. One day she wrote of her work there:

> *Oh—wow—the last thirty hours have been the most stressful/anxious hours I have ever had. I've actually had physical anxiety attacks—hyperventilation, increased heart rate, nausea, tears. Yuk! I hate it. The agency business is definitely not for me long term—nor is any job that has constant pressure of deadlines.*

It got worse the next day:

> *More stressful because I had to write about things I don't know. I went crazy at noon about anxiety. Well I could go on and on. But the point is I know it's not my kind of environment. I overreact negatively—don't view it as fun—and can only see a life of always being pressured to meet a tight deadline.*

Enough already, Margo thought.

To address her situation, she decided to sell her house in New Jersey—which I once was "ordered" to go see when I was courting Margo—and moved back to Minneapolis. *"The traffic and population is continually bugging me."* It was in Minneapolis that she had to come to grips with a strange realization: *"It's almost schizophrenic my confidence in myself to travel the world alone vs. my lack of confidence to perform on the job. If I could only untap the confidence for a job!"*

During this time, she felt terribly alone and unfocused—the trip to Asia gave her a focus, but now she had to deal with the unknown. She penned a graph which expressed her frustrations and where she brought out the unwarranted fear of dying alone. All the other demons expressed in that graph were successfully dealt with, and as we shall see, she did not need to fear dying alone.

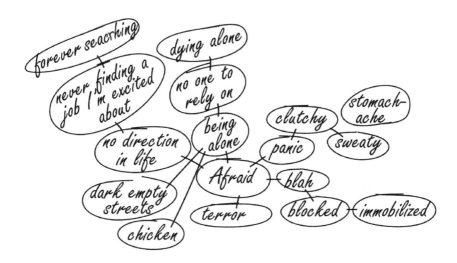

Margo didn't fashion herself as much of a writer but I think she did quite well in repackaging her time with the ad agency to read:

1987 to present Marketing Consultant

Researching, developing and writing market analyses and promotional/educational program proposals for pharmaceutical and health care companies; managing the development and execution of programs within the advertising agency.

Her longtime friends, the Barkers, took in this now refugee from congested New Jersey and let her spend many months in their home in the improbably named Lake Elmo. *Wikipedia* says, "Much of the area within the city limits has a very rural feel to it." A perfect place to go hunting for an international job? She found living in Lake Elmo challenging because she was once again living out of a suitcase and in somebody else's house. She wrote a lot and fantasized finding another *"bird of a feather that flocks together."* She felt very much alone as her graphic shows.

In a subsequent journal entry, she described her meeting with another of *"the same feather."*

136

Can't you just imagine a coat made of peacock feathers? The colors would be brilliant aqua and royal blues and red. Quite striking on this tall, lean lady, don't you think? Silky, soft and sensuous to the touch both the coat and my skin would be. Both so easy to touch as underneath the coat of flocked feathers would only be me... A sense of freedom. Just you, me and our birds out in the wooded hills or along a cool, deserted ocean beach. Searching and sharing our souls. Yes, we two birds of the same feather will flock together in our dreams at last.

She also wondered where she fit in socially, as she came back from her Asian trip just as she had left—alone, without a relationship. She was afraid. *"I'll be alone always with no one to rely on but myself. Dying alone will be the final culmination of being afraid."* The graphic below describes all her fears upon returning as well as anything could.

I suppose we all have had the same fears. I know I had the same ones, but it was something Margo overcame. Boy, would I have loved to see and discuss those graphics while she was alive so I could ask, "What did you mean by that?"

This sincerity, then, extended to writing, not only the fantasy letters I would get, but amusing things she would do when she got back. Just a few short months after her return, in August 1987, she found herself wondering where and how she would fit in and where she would find *"birds of a feather that flock together."* She penned this:

> *Literal definition—members of the bird species will stay together— live in the same community; fly together and will not stray away. How strange to associate the proverb 'birds of a feather flock together' with sexual fantasy. But then writing is to be creative.*

These journal entries explain Margo's almost metaphysical desire to live alone with me—a "bird of a feather"—on the mountain, as we shall see.

In Minneapolis she began networking as soon as she arrived and met up with an investment banker by the name of Tom Martinson. He ran his business out of his spacious home in the wealthy Minneapolis suburb of Wayzata. He knew the money folks and was always bringing them deals.

At the time I ran the Minneapolis office (which consisted of me!) of a division of Ogilvy, the famous advertising agency. The division I worked for did international advertising and language translations and thus I pretty much knew all the international folks in town. Part of my job was to have lunch and dinner with people and tell them what we did. In fact, my boss got on my case if I didn't take enough people out to lunch. That's what I was doing at the American Café that day—schmoozing.

Tom invited Margo to lunch at a very business yuppie watering hole which I frequented. It brought all the eager business types together during the day and Rupert's Night Club brought the same people for fun, drinking, and dancing at night.

Tom remembers the lunch with an eager Margo that sunny day, April 22, 1988, and her asking: *"Who should I be talking to about international jobs?"*

"That guy over there talking to my partner," he pointed towards me.

I barely noticed.

They both came over, cherubic Tom and tall Margo. I told her, without much thought, to come to my office and I would be happy to meet with her. I gave her my pretentious business card (it had a high linen

138

content by design). To my surprise, she came to my office the very next day. The details and implications of that meeting will be explored shortly. Anyway, that's how Margo and I met on April 18, 1988. At the time neither of us knew how profoundly this meeting would affect the future course of both our lives.

She beat the streets for a few more months until July. Finally she decided to go back to work for Mead Johnson—for whom she had worked before taking the New Jersey Biosearch job. She would become an "institutional sales territory manager" based in St. Paul, Minnesota.

Mead Johnson is a low-profile company without a brand name like Coca Cola, though every mother knows Mead Johnson as the manufacturer of Enfamil—infant formula. It then was a division of Bristol-Myers Squibb, the pharmaceutical giant. The company started out in New Jersey but moved to Evansville, Indiana, to be nearer agricultural raw ingredients needed to make the formula. Busy Evansville is on the Ohio River at the extreme southern part of Indiana—it's really a southern town of some 150,000 as Kentucky is just across the wide Ohio River. Gravy is always served with breakfast.

Evansville lies at the huge bend of the Ohio River which seems to be over a mile wide. Since the river never freezes over, there is constant river barge traffic going up and down, and the deep powerful groan of the diesel engines is always heard. A block-long group of stately Victorian houses face the river. Called Captain's Row, this is where the riverboat captains lived when not piloting one of those flat-bottomed, stern-wheeled boats.

While Enfamil was the bread and butter of Mead Johnson—expectant mothers would get a Beatrix Potter emblazoned goodie bag from their obstetrician—it also sold adult nutritionals. One, called Sustacal (later known as Boost), was given with meals in hospitals and also to patients so wracked with cancer they had to be fed through a tube. To show you how technical her products were, she wrote this to a friend who was wracked with cancer:

> *Here are possible helps for lack of appetite. It is a very common problem for folks recovering/receiving cancer treatments. I have to assume they are pumping her up with calories and nitrogen and vitamins/minerals with TPN or total parenteral nutrition which goes*

directly into the bloodstream through an IV. Sometimes that will help stimulate appetites. But there are oral supplements which one sipped over time (if you have no appetite you don't want 8 oz. at once). The Boost line is what I sold. There is Boost plus which is calorically denser than plain Boost at one and a half calories per ml or Boost high protein or plain Boost. The high protein and regular are one cal/ml but protein is 14 gms.

Little did Margo know that one day she would have to take her own advice.

What did she like and dislike about her work? Some things she liked were: the freedom to plan day activities (something she demonstrated very well during her Asian trip); she could identify successes and failures; no one watched her day in and out; it played off her well-liked personality and the challenge of being turned down by customers and then turning them around.

There was also, however, lots to dislike that those of you who have sales jobs will recognize. Margo did like to make appointments ("CONSTANT!"), write reports, and account for her days' activities:

Doing things that a sales manager told us to do that made no sense; not having a group to work with and socializing with big name customers. You know, Fred, how are you and so forth and excessive back slapping.

Although still vibrant and strong, the handling of samples in her Minneapolis sales job for Mead Johnson really was for weight lifters:

The job required the lifting of 10 to 20 sample cases which I delivered to clinics. Then I had to unload them and each day I figured I had lifted a ton of product.

It did not help matters that some "sales reps" were given those Pontiac 6000s with deep, awkward trunks out of which they had to reach down and clumsily lift cases of product. Whatever her likes and dislikes about the car and job, she was able to write on October 19, 1989—a little more than a year after joining the firm again in July of 1988:

I am #6 in the country as of the end of August!!! Wow! Hallelujah, it feels wonderful. And in September my sales index climbed from

101.5 to 105 in August. So—for the record month in a row I am #1 in the district.

Her territory was a good one—most of Minnesota and Wisconsin, including the crown jewel: the Mayo Clinic. The Mayo Clinic, according to Leonard Berry in his book *Management Lessons from the Mayo Clinic,* "is the first integrated not-for-profit medical practice in the world and one of the largest. As a multi-specialty group it brings together doctors from virtually every medical specialty—joined by common systems and values who work together for patients."

For many heads of state, particularly in the Middle East, the Mayo Clinic is their "emergency room." The international center has excellent bilingual staff and offers daily newspapers in Arabic and Spanish. It then and now welcomes Arabs of whatever ilk and dress knowing their importance to the local economy. Mayo draws 150,000 out-of-city patients a year. Margo and I would both become patients there ourselves.

Margo's efforts in this territory began to draw the attention of top management including our Luis de la Cruz. The big bosses began to take notice and be impressed. I asked Luis de la Cruz about Margo. He was a regional sales manager for the Midwest for Mead Johnson with ten states in his region including "most of the baseball cities," as he put it. Luis, who now lives in Florida, told me that when Margo interviewed for the sales position, "I hired her on the spot. She had an opportunity to be home in Minnesota, work in an industry that she had helped develop in prior years and have a tremendous and very large sphere of influence both within the country and with customers." And he added, "She was a smart world traveler and strong—she fought off the entire Indian army defending her honor."

Since the Mayo account was a big and important one, Luis decided they should make a number of sales calls together. This is how he remembered one such trip.

"Deep in the heart of winter Margo and I went to the Mayo Clinic for a series of talks and product presentations about nutritional support. We knew we were close to converting this prestigious account and that the ripple effect to convert other clinics would be huge. We were very excited that day as we parked in one of the four parking garages (there is one in every corner of the clinic site) and quickly walked into a side entrance of the clinic.

As expected the day was very productive and Margo got commitments from department heads and clinicians and an initial purchase order was drafted. Those were the days before cell phones and we wanted to tell everyone back at corporate about our newest conversion and we were in a celebratory mode the moment we walked out to 26 degrees below zero. As we walked up the ramp at the parking garage, Margo began to realize that her car was nowhere to be seen. There was snow and ice all over the campus, the wind was picking up and the cold went through our clothes like ice picks into our skin.

That is when it struck us. We could not remember in which of the four parking garages we parked the car; we got turned around inside the clinic as we worked the different departments and now it was impossible to tell where the car was. As we started walking to the next corner's parking lot, Margo started laughing with that contagious style that made everyone around her laugh, and she said, 'Boy, this is great, I don't know where I parked the car, it is 26 below zero in Minnesota on the day that my boss comes to work with me. This is going to look great in my appraisal next year!' We both started laughing loudly and just then a security vehicle came close to us and after explaining he took us around until we found the car."

The memories didn't stop in Rochester. Fast forward to Milwaukee where they called on that city's biggest hospital and convinced them to convert to Mead Johnson in merely a morning. That left a whole afternoon and evening.

Margo, knowing Luis's love of baseball, said, "*Want to go to a ball game?*"

So they went to the game in their business clothes, but Margo always came prepared. She said, "*Excuse me for a minute.*" When they got to their seats, which were right alongside the Milwaukee Brewers dugout, Margo had changed into a mini-skirt and with those long legs (36" inseam) immediately caught the eye of Milwaukee's future hall of famer, Paul Molitor. Luis recalled that Molitor didn't play too well that game for every time he came up to bat he would ogle Margo's long legs and then hit the ball miserably. Luis remembers telling Margo on his last time up, "If you want Molitor to get a hit, cover up those legs."

She rented the top floor of a spacious remodeled house in a tree-lined section of St. Paul, the capital of Minnesota. She lived maybe a five-minute walk from a magnificent bluff overlooking the Mississippi River and St. Paul's High Bridge, which the local *City Pages* newspaper dubbed the "suicide hot spot."

Margo's success in the work field stood in painful contrast to the lack of success I was having in freeing myself from the bonds of an unhappy marriage. We had been seeing each other and our proximity was too frustrating for her. She wanted to get back into the international game because it put more distance between us. Mead Johnson wanted to beef up its international presence and created a new position for an international development manager which Margo applied for early in the summer of 1990. We had planned to meet in the little Wisconsin town of Abbotsford somewhere in the middle of Wisconsin in the middle of the hot summer when she cancelled and said: *"I have to go to Evansville. I've accepted an international position."*

We knew we would still be seeing each other, but much less often than we had before, and both she and I could take a time out! She really wanted to see what she could do as an international development manager.

She later wrote on moving to Evansville: *"I realized I've done it to get away from John—so that I don't get so caught up with him knowing that it just caused pain."*

Almost immediately after getting the international job offer as Manager, Nutritional Business Development International, her bosses recognized in Margo what is now called "erotic capital." There is a book out by that title. The author, Catherine Hakin, defined the term to the "complex but crucial combination of beauty, sex appeal, skills of self presentation and social skills—a combination of physical and social attractiveness that makes some men and women agreeable company and colleagues, attractive to all members of society and especially to the opposite sex."

Margo was slowly beginning to realize herself what I and her bosses, Luis de la Cruz and Rida Ali, were telling her and which Catherine Hakin sums up by saying: "Attractive people draw others to them as friends, lovers, colleagues, customers, clients, fans, followers, voters, supporters, and sponsors. They are more successful in private life but also in sports, the arts, and business life."

While she would never admit it publically, Margo subconsciously knew the attractiveness game. Her infectious smile, which she became famous and loved for, was not all that natural. She once wrote: *"My pasted smile was learned behavior as a child—quit frowning, you're much prettier when you smile. No need to have such a sad look on your face."*

Margo's first trip as the international development manager came on September 17, 1990—about 2½ years after stepping off the plane in Los Angeles after her year in Asia. One of the biggest differences in the two trips was that she was now flying first-class from Evansville, Indiana, to Athens, Greece.

> *A rite of passage, my first business trip abroad first class to Athens. Wow, it was like Christmas—porcelain Dutch house filled with liquor, the captain introduced himself and served delicious Indonesian dinner—too much.*
>
> *I vomited just before getting off—gave us socks, neck rest and goody bag.*

Hey, give her a break; it was her first flight in her new job as the international developer of business for Bristol-Myers. This trip also took her to Munich, Germany (where she sped along the autobahn at ninety miles an hour to a meeting) and then on to Madrid, Spain. The enormity of and cost of her trips amazed her—this one was US$10,000. But upon returning, her boss, Rida Ali, told her he "wants me to go to Canada for five to seven days and research a project and that she'll be adding Paris to her Asian trip in November."

All her flying, of course, was first class. I can't help but think how funny this is as this same woman endured a filthy 9½ hour bus ride in India just three years before. She then realizes, *"I definitely will work on improving my classiness—leather brief case, shoes, purse for documents."*

Upon arriving in Evansville to accept the international job, Margo registered herself at the Riverview Motel where she would live for a couple of months—at company expense. The hotel and room were cool, as I went to see Margo when she called it home. "Each room has a spectacular view of the Ohio River or the historical homes located in the historical district...Atop the River House sits the Sunset Restaurant and Lounge which overlook that Grand Old River. The atmosphere is as delightful as the view."

I'm sorry the people in Evansville are kind of dour and Margo re-thought having a condo in the city. She had dreamed of a house on the water and she wanted one but bad.

There was nothing to be found in Evansville, no real waterfront de-velopment had started, so she went exploring up and down and even across the river from Evansville. In funky Newburgh, Indiana, ten miles north from downtown on the river, she found four new three-level con-dos with elevators no less.

Newburgh had a population of 3,000—a Margo-sized sort of town. And just up the road from Margo's house was the popular if not rustic (OK, it's a hole in the wall) Knob Hill Restaurant which offers a local delicacy—fiddlers. These are catfish "fried in a batter which is top secret." More to her liking were broiled fiddlers but the head "chef" noted this is the south and few people save Margo requested them...Margo took many an out-of-town visitor there including me.

August 7, 1988

It gets better each day being in here. I decided to lease 100 Water Place #3. It's so pretty here—I'll feel like I'm in heaven. I'll have a re-frigerator and washer and dryer again... I love the water and always wanted a place on the water.

It was US$800 a month rent, but much cheaper than in New Jersey.

What a gorgeous place—the living area was on the second floor, bed-rooms and balconies on both floors overlooking the Ohio which was only a couple hundred feet away. And it even had an elevator to connect the two-car garage with the upper two floors. She was in heaven and wrote a friend:

I now have traveled Australia, Europe and Canada. I am back living in Newburgh, Indiana, in a small town outside of Evansville on the Ohio River. Besides playing tennis and hiking, a favorite activity is watching the river barges and the changing character of the Ohio River.

And on the occasion of a reunion with a sorority sister, she summed up the last couple of years nicely in a letter:

> *I have had the opportunity to travel extensively around the world. After working for a small medical products company from 1983-86, I had myself a sabbatical. I quit my job to travel the Pacific Rim for a year. A few highlights were the wonderful friends I made in New Zealand; trekking in the Himalayas in Nepal; exploring Australia, Thailand and China.*
>
> *A year of international travel told me I would love a job in the international business arena. Two years ago I was fortunate to be offered a position in international business development with Mead Johnson International, a division of Bristol-Myers Squibb.*

What to put in the garage?

She had to give up the company car, a clunky Pontiac, and when she passed a Chrysler dealership she saw an Eagle Talon—a two-person, low-slung sports car. OK, it had four seats, but the back two were marginal and only suited for people who had no legs. It had a sexy hood air intake on the left side of the car in order "to provide adequate clearance for the camshaft/timing belt on the 4GB3." Translation: the turbo made it faster than a Porsche at a fraction of the price—US$17,000. One enthusiast wrote, "But when I saw this car I was in total disbelief. It was lightweight, inexpensive, had a tiny engine with something called a 'turbocharger' and was seriously fast." I got to drive it a lot and got it up to 135 mph while Margo topped it out at 125 mph on a lonely Montana interstate two years later.

It was the only car I've driven where you could put your foot on the gas—not the brake—to get out of trouble. Margo was very flexible when she bought this and had fun looking at people's expressions of this very tall woman getting out of this low-slung car. So again this blows my mind: Margo zipping around in this sports car with racing tires just a couple of years after going through India in a slow-moving bus—or being stuck in traffic in New Jersey in her beat up Camry.

One of the very few times I ever saw Margo visibly angry was when she was driving this turbocharged speedster in the wide open and empty spaces of Wyoming. She wanted to know how fast she could drive it. Montana did not have a speed limit after the nationwide 55 mile an hour was lifted on interstate highways. Instead the only rule was "reasonable and prudent."

In any event Margo got it up to 125 miles per hour and watched the world whiz by on Interstate 94. She let up on the gas and brought it down to 95 mph when she saw flashing red lights in her rearview mirror. The Montana state trooper pulled her over and said she was going "too fast."

"What's too fast? There's no traffic; the road is dry."

"Eighty would have been OK," responded the trooper and gave her a ticket for US$77. After he left Margo said, *"Who is he to tell me what reasonable and prudent is?"* Eventually that rule was overturned as too arbitrary. I always remember the anger in her face and voice for someone having the gall to tell her what "reasonable and prudent" was.

What to Wear?

As to clothes, Margo realized on her first trip abroad—to Paris, just a month after joining the international group—that she needed a classier wardrobe. International fashions were not the *in* thing in Evansville, Indiana, so off it was to Neiman Marcus in St. Louis. In addition, she made a list—one of hundreds I found—of travel clothes necessities which included:

> *Pressed jeans or jean skirt, comfortable black flats, briefcase that's also purse—no separate purse, no hair dryer, no iron and a non-hanging bag.*

So what does an international development manager do?

Travel. The travel was grueling yet exciting—twenty-seven major international trips to sixteen countries in three years My favorite photo of her at work shows her standing her head and shoulders taller than a bunch of Swiss businessmen. You cannot develop much of a social life with that pace so Margo would frequently call me—I would get calls in the middle of the night due to the time difference. I have listed the trips Margo took—all first-class around the world to carry out her job:

147

Margo's Dream Job International Travels

Travel Dates	Country
September 1990	Greece
	Germany
	Spain
November 1990	France
November 1990	Japan
	Singapore
	Malaysia
	Taiwan
November 1990	Korea
February 1991	Toronto, Canada
March 1991	Switzerland
	Paris, France
	Denmark
May 1991	Korea
	Taiwan
June 1991	Madrid
	Thailand
July 1991	Australia
August 1991	Mexico
October 1991	Madrid
April 1992	Indonesia
May 1992	Singapore
	Australia
	London
	Spain
July 1992	Japan
	Malaysia

She did reflect on her travels. She wrote this when in Taipei:

I am ready to go home. But miss Chelsea (her cat), the river, my car, my food—a grilled cheese sandwich—a walk in a clean environment, a hard swim, racquetball, my friends, John—I wonder what he's up to this weekend.

Luis recalls when he and Margo were in Madrid together. At the end of the presentation by a group of Germans, she said to Luis: *"Let's get out of here."*

They drove an hour to the medieval town of Toledo and toured everywhere. Finally they came to the top of a hill overlooking the city and he heard her say: *"This is the most wonderful job on earth."*

Some of the strategic issues she faced were:

Infant formula is nutritionally inferior to breast milk but superior to other substitutes, such as milk from cows. Besides breast milk, infant formula is the only other milk product which the medical community considers nutritionally acceptable for infants under the age of one year.

Margo best explained what she did to the conference of Australian dietitians (think back to her meals at Ayers Rock with Titus just a few years before). Boy, I would have loved to have read this presentation before—it gets into how peanut butter was "invented," but again it was tucked into the steamer trunk. Here are some cool parts from that presentation:

In my position in International Business Development with Mead Johnson, I travel fairly extensively in the Pacific Rim countries and Europe. So I personally encounter a wide range of foods, parts of plants, animals, fish, etc., tastes, textures, food combinations, etc. which is increasingly fascinating to me.

But more importantly, I and the company are challenged to try to integrate some of this knowledge into product development activities for specific markets or regions of the world.

But how does that play out when it comes to developing products for an international market? And this does not relate only to foods, but to all kinds of products. The book Medicine and Culture *by Lynn Payer makes the point about the wide variations in medical practice between the U.S., U.K., France, Germany and Italy amongst each of those countries while life expectancies are equivalent.*

For example, low blood pressure is rewarded with reduced insurance rates in the U.S. while it is treated as an ailment in Germany; supposi- tories are a relatively common method of administering drugs in France and Belgium, etc. Understanding differences can affect a company's suc- cess or failure in the market place. And even within one country the cultural differences of the population can demand modifications.

And Margo took a painful cue out of her past to say that whatever the cultural circumstances, success only comes from listening to the customer.

Listen to the customer—both to what they actually say and to what they do not say. A short experience with TV taught me this latter lesson: 'Marketing with Margo' was a short test-marketed 60-minute segment on a local TV station that I did in the mid-70s. I talked about and showed the best nutritional buys of the week. To keep the series going, the station wanted to know someone was watching—even if they did not like it. They received no comments on the segment! Thus 'Marketing with Margo' had a very short life—eight segments.

She would have to keep up with her grueling travel schedule and then greet Mead Johnson visitors from all over who she would promptly take to eat fiddlers at the Knob Hill Restaurant in Newburgh. To wit a thank you note in Japanese-English.

"Dear Margo,

Thank you so much for your kindness for [sic] our trip. The visit to USA have [sic] taken great success by your support. Japanese dietitian and nutritionist participated to [sic] this tour got strong impression [sic] on every places [sic] to visit. It was very usefull [sic] to discuss the role of dietitian [sic] with together [sic] USA dieti- tians and Japanese dietitians. And we could study many significant things for preparing to start the professional education systems for clinical dietitians and nutrition support dietitians in Japan.

I never forget all your kindness [sic] and your friendship.

I send [sic] the book about 'Japanese Nutrition and Dietetics' and please send me the documents of Mayo Clinic.

I look forward to meet [sic] you sometime and somewhere.

Sincerely yours
Teiji Nakamura, Ph.D.
Japanese Dietetic Association"

Between her hectic schedule and the frustrations and successes it brought, she received in Evansville on July 7, 1992, a reassurance in her ability when she was given her workplace evaluation:

Lordy, lordy what a crazy life I lead, Rida gave my evaluation at end of day—no warning; I'd been paranoid about it worrying myself sick and it went great, I feel suspicious that it is not for real or will get reversed. Yuk! He gave me a promotion and a 23% increase in salary! Unreal but very nice. I do deserve it as I have worked very hard.

Celebrating Success

When it came to celebrating her success, Margo did it in Margo fashion. She created a list titled Possible Celebrations. On the list she included:

- New stereo
- Running shoes
- Exercise outfit
- Flowers
- Aboriginal art

She also managed to give herself a few interesting vacations. She made quite a few friends in Evansville including a woman named Christine Helfrich. (She now lives and works in Salt Lake City at the Huntsman Cancer Hospital.) When Christine and Margo met, they discovered their mutual love of mountains, of which Evansville, Indiana, had none. So one day they decided they would go to Utah where Christie is originally from and go camping. There were lots of places to go camping in Utah, but which ones to go to? They picked out a number of destinations, wrote them down on pieces of paper and then threw them into a hat. They would then pick out two and visit those destinations for a week. The winners were Zion National Park and Bryce Canyon.

It was the beginning of fall so the brutal temperatures of summer were gone, but evenings were cool, dropping into the forties. The idea of campfires at night sounded intriguing. So how do you get to Utah from Evansville? First you fly to Chicago, and from Chicago on to Salt Lake City; then you take two fourteen-seat puddle-jumpers to reach St. George, whereupon you rent a car.

They brought sleeping bags, air mattresses, backpacks and a tent. Christie, who was slim and attractive but shorter than Margo, does not recall Margo telling her about her yearlong travels with a backpack through Asia.

From the airport the two women finally headed out by car to spend three days at Bryce and Zion. The scenery was beyond scenic and soon Christie realized (as I later did) that low-key Margo was "exhilarated" by danger.

At Zion they have this wonderful red rock monolith called Angel's Landing sitting out in a similarly rugged valley if you want to call it that. Basically it's a 2,000-foot hike up a steep trail which at one point has an 800-foot dropoff on one side and 1,000-foot drop on the other. Margo went up it like an experienced rock climber while Christie watched in awe. People do die at Angel's Landing, raising questions for the Park Service about who should be allowed to go up it, though chains have been installed at the most treacherous sections. I like what one blogger wrote: "It scared the hell out of me the first time I went up Angel's Landing. That adrenalin rush not only heightened my cautiousness but it also let me know how alive I was. When my time arrives, I hope it comes at Angel's Landing and not while driving down the highway or crossing the street."

Christie recalls Margo's devilish smile as she scampered up the treacherous path that led to the top of Angel's Landing. She recalls one photo she took. "There is one picture that makes me smile. It only shows Margo's hand on her backpack but also a squirrel that is trying to get to the 'trail mix' in her backpack. I recalled that Margo calmly watched the squirrel inch closer to her hand because after all we are sitting atop Angel's Landing where getting alarmed or nervous could be deadly to human or animal. Mere rodents were not going to ruin her moment at the top of the world."

In my townhouse in Minneapolis, I have a poster Margo bought at Zion, and I also have made a scale depiction of Angel's Landing on the reproduction of Zion that I constructed for my train layout. I cherish a photo of a barefoot Margo dipping her toes in a cool mountain stream while pensively reading a book. And it scares me to put those scale figures climbing up the landing, even though there were chains to hold on to. But how strange of Margo not to mention her trip to Zion even though I saw her throughout her time at Zion. Too much going on elsewhere I guess. But it does warm my heart that over the campfire one evening she told Christie that I was the love of her life.

Our professional careers intertwined while Margo was in Evansville. I was working for a language service firm and wanted to know how our prices stacked up against the competition. I couldn't call up our competitors and ask them. So I wrote a letter using her letterhead, included a document to be translated and asked for a price quote and other key information. All the competitors were frothing at the bit to do work with Bristol-Myers so we got immediate responses. I saved Margo a lot of grief by making it clear that no one should call.

Being an international company, Bristol-Myers needed manuals, labels, et al., translated into other languages, and lucky me, Margo gave me the business. Boy, did I look good. My coworkers asked, "How'd you get that business?" If they only knew.

So when not flying (Oh! The advantage miles!) and receiving visitors and entertaining them with fritters, Margo had to evaluate proposals from scores of companies wanting to do business with Mead Johnson.

If you can get through the following paragraphs, I applaud you and give you a degree in intuition.

Summary of April 2, 1991 meeting with Ferrsosan, a division of Novo Nordisk, Copenhagen, Denmark

It was because of Novo Nordisk's experience with enzymes, which started with insulin, that they began exploring other uses for their enzymes, and specifically using them in enteral products. They developed four products using hydrolyzed soy protein: Orange Plus, a protein fortified juice; Restore, an isotonic hydrolyzed protein standard tube feeding product; Top-Up, a higher protein version of the Restore; and Restore Oral, a fruit flavored version of Restore.

They brought these products into test market in Australia and Denmark to prove/test whether they had viable products. They are also doing significant work with structured lipids and are supplying the Boston group with their structured lipids. Their enteral products were packed in tetras in Australia and in Denmark the orals in tetras and the tube-feeds in Bottle-Pak.

Did you get all that?

The pressure, the travel, the visitors, the analysis were constant, and Margo wondered if she should just be running an art gallery as someone in New Zealand had suggested during her Asian trip. She was dealing with the turmoil in our relationship as I had not yet been officially divorced; her cat Chelsea urinated all over her carpets because she was away so much, and she feared that she had botched this new job—her dream job—and they would find out that she knew nothing and would fire her.

With the amount of self-doubt she had about the security of her dream job, one would have thought she was mismanaging her international business accounts. It doesn't appear anything of the sort was happening—there was the odd hiccup but that's about it. She analyzed her dream job thusly:

International:
I liked: sense that my opinion/business sense was respected and that I was expected to make judgments and make decisions and act
— job had a mix of tasks—some mindless, some thinking
—loved team work aspect of first—second year
—loved interfacing with the markets, learning market dynamics, being challenged by DIFFERENT perspectives; being viewed within company and in Evansville as different because I traveled and worked with foreigners
—being busy
—being a mediator between groups
—challenging what is being done or said

And for dislikes there were a few:

Dislike: details, keeping track of information, business socializing for weeks on end (overseas travel or lengthy deals); worrying about political rightness of actions or words, procedures (who can tell you what, when, etc.)

I asked her boss, Rida Ali, who now is the franchise owner for Gold's Gym in Cairo and professor emeritus at Cairo University, to provide some anecdotes on Margo's dream job. He came up with a couple—one from the Philippines and the other from Japan.

"The image that is everlasting in my heart for Margo is her kind heart! On a joint business trip with her to the Philippines, we went together to visit the general hospital in Manila to approve it as a site for conducting a clinical trial. I was walking with the hospital director discussing the study when I noticed that Margo was no longer behind, so we back-tracked to find her sitting on the edge of a hospital bed holding the hands of an old woman patient! The woman was in pain, calling for help and no one was listening to her cries! Margo stopped and called for help; she was waiting with the patient for help to arrive! That was an act of kindness only Margo can do!

On a lighter note, we were together in Tokyo on another business trip and we went out at night with a group of Japanese business friends. All were at least two feet shorter than she was and all wanted to dance with her! She never turned an invitation down, though she was tired and looked so funny trying to keep up with dancing partners much shorter than she was! At the end of the evening she was complaining to me about her back because of leaning forward not to make her dancing partners feeling bad because of differences in height! That was Margo at her best, very kind, very accommodating! God bless her soul.

–Regards, doc Rida"

And this is what Margo wrote on a résumé in May of 1996 when she was asked to write a résumé for a new job within Bristol-Myers:

1990-1993 Senior Manager International Business Manager

Responsible for strategic planning, identification of new product/ business opportunities, providing assistance to local markets in developing the US$40 million enteral nutritional business as part of a US$350 million international business.

Accomplishments: Increased sales 40% first year, 46% second year. Developed five-year strategic plan, worldwide label graphics and quarterly newsletters for customers; expanded product line in Taiwan, Philippines, Thailand, Australia and Japan; guided development plan for Indonesia, initiated development of three major new products, developed sales training materials for markets.

What Margo Missed

While she was working in Evansville and I was alternately in Pittsburgh and Minneapolis, the separation was getting to us. So when we finally decided to live together, Margo got a domestic assignment to be a sales representative (like she did before) working out of the Twin Cities.

Writing in a stenographer's green notebook on March 3, 1993:

I miss being the 'international marketer'—the fame and the glory of it; the power of it compared to being a U.S. marketer or salesperson. I miss not working for a unit I respect and like—although I had concerns about people and actions in international I basically liked our group and our role. I miss not being part of the home office team—being on the inside and I miss not calling or hearing from them.

Her previous ties to the home office—and the salary she kept—made a future boss very jealous of her, and he went out of his way to keep her miserable. But for now she could gloat.

When she wrote out her twelve-page epistle in 2009 called My Life she concluded: *"This was one of my best jobs and times of greatest happiness."*

10

take a chance on me (and my considerable baggage)

*If you change your mind, I'm the first in line
Honey I'm still free
Take a chance on me
If you need me, let me know, gonna be around
If you got no place to go when you're feeling down
If you're all alone when the pretty birds have flown
Honey I'm still free
Gonna do my very best and it ain't no be
If you put me to the test, if you let me try.*

– ABBA, "Take a Chance on Me"

*A*s previously mentioned, in 1988 I worked for a division of the Ogilvy Advertising Empire: I ran the Minneapolis office for the subsidiary, Euramerica. My office was housed inside the headquarters of the hotshot advertising agency, Fallon McElligott, in a spanking brand new office building with pink reflective glass in the windows and yuppie bars and restaurants downstairs. It was at this office that Margo first came to visit me on April 19, 1988.

Margo cautiously opened the solid, industrial-strength, heavy, dull brown door and inquisitively said, "Euramerica?"

"You got the right place," I replied and pointed to the chair on the other side of the desk. She had a wide, cautious smile on her face as she entered and sat down.

Looking back today on that first meeting, with me on one side of the desk and Margo on the other, I can't help thinking how self-centered and egotistical I must have appeared. After all, I did work for a New York ad agency that was not known for humility. I guess there is a sense of self-importance that emerges when you work for and with some of the largest international businesses on the planet. In many respects, every day was an intellectual and international adventure in which I felt I could either influence or shape, if not entirely control, the outcome of any number of contracts. Let me give you a sense of these adventures and their impact on me before describing my first business meeting with Margo.

One day the account executive for Timex came into the office and asked if I knew anyone who could help them film a commercial in the Amazon jungle. Timex had the advertising theme, "Timex: It Just Keeps on Ticking." And they wanted to put a Timex on a ham and throw it in the water and watch meat-eating piranha fish devour the meat, then pull out the bone and see the Timex watch still ticking.

Wouldn't you know it, I *did* know someone who could do that. George Sluizer is a Dutch movie producer and director who had bought the movie rights to my novel *The Famine Plot* several years before. He did a lot of things and was the Amazon production manager for a Werner Hertzog (famous German director) film called *Fitzcarraldo,* also filmed in the Amazon. The account executive was impressed. Initially, Fallon wanted to send seven people to the Amazon to shoot the commercial, but then Fallon presented the cost to Timex. Mama Mia Santa Maria! Timex elected to do the commercial in an aquarium in London—much cheaper.

Another time an account executive for FedEx gave me the assignment of finding out how FedEx could be a sponsor for the 1988 Olympics: who to call, how much, etc.

The sum total of these kinds of visits, plus the sales we made to Medtronic and other top accounts, plus an unlimited expense account, made me think I was really hot shit. This is the man who humble and insecure Margo met when she cautiously entered my office on April 22, 1988.

My office was huge—some twenty feet square—but had no windows; you had to walk down a long corridor to get to it. A sign read Euramerica and underneath *International Advertising and Language Management* in cardinal red letters on a black background. Inside were two desks. One was for a constant stream of interns I employed; the other was mine. It sat in front of an 8x12 laminated wall map of the world. It was really handsome and pointed out to all visitors that we were international—and that my ego was world scale.

Margo and I had our meeting in this office. I may have thought myself "a man of the world" but let me tell you, her entrance into the room was mesmerizing. She was simply stunning. I was instantaneously attracted to her and the feeling just got stronger as she started talking about her Asian travels and interest in an international job. I was to be part of her job hunting networking process.

Oddly, my perception of her at that moment stood in stark contrast to her perception of herself. In her diaries from that time, she appeared to be a totally disorganized, scattered person who would be living in a friend's house and out of a suitcase. Just a month earlier she had written, *"My beautiful smile is pasted on a face full of pain."*

But to me she was radiant and totally composed and her body language told me she was looking for love and companionship, not just a job. She recalls that I said, "You generate electricity that's fun to be around."

We blabbed on for an hour about world affairs, people she should contact, and an upcoming seminar at a fancy hotel, the Whitney, which I was hosting. She took notes on a stenographer pad as we talked, and that same notepad ended up in the steamer trunk. I'm using that notepad now as I write to help me recall details!

Then we were done. As she elegantly and slowly got up from the front of my beat-up desk, I was amazed at how tall she was. Wow!

She walked confidently out of the room and headed for the elevator. I said to myself, I can't afford emotionally not to see her again and ran out the door and said, "I like you, can we have dinner some night? I'm divorced and would love some company."

I lied. I wasn't legally divorced and wouldn't be for another three-and-a-half years, and my personal life was a mess. I had been married for twenty-two years, but all the love had gone out of our marriage years earlier. I was under tremendous work and financial pressure, raising three active teenage daughters and traveling the country, if not the world, to make sales so I could pay the bills that were coming due.

Margo took a chance on me in spite of my background and then took an even bigger chance when all of my past, children and the rest of it, became a fixture in her life.

I wasn't interested in sex when I met Margo, for I had been in steamy yet unfulfilling relationships with different women: a travel agent, a former clerk, and a model, all of whom approached me first, as if that mattered. The former clerk was in fact a preacher's wife no less, and she actually became a friend of my ex-wife until she found out about our relationship. My ex-wife promptly slammed the door in her face when she tried to explain our affair. All of these empty and willing women put up with my bloated yet insecure ego and heavy-duty temper tantrums. With Margo, I could tell there was intellectual substance, athleticism, a sense of adventure, and kindness. I had never been so attracted to a woman before.

In a couple of days, I put on the well-attended seminar, and with her heels on Margo, at 6'3", was the tallest person in the room. I remember walking up to her in that crowded room of well-dressed, name-tagged individuals and welcoming her, and then asking her if we could have dinner some night. After the seminar, she wrote me a note I still cherish.

> *Thanks for your time and ideas last week. I thoroughly enjoyed our meeting and you. I hope we are able to have dinner as you suggested. I would like that very much... This week I am house-sitting for some friends in Lake Elmo. Look forward to talking to you and seeing you again. I can be reached at 779-6156. Regards, Margo.*

I melted when I read this note. I just had to call her. So I did. Meanwhile, Margo pondered in her diary.

> *Now, what kind of man is John Freivalds going to turn out to be? It seems he could be a major jerk – egotistical – only into himself – so bright – so crazy. On the other hand he could be a gem: he thanked me for my nice note, called to apologize to me for not talking to me at luncheon... then the statement about my generating electricity in a room – all of that is more open than any man I've met in a long time – I mean really – that day at the elevator he said he <u>liked</u> me. Quite amazing that he's that out front. Well tomorrow P.M. will be interesting to say the least. Wouldn't it be great if it went well and saw more of each other? One day at a time!*

But then she added she still wanted to pursue a fellow by the name of Tom Vance. So I was not the only game in town.

The Saturday night date came and I picked up Margo in Lake Elmo on the east side of St. Paul, probably thirty-five miles from where I lived.

I was driving a dented 1980 four door Buick Skylark with blue velour seats and a stick shift. It had a tacky four-cylinder engine I couldn't even pretend was sporty. Margo also drove a beat-up older car, a Camry, to be exact. In many ways, Margo and I were as beat up by life as our cars were by the road. Of the date, she wrote:

> *My Saturday date with John Freivalds was exciting and fun – as well as a bit nerve-wracking. The latter due to the fact it was my first real date in a year and the first sexual turn on since Mitch David (remember Ko Samui and Thailand). John's intriguing because of his experience and feedback to me. Last night he said he was 'smitten' with me because I was so nice, honest, fun, sensible and good moral judgment and you did everything right on Saturday.*

She was a magnificent woman, a keeper, and I knew it, but as the relationship developed I was afraid I would scare her away. I found myself in a horrible dilemma. I dare not tell her I was still married for fear of losing her; yet the longer I refused to tell her the truth, the more quickly I found myself being dragged into an ever-thickening quagmire—one I might eventually drown in. I was worried I would lose this wonderful person and was unsure of what to do.

Margo again made one of her illustrative graphics to show where I stood in her life. Her confusion is also quite apparent.

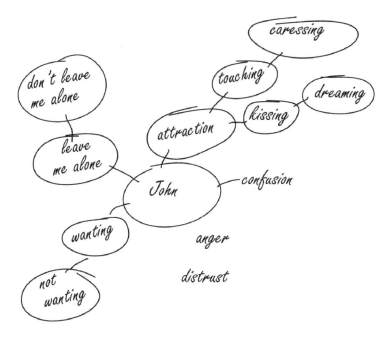

Our relationship was getting deeper and richer rather quickly, for on May 4th, barely two weeks after we had met, she wrote: *"I bought John a red rose yesterday which was a hit, I believe, and so fun to do. We had a quick drink in a downstairs bar. He said he was trying to avoid my eyes – I said I was ready to devour him – he returned 'that sends a sensation from my heart to my groin.' I LOVE IT."*

We began to see each other as much as possible and went on walks, bike rides, worked out at my club, dinners and lunches. I profoundly enjoyed our time together and so did she. Margo wrote:

> *Playing racquetball for the first time in six months was glorious even though I was afraid for my body – GOD I LOVE THAT INTENSE ACTIVITY. It's a great thing to do with John – I actually find it sensuous – as I seem to do with most physical activity I do with a man. I think part of it makes me feel so good – anyway it's pure clean exhilarating fun. That was followed by a roam thru the JCC art gallery and a walk.*

We were physically attracted to each other, but neither one of us had a place where we could go to spend quiet time alone. In some ways we were like teenagers still living at home. So we snuggled in my office, car, woods, fields, and in the house she was staying at when the owners were away.

But all this deception was driving me crazy. I had to make up stories to tell my wife as to why I had to leave early or arrive late. She probably knew something was up, but didn't really say anything. After our divorce, she told me that she hoped my plane would crash so she wouldn't have to see me again.

I was twisting in the wind, tormented by lies and deception. Margo, however, had righted herself by moving into a neat, tree-lined apartment near the High Bridge in St. Paul. One among many neighborhoods through which we frequently walked. I would visit her apartment many times for marvelous dinners (lemon chicken was my favorite) with her cat, Chelsea, jumping all over me.

We got closer.

The stress I was enduring was growing greater and greater. Like my ex-wife who was growing suspicious of my early departures and late arrivals, so too was Margo getting suspicious of all my strange comings and goings, and even stranger explanations for them. I also felt the need to be with my girls, do things with them, but that was becoming more difficult as I was spending more time away from home. I knew getting a separation would be painful and the financial pressure associated with it would be overwhelming. Yet I wanted to be with and snuggle with Margo. I felt alive again with her. All of this was eating my insides out and would eventually result in my first ulcer and a trip to the emergency room.

Then the unthinkable happened. Margo asked a sorority sister of hers, a judge in Minneapolis (who later would marry us!), to investigate whether I was truly divorced. My awful secret was revealed. Margo screamed in anger when she learned I was not divorced. She had been with married men before but at least they told her they were married. I had lied and that was unacceptable; more unacceptable than being married. I tried to explain myself out of the mess the best I could. Margo then pondered: *"John, why should I trust anything you say to me? Your actions were totally selfish. All I asked from you was honesty and to listen to me and you didn't do either. What do I have to gain from this? What was going to give you the strength to tell me? If all you wanted was to take me to dinner and friendship, why did you pursue me sexually and call me so much?"*

Yep, I was a real gem.

Margo decided she would move to create space between me and her. She was very much saddened by the turn of events. She wrote in one of her journals:

> *For the reality of how much I want John to be available to me and the realization of how impossible that is – it will never happen – plus he can't meet my needs – but the dream of a nice house with a husband is so far from being – and so why do I continue to take the tidbits from John and others. Oh I would like to inherit a family since I will never have my own.*

We saw each other after that truth was revealed. She was very angry, and rightly so, and I was in some sort of emotional coma. Margo was fed up with my inability to change my lifestyle and to keep my emotions in check so this inevitably happened.

I Have to Say Goodbye

10/30/1989—Oh God – I did it! I told John goodbye without a discussion or attempt last night. I met him at the door and said, 'I didn't cook dinner.' 'You look awful, what's wrong?' he said.

'I can't do this anymore. I have to say goodbye.'
'Oh, OK, goodbye.' The end, and away he went.
I watched in tears and sadness. Feel guilty and yet it's right. Have somehow given him lots of opportunities and yet nothing.

I had nothing to say. I was ashamed; I was selfish; I was to blame for all the heartache I had caused. Yet deep down I knew I was in love with Margo. In the midst of the heartache brought on by the breakup, my health started to crumble. First, the perforated ulcer and then the panic call to 911 as I lay on the living room floor floating in my own blood. When the ambulance arrived, I was rushed to the hospital and underwent emergency surgery for a bleeding ulcer. The loss of blood was so great that two units of blood were needed to stabilize me. Needless to say, I was a mess and I needed help.

Regardless of my plight, Margo remained pissed and perplexed, and a week after showing me the door wrote an obituary of me. She never told me she had written one—I found it in the steamer trunk.

Memorial Service
for
John

I was alone, walking in the park
You were sitting by a tree
Our eyes met
You smiled

And invited me into your
world of deception

Only I did not know
at the time that that was where
you were leading me

I was vulnerable being without a job, a place of my own – working to re-establish myself in the Twin Cities community amongst old friends and colleagues and certainly eager to make new friends and connections.
Yes – and connections is what I wanted then and want even more now as I search for intimacy.

164

What a sham our relationship was – there was no true intimacy as there was dishonesty and untruthfulness on your part.

It is truth which makes man great – for in truth lies all the virtues of the human soul.

Your death is the first real truth in my history with you and that is painful for me to admit.

You even admitted on a number of occasions that you were not always truthful – were you proud of that? How could I continue with you with that knowledge? I no longer can – that is for sure.

What is the truth about you? I will never know – it is no longer important. You are no longer alive for me.

How disrespectful you have been to me and so many others – including yourself with your dishonesty.

I must also wonder if you're that way in business as well as in your personal life.

I was swept away by your experiences with the Peace Corps, Latvia, international marketing, public relations connections, etc., etc. – and yet how empty it all really is – there was no depth of meaning to any of it.

It pains me that you've been so egotistical, judgmental.

I guess I thought I could break that down – but of course I couldn't – how do you correct lies when the liar doesn't see a need to change?

What I grieve most in your death is the dream of what might have been.

But there are also good memories – Dear John.

The good ones are wonderful:
- *Exhilarating and sensuous bike rides down the country roads and bike trails of Wisconsin sprinkled with refreshing dips in the river*
- *Brisk walks through county and city parks*
- *Picnics along the river*
- *Dancing in country bars*
- *Strolling along the New York streets*
- *Decorating your office with wonderful prints from Latvia*
- *The night at the Latvian Cultural Center*
- *Occasional mutual sharing of painful experiences with our families*
- *Supportive calls during my long job search*
- *Stimulating conversations about international marketing and agriculture – you brought me a world I've wanted to know and experience*

(relatives and friends, foreigners with no resources) and yet you're so judgmental and uninterested in so many things I do and often gave the impression of being totally disinterested in anyone but yourself.

I grieve your death but sadly it's more the death of the dream of what might have been that I grieve the most.

I miss already being able to call you to share a sales success or failure – a moment to connectedness brief and frustrating as they often were.

I miss the aggravation I had when I couldn't break down your barrier to your emotions – and your monologue reporting on your business.

I miss your intense beautiful eyes, your willingness to poke around back alleys and small towns.

I miss the chance for an occasion of romance, the distant affection.

I really don't know what I meant to you and I'm sorry I'll never know – but I don't even know if you know the truth about that or anything else. Pain Be Gone.

Goodbye John

Even though I had been literally written off if not buried, Margo called me on January 4, 1990. In her My Life memoirs Margo wrote about this whole business:

It took me about a month to see the writing on the wall, that he was still married. When my judge friend gave me the info, which I had requested, I was livid – probably one of my most angry times. For days I swore about him, went swimming and kicked and hollered at him (in presence of friends). So I quit seeing him for a few weeks and then somehow allowed him to creep back into my life. At one point I met him at my door and said I can't do this anymore. He turned around and walked away without saying a word. A few months later I called him to see how he was and of course that started the whole thing up again slowly.

In the meantime, Margo had been going to group therapy. She told her group that I was being "reincarnated." They did not agree. What's really weird is I found the audio tape of Margo telling her therapist all about her relationship with me. After finding and listening to all the written materials, audio and video tapes, Margo seems almost alive as I write this—too weird. I told one of her former friends about this and she told me I shouldn't publically reveal what was in the steamer trunk,

"Those were private moments," she said. I disagreed. I don't believe, at all, that this women's inspirational history should remain locked up in a steamer trunk.

Once again we began to see each other quite a bit. Margo wanted to tone down the romance so we began to do a lot of sophisticated and athletic activities together. It helped somewhat that Margo knew what the deal was with me, but she was still mystified as to why I remained in my loveless marriage. I started going to see Scott Kamilar, a psychologist, to work out the weirdness in my flawed brain.

I wrote Margo lots of letters (no email in those days) and she saved all of them; I dove into them when I began to write this book. One pathetic one went as follows and then begs the question why would Margo take a chance on this loser?

"Dear Margo:

I feel terrible. I miss you and have got my lousy past weighing me down like a ball and chain.

It's like a cold day at the beach. The water is cold and you are afraid of jumping into it. Nothing is going right for me. I just have a penchant for making myself and everyone around me unhappy. Sometimes I think you must really hate me for the way I have mismanaged my life.

– John

P.S. I know, I know, go see Scott. I will."

After a couple of months, I realized I had to move out of the loveless house I had helped create. As time unfolded, the idea of leaving home seemed to be a logical next step. In addition to the disintegration of my marriage and my positively evolving relationship with Margo, a third factor involving my job and its instability helped influence my decision. The long and short of it was that Euramerica, the firm I worked for, had been sold, and my future with the firm that had purchased it was tenuous at best. As a consequence, I decided to join a firm based in Pittsburgh. My physical presence in Pittsburgh became absolutely necessary.

I was beyond a total emotional mess, yet Margo still took a chance to keep seeing me in the worst time of my life. It really was. I was now the national sales manager for this company and I really enjoyed what I was doing and it paid good money—US$120,000 a year plus expenses. The guy I would work for could qualify as a crazy boss, but I had to do something to change my life, so off to Pittsburgh I went. How crazy was this guy, you ask? Here are two stories that will give you a sense of this guy's character.

We were heading back from a business trip and it was 2:00 a.m. He had fallen asleep and I stopped for gas. I was driving his Volvo station wagon. I pulled up next to the pumps before noticing that the gas cap was opposite the pumps, but I got out and still managed to get the hose over. I started pumping gas. My boss woke up and demanded I stop, turn the car around and put the gas cap closer to the pump. He screamed, I did it, and then he went back to sleep.

And he would always try to cheat you whenever he could—something about his Polish Russian ethnicity. I was bringing in big accounts—UPS, Rockwell Automation, American Airlines—due to my many sales calls from a tiny office that had lots of boxes in it. As a consequence we needed more and better office equipment including a US$12,000 copier. At the end of one month I was going over my commission sheets and saw he had deducted the US$12,000 from my commissions. I protested, saying, "This is for the office." His response was, "Yeah, but if you hadn't brought in this business, we wouldn't have needed a new copier." I won, but it was always like this. We had a small staff of perhaps five people and we were always telling each other "crazy boss" stories.

But in spite of having a crazy boss like that, Pittsburgh was only four hundred miles from Evansville and Margo—an eight-hour drive instead of twelve. So I packed my little eight-foot-long trailer, which was equipped with a table, two chairs, a little dresser, a fold-up bed, bedding, some silverware, an old TV, and cooking utensils, and set off for Pittsburgh nine hundred miles from Minneapolis; I once drove that distance in fifteen hours straight.

When I got to Pittsburgh, I went to my crazy boss's house in a fancy part of Pittsburgh called Fox Meadows. I stayed a couple of days with my crazy boss and his wife, equally crazy, who would come into my room at 3:00 a.m. in her negligee with her boobs showing to offer me a glass of water. And I suppose herself.

Just as my job was in flux, so too was Margo's. However, she transitioned into a job that was far more stable than mine. It was at this time that Margo landed her dream job at Mead Johnson, as mentioned earlier. In June of 1990 she moved to Evansville. She later admitted to me that although the job itself was great, she also wanted to get away from me and give me an opportunity to get my act together before we got more deeply involved.

When Margo started her international travels, I suggested she stop by to see one of my closest friends, Jack Martinson, in Korea. (Incidentally, Jack's brother Tom had introduced Margo and me.) She did, and the visit gave her a new perspective on me and where I was coming from:

> *Jack Martinson was fun to meet; kind of off the wall funny; good natured; was willing to talk about John's distance from his wife and non-involvement with family as a group. Had been to his home a number of times – not a real fun affair it sounded like. It was neat to talk with someone who knows John. Didn't change my opinion of what I had one – must keep it that way.*

In Pittsburgh I ended up living in a one-bedroom apartment at the Wentworth, a dim, stodgy, moss-covered, 1940s-era, red brick apartment building complex in the heavily Jewish section of Pittsburgh called Squirrel Hill. There was a Jewish Community Center with a gym, and since I belonged to one in Minneapolis, I had reciprocal privileges at this one. But I didn't use it much and in two months gained ten pounds from lack of exercise and drinking too much. Margo once came to visit me and said my apartment reminded her of a prison cell. It was solitary confinement, for I didn't know anyone in the complex or the restaurant-rich neighborhood. Very quickly I came to really miss my huge comfortable house in Minneapolis and its privacy. But what I really missed—I mean, *really* missed—was the enthusiasm of my girls telling me about their day's adventures. Good God, it sure did feel like solitary confinement. Looking back it was a form of masochism.

Instead of experiencing the comforts of my house and the love of my children, I would pick up a few slices of pizza or some other takeout food after work and then go home. I would drink Myers rum with Diet Pepsi, watch mindless TV, and then go to sleep. I would often call Margo—bless her 800 number, for if her company didn't have it I certainly would be declaring bankruptcy. I lived in this prison cell for nine months.

Meanwhile Margo wrote this about our lives in her memoirs.

I lived in a new townhouse 20 feet from the Ohio River in a little burgh called Newburgh north of Evansville. It was heaven. I traveled fairly extensively for three or four weeks at a time. The job was demanding so I had little time to worry about a social life – also I had to conduct business often at 10/11 at night to talk with the Pacific people. John was asked to move to Pittsburgh for his job, which he did without his family. His marriage continued on very rough ground. He came up for weekends occasionally. They were great times as we just played during that time and did not talk about failed marriages or business at all. This was one of my best jobs and times of greatest happiness.

Coming to see her was like going to Shangri-La; I could leave my cell and a city where I knew no one and be with someone who loved me. Since Evansville was in the Midwestern time zone, I always got a free hour by driving there. Of course, it was depressing when I went back to Pittsburgh and lost an hour.

Wow! The condo was simply gorgeous, huge windows with porches overlooking the wide river where we would sip wine and eat cheese while watching the sunset. We would then zip around town in her turbo-charged sports car and she would tell me stories about flying around the world on business—all in first class. She had bought an expensive Toshiba laptop computer for US$2,600. Even though I used a computer at work, her laptop was a mystery. It was a brownish monochrome that could do little more than type letters. I still have that computer which would now be considered a museum relic.

Margo fell in love with watching in awe the heavy barge traffic going up and down the wide river and the rumble and throbbing of the huge diesel engines of the tug that would push up to fifteen barges. We would go up to the local dam and watch the barges being raised and lowered. For us, it was more fun than going to a Broadway show. Yep, we were both nonlinear!

I often would prepare an agenda for my visits and fax it to her for fun. Here's one:

Fifth visit of John Freivalds to Margo Brown's condo

Friday, March 13 (had to be 1991)
6:00 p.m. Registration at Front Door
6:15-6:30 p.m. Welcoming Hugs

6:30-7:00 p.m. White Wine Reception
7:30-9:00 p.m. Dinner (selected Evansville eatery)
9:00-12:00 p.m. Dancing
12:30 Curfew
Saturday, March 14
Dawn hours snuggling
8:00-12:00 Breakfast (selected Evansville location)
10:30-Afternoon Physical Activities, Walk, Racquetball, Tennis
6:00 Sundowner
8:00-12:00 Socializing and General Relaxation
Sunday, March 15
8:00-10: 00 a.m. Breakfast
10:30 a.m. Departure to Drudgery

By far the activity we enjoyed most was dancing. Before going, Margo would doll herself up in some smashing clothes, put on a beautiful scarf, and spray herself with Paco Rabone perfume. We usually went to a hopping place called Gloria's where they played rock-a-billy music— lots of men in cowboy hats. The club's official name was Gloria's Corral Bar. It was already a local institution at the time and it's still around; a neat lady named Gloria Altman has been running the place since 1962.

We requested that the band play a number of dancing songs we like: "Pink Houses" and "I'm Not Running Any More" by Mellencamp, "Old Time Rock and Roll" by Bob Seeger and "Sweet Home Alabama" by Lynrd Skynrd. If we had to pick a theme song, it would have to be "Pick Cadillac," which was made famous by Bruce Springsteen. One line went, "Honey, I just wonder what you do there in the back of your Pink Cadillac."

You could say that we got back to the condo in a very aroused state.

I recall specific wonderful visits:

- My first trip to Evansville was when Margo was still living in a hotel – she hadn't yet found a place to live and sent me many love letters on the hotel's stationery.
- My second trip was when I brought her beloved cat to Evansville. I picked her up from her parents. This was the first time I met them.
- On another occasion, I was making a sales call on Deere and Company in Moline, Illinois, and I called Margo to see if I could spend the weekend since I was in the neighborhood. *"How close?"* she

asked. "Only 340 miles," I responded. I left Moline at around 8:00 p.m. and got there about 1:00 a.m. always listening to the wonderful fusion music tapes that Margo had given to me.

- On yet another occasion, I arrived the same time as the wonderful black screen that Margo had bought in Bangkok which really became her prized possession. The screen came with the motto, "Successful people are like screens, they have to bend in order to stand." I was on my way to pick up this screen and put it in Margo's room at the hospice when she died. And the screen still stands proudly in my living room.

For the most part, I made the pilgrimage to Evansville with the thought that if both of us were tired from driving we wouldn't have as much fun. It was always better if Margo was fresh. But on occasions Margo did drive to meet me in Bloomington, Illinois; Charleston, West Virginia; and St. Louis, Missouri.

She constantly wondered when I was going to get out of my situation and move on. I think somewhat of a turning point came in how Margo and I celebrated her birthday in Minneapolis on December 31, 1991; Margo had turned forty-seven.

> *John was a sweetheart, brought me flowers along with Christmas presents... gave me Australian Monopoly; a book* Culture and Medicine, *bath oils, and an amber necklace from Latvia. They were a wonderful blend of presents, fun and personal.*
>
> *Yesterday for my birthday I decided to relax and spend a day with him – it was the most at ease I have been shopping with him – Got him to help me pick out a coat and ended up buying a red cashmere coat! Wow! It is striking.*
>
> *He gave me a scrapbook which traces his feelings about our relationship. He put a lot of thought into it – very special! And then took me to lunch at the Monte Carlo – sat in a booth next to former Vice President Walter Mondale. It was class!*

We were in each other's dreams continually from this point on. She was in Denmark in March when she wrote: *"Oh baby I want you to seduce me on the street...my oh my last few days I have been obsessed with sensuous thoughts. I'm seriously hungry for John."* And then she called and told me about this.

This of course is the PG13 version of what she was thinking that day. But strange as it is to talk about now, she no longer was thinking about anybody else. She had cast her fate totally to me. We were birds of a feather as that diagram once again shows.

I remember the last weekend I spent with Margo before my wife made the momentous decision to end our marriage. On that weekend, I was living in the basement of the comfortable house with my girls. I can distinctly remember their energy and the joy it brought me. Nevertheless, I felt stuck in the muck—that is how I described my situation to Margo. This sense of helplessness only grew in intensity as I contemplated the impending surge of yet more expenses that a divorce would bring. I hardly spoke to my wife anymore and Margo wondered what impact all this was having on the children.

On that weekend, I hadn't called home for four days. On Monday I left for Fond Du Lac, Wisconsin. I was wearing a knock-off Rolex watch Margo had bought me in Hong Kong on one of her previous Asian visits. It cost US$15 and looked smashing. I went in to see a client, Mercury Marine, who made all those outboard motors for boats. My client kept looking over at me during the meeting. He finally said, "I'm admiring your watch. Those Rolexes are beautiful." I didn't tell him that the watch was phony, nor that my marriage or the relationship I was having with Margo were also phony.

I drove home after the meeting to discover that two of those three phony things were about to change forever. My ex-wife asked:

"Where have you been? You haven't called," she said.

"I was with Margo. I needed my spirit renewed."

A couple of days later she went to see a divorce lawyer and filed the paperwork—irreconcilable differences—and that they were.

Communiques with Margo from Jakarta, Indonesia on May 5, 1992

Amazing news tonight from John. He will be moving out of the house and be divorced in August. Incredible! The story I got tonight is that she told him this am that she'd gone to an attorney yesterday. She finally realized that they were on different boats.

We had the most amazing conversation of our relationship two hours talking from Jakarta. Make list of issues he says – money, communications, frequency of seeing each other, concerns, children, friends, similarities, dissimilarities.

How do we share a life? I'm scared yet calm. Part of me wants him to date others for a time. Here's my chance for the dream I've wanted these past few years, yet I have lived a life so freely, so independently hardly a soul has known my whereabouts, changing that is wild!... this is first time I have been involved with an unencumbered man. And now I have for my second dream – a real relationship. I'd better act on it like I did the job dreams – life will be more interesting with more factors affecting it – go for it!

She made a rough chart in her diaries which compared what we were like.

In addition to expressing how we were similar and different, she also expressed her dreams, hopes, and visions for the future. She wrote:

MARGO'S CHARACTERISTICS	HOW JOHN IS DISSIMILAR
Loves cats	Higher verbal energy
Slower to speak	Fast eater/drinker
Take time for eating/drinking	Not a particular connoisseur of food/
More interested in romance books and	wine
movies	More driven on business level
Large circle of good friends – I spend	Few real friends
time nurturing that	Early riser – needs less sleep
More interested in arts and classical	Voracious reader and remembers!
music?	Doesn't dry self coming out of shower
Slow reader; forget a lot	Fast, efficient and creative writer
Much neater	
Have harder time talking about my	
work and accomplishments	

Ooh do I have many – I've lived moment to moment so much maybe the closest thing to living a dream is trying to make a relationship with him. I do dream of a house in the woods where we can canoe, sail, swim with all kinds of kids of all ages visiting; I dream of hosting people from all over the world, sharing ideas; I dream of hiking in the mountains, bicycling locally, touring, whitewater rafting, beautiful dinners in beautiful places, dinners at home with friends we both enjoy and are relaxed with having a house with lots of warmth, light and airiness.

All this may appear too lofty and unreachable, but let me assure you, she had all that by the time when we went to live in the mountains of Virginia. She had her dream job, a committed man, and a peaceful home in the mountains. In essence, all of this became possible because she took the risk to travel to Asia for a year. Margo gave in to some reflection on what had happened when in London on May 17th, just ten days after the freedom call on May 7th.

This AM I let myself take in the feelings re Jani. He has encouraged me to be strong, to state my opinion and feelings – no man has ever done that before. We have grown so much together and I do feel we complement each other a lot – he brings creativity – great intelligence – entrepreneurship, world experience and love of that – different cultures – a strong tie to his heritage and sense of family.

I bring warmth, gentleness, class, adventure, emotional growth, encouragement of communication – have never really had someone with whom to dream and plan – I am unaccustomed to that – have always either been self contained and quiet or felt I was totally on my own – with few plans for the future – he's opening up my mind to possibility of sharing a life together with common goals: house in the woods, bicycling, snorkeling, vacations, hiking, culture, theatre, music, kids.

I then started to get faxes like the one below from Margo when she was traveling – they just gushed with joy. (Fax from Tokyo)

Jani–

What a nice conversation – it was the kind that made me want to call you back to talk some more and tell you how much I love you!

I'm eager for the day when I can meet you at Northwest Tennis Club after work – you play basketball and I swim – or we play tennis/racquetball and workout on the Nautilus together and then go on home for dinner and a quiet evening at home – nights when one or all three girls are with us – dinner on the patio with them and their friends.

And other nights when we take a walk around Harriet – stopping at Sebastian Joe's for a Café Latte – meeting friends along the way.

175

And days of hosting our friends from around the world – touring them about whatever city we live – inviting other friends over to meet them.

Evenings of lively discussion between you and me about the world situation – being able to cuddle up together as we discuss – ooh-ooh what fun I see ahead!

– Love, Margo

I consider that day when Margo called from Jakarta to be our wedding day. We both cast aside our past lives and announced that we would love one another forever. I asked her to call me Jani, my Latvian name, from now on and she did. I was only called John when I did something stupid or she was mad at me. Our honeymoon was on Saturday, June 7, when Margo had returned from her latest Asian trip and we found ourselves in Menominee, Wisconsin, at a bed and breakfast. Margo best described the breadth of our love and commitment to each other first in one of her classic graphs and then in her diary.

Saturday, June 7, 1992 was the beginning of our new life

It will be an anniversary to celebrate. A wonderful 4-5 hours of lovemaking on Saturday. I woke up wide awake around 4:00 a.m. and initiated.

Eggs Benedict with asparagus, walk on Red Cedar trail, long talks and sat on sand bars. Stupendous lunch at Harbor Inn. We really were one there. Shared a sensuous cream caramel. We laughed hard several times. 'Brownie is a ding because he doesn't have a functioning dong'!

Sat and watched boats, sang poorly to his guitar playing, walked around Lake Pepin, actually a wide spot on the Mississippi River. Then spent a couple of hours at Corral Bar in Durand, Wisconsin alone on deck dancing and talking.

I remember the bar and its juke box well. We played our anthem, "Pink Cadillac." That day there was no drug on earth that could have made me feel any higher—I swear, our feet never even touched the ground. I was free of all the pain and torturous emotions I had been living with. I no longer had to hide anything from anyone and could just look forward to a wonderful life with "Mookie," as I had begun to call her.

June 8th

Our discussions were fast and furious, and the very next day Margo wrote this:

> *Wow what a weekend. Each moment I have with Jani I feel more comfortable that there is a life for us. The divorce is happening. He's processing a shit load. This three way relationship has been far more agony for him than I realized. He dreaded my regular comment 'we have to talk.' Interesting that he didn't stay away as a result of it. He's really rediscovering his old enthusiasm for life and joy. I'm still feeling skeptical and reserved – a bit afraid to let go completely - tho I think I have let go some.*

She did let go for on June 26th Margo wrote:

> *I have less of a need to talk with Margaret or any therapist – feel strong and in control of myself again* (but she added) *I was sad and melancholy today – have been tired all week. This afternoon I had a comfortable longing feeling that I wanted to be with Jani, not 735 miles away. He said these long trips will begin to have an effect on our relationship. Why don't you talk to Rida* (her boss) *about it?*
>
> *Well I admitted it's my own doing. I later realized I've done it to get away from John so that I don't get so caught up with him knowing that it just caused pain. The more I see of him and talk with him – the more I want him. It has been a way of coping with the loneliness and sense I was going to lose him because I would have to walk away. I can change that now – he is getting closer to being really available. Friday p.m. was miserable. I felt his now ex-wife's presence with us. I think it must be because we have talked about her so much. Jani just keeps talking. He's kept it bottled up for 4 years.*

Then right after that she wrote an affirmation. So consider that two and a half years before she had written an obituary and now I had this wonderful affirmation. She never showed it to me and I just found it in the files.

MARGO BROWN
Personal Objective:

To be loved by John Freivalds for the rest of my life

Emotional Accomplishments:
- *Survived four years of marital indecision on significant other's part*
- *Learned to say no even though I wanted to say yes*
- *Have stopped shopping around for men*
- *Have decided that it is more fun to live with someone than to live alone*
- *Have become more sexual and sensual as I have gotten older*
- *I am still really a big kid*

Sensual Accomplishments:
- *Have made love to John over 100 times*
- *Know what turns him on*

Dancing Accomplishments:
- *Have danced with John at Gloria's nine times*
- *Have danced with John in Evansville, Chippewa Falls and surrounded by a bunch of Philippine teenagers in San Francisco*
- *I have danced with John alone on a pier in Durand, Wisconsin*

Sports Accomplishments:
- *I have been biking with John throughout Wisconsin*
- *I have swam with him in Wisconsin, Indiana and Minnesota*
- *I have played tennis with him in West Virginia, Minnesota, and Indiana*
- *Kayaking on the Gulley River in West Virginia*
- *Walks of varying lengths in California (including Golden Gate Bridge), Chicago, New York, Minnesota, Indiana, Wisconsin, Illinois, West Virginia, Kentucky*

Vehicular Accomplishments:
- *I have known John through a variety of cars from Toyota Camry to Pontiac 6000 to Voyageur van to Talon.*
- *In turn I have been present when his motor froze up in his Cadillac and listened when his wheels fell off in West Virginia.*
- *I have driven through ice storms with him and I bounced a check so that he could get his car painted.*
- *I have discovered that however you try it, it's always 13 hours to drive from Minneapolis to Evansville.*

Therapeutic Accomplishments:
- *I have learned to love and respect myself which in turn has made*

people feel better towards me. I can be a tough bitch or a gentle pussycat depending on how I am treated.

Things were wonderful after this—no hiding around emotionally. We could say we were engaged and, best of all, no more Margo asking, "When are you finally going to move on from your wife?" and me having to lie.

Soon thereafter, I invited Margo to come and join two of my daughters and me at the Wisconsin Dells, which had become the water park capital of the world. There was a strong vibrant Margo having the strength to cavort with a thirteen- and fifteen-year-old. She then wrote this to her dad on October 13, 1992, some four months after the Jakarta phone call on her new Toshiba computer about her day at the waterpark:

...Talking about physical activity, I have included a picture of John's daughters (left to right) of Karla 15 and Maija 13 and me at the water park in Wisconsin Dells. Were we having fun? Indeed! It's fun thinking about being their stepmom one day – also a bit weird. But also something I never thought I would have the opportunity to experience. It is a very nice feeling.

And while I am on the subject, I want to address one of your comments, Dad, of a couple of months ago regarding my talking about a marriage to John. I have to laugh a bit since to many people I have taken a LONG time to consider marriage an option in my life or to open myself up to that possibility (16 years!) And you comment which may have been related to this particular situation with John (which is not a situation I would recommend to anyone) and yet here I am in this wonderful relationship which has certainly seen its ups and downs. However I want you to be assured that tons of work, talk, emotion thought, and challenges have gone into this relationship and continue to. It is far more than I ever imagined being able to experience and enjoy – and we have a great time growing in it as we face different and new challenges. I mean this man talks to me, listens to me, respects and loves me the most when I challenge his way of doing or thinking about something. He demands that I am respectful of myself and proactive and loves the vibrant, alive Margo that I have found these last years and grown to love myself. Anyway, I just want you to know that this is not something I do or have taken lightly and that I am taking care of myself in this relationship like I have never before in or out of the relationships I have had. And I look forward to you both getting to know and enjoy John.

But then the new reality of what we had done and where we had been crept in. Margo wrote this later in 1992:

Today I was struck with my own guilt about this four-year relationship with Jani – now that he is sharing our friendship with his daughters and ex-wife I am the one that is uncomfortable. I don't know how I can think that they wouldn't figure it out whenever he shared me anyway? And isn't it better he be straightforward and not hide anymore – plus I don't want to be a secret when I come back to Minneapolis or when he visits me. We need to be done with secrets. I guess I'll be viewed by his family as a family breaker – the source of problems and that the kids will not like me or accept me and that will influence Jani's feelings about me – that he will be put in the middle between the girls and me. I want to be able to be a unit – should have brought the book on step families and me – I bought it because deep down I know I have a concern…I am a good, loving person though again I have not had much exposure to teenagers – Paul, Annie and Johnny like me… John's daughters like some of the same things I do – and all we want is to be comfortable with each other.

So a whole new series of risks appeared—trying to live with an emotionally battered man who was essentially broke, with credit cards maxed out, and to fit in with three hormonal teenage girls.

In August Karla, our middle daughter, sat down with Margo, and Margo later described everything that happened this way.

August 19

Karla told him she really likes me. Margo looks happy just standing on the street – dad, she's pretty. It was so neat to see her walking on the doughnuts (this refers to the day at the water park).

She admitted that she knew Susan and I were unhappy—they didn't like the fights—and she asked her mother, "Why don't you and Dad get divorced?" Yes, kids are smarter than we think.

Margo and I had decided to take a vacation together in Wyoming to further cement our bonds and to do it after school started so that there would be fewer tourists. So think about this; we got married meta-phorically in May, had our honeymoon in June and now we're going to have our first vacation together in Wyoming in September. We were crawling out of our skin with joy. Just imagine the emotional turmoil we had been through (all caused by me) and now to be free as birds. It was almost too much to bear. Then her boss told her about a new assignment. *"Japan for six to nine months. Rida asked me today! God – not when my personal life is finally giving me what I have wanted for so long."*

9/13/92

Finally. I'm on my way to meet Jani – to our first real vacation. We're both excited. He whooped over the phone last night; I've been all smiles. A week of being away from work – it'll be interesting to know how much he and I talk about our careers or really our jobs.

Margo and I were already thinking of where we would like to live someday and picked Wyoming and the part where fewer people go to—the Big Horn Mountains; Sheridan (population 13,000) was the jumping off point. We took my big blue Cadillac and packed the huge trunk with everything, a huge cooler and lawn chairs, blankets and whatever—lots of whatevers. This first trip led to at least four subsequent ones, one of which Margo took by herself.

We stopped the first night at some little motel in the South Dakota Badlands. The stars were beautiful and we escaped at midnight to look at them; as was our custom, we made love under the stars. Give me a break, was all this good stuff really happening? What planet were we on? Our hearts just opened up and all the truths and untruths of the past four years just kept pouring out. For years Margo wanted me to talk and tell her all that was on my mind, and I was afraid to, but now she wanted me to just shut up as I wouldn't stop talking!

The next day we got to Buffalo, Wyoming, which is the jumping off point for the mountains. We couldn't sleep and at 4:30 a.m. got up and started wandering around the town on a cool, very early morning. We even found an art gallery run by a woman named, wouldn't you know it, Margo Brown. One of those mathematically improbable coincidences you read about that happen in life. We considered it to be a good omen. More wanderings in this beautiful land and we were ecstatic when we found a place called Cappuccino Cowboy in Sheridan—the West was changing, as we were. However, the Old West was always nearby and

Margo loved it when we would have to stop our forward progress to let a herd of cattle cross the road. And then in Sheridan we found the historic and drop-dead beautiful King's Saddlery where every imaginable piece of cowboy gear from a US$10,000 silver-embossed saddle to US$20 lariat ropes were for sale. We would just watch as cowboys came in to "test rope" lariat on a horizontal fifty-five-gallon drum. I bought a cowboy belt which I still wear when I'm in a Western mode, and wore constantly when penning the book on Paul Engler, the world's largest cattle feeder—one million head of cattle a year—who supplies all the beef to Wal-Mart.

And then another omen appeared. We were heading back from our drive through the mountains to visited the Shell River Canyon and on our way to spend the night in a mountain-top community called Ten Sleep. It was dusk and we stopped to look at a high bluff on our left that was changing colors: red, purple, yellow, brown, yellow and as so on. We couldn't keep up with this rainbow. We just stood mesmerized and in awe as we watched this light show.

From Ten Sleep we thought we could make it back all the way to Minnesota—a drive of some 802 miles—with both of us driving. Well as soon as we hit I-90 we got real touchy feely and I said, "Do you want to stop and make love?"

"Why not!" Margo answered.

About this episode she later wrote:

Wow – ooh – I think Jani and I both feel we can be like teenagers in love – be gushy – it is fun to have him acknowledge how he's feeling – and to loosen up myself – we both want to have a lifetime of hand holding, stroking – fun – live today and enjoy.

We were both forty-eight years old, but on that drive we had the hormones of eighteen-year-olds at the drive-in. Man was that fun! Remember we had the big Cadillac Eldorado which had tinted windows and a huge back seat; Margo called it a *pimpmobile*. We would just pull to the far end of the rest stop and go at it. We did that four times, and when we later drove back to Wyoming we would say to each other, "Do you remember that stop? How about that one?"

The drive took us two and a half days, and we did get out of the car at a rest stop in Chamberlain, South Dakota, to go for a walk in the tall prairie grass overlooking the Missouri River. You guessed it. We got it going again. Somehow Margo lost her sunglasses in those tall grass snuggles and I always wanted to go back and see if we could find them.

You would have thought it was a petting zoo in that car. We could have been definitely charged with DWI—driving while intoxicated—with each other. Margo reflected on this jaunt on her flight back to Evansville.

9/27/92

Oh – so hard to leave Jani today. I have such a feeling of aloneness. We were so close all week. Had such good times all week from 4:30 AM breakfast and walks to hikes in the mountains – love making outside – behind rocks, on hills, in fields, at rest stops, church at Unitarian Universalist – Jani's church, it felt safe, welcoming...I was the most at home/at ease than I have been with him in the presence of my family and friends... Jani was quiet all the way to airport – was it all the re-entry; the strangeness of meeting the new extended family, still trying to figure out how to disentangle from 25 years of marriage?

Yikes, what do I do now and how do I behave? Now I had to find a place to live. I had found a cheap apartment with a six-month lease (whose dumpster I still use on occasion) but needed something more permanent. A condo sounded nice and I did find a small one—very small—in a development called Amherst. I wanted some place where the girls could come and stay (that joint custody business). Margo was considering moving in.

I now live in a 3,000-square-foot condo by myself in Minneapolis, but then I had to get what I could afford and that was a 1,200-square-foot, two-bedroom condo. Upstairs we had two bedrooms (one for the girls with a bunk bed and a single bed) and one master bedroom which also served as my and Margo's office. It was more hers, as she was on the road and I still had an office downtown. What we painfully learned was that this small condo could not hold all the baggage I brought with me. Something Margo would now have to face. But more of that in the next chapter.

Our Wedding

Oh, yeah, did I mention we got married on November 11, 1993? I didn't propose, we just decided to "sanctify" our relationship—not in the eyes of God, as neither of us was very religious at that time, but to each other

183

and our families and friends.

We decided to make the wedding a non-event event. It was to be at the Minnetonka City Center; a karaoke guy did the music; our favorite restaurant, the Port of Beirut, catered it with Lebanese food; we did the photography ourselves; and Margo's sorority sister, a judge, did the "vows." It cost around US$5,000 in 1992 when the average for weddings in those days was US$20,000. Margo's dad gave us US$5,000 for our honeymoon which was on the big island in Hawaii.

Some seventy people came, drank, danced, and whopped it up. Margo gave a big "whoop" when she walked down the aisle. By the way, Margo looked absolutely stunning in her wedding gown, which I have preserved and cherish dearly.

Unfortunately, love does not or did not conquer all. Margo left her spacious condo with an elevator in Newburgh on the Ohio River and moved into my 1,200-square-foot condo. And if that wasn't bad enough, she went from an international job with first-class airfare and hotels to a sales job driving clunky company cars and spending the nights at a Motel Six in places like Abbottsford, Wisconsin, and setting up display stands in shopping malls. But I'll let Margo tell the rest of the story as she did in her opus My Life.

Unfortunately that job ended in two and a half years. I was offered a job as district sales so I returned to Minneapolis as a sales rep working for a nice guy out of Madison. The smart move for me would have been to find myself an apartment but instead I moved right in with John who by then had officially separated from his wife and was in the midst of a nasty divorce. He has three daughters who were in their teens at the time. When they stayed with us we were crunched together. For my sake it was good that their mom told them they did not need to spend time at their dad's so they were with us very little except for the oldest who happens to be the one with serious problems. She likes being away from her sisters.

Margo wasn't into the corporate game at all and found relief in a lot of ways: travel, gardening, wine, and even tap dancing as the sidebar illustrates.

If all of the above was confusing as to dates and times, here is a recap of all that went on from the time I met Margo until we started to live together with all my baggage.

Margo and backpack

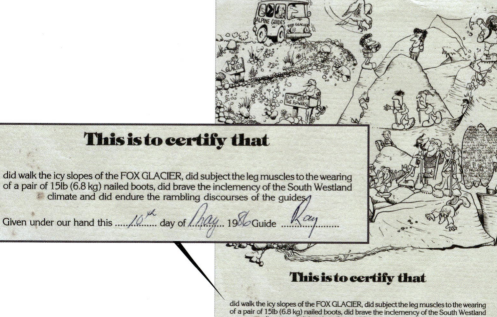

Fox Glacier Certificate

Margo in New Zealand

Margo in New Zealand with tall trees

Margo and David Cranna in Australia

Margo's promotion at Bristol-Myers Squibb Company

Dream house

Dream life

Dream car

Margo taller than most men

In Philippines

Bristol-Myers Malaysia

Margo and John finally together

Margo and John at Mead Johnson

Margo in her wedding dress

Margo, John and family in Golden Valley

Margo at play with the girls

Margo and John just resting in Virginia

View from our home

With grandson Joshua

Building Margo's studio

Margo and John dressed as clowns

In her flower garden

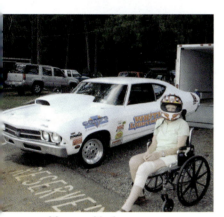
Margo with the race car

On her trike

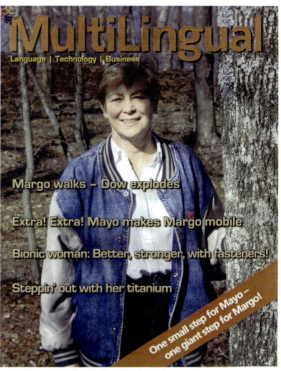
On the cover of MultiLingual magazine

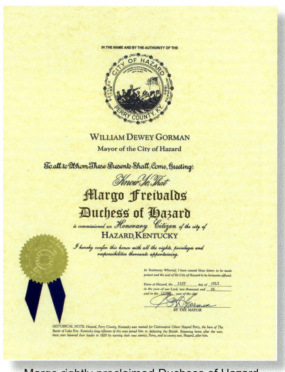
Margo rightly proclaimed Duchess of Hazard

In Panama

Paul Engler's yacht

Margo in Canadian Rockies

Where Margo's ashes lie in
Northern Minnesota

Plaque at church in Dubuque
honoring Margo

THE MOST PAINFUL – YET IN THE END MOST JOYOUS CHRONOLOGY

04/18/88   Margo Brown and John Freivalds are introduced at American Café in Golden Valley, Minnesota.

04/24/88   Margo's first date with John at Port of Beirut which years later would cater their wedding. Her first real date in over a year. John tells Margo he is divorced.

06/14/88   Margo learns John not divorced as he told her.

09/06/89   John hospitalized with perforated ulcer as stress starts to break his body down.

10/30/89   Margo tells John she can't do this anymore and for John to disappear.

11/01/89   Margo writes John's obituary.

01/04/90   Margo calls John to see how he is and tells her group therapy he has been reincarnated.

06/04/90   Margo accepts international job in Evansville, 735 miles from Minneapolis, for the job and to get some separation from John.

06/25/90   Margo buys her beautiful and precious Chinese screen in Bangkok.

08/07/90   Margo moves into fancy condo at Number 3 Water Place in Newburgh, Indiana 20 feet from the Ohio River. Buys turbo-charged sports car.

10/05/90   John moves to Pittsburgh. Separates from wife.

11/03/90   John hospitalized with bleeding ulcer in Pittsburgh. Stress is further weakening his body.

06/09/91   John moves back to Minneapolis from Pittsburgh and lives in basement. Goes for intensive therapy. Margo apprehensive.

12/30/91   Fabulous birthday with Margo at Monte Carlo in Minneapolis. Gets the ball rolling to resolution. Margo begins to trust John.

05/05/92   Margo calls from Jakarta, Indonesia. John announces he is leaving wife – is free now to pursue Margo but is broke. Moves into motel, then cheap apartment. Looks for condo.

06/07/92   Margo and John spend marvelous weekend together at a B&B in Menomonie, Wisconsin. Margo says this will be our anniversary.

07/01/92   Margo writes her love letter to John, no more men chasing. John is it.

07/15/92   Margo meets with two of John's daughters at Wisconsin Dells water park.

08/01/92   Margo writes her father about John.

09/15/92   John moves into his condo and all his baggage continues to come in.

Joy takes over their lives

11/19/93   John and Margo are wed at the Minnetonka, Minnesota Community Center.

11

almost heaven

*Twenty years from now you will be
more disappointed by the things you
didn't do than the ones you did do so
throw off your bowlines, sail away
from the safe harbor; catch the trade
winds in your sails.
Explore. Dream. Discover.*

—Mark Twain

"*I hungry,*" a weary Margo gently said about 7 p.m. one spring Saturday in 1999, joyfully pointing her long right-hand index finger at her flat, sensuous tummy hidden by a soft and cuddly pajama top. She had just groggily woken up from a little nap after driving for a couple of hours to a Country Inn and Suites Motel somewhere off Interstate 64 down south along the Blue Ridge Mountains in Virginia. We had left Washington, DC, earlier that Saturday morning, going west on congested condo-lined and suicidal I-66 until we hit I-81 and headed south down the Shenandoah Valley until we were safely on I-64 surrounded by 28 million-year-old mountains. Red painted barns with signs touting Mail Pouch Tobacco started to appear.

We didn't know what town it was as we just followed the signs to the most known motel. Country Inn and Suites was owned by Carlson Companies, one of my clients, so I felt some loyalty in staying there. The parking lot wasn't full of tank-sized SUVs; all schools were still in session, so our chances of finding a room on the spur of the moment were good. The place had a glimmering indoor pool and whirlpool which you could see from the front desk; Margo's tired body was sure to find its way there in the morning.

We checked in, brought in our "day bags," gym bags stuffed with stuff for the night, and crashed into soft beds and pillows without looking at our typical antiseptic motel décor surroundings. I didn't take my clothes off, but Margo, Ms. Prim and Proper, did. She folded her driving clothes, jeans and T-shirt neatly on a chair and had already laid out her toiletries, endless amounts of different facial creams and moisturizers in the bathroom. I think applying all that cream had a calming effect on her soul, though I doubt that it do much good for her already silky skin.

Our day-long drive around the verdant lower Shenandoah Valley had taken us past some spectacular scenery; blue-green mountains and spring-flooded rivers were everywhere to be seen, smelled, and heard. There were cattle of every hue—black, tan, brown, and grey—and woolly sheep (all facing the same way, it seemed) were everywhere munching on the newly invigorated pastures. It was like driving through a bucolic picture postcard with spectacular backdrops. The forsythia all around us were screaming yellow and we enjoyed the early spring all the more, knowing that our home back in Minnesota was still mired in winter. The season was also further advanced in the valley than in hectic, urban Washington, DC, some 180 miles to the northeast where we had started the day. My spring hay fever was starting to set in my itchy eyes. It had been a beautiful, sunny, day-long drive through the valley, but we had no intention of living there...yet!

We were ostensibly headed to Floyd, a little country town farther down truck-clogged Interstate 81 which was home to Floyd Fest—a musical festival that would begin the next day. I was enthralled with Floyd after a previous trip I took from Washington, DC, where I grew up, to see a client in Winston Salem, North Carolina. I wanted Margo to see, if not experience, that melodious mountain hamlet.

Before completing the drive to Floyd, we decided to stop in Lexington for the night. Since Margo drove the last couple of hours in our blue and now dusty Jeep Cherokee, I had to go get the food; that was a rule we made—the last driver crashes, the other guy goes out to get the grub. Neither one of us wanted to go to a sit-down restaurant and be greeted by, "Hi, I'm Chad and I'll be your server tonight." Margo had already stretched out her six-foot body in her night clothes and was now watching—or should I say staring?—at some mindless TV show with channel clicker armed and ready in hand.

There was a char-broiled Dairy Queen glaring across the street but we both wanted something more substantial than that. I decided to trudge downstairs and ask the desk clerk where there was a place to get better food. I promised Margo I would get something. "You better!" her blue eyes seemed to say as she looked up at me. We had brought up a nice bottle of Kendall Jackson Chardonnay with us and it stared invitingly at me on the desktop. I had forgotten the cork screw in the car. Margo once met Jesse Jackson, the man who started the famous vineyard (not to be confused with the politician of that name) and the wine quickly become one of her favorites. So off went Neanderthal man in search of food.

And really it's as simple as that—how Margo's constant hunger for something different, metaphorically and physically, led us to end up living on top of a mountain (Mt. Atlas) in Southwestern Virginia hard on the border with West Virginia. Yep, almost heaven, almost West Virginia. Margo wrote that *"this trip turned our lives upside down."*

In fact, it was her geographical if not her cultural curiosity, financial engineering skills, tenacity, and ability to make friends in the darndest places that gave us perhaps the best years of our lives together. Looking back it always amazes me how the slightest decision you make can change your life forever; what if Margo had said a greasy burger from the Dairy Queen would have been good enough that night? But she was a dietitian by education, a master's from the University of Minnesota if you please, and in 1975 was voted Minnesota's outstanding young dietitian of the year. So getting a greasy burger from DQ (OK except for an occasional Blizzard) wasn't going to happen tonight. A snack for Margo was a handful of shiny orange baby carrots, not French fries. Her slim and bicycling-toned body was proof positive of that.

"Well, to get something better you might just head downtown," the night clerk indifferently twanged at me after probably having said the same thing to hundreds of weary and hungry travelers. People shuh enough spoke differently down here. "Jeeest go right at the foooork in the road." So I drove out and almost immediately met up with a huge, tasteful sign: WELCOME TO LEXINGTON, VIRGINIA POP. 6024. We had driven by the signs pointing to Lexington many times before but never went further than that to find out about it. There were historical markers everywhere as the Civil War was fought up and down the valley and right on into Lexington, or so it seemed. Robert E. Lee, the famous confederate general, I later found out, was buried here—along with his horse.

It was too dark to make out all the signs and what they said. Then all of a sudden, I found myself surrounded by gray-green, gothic-castle-type buildings, and quickly realized I was passing through VMI, the Virginia Military Institute, the West Point of the South. As soon as I drove past the looming gothic buildings, I entered a stretch where colonial buildings predominate. There were plenty of white colonnades in front of majestic red brick buildings with wide, expansive, manicured, pasture-sized lawns stretching out in front of them. It smelled of rich and donating alumni.

There was a gentle rise to the road and I entered downtown with handsome painted buildings, all blending in with each other. They all bore an architectural consistency you don't see in many small towns. I then noticed that the calm Main Street beckoning me wasn't marred by a jungle of utility wires crisscrossing the streets. In fact, there was not a utility wire to be seen. It was a Saturday night and lots of college students were milling about, some in military dress and some in properly disheveled college clothes with flip flops on their feet exposing painted toe nails (guys, too). I came to a little restaurant called the Palm's Lounge which was busy with people waiting outside to get in. Nothing here.

I turned onto a side street and passed a bunch of frat houses: Washington Lee has gained notoriety as the number two party school in the U.S. Then the road went downhill and every fast food place known to mankind stretched out before me. I had reached the commercial distinct that obviously wasn't restricted by zoning laws. It was an immediate turnoff. Discretion is the better part of valor and I turned into the Kroger grocery store parking lot at the edge of this neon mishmash. I thought I'd just get some cheese, apples, and perhaps some salami, bread and baby carrots, of course, to take that back to the room. Instead, once I got into the store, the smell of a rotisserie chicken overwhelmed me. Did it smell appetizing!

I also noticed the customers who were in the store, and I liked the mix. There were ironed and pressed military types (everyone at VMI has to wear a uniform, I later learned); college professors with salt-and-pepper beards, pony tails, and mismatched slacks and suit jackets with leather patches on the elbows; frat boys buying beer in shorts; local ladies wearing hats; and tired farmers wearing grimy and torn overalls with a chaw of something bulging in their mouths. There were benches throughout the store and people seemed to just come in and "set" with their friends. This is something you would not see in a big crowded city.

I loved mixing with this eclectic group; I can't even remember what I was wearing, but I must have been invisible as I picked out a rotisserie chicken in a warm plastic container and was off in search of some vegetables and fruit to take back to the room. I couldn't wait to get back to Margo with my harvest.

It turned out that all the main streets, north and south, were one way streets, so I had to drive on the Main Street to return to the motel. The return drive was even more impressive than coming into town. The same magical consistency appeared as did a couple of neatly painted churches with white steeples pointing to the heavens, no crisscrossing of utility wires to mar the view, and I began to wonder why every little town didn't spruce itself up like this. I drove slowly and super analyzed every storefront as I went back to the motel. Lots of restaurants and art galleries—the visitors who came here had money to spend.

What a contrast from where we'd spent the last two hectic months. After my mother died, we had to clean out her house in Washington, DC, where she had lived and accumulated stuff for thirty-five years. I was born in Latvia and along with my parents was a refugee after World War II. We ended up in a displaced person's camp in the mountains of Austria before coming to America. This war-time mentality with its attendant scarcity followed my mother and me to America.

The only remnant of that past life is a handmade chest of belongings that came to Boston Harbor with us in 1951. That chest is the only relic of family history that my daughters are already fighting over— who gets the immigrant chest when Dad dies? But my mom's mentality was to save, for who knows what will happen? So for over thirty-five years she saved every coffee can, patched together rolls of aluminum foil, balls of string of all thickness and colors, piles and piles of clothes of different sizes, plastic dishes and assorted nuts and bolts put into coffee cans and properly sized. I found two big steamer trunks full of pictures that we had sent her over the years—she had no place to put them; I remember her saying, "No more pictures!" And that was just the storage room.

The house was full of mismatched (well, to me) furniture that she had acquired at neighborhood garage sales. It was easier to walk on top of the furniture than on the carpet—it was almost impossible to *find* the carpet. My mom also saved clothes of all sizes by the armful. Whenever someone tall would die, Margo would get a call from my mother asking, "Would you like some of Ms. So-and-So's clothes? She was tall like you."

The walls had three layers of wallpaper with dizzying patterns affixed by my mother herself which just begged to be torn off—and which Margo eventually did. OK, my mother was an eccentric; she spent thousands to have new Pella windows put in the house and decided to keep the Pella window stickers on. "They look nice," she said. Her bank was a stash of cash hidden under the rug in her bedroom; this lady managed to save US$80,000 while on social security. But who is to argue? She lived to be eighty-seven and died in her own house, not a nursing home. We actually did realize while cleaning out this house that we didn't have to live in Minnesota, we could live elsewhere.

My Minnesota scene was not the best. I was coming from a failed marriage and my three daughters initially blamed Margo for the break up. I was in a very confused mental state which led to two life-threatening ulcers. Margo felt she would always be a step-mom who would feel out of place. It was in the back of our minds to make a clean break from that entire life if the right situation ever came long.

The previous fall Margo even wrote this in her diary.

> *I want to go away – move away from John's family and its negativity. I want John and I to go to Wyoming to do our own thing – writing, walking, painting, reading, discussing, walking in the woods up in the mountains, helping others but away from the negative vibes of John's family. I want OUT! How will this ever even be possible?? I want to focus energy on Jani and me – I want passion in my life, spontaneity, happiness, glee.*

When we left my family and the turmoil in Minneapolis, we had all sorts of grandiose plans. We were going to walk evenings in Rock Creek Park, which ran the length of the city. Margo was going to take some courses at Georgetown, my alma mater. We were going to go bike riding along the C&O canal, and Margo wanted to go to the National Gallery of Art. We did none of those things and in two months we

192

went out to dinner once. It was work, clean, clean, clean, and on most days in bed by 7:00 p.m. and up at 6:00 a.m. So to relax on weekends, we would go to the shore or the mountains. We found Lexington on one of the mountain jaunts.

But imagine Margo and I trying to yuppify a house like this surrounded by jammed freeways and you understand the reason we fell immediately in love with the grace, quiet, charm, and order of Lexington. When I brought back a bag of culinary largesse that evening, I said to Margo, "This town is too cool. We need to drive around it in the morning." We did. I had an immediate trip to Europe planned, and while alone Margo said, *"I am going to come back and explore this place."* She hated Floyd, by the way.

I Gotta Have It

"So what are you interested in?" asked the thin, striking, and always fashionable Lucy Turner, an experienced agent with Mead Associates, the leading Real Estate Firm in Lexington, Virginia, at the time. It was a sunny and warm day in April 2001. Lucy just oozed confidence when Margo first met her. She had her own twenty-six-acre horse farm and knew Rockbridge County, Virginia, like the back of her gracious hand.

Lucy, not very tall, was always decked out in some neat linen pantsuit outfit, which stood in contrast to the frumpy mismatched clothes and tennis shoes we usually wore. Hey, we'd come to Lexington via DC after cleaning up and cleaning out my mother's house. We only had work clothes with us. To boot, she drove us around in a green Land Rover with comfortable leather seats. Did we look a bit odd.

Lucy would later become a lifelong friend and the hostess of the best Halloween party, heck best party, we ever went to several years hence, but for now Margo was just fishing round for properties and did not know what she would find. We had just about finished cleaning out my mother's three-bedroom house and had put it up for sale. The realtor in DC said it would go quickly (it took two weeks!) as the U.S. government never stops growing and keeps bringing new people into the area. The house would easily bring US$200,000 plus. My frugal, eccentric mother had no debts, no mortgage, so this would all be cash in the pocket, with me (us) as the only beneficiary.

While we worked at my mother's house, we—well, at least I—realized that we could live somewhere other than Minneapolis; it was nice enough, but we longed for something even more private.

This is how Margo once described our land in Minneapolis.

> *It was unusual (our friends and family say our houses are always unusual) it was 10 minutes from downtown but sat on about an acre and half of woods behind houses on an actual street. It had a magnificent gazebo with a huge stone fireplace that held magnificent fires all year long. We'd go down in our down coats and jackets and drink sometimes with others on the coldest of days or just go ourselves.*
>
> *We had great neighbors…but it wasn't in a brave new world and a chance to start over, meet new people and have new experiences whatever they may be.*

Once we cleaned up my mother's house, we both entertained the thought of living in it – I am glad to say that thought was fleeting. What were really alluring were the mountains we had seen in Virginia. They were calling Margo in her dreams, all the time. Fifteen years earlier she'd once described what her dream house should be:

- *on a lake/pond/stream in heavy woods*
- *very light and airy*
- *fireplace in main sitting area*
- *large kitchen with windows on to woods*
- *center island Jenn Air*
- *room for house guests*
- *good walking area; pool nearby*
- *huge screened porch*

I had gone back to sedate Latvia, my homeland, for business for a week. We had property to sell there as well, and Margo took it upon herself to drive back down the 180 miles to Lexington and to start looking around. It was not a hard decision to leave congested, noisy, rude, and overcrowded Washington, DC, in search of some peace and quiet. Margo told me she once got the finger for *doing* the speed limit leaving town. The mountains we had seen together earlier had infected if not infatuated her, and they had the same effect on everyone who later came to visit us. *"We are looking for something modern, not too large, remote, wooded, with about 10-15 acres of land and that has a mountain views,"* she responded to Lucy.

Margo was ready for a new challenge and mountains had always enthralled her. A side benefit was Virginia's longer growing climate; the blooming plant life all around hypnotized her. And, of course, getting away from all the family baggage issues I had was an added plus.

"Come with me. I have just the place," Lucy responded and off they went in that green Land Rover with tan leather seats. They drove north out of Lexington for about five miles on U.S. 11, the old road that ran up and down the Shenandoah Valley paralleling I-81. They turned left at the antique store on Mt. Atlas Road, went past a couple of farms replete with those black Angus cattle munching on pastures, and then took a left on paved but much narrower Reid Road. They scooted past Caboose Lane and a cluster of houses where the quaint old Timber Ridge railroad station had been (now converted to a funky house) and came by a new farm house sitting strikingly alone in the middle of an alfalfa field. A strange ammonia odor could be smelled, if not felt, deep in your nostrils; it came from a big red truck parked by the house.

"That's Reid Mackey's house and farm and he hauls poultry manure on the side," Lucy told Margo. There were no trees or flowers or bushes around it, and Lucy explained, "Jeannette, Reid's wife was afraid of snakes and wanted the house to be away from the woods." Lucy knew everybody's business.

After Reid's house the pavement ended. They were now on a dusty gravel-dirt road hardly wide enough for two cars to squeeze by one another. We later learned that half the roads in Rockbridge Country were unpaved and Margo wasn't quite used to unpaved roads yet and didn't know that spectacular properties could be found at the end of them. They came up to a smaller road and took a sharp right turn. Huge 150-foot red and white oaks lined both sides of the now one-lane road. Rays of brilliant yellow sunshine occasionally penetrated the deep forest and Margo kept looking for a blooming mountain laurel, but it might have been too early yet. The road had lots of twists and turns and kept going up and up and went over two of those menacing and noisy cattle guards. The temperature fell as they kept climbing. This road has eight culverts to maintain but you can see the swales have been kept clear. This was the first time Margo had heard that word which meant sort of a path for the rain to follow away from the road. We were to learn many new words, a whole new vocabulary, while we lived on Hickory Ridge. I became intimate with the terms "crush run" and "money trees" later on.

In fact, from the turning point to the top of the ridge it was a 500-foot climb in elevation in less than a quarter of a mile. I can still visualize every twist and turn. Since tall trees lined both sides of the road you couldn't see much, just leaves and leaves and very tall trees, mostly stately oaks which I later called our legacy trees. The sun barely filtered in, and ferns and green, moist, fuzzy moss grew everywhere.

Margo eyed the thick, twisted vines hanging from the trees suspiciously and her immediate instinct was to get out of the car and pull them down. Talk about being passionate! Lucy noticed Margo's intensity and said, "Around here we call those Virginia creepers." They were near the end of the road and a thin layer of dust now covered the green Land Rover.

Right after the second and last clattering cattle guard, they passed a half-broken-down sign tacked onto a Hickory tree which said "Welcome to Hickory Ridge."

The house they came to looked small and unassuming from the outside and was painted in grey. There were two small windows and a wide front door. Nothing special there. Then Lucy opened the very wide sort of Redwood stained front door for Margo.

"Oh my gosh," Lucy recalls Margo's first gasping words when they walked into the living room with the big picture windows and saw the view. Then she heard Margo shout out, *"Gotta have it."*

You could see for miles—at least fifty—and deep down into the valley below. You got glimpses of I-81, but the semis looked like little ants as they labored up and down the valley. It was quiet, so quiet. The nearest neighbor was over a mile way and the house was surrounded by those immense legacy tress that ominously seemed to be closing in. All kinds of birds were darting around and hawks were riding lazy thermals in the sky, making endless loops as they looked for something to eat. Later when we had visitors come, they would stare and become misty eyed, if not outright crying in joy, the view was so spectacular. The mountains you looked at were smooth, and no wonder. They'd been eroding for almost half a billion years, unlike the young and still-rugged Rockies. Straight out in front of us, some thirty miles away, was Mt. Baldy at 3,200 feet. We were at around 2,000 feet above sea level. Yep, we later bought an altimeter, as guessing elevations was fun in that part of the world.

Margo was so taken by the view she almost missed seeing the aqua-marine lap pool. "You know there is a forty-foot heated lap pool and twelve acres of land that come with this." Lucy went on. "You have deeded right of way for most of the road you came up on and on the lower half you own fifteen feet on either side."

Then Margo noticed the decks—a thousand square feet of multi-layered decks, part of which surrounded a huge fish pond and rock, or should I say boulder, garden and a huge screened porch. Margo didn't use my favorite exclamation "Mama Mia Santa Maria," but she was thinking it as this all sunk in. The deck was amazing for as soon as you stepped on a different level the view changed dramatically. Later, when we would sit on the decks, we would move around just to get a different and equally spectacular view.

There was more. The vendor's daughter was a landscape architect and had planted four hundred feet of gardens ten feet wide in front of the house, planted with the thought that something should always be blooming. There was very little lawn to speak of. Margo would later keep a diary of what was blooming every day in the garden and in the woods all around us. After stark Minnesota, this was a Garden of Eden. It made even a master gardener breathless.

The inside had one huge great room with a very high white ceiling, an open kitchen with a Jenn Air island off to one side and the master bedroom off to the other. Huge sliding doors faced the mountains. When you sat in the Jacuzzi tub off the master bedroom, you viewed the mountains through a huge picture window looking out over the mountains. Spectacular! Then there was something that Margo and I have never seen before: a huge picture window in the garage that over-looked the mountains. There were no privacy shades because there was no need for privacy. Downstairs there were two smaller bedrooms—with views of the mountains—and a large concrete patio leading to the pool.

Then Margo, the business woman started in, *"What do they want for this?"*

Margo had bought and sold many homes in her life, but all in urban areas. In fact, Margo wanted me to visit many of these before we got married so I would know something of her previous life. But this rural property was totally new.

"US$400,000," Lucy said. Margo began calculating US$200,000 from my mother's house and we could get US$200,000 out of our Minneapolis house after paying off the mortgage. My mother's money was close by and we had yet to put the Minneapolis house up for sale. We wanted to buy this outright and not have a mortgage. I was pretty broke after the messy divorce and was helping to finance a college education for two of my kids and to support another daughter and grandson. My inheritance from my mother was my cash cow.

This was the dream retirement home of a local couple, but the husband's heart problems scared them and they wanted to be close to the hospital and medical care in town. It broke their hearts to have to sell. At that moment, Margo had no doubts about buying it.

It was right from the first thought, it was right to get away from all the family badgering. We were buying this for us not to have hopes that my daughters would sometimes stay with us which was the hope in Minneapolis. So it was like starting anew. It would be like living in a resort.

But how to pay for it? And before that, *"Would John like it?"* Margo asked herself. It was a no-brainer to me when I got back from Latvia and saw the place for the first time. I was awestruck as I walked through the silent and mysterious woods. I saw something that Margo missed, an animal viewing (heck, a hunting platform) hidden deep in the woods. The previous owners had built what amounted to a large tree house up a 25-foot ladder so that you could watch deer, foxes and, yes, bears that prowled the property in quiet. Heck you could watch in the nude if you wanted to.

After I saw the house and property, we both agreed and said let's make an offer. We drove home, did, they countered, we accepted, and they proposed a close date. That was a challenge. We doubted we could sell our house in Minneapolis by the closing date, nor round up the extra cash we needed. At that point, we hadn't even put our house up for sale. We needed a bridge loan fast, if not, faster.

"That shouldn't be hard," Margo said optimistically. We tried to arrange financing at a local Lexington bank, and called a banker that Lucy recommended. He gave himself the name Butch because his given name was Francis, which for a Southwestern Virginian was too prissy. But Butch was not interested in a US$200,000 bridge loan where the

collateral would be a house we had not yet sold in Minneapolis. "No," was his answer. Other local banks took the same view. Thus Margo knew she had to find the money in Minneapolis.

I had lost hope, but Margo wanted Hickory Ridge badly, so she went into her network of friends, one of whom was married to a banker at a local bank.

House Buying and Selling 101

Margo and I would later boast that we made an offer on Hickory Ridge in April and moved in in June. But the truth be known, if it were not for Margo's ability and knowledge, the deal might not have happened. As your basic hormonal male who is full of himself, I left the financial issues and the paying of our many bills to Margo. I was the ceremonial head of state but pretty useless when it came to money matters. Insofar as buying Hickory Ridge, it was all Margo.

Frankly, after the rejection by local Virginia banks to give us a bridge loan, I gave up hope in buying 887 Reid Road, Lexington, Virginia 24450. Margo didn't, and her talent at buying and selling homes became quite evident. She was always wearing a big smile but was constantly interrupted by phone calls. She often quoted Tom Veblen, a family friend who would invoke the phrase "Press On" as "Nothing in the world can take the place of persistence... persistence and determination alone are omnipotent."

Her persistence, combined with two other factors, got her to understand real estate buying and selling better than me. Her commodity trading father taught her a lot as did her own experience and a friendship with Joel and Susan Barker. Nonetheless all of the above got us to move into Hickory Ridge.

Buy Low, Sell High

John, Margo's dad, was quiet, if not taciturn; he had been raised in the hardscrabble world of the Iron Range in Northern Minnesota. He worked thirty-eight years for Cargill, the world's largest commodity trading firm, where he was a star trader. He had mastered the art of buy low and sell high. He didn't show much emotion towards Margo and didn't speak much, which sometimes drove Margo into a tizzy.

He was old fashioned in his demeanor, style, and values. Growing up, Margo's mom would dress Margo and herself each day before dinner and await her father's arrival home from work. Her dad had a hard time understanding anyone who wandered around as much as Margo did and he was very suspicious of me at first because I had worked in a lot of places doing lots of different things.

He never sat Margo down and said, "Looky here, I'm going to teach you about business," although she wished he would have. She learned through osmosis and being around him. From him she learned the difference between price and value. America's inability to understand that difference led to the housing crisis of 2007.

The next thing a commodity trader learns after "buy low and sell high" is how to gauge the difference between the price and value of something. Just because something is priced high doesn't mean that it's worth that.

Practicing these simple concepts led to his successful career at Cargill and later as an astute stock market investor. His investment strategy steered him away from numerous bubbles. Thus, when John Mogush died and we had a celebration of his life at the funeral home, all the former presidents of Cargill came to pay their respects.

While he lived, though, he was frugal, and we dared not ask him for the bridge loan we were seeking. But his wisdom went into Margo's thinking. She knew the value of Hickory Ridge far exceeded its price.

Paradigms

Early in her business career Margo met a woman named Sue Barker and considered going into the nutrition consulting business with her. Sue's husband, Joel, who eventually romanced Margo, was also a successful lecturer and author about the future.

Apart from her convoluted relationship with that couple (more about that later), Margo learned about managing her future from them, and also, by watching them, much ado about house buying and selling. It was Joel who in 1977 encouraged Margo to start writing down everything that happened to her—which she did.

Margo moved in with them when she got back from her Asia trip in 1986. In fact, she was living in one of their houses when I first met her in April 1988. After she finally found a job eight months later, she moved into a condo they owned in St. Paul. Joel Barker's income from writing and speaking enabled them to buy, renovate, and sell numerous houses, many of which Margo visited. She quickly learned how they did it. Their last and most innovative purchase overlooks St. Paul. Its uniqueness led a writer for *Midwest Home* to conclude, "Joel and Susan Barker had the best view in town."

Margo wasn't about to let the view on Hickory Ridge go to someone else. So she took what she knew about buying and selling houses and embarked on selling our "not so bad" house in Minneapolis and finding the US$200,000 we needed—fast.

She would have her dream house.

12

bad assed rocks and cliffs / people / events

Remember that you are always a visitor here
A traveler passing through
Your stay is but short
And the moment of your departure unknown

— Buddhist saying

When first we moved to Hickory Ridge we put the big bed on a wall parallel to the mountains, but then we changed the bed so that we saw them as we looked out over our toes. It was simply glorious. Every morning we would wake up and the view would be different. Through our bedroom doors we could see the sun rising and setting. We hung a bird feeder right outside the door so a variety of birds would come every morning and wake us with their chatter. I don't think I will ever experience anything like that again.

Whenever some sort of natural catastrophe hit Rockbridge County, in southwestern Virginia, where the soft sloping blue-greenish Blue Ridge and Allegheny mountains converge and then gently squeeze the Shenandoah Valley out of existence, armies and convoys of utility crews from throughout the southern U.S. would rush in to help, get the downed and traumatized power lines back up and get the electricity back on. There are a lot of catastrophes that knock down power lines and disrupt electricity: fires, hurricanes, thunderstorms, floods, and worst of all, paralyzing ice storms. We lived through one of the ice storms that hit the region: we lost power for a week. Of course, there was always those armies of pesky, hungry, and toothy brown and gray squirrels that would occasionally chew through the power lines, electrocute themselves, and bring the power grid down—but that was easily fixed.

Our electricity company was *BARC* which stood for Bath, Augusta, and Rockbridge Counties. But we locals (we loved considering ourselves locals) would explain to those busy out-of-town work crews that *BARC* really meant "Bad Assed Rocks and Cliffs." It's just a 600-square-mile county, but you would be hard pressed to find a more beautiful one in Virginia. *"It's just simply breathtaking,"* Margo would exclaim with joy.

The Appalachian Trail goes through the county as it runs its 2,500-mile arduous course from Georgia to Maine. Margo and I would sometimes drive the colorful roads to where the trail crosses a winding state highway over the crest of the Blue Ridge and have our lunch, usually grilled cheese sandwiches and a pickle. Our legs and knees were not in shape for the incessant ups and downs of the sinuous trail, so we vicariously enjoyed meeting with the real hikers. They were invariably disheveled, pungent, and tired, with two expensive Cabela's walking sticks—one in each hand—and wearing enormous backpacks like the one Margo wore on her Asian jaunt. When they came by, they would sit with us at the several weathered, knife-inscribed picnic tables and tell us their tales of woe: "The sun never shines on the trail and it's always raining and I'm starting to get foot rot."

Rockbridge County has mountains, the Allegheny and Blue Ridge, running down the narrowing Shenandoah Valley (a Native American term meaning "daughter of the stars") and the wide, bubbling, shallow James and Maury rivers flowing across it. Then you find neat little picture postcard towns like Lexington, where we lived, and Buena Vista (the locals pronounce it Bewna) home of a growing Mormon colony. Three mountain monoliths dominate the Lexington skyline: House (a huge rectangle), Hogback (a sloping hog's back) and Jump (it has one steep cliff edge where the legend goes a Indian maiden jumped to her death rather than be married to a man she didn't love). During colonial times it was the iron-producing centre of America with metallic-named towns like Vesuvius, Clifton Forge, and Longdale Furnace. They are just industrial relics now, with little more than brick smokestacks remaining, and the surrounding topography, while beautiful, doesn't allow any intensive row crop farming. The county does provide 40 percent of Virginia's cattle which munch on all the verdant grasslands. Ironically, it was in Raphine in Rockbridge County that Cyrus McCormick invented the mechanical reaper in 1834 which replaced the manual cutting of grain with scythes and sickles. Even though McCormick left Rockbridge to seek greener and flatter pastures in the Midwest and founded International Harvester (the red tractors you see in farm fields), the land, due to its scenic value, commands US$10,000 an acre as you always have a mountain view of some sort. The views are always being painted by the scores of real and wannabe artists who live and thrive here and I have many of their pictures on my walls.

Finally, Rockbridge has three universities which brought all sorts of interesting people (OK folks, our lexicon was becoming increasingly rural) to town in the form of professors, speakers, and students: Washington and Lee (W&L), where rich kids from the East and South go; VMI (Virginia Military Institute), a state school; and Southern Virginia University, which is Mormon and often referred to as the Brigham Young of the East.

We liked Southern Virginia the best. The W&L kids are mainly effete snoots, beyond fraternity and sorority oriented, and given to huge drunken beer bashes. W&L is basically the school you go to if you don't get into Harvard, Yale, or Princeton. One student once wrote he didn't like Lexington because he was once forced to drive behind farm tractors. Interestingly, Kuwait has thirty-five Starbucks, Lexington has none, and the *Princeton Review,* which grades all universities on their social life, ranks W&L as the number-two party school in the country. They also note that W&L resides in a village and not a town. But the school is well endowed and has great professors who wanted Margo to audit classes (for free) and invited me to talk about this and that. We represented "real world perspective!"

While VMI brought in good speakers, the restrictive policies of the school forced everyone on campus to wear a uniform even if you were not a soldier. As to Southern Virginia, we are not Mormons, but the school was fun to go to for the music and to witness the change it brought to a small, sleepy town like Buena Vista. "Bewna" has a lot of Evangelicals and they would rant about the influx of Mormons—one radio preacher I heard would caution, "The Mormons are sneaky and they will indoctrinate your kids while they are young and you are not watching."

So what types of things does the Bewna city council discuss? Well, in one session while we were living nearby, it postponed taking action on a proposal to include cats in its animal control ordinance. As the local paper wrote, "The changes would require cats to be licensed and would forbid dogs from biting pet pussycats." Bewna also has Glen Maury Park where every spring and summer some sort of Blue Grass Music Festival would be staged on the bandstand. Singers, bands, and just pickers, including Pete Seeger's brother, would come from all over the country to strut, or should I say pluck and pick, their stuff. Our orthopedist, Ned Hooper, about whom we shall hear more later, would always be there; he was a good guitar picker in his own right. But the real joy was to walk through the campgrounds where the grills were always cooking something fatty, smelling wonderful and not good for you, hear the hundreds of performers, look at the rusted-out RVs and campers with bumper stickers galore (Fiddle Fest 2004) that would be parked everywhere and just go pick up on a number of jam sessions. We would always be welcomed by bandana-wrapped musicians, handed a cold brewski out of a cooler, offered a brat, and invited to "set" while they picked and played. I would often request two of my favorites: *Bringing Mary Home* and *Banks of the Ohio*. Margo had scores of CDs with soothing Bach and Beethoven concerts, but as soon as she heard about bluegrass being played anywhere in the vicinity (that meant within a hundred miles) we were off.

The demographics of Lexington could easily be divided into thirds. One third of the town was expatriates from somewhere else, mostly college educated; one third were the longstanding locals who ran things, also college educated, but hailing from somewhere in Virginia; and one third were good ol' boys—nice people, but poor, with very bad teeth, who didn't gripe about "nothin." Strangely, I found much more affinity with this segment than the expatriates. My daughters, who sometimes came to visit, disagreed, seeing this group as rural bigots. I saw them as making no bones as to who and what they were: "What you see is what you get." One daughter once sent me a Ralph Lauren polo shirt so people wouldn't think I was a hick.

In any event, I doubt that the horse center, the universities, the artists and the musicians would have settled here if it was just some dry, dusty and flat, boring locale. It's just plum drop-dead beautiful, which is why we stopped to live here and meet and enjoy people you can't find or even imagine elsewhere. Many people who drove through on their way back to garden spots like congested New Jersey would just say, "Do I want to go back there?"

My daughters would lose patience with me if I started waxing nostalgic about Virginia, yet those first couple of years—before my burns and Margo's falls—were the best times of our lives. One day, as we were lying in bed, Margo said: *"It's snuggles and scenery and it just doesn't get any better than this."*

The county was named after the Natural Bridge which is found in the county and was once owned by Thomas Jefferson who called the area "sublime." Many who passed through came back to live out the rest of their days there, like us. You may have already seen Rockbridge and didn't know it: *War of the Worlds* starring Tom Cruise was filmed here as was *Heaven Can Wait* with Morgan Freeman.

The beauty and the remoteness of Rockbridge transformed even the people who once lived in urban areas. Some people like Margo thrived from the get go, yet many go back to urban comforts—our closest Target store was sixty miles away. Heavens to Betsy! But Rockbridge also has Hull's, the only nonprofit drive-in movie in the whole United States, which is always jam-packed on summer evenings. With a good pair of binoculars, we could watch the movies from our house on the top of Mt. Atlas—no sound, however. During the day the theater served as the site for numerous flea markets.

The main wordsmith for Rockbridge County is Doug Harwood, the very nonlinear editor of something called *The Rockbridge Advocate* whose motto is "Independent as a hog on ice." There is a traditional country newspaper in town, *The Lexington Gazette*, but *The Advocate* requires a little deeper reading. According to its website, *"The Advocate* draws its material from the culture of Rockbridge County, the people, news, gossip, troublemakers, and way of life. Without the county and the kinks that make it unique, there would be no *Advocate*. *The Advocate*, then, shows the local color of one corner of the globe, something that some folks seem to be trying to stamp out or ignore these days most everywhere. Walmarts and interstate highways, two of which pass by Lexington (I-81 and I-64), come in for equal amounts of disdain. Years later I still subscribe to the *Advocate*.

Margo was destined to thrive in a place like this. She wrote of herself years before: *"The good parts of me are that I am adventurous, willing to explore new places and concepts, tolerant, kind, good sense of direction, respect others' choices, and not afraid of work or doing with less."*

Every day was an adventure and we gradually increased our contacts with the people living in this remote and much focused part of Virginia; not a lot of multi-taskers were to be found here. We had Peter Mayle's book *A Year in Provence*, and I remembered a page from the book which struck me as remarkably similar to our living in Rockbridge County: *"A Year in Provence transports us all into all the earthly pleasures of Provençal life and lets us live vicariously at a tempo governed by seasons, not by days..."*

Three people stand out, as well as our pool and one event.

Lower Than a Rattlesnake in a Rat's Wagon Rut

Having been in the Peace Corps and having worked in strange and exotic places like Iran, Afghanistan, and Kazakhstan, I thought I was hot shit in knowing how to meet and talk to people. Margo once stood by me as I was speaking to our mile-away neighbor, Reid Mackey, a hardscrabble farmer whose land surrounded ours. He had given us the deeded right of way across his land that got us to the top of Mt. Atlas. Our first summer there was very dry and I related to Reid some of the river-flow volumetric readings (that sounds rather clunky, doesn't it) on the Maury River which flowed not far from us. I thought I had found something to talk to Reid about; I gave myself an intellectual pat on the back. He just stood there with his strong hands deep in his faded overall pockets, feet spread wide apart, tilted his head and prepared a response.

Reid, always clad in ripped, dirty, and stained bib overalls that had a pungent chicken ammonia manure odor to them, and a twice-faded baseball hat, quizzically looked at me and said with his unique twang, "Weeeeell, that's interesting, but all I care about is how much it rains into the rain gauge in front of ma house." So there!

Every evening, Margo and I would cuddle with a (OK, many a) glass of white wine on one of our many porches, stare at the stars, talk through who we'd seen and what we'd heard that day, and ponder tomorrow's fate. This was a brave new world and a unique total adventure not unlike her solo trip to Asia a decade earlier. She kept copious notes which have enabled me to recount some of the conversations and caricatures.

Margo adapted to Rockbridge County quicker than I did for she was not judgmental, a closet Buddhist if you will, and even though she spoke without a twang, she adapted very quickly just as she had elsewhere in the world. She developed a better relationship with Reid than I did for perhaps he saw me as a threat if not "too smart for his britches." Reid did not share the limelight with anyone, not even himself at times, but he did share everything, and I mean everything, and he knew about everything. If you stopped to talk with Reid, which we often did—we had to drive by his house to get into town—you were assured of a half-hour discussion while he stood with his legs far apart and rocked back and forth and yakked about: the weather, status of the hay crop, his no-good cousins, what equipment broke down over the night, the runs he had to make in picking up and delivering chicken manure, the imminent dangers to the hay crop, how his cattle and sheep and baby goats were doing, the weather, why Washington was clueless in its policies, and how Virginia Tech (his alma mater) was doing in sports and, of course, how the hay crop finally turned out. Any mention of these topics would get Reid going and then it was very hard to stop him—get out your lawn chair and listen because you won't be asked to comment. When I had the audacity to say the manure sitting in his red truck stunk, Reid responded, "That's the smell of money, my boy; the sweet smell of money."

Reid was not a big man, maybe five-foot-eight, with deep crow's feet wrinkles etched into the back of his neck. He was highly opinionated, and someone you didn't want to get on the wrong side of, though I inevitably did at the end of our time in Virginia. Margo would constantly urge me to "be patient with Reid." He was also a busybody and probably knew and wanted (and insisted) to know everybody's business. Well, almost everybody's. When Margo inquired about who was living in a little wooden house down the dusty gravel road from us, Reid said, "Don't worry about dem, they're renters." He wasn't kind about some owners either. When Margo asked who lived in the big house down the other way on Red Road, Reid said, "He is a professor and I guess he professes something." We later learned Reid had a run in with him on some matter or another as had everyone in the "neighborhood" or should I say immediate vicinity (again within a hundred miles). He is the only person I know who was thrown out of his church—too many arguments with the minister.

He always put Margo and me on edge by saying, "Daddy (Reid's father) never should have sold the twelve acres you own on top of Mt. Atlas nor given the deeded right of way to cut through our land and get to it." This, however, was common practice in Rockbridge County where farmers couldn't do anything profitable with their land on top of a ridge line and thus sold it to someone who wanted to build a house with a view.

He was as hardscrabble as the 190 acres he owned and the 60 he actually farmed. Reid represented the fifth generation of a family stretching back to 1756 who had lived on the farm, and he would pass it on to his son Drew. There was another son, Jody, who had Down's syndrome. Reid cared for him lovingly and took him along in the pickup during his many deliveries throughout the valley. Actually, I think he loved Jody so much because Jody was the only person who didn't argue with him.

His twangy English is hard to describe, but on days when he didn't feel good he would say, "I feel lower than a rattle snake in a rat wagon's rut." To speak properly, you never said something was five miles away, it was always "five mile" without the "s." His philosophy on equipment was useful for both of us. "If you own something that runs, it will eventually break down."

His wife, Jeannette, was in her late forties. She had bleached and heavily coiffed hair. Margo got to know her quite well. Where Reid didn't care for neatness, Jeannette did, and their house showed it. The house was set off in a field with no trees around it for Jeanette didn't want any creatures coming around. The house had many cabinets filled with tiny and intricate glass and ceramic figurines, very clean carpets (you always took your shoes off when you came into the house), and overstuffed, old-fashioned, tan-colored furniture. Reid had a workshop by the side which was filled with stuff, every piece of discarded equipment he ever had he saved ("never know when you might need it") and Reid's woods were full of discarded appliances and junk cars sitting on blocks and entangled with ugly vines and very sharp thorn bushes. When not driving one of the two huge Mack trucks which he used to deliver chicken manure, he drove a little yellow pickup truck that looked like it had been rolled several times.

Whereas Reid was as thin as a rail, Jeannette was a little chubby. Reid hardly drove more than a hundred miles away from the farm, while Jeannette was a sales rep for a food service company and drove all over Virginia. Whereas Reid had a deeply rutted face and a sun-dried, wrinkled neck, Jeannette's was smooth and white as a ghost as she stayed out of the sun. Reid once came to our house in Bermuda shorts and it was the funniest if not the strangest sight you have ever seen.

Our first guests to Hickory Ridge were Jeannette and Reid on August 4, 2002. Jeannette wrote in the guest book that Margo covetously maintained, "The Reid Mackey family welcomes you to the top of Mt. Atlas. Looking forward to having you in the neighborhood."

She and Margo bonded immediately. Both worked on the road and had stories to share. In Margo's case, she had spent time (seven years, to be exact) suffering on the road while selling drugs for Bristol-Myers Squibb. For Margo it was the most miserable job experience ever, but the money and the medical benefits were too good to pass up; Margo kept her executive salary from when she worked at headquarters, and though only a sales person now, she earned more than her boss, which pissed him off greatly. She once wrote of her job selling and had probably shared this with Jeannette:

> *Sales jobs are the worst. Having to see the same people over and over again on a regular basis; having basically the same info for them; the stress of not interfering with their work and patients, talking the same subject every time...boredom and repetition are dreaded components for me.*

Reid did reach out to me sometimes for he knew I wrote for *Successful Farming,* the leading U.S. farm publication, and they eventually did run a story I did on Reid with the sexy and catchy title, "Money From Manure: Hauling poultry litter proves profitable for Virginia farmer." Now doesn't that twinkle your toes?

Reid would sometimes call to ask if I wanted to go to cattle auctions, go with him to buy barbed wire, or spend a day picking up and delivering chicken manure all over the valley. Given that Georgetown University, my alma mater, expected me to become well rounded, I went along. And I finally knew someone whose business was "chicken shit."

In the early years, Reid and Jeannette did care for us. One day, Jeannette called Margo to say that a group of hungry black bears were on the prowl near us and "you be careful up there." When I rolled our

"Safari Tested" Jeep Grand Cherokee over during a snowstorm and was hanging upside down, I called Margo and told her of my plight. She said, *"I'll call Reid and an ambulance."* Reid came right away and saw my predicament, and that I couldn't get out of the jeep. I had managed to get out of hanging upside down and was trying to kick the door window glass out but that was proving impossible. "John, you want to get out of there?" he said sardonically. My ego was really hurt for as a former Minnesotan you would think I knew something about driving in the snow.

CJ the Savior

Having twelve wooded acres, a steep, curvy, three-quarter-mile gravel road, and eight culverts was daunting, even to me and my self-image as Macho Man. Once Margo found her intellectual mentor at the University, we both needed a physical backstop to complete all the physical tasks we wanted to do. I had a standard of neatness even while living surrounded by a deep, dark, and very tall forest, and we simply had to keep the place up to the standards we both set. We found it in CJ Goad, or just plain CJ. Here is how Margo and I came to meet him.

On the day that I rolled the Jeep and Reid Mackey came to get me out, the car had slipped on the ice, flipped, and landed upside down, leaving me wondering what to do next while hanging from my seat belt. Although the roof was crushed and all the windows broken, the insurance company decided not to declare the Jeep a wreck but pay US$11,000 to fix it. Goad's Auto Body did the work, which took several months; the parts had to be found.

You can't miss Goad's Body Shop as you approach Lexington from the east on Highway 11 which parallels I-81. It's a compound of several big metal buildings mostly stark white with armies of cars of various vintages parked out front in different stages of disrepair. There are always some cars for sale and usually a big rock star bus outside. There was always a huge pile of amputated auto and truck parts, fenders, side panels and bumpers which a recycler would pick up now and then. After I wrecked the Jeep, Goad's became my second home as I constantly went there to check on the repairs.

You might as well call it "Goad's World" for Goads were all over the place. J.D., who ran it, was so big that he not only filled a huge high-back chair but the whole room, it seemed. He was close to 400 pounds. His son W.D. did most of the estimates and drove the family race car (really a rocket on wheels) and Charley, J.D.'s brother, worked there as well. I became somewhat of a welcome oddity by coming by as my clothes were far from the pick up and cement truck casual style they wore. One day I told J.D. I needed a helper on Mt. Atlas and asked if he knew anyone who could help me out.

"Well I have a no good nephew, CJ, that is looking for something to do. But I warn you he's lazy, lazy, and lazy." J.D. was like Reid for you don't ever give your in-laws any credit.

"Well, have him come up and see me," I said.

Although people had cell phones, a first visit was most often done in person in that part of Virginia. Sure enough the next afternoon a shiny old red Chevy pickup truck without any dents drove up to the house. A very large man/boy got out of it. I guessed six foot three and 225 muscular pounds.

"Hi. I'm CJ"

That's how it started that first year, and CJ became a constant and welcome feature at our house. He liked coming up because there was always something to do. He didn't have to be called. He once told his father, Charley, the only senior male member of the Goad's who wasn't known by initials, "Well I'm going up to John and Margo's to see what needs to be done."

Let's see, I had CJ do the following: mow grass, clear brush, rake tons of leaves, build shelves, burn huge piles of brush and fallen trees, smooth out the road, dig out culverts, clean the filters in the pool, build ramps for Margo, serve as parking master for our many parties, put a tarp on our convertible when winter came, gather huge piles of firewood, paint, install insulation in the art studio we built for Margo, and clear the road when ice storms blocked it. After one such ice storm, he and a friend started at the bottom of the road clearing trees and branches that were blocking the road while I started at the top; it took us six hours to meet at the middle.

When Margo started to have troubles maneuvering stairs, CJ built ramps to help get her into the house and from the house onto the porches. Margo and CJ really bonded when we decided to build Margo her own studio. He was instrumental in its installation and maintenance.

CJ also taught me to be neat and tidy. When he finished his work, he always put the cleaned tools back where he got them. I had never met anyone like that, ever.

Like most young men in Rockbridge County, CJ was into guns and drag racing. Hunting and guns go together in Rockbridge and CJ took full advantage of our land to hunt deer. He had a powerful 270 rifle with a scope with special bullets for hunting and also a bunch of weapons for fun—like a sawed-off shotgun. CJ would bring those up to the mountain now and then and we would blast away. He lived in a crowded double-wide trailer home and it was heaven for him to come up on our land and be able to shoot at will.

During hunting season the surrounding woods would reverberate with the sound of gunfire—no rebellion going on, just hunters. With his help, I bought a Stainless Steel Marlin 22 with a scope that I would use for target practice. CJ adjusted the scope for me. Margo fired it a couple of times but really wasn't into guns.

She did like drag racing, though. CJ's hobby was drag racing and we ended up sponsoring his dragster. So you can go to the Waynesboro Raceway today and see "JFA" on the back of his race car. And boy did I learn just how sophisticated the sport of drag racing was—it's not just a bunch of good ol' boys making noise. Here are the track requirements at Waynesboro, if you wanted to compete:

SUPER PRO E.T. (7.99 ELAPSED TIME AND QUICKER):
Electronics permitted. No stutter-boxes or similar devices. If vehicle performance falters and picks back up you will be disqualified. If in doubt don't use it.

1. Must have driveshaft loop. Must be 360 degrees.
2. Must have fire extinguisher mounted within reach of driver.
3. No holes in firewall or floor pan permitted.
4. Four or five speed transmission must have a blow-proof bellhousing.
5. All fuel lines must be located outside of driver's compartment.
6. All cars running aftermarket transmission coolers must have steel or braided lines. No rubber lines.
7. Must have a minimum of three inches ground clearance.
8. Front engine roadster must wear gloves.
9. Any open wheeled cars drivers must have shield on helmet.

10. All S/Pro drivers must have a Snell 90 approved helmet.
11. Must have hood or flash field over carburetor.
12. Radiator catch can be mandatory.
13. Protective clothing: Fire jacket required.
14. Seatbelt and shoulder harness required.
15. Roll bar required. Minimum 4 point cage, recommended 6 point roll bar.
16. Neutral safety switch required.
17. Wheel studs must protrude through wheels at least one thread.
18. External kill switch on all cars 7.99 E.T. and quicker required.
19. 7.49 E.T. and quicker must have rear end c-clip eliminators.

Still think NASCAR is for dummies?

Margo would go out to watch the races with me, and for fun CJ would put a racing helmet on her head while she was in a wheelchair. I remember one crucial point CJ taught me—for every hundred pounds you get rid of, you gain a tenth of a second in speed. That sport is so precise, and now I know more about it than I need to.

Kayla Finlay

The grocery stores in Lexington were rather pedestrian, so a store offering sushi, *foie de grais*, stuffed lamb chops, and expensive wines seemed like a sure thing—at least to its quixotic owner, Foods International, for whom Kayla worked. However, it failed because Lexington, with its population of 6,000, just didn't have enough rich people. The owner and several rich investors burned through US$1 million in just a couple of months. It was located on the way out of town, squeezed in between a farm supply store and Peebles, a very low-end clothes store. Wonder why that didn't work out?

Kayla left and started up Patisserie, a French deli, in a deserted and somewhat spooky bowling alley. Ever try renovating a deserted bowling alley with a limited budget and make it feel like a French deli? Though it was a neat place to stop for a morning coffee, Patisserie didn't last long at that location, so Kayla tried the same concept in a deserted gas station.

We kept coming for coffee and pastries, and Kayla, seeing Margo struggling, asked her had she tried spiritual healing, deep stuff. Kayla described herself as an "alternative holistic psychic healer event planner," and on her website you could read: "If you plant a flowering bulb too deeply and then every year cover it with more and more mulch even though the bulb exists underground, it is hard pressed to send a shoot to the surface when it cannot be seen visibly by all. Our inner voice or Divine Intelligence is often covered with so many layers of our unconscious lives it becomes invisible."

She and Margo developed a close bond and Kayla would drive to Margo's studio and have healing sessions during which Margo would "recharge, regenerate and restore." It helped Margo, and Margo reciprocated by investing US$10,000 in Kayla's plan to reincarnate her French deli in a renovated gas station. Alas, that didn't work either.

Then, some time later, Margo's health deteriorated when cancer crept into her body. Kayla came to the Mayo Clinic and the hospice where Margo was. In her brochure Kayla put it this way:

"Kayla Travels to Clients
September 2010. Kayla drove from Pennsylvania to the Mayo Clinic in Rochester, Minnesota to offer her services and love to a dear friend and family during her final transition from earthly life to an eternal soul in the spirit world. Kayla was bedside both at Mayo and at the hospice in Minneapolis offering support and love throughout the process."

The Pool

OK, the pool. When we bought Hickory Ridge it was for the magnificent view, not the forty-foot long, four-foot deep lap pool that went with it. After five years of maintaining the pool, I finally learned to manage and know all about it. Now knowing what it takes to have a clean pool, I would never dare swim in a hotel pool ever again. That murky water you encounter usually means the proper chemicals aren't used, and, to be polite, that it's polluted by humans. Our pool in Virginia became as important to our social lives as the hunting platform became to having good relations with our tradesmen.

There was a public pool in Lexington which was dirty, loud, and crowded with teenagers. Our pool was quiet, clean, and with mountain views. Our ultimate high with the pool was when Margo and I would walk down to get the paper and mail (half hour) and then walk back up the mountain (forty-five minutes) and arrive totally sweating. We would strip off our clothes and just jump into the pool nude and enjoy the cool, clean water cooling our bodies. We never got caught nude in the pool by visitors as cars made a lot of noise crossing the second cattle guard, giving us time to scurry in to get clothes before it arrived.

Since we lived in the middle of a forest and on top of the mountain, there were lots of little creatures in search of a quick drink. So even though I used the powder-blue pool cover every night, all kinds of critters—snakes, squirrels, mice, rabbits, frogs, worms, birds, and every type of bug—would seek the pool out...and then die. The chlorine would kill them. Sometimes they would just be floating in the water and sometimes we'd find them on the bottom of the pool. Most often they would be found in one of two white perforated plastic buckets on either side of the pool. Over time, it became my job more than Margo's to clean out the dead critters, as it became harder for Margo to bend to get them out.

Pools are kept free of green and cloudy scum by consistent pumping and filtration. Understanding what went on at the pumping station with its many handles and dials was a chore and a science lesson. Since Margo was the scientist in the family, she gave herself the task of analyzing the water. Remember those litmus tests in high school? We used that for pH and others to test for chlorine. We always had to soften the water after a rain as acid rain was prevalent on the East Coast. We stored all the chemicals in a safe, dry place, but boy did they smell—and cost a lot.

There was also a basket where junk was caught at the pumping station. We'd also find dead critters there. I always remember that the pressure gauge had to be at between twelve and fifteen for the pump. If it wasn't, there was a blockage somewhere.

We cleaned the pool with a robot called a Navigator. It was attached by a hose to a suction device in the pool and in a couple of hours could clean the whole pool. It would pick up all the little stuff the baskets wouldn't catch and clean the vinyl lining of the pool. The pool would glisten. When the pressure was right, it would climb halfway up the pool wall.

Did we love that pool!

Jana Diena – The Perpetual Draw

Here's how we announced our annual festival.

St. John's Day (Jana Diena) at Hickory Ridge
June 21, 2003 5:00 p.m. Until Midsummer Nights Dream

St. John's Day (aka the summer solstice) is celebrated in Latvia as the longest day of the year and people gather together to weave oak wreaths and make daisy chains (something to do with fertility), sing songs, talk about how good it is to be alive and dance around the bonfire. The fire is important because it chases the night away.

> Directions
> We live on Mt. Atlas about 6 miles from Lexington, Virginia. Get off on exit 195 on Interstate 81 and go north on US 11. About a mile up the road after the Sam Houston Wayside is Virginia 716 by an antique shop. Turn left and go to the Y in the road. Go left here; this is County 622. After the asphalt ends about a mile later, turn right at the second drive; this is 877. There is a big green sign directing you up the mountain. Don't lose faith going up the mountain as it is about a mile. The views are great.

We even had Latvian diplomats drive 180 miles from DC to come to this Jana Diena. Making it wonderful for Margo in 2006, our best ever, was the attendance of two of our friends, Uldis and Ilze. I met Uldis in my role as special representative of Latvia. Young and energetic, they eagerly cooked food like sweet and sour Latvian sauerkraut, pieragi (little meat pies), and handed out big frosty bottles of Latvian beer.

It was the first Jana Diena we gave and it was a fabulously enjoyable event for all. To deal with the inevitable rain showers that were common during that time of year, we had a huge tent put up over the deck—ten feet by fifty feet with internal lights. As Margo and I had to be hosts for the day, CJ and his friend Stephen handled the fire— very important—the parking, and all logistics. These two guys figured out that we could park forty-eight cars on top of the mountain and acted as traffic cops. Congressman Robert Goodlatte, Chairman of the

House Agriculture Committee, was given a premium space in front of the house. His license plate was Virginia number 6—the congressional district he represented. We celebrated June 21st every year we were on Hickory Ridge, but our last event, in 2006, was the best. We invited a hundred people; some seventy came.

For Margo, always worried about being accepted, our Jana Diena celebrations were wonderful. We had brought something "cultural—non-hillbilly" to the mountains which was much appreciated. Although we invited our tradesmen friends to these celebrations, they never came. It was the more urbane part of Lexington that came. Margo told me, *"People must think we're hot shit to have a congressman show up."*

But as wonderful as Hickory Ridge was for us, it did seem like our stay was doomed from the start. The first indication was my almost dying from a fire on July 5, 2003.

Burned Alive (well almost)

I am a Latvian neat-nick like my parents; we couldn't stand disorder in our woods. The backside of our land was a steep slope covered with tall red and white oaks. Margo and I decided to cut down five acres of those woods to improve the view. I'll let Margo describe what happened via a text she put on the Caring Bridge website (www.caringbridge.org/va/John) she developed for me.

> *Thursday, July 10, 2003 9:36 a.m. CDT*
> *I am going to recap the last five days since John was admitted by helicopter to the University of Virginia Medical Center in Charlottesville, VA.*
>
> *He had been burning trash trees on Saturday, July 5, got impatient (a usual male gene, as per the head nurse here), threw gasoline on the fire, backed up away from the fire but was apparently knocked over by a huge blast of hot air and sustained what we now know as a major 'flash burn.'*
>
> *He came and found me and said he needed to be taken to the hospital because he had some bad burns, and that I should call the local Lexington hospital and alert them that we were coming. We got there in 15 minutes, the staff was waiting, fortunately the ER was quiet, and on immediate assessment the ER doc said to us, 'You need to be at the UVA Burn Center…we are calling the helicopter.'*

John's comment, 'Well, I guess I'm going to be there for a week or so, so get me some clothes and books and come tomorrow, don't come tonight. I'll be okay.'

Burns are an ever-changing drama so nothing is for sure. So the long and short of it is initially we were told that he probably had first, second and third degree burns. Total body surface being burned was about 60%. And that most were second degree. He would have to have skin grafts on the third degree burns since skin will not grow back over those burns.

We were advised that he would have five to six surgeries, thus being totally sedated and immobile for about a month – with at least another month of hospital recovery.

He is resting quietly, totally sedated which means that we can talk to him but he can't respond to us. He is on a respirator and feeding tube, and completely covered in gauze, except for much of his face which was spared from the heat (we think when the heat hit him, he turned to his right and covered his face with his left hand and arm because that side of him is worse than the right and his face is pretty much okay, although not looking 'normal' – he is very swollen). You could not see his eyelashes. But now his fluid is subsiding and you can at least recognize him. All along he has been in reverse isolation, which means that everyone who enters the room has to put on a gown and gloves as a protection for him. Then every time you leave the room, you have to throw them away and then take a new robe and gloves when you enter again.

Friday, July 11, 2003 8:57 a.m. CDT

Yesterday many nurses and doctors would say to us, 'we heard the good news!' It's becoming quite clear that they didn't expect him to improve this much – or to make it at all. Our nurse says the whole unit is so happy at how well he's done. They told us the usual survival predictor is age plus percentage of burns – if it's over 100, you are sure not to make it – He was 119.

We will try to quickly update you all again before we leave after we talk to the trauma team. Thanks for all your warm wishes.

What happened to me was a tragedy but I also learned how to become a caregiver. For example, on the Caring Bridge site, Margo asked for help from the community and many people offered to support her

219

during her time of need. The help people offered would be the same type of help I would need when Margo wasn't mobile.

Margo wrote this about two weeks after I was burned.

> *For all of you who asked 'what can I do to help,' here are some things that definitely would be helpful:*
>   *weeding (the weeds are overgrowing the yard)*
>   *vacuum*
>   *dust*
>   *invite me to dinner while John's still in the hospital and after he's home or bring dinner to stay to share*
>   *clean the fish pond*
>   *water yard and flowers*
>   *weeding*
>   *encourage me to get out to take care of myself*

Really the end of our stay in Virginia came after Margo had hip surgery in Richmond—a place you really don't want to go to. The surgery was unsuccessful, and the food, even for hospital food, was awful. The place was so bad that I had to pull Margo out of the hospital and take her home.

When we got home, Margo was confined to a wheelchair and could not get down to the pool, much less swim in it. The pool became my responsibility, but that was OK because only I could use it—it was no fun to swim alone. Our friends still came up to use it but it was primarily me and the pool. I started to think: Do I really want to take on everything by myself? It was pure torture to think like that, for Margo had found the mountain home she loved, a bevy of friends, tutoring, intellectual activities, and freedom from all the nagging issues of my family.

We drove to Minneapolis for a family function and a respite from the work, and on the night we got back the county was hit with a tremendous ice storm. Hundred-foot trees came crashing down all over the mountain top and on our home. We couldn't sleep that night for all the noise, and then—"click"—the lights went out.

When we woke up in the morning, we couldn't believe our eyes. Everything was covered with ice—it was beautiful, but destructive. We got into the Jeep with the chain saw in hand, which I had gotten very adept at using, to see how far down the mountain we could go. I wheeled Margo out to the car and had her drive. I got out and picked up branches until we encountered whole trees blocking the road. This was serious. We couldn't get out and Margo couldn't walk. We called CJ, and he and his friend Stephen put down what they were doing and came as quickly as they could. The ice storm had only hit the higher elevations—Lexington, a thousand feet below, was ice free.

It took us three exhausting hours, starting from the top, to meet up with CJ and Stephen, who had started from the bottom. It took four and a half days for crews to come and restore power. We spent a lot of time in Margo's artist studio. We had installed a gas fireplace with an 800-gallon propane tank there that kept us warm and comfortable. Eventually, the power came back on, but this whole ice storm business was the second strike.

The third strike came in the spring. Margo now could get around with a walker and even drive—this information becomes important later. Our neighbor Reid Mackay started cutting down trees. He cut down five acres which took a couple of weeks. Reid was going to cut down fifty acres on some very steep land, and he was going to use our road which I maintained and Margo and I used. He had the three huge Deacon brothers cut the trees; when you shook hands with them your hand disappeared in theirs. They overloaded the lumber trucks and to get them down they had to attach a chain to a bulldozer and inch the overloaded trucks down because their brakes alone would not hold.

We would wake up in the morning to the sound of chain saws and watch the spectacle of trucks being lowered. Then one day when Margo was driving up the road, she came upon a fully-loaded and top-heavy logging truck coming down. It pained Margo to back up, but the logging truck couldn't and the road was too narrow to allow vehicles to pass. She had to meander down the hill in reverse, and that painful and uncomfortable feat became the proverbial straw that broke the camel's back. First, there was the pool that only I could use, then there was the fear of being trapped by another storm, and now this.

I didn't like the dangerously over-loaded lumber trucks using our road. There is something on deeded right of way that you can't "increase the demand," (for example, I can't build a resort on top of the mountain and have tenants going back and forth) and Reid certainly had no right to have lumber trucks going back and forth on it.

The incident when Margo with her aches and pains had to painfully twist around while backing down the mountain brought all this logging intrusion to a head.

I drove down to Reid's house and had Margo get out of the car and sit in her wheelchair so she could witness what was about to happen. I knocked on the door and Reid came out. I didn't mince words.

"I'm pissed."

"'Bout what?"

"The logging trucks constantly using my road."

"But the road crosses my land."

At this point, I knew the conversation would quickly go downhill.

When I asked Reid if he said it was safe for loaded lumber trucks to be lowered down by a chain affixed to a bulldozer because the brakes wouldn't hold as the loggers were doing?

"Sure."

Then I asked, "Would you entrust your life to the loggers, which is what we are being forced to do?"

"Sure."

After that testy conversation, I contacted my lawyer.

That night I told Margo I had to get out. She didn't like my decision but she understood. She also understood what was going on with her body, and that the physical and emotional strength I had was quickly disappearing. Resigned, she said, "I'll call Reid to tell him we're moving."

And in two months we were gone. We sold at the height of the housing bubble to a couple who had gone to Countrywide Mortgage and gotten a loan. In fact, we made US$150,000 by living in Virginia those five years. The owner of a fancy eatery, housed neither in a deserted bowling alley nor gas station, bought our house.

So where to go? We weeded out Minneapolis because of the housing bubble. My commodity trading background—buy low, sell high—told me it made no sense to move back from whence we came, the family issues and all, and pay a high price for a house knowing that its value would come crashing down soon enough.

We looked around Lexington, comparing what we saw to where we had lived. There were no comparisons. We couldn't live in an ordinary house in the mountains, and we decided if we can't look at mountains, let's look at a big river. Margo's best professional years were spent while she lived on the banks of the Ohio River in Newburgh, Indiana. So where do we live: on a river? Which river? We picked Dubuque, Iowa, on the Mississippi, as a place to start looking. It was only a couple of hours from the Mayo Clinic where we hoped Margo would finally get her hip fixed and have some relief from pain. Dubuque turned out to be a good choice, as Margo's dad, we would soon find out, was dying in Minneapolis, and she would get to spend a lot of time with him.

A couple years after Margo's death, I went back to visit our home on Hickory Ridge. It was different—its charm seemed to have disappeared. Regardless, I will never forget the wonderful memories we created there and will cherish them for the rest of my years.

13

the blessed mess

You see the smile that's my mouth
It's hiding the words that don't come out
All of the friends who think I'm blessed
They don't know I'm in this mess

No they don't know who I really am
And they don't know what I've been
through
Like you do, and I was made for you

– Brandi Carlyle, "The Story"

"*J*ust the facts, ma'am." Those were the famous words spoken by deadpan and ashen-faced Sgt. Joe Friday on the 1950s TV show *Dragnet* that I watched on a black and white console RCA TV when I was growing up. He had a beyond-matter-of-fact style, with his five o'clock shadow look, as he gathered info at the crime scene or interrogated witnesses. "Just the facts," he would ask if not demand. And so here below I list just the medical facts on The Blessed Mess that Margo and I lived through in our years together. Every medical event could be a short story or a book by itself. At parties and family get-togethers, Margo and I would tell people we would limit medical talk to ten minutes; otherwise, we'd go on all night: "Would you like some piriphormis, or how about a well-differentiated tumor, or should I add chronic osteomyelitis of the left hip?" It got so we didn't tell our families or friends any more about the new facts, incidents, diagnosis or whatever they were, as they were overwhelmed with them just as much as we were. Needless to say, this chapter of the book has been the hardest to write about emotionally. The medical situations I write about are full of "could a, would a, should a," events, but Margo is gone and there is no reason to hypothesize; we do anyway. What is remarkable, however, is that regardless of how Margo got kicked down by events, she always got up—as did I.

MARGO FREIVALDS' SURGICAL HISTORY

03/86	Tubal ligation
04/00	Right breast lumpectomy (stage 1 breast cancer)
08/01	Right knee replacement
11/01	Right knee replacement removed due to infection
01/02	Right knee revision
04/04	Partial left hip replacement
05/04	Infection cleanout of left hip
08/04	Broken left femur
12/04	Surgery on right breast to attempt to eliminate fistula that had developed
05/07	Left hip and left knee replacements
11/07	Skin graft, left knee
12/07	Left hip revision
03/08	Left breast lumpectomy (stage 1 breast cancer)
01/09	Left hip revision
08/09	Cataract surgery
09-11/09	Seven left hip dislocations
11/09	Left hip revision

JOHN FREIVALDS' NEAR MISSES

07/05/03	Explosion with burns covering 60% of his body
09/07/09	Accidental near fatal drug overdose

Or put another way, our blessed mess included my two near misses with death, bone breaks and fractures, falls, hip and knee replacements, burns, breast cancer, dislocations, wounds that would not heal, a hearing aid, emergency rooms, home nurses, skin creams for eczema and severe burns, carpal tunnel surgery, cataract eye surgery, home IVs, two helicopter evacuations (for you budget-conscious readers, US$17,000 each), many 911 calls, ambulances, crutches, Margo's black and blue arm from so many attempts to draw blood, bleeding ulcers, extra large wheelchairs, wound suction pump, blood clots, elevated white counts, braces, wheelchair ramps, portable toilets, specially raised toilets, every type of gauze bandage ever invented, psychiatrists, ulnar nerve transposition surgery, intensive care, hand splints, therapy upon therapy, cold packs, heating pads, double vision (both of us), grabbers of various lengths, getting out of one therapy location to go to another, ventilators, reaching contraptions to put your socks on without bending, every type of elastic wrap known to mankind, being denied help by a surgeon, buying a new SUV large enough for Margo to totally stretch out and to easily put a wheelchair in, carpal tunnel surgery, a variety of walkers, compression garments (two pairs, each pair was US$1,000), TENS units, accidental drug overdose, being sent to a surgeon who once saw fifty-one patients in two hours at his clinic, every type of drug to relieve pain and thicken bones and thin blood, faith healing and Zen Buddhism sessions, five hospital stays in five states, almost permanent residency at the Mayo Clinic on the fourteenth floor, and of course:

THE GRAND PRIZE: cancellation of our health insurance for we had reached the lifetime limit—US$1 million dollars!

We lived through them and with them all, and only after Margo died did I fully grasp the totality of it. We just went from one blessed mess to another and didn't keep score; we were too busy living. Brandi Carlyle once again:

> And they don't know what we've been though like you do
> And I was made for you

Even though we would sometimes hold each other in our arms and cry ourselves to sleep at night, we somehow got up the next day with our always beautiful mountain views and would try to lead as normal a life as possible.

Normal? Us?

> *I've never really wanted to do what the masses want – explains why I love Jani – he's not of the norm and yet I've never been totally comfortable with that and have fought it all my life. It's obvious I have been unhappy in accepting of who I am. Now maybe I can change all that and begin to embrace me.*

We both laughed when we saw that cartoon in the *New Yorker* of a doctor addressing an obviously distraught middle–aged flabby patient sitting on the examination table and with a straight face looking at a paper in his hands saying, "Why not you?"

But believe it or not, after all that, we considered ourselves healthy—our tickers worked, blood pressure was normal, and most of our issues had to do with bones or burned skin. We always worked out, swam, didn't smoke, and although we drank wine and aged mellow scotch whiskey, it wasn't to excess (OK, just sometimes). We would cuddle up and make love several times a week, mostly in the mornings, and fantasize about being on a magic carpet floating high through the clouds. After which we would gaze out the window at the blue sky and wispy clouds, hear the morning birds serenade us, and thank God, celestial algorithms, the Lord, Sky Chief, Buddha, Allah or whoever he, she, or, it is that is in charge for this glorious time we had together.

We never thought that we would ever die any time soon; we just thought (particularly me) we would have to adapt to new circumstances. I would have been happy to have Margo in a wheelchair for the rest of her life for I loved her so. I intellectualized it all by saying we had to develop "compensating mechanisms" for our new reality.

After Margo's first big hip surgery in Minneapolis (one of three big ones, by the way), her friends put together a collage of get well cards and one had the inscription which I liked: "Perhaps I cannot control the wind, but I can adjust my sails." And she only did—sort of. As for me, it was one big numbing caregiver fog, as I went from one thing to another and yet another. All the while Margo tried to keep her true feelings hidden from me as much as possible. It was very hard to live through it all with Margo, and, because of the benefit of hindsight and insight, it is even harder to write about it now. Oh, my poor baby!

The Aging Self

Every day Margo would look at a framed picture collage that I'd made for her which she kept by her mirror. It showed Margo biking, hiking, skiing, rock climbing, swimming, snorkeling, and playing tennis in different places around the world. It made her happy but also sad, because as her medical issues grew, she could no longer do all of the things she wanted.

It was hard for her to transition from an Australian rock climber, New Zealand glacier explorer, Zion National Park daredevil, Minnesota Iron Man biker, and accomplished cross-country skier to a limping aging person with broken and fractured bones. It was a transition that she grappled with:

> So much of who I am and how I see myself or at least have in the past is based on physical activities. I prided myself in being able to move heavy things, garden as much as I wanted, hike, bike, cross country ski, etc. as well as reach high awkward places in the house. Now I need to redefine myself as so much has been severely diminished. Also the constant vigilance of safety. However is it reality as Jani says so what to do?
>
> For the first time in my life, I really do need to rely on help from others – something I always struggled with as well as knowing I need physical activity for my emotional well being. Moving to Virginia happened at a good time for me... Swimming becomes a must – it is something that I can do with ease. The things I need help with are carrying things – tools, laundry, etc. The good new is that means I need to think about what I am going to do and how I'll do it. A major goal has been to increase the amount of walking I can do at a time as this is one of the activities that Jani and I have always shared.

But complicating all of this was Margo's clinical depression. Way back in July of 1985 her therapist "John" led her to worry, *"I may indeed have clinical depression* (which I do believe) *rather than an environmental depression... I do have a zest for life but if people do not respond the way I like/want/need, then it squelches me. I withdraw and out comes depression."*

Margo sought help in Virginia with the Department of Psychiatric Medicine at UVA in Charlottesville. They put it this way:

"She was first diagnosed as depressive in 1988 within the context of vocational; and other life transitional stresses (that be me). She also noted that she has had psychological counseling off and on since 1970 discussing basic self esteem issues. She recalled that a major depressive episode was recently triggered when working with pharmaceutical sales representatives who, she said, were working to destroy her, as well as with a supervisor who she stated eventually sided with her peers rather than herself. She said that this experience ultimately challenged her belief that she is a likeable person and ended up receiving psychiatric care in an emergency room, and eventually going on medical leave. ... Ms. Freivalds stated she is severely distressed that her physical health is not what it used to be and she fears her body is falling apart."

228

There was a good side which was underlined by Margo. To wit…"Ms. Freivalds appeared younger that her stated years (sixty)…demonstrated a statistically significant strength in her visual perception processing of symbolic stimuli, recognition memory."

But there was a cautionary sentence as well and this *was* Margo:

"They see themselves as being self reliant to a fault and when they frequently end up becoming overburdened, they do not ask for help."

This depression also meant that Margo always thought there was something wrong with her. At times I wasn't much help. My sour moods, sarcastic statements, or glaring looks often had a crushing effect on Margo—even though these moods, statements, and looks were never intended into bring harm to her. One of the worst thoughts she had was that she often believed the medical messes she was experiencing happened as a punishment because she was a bad medical sales representative! Of course, she kept all of this well bottled up inside of her and would tell it to a therapist and on occasion to me. I think she saw too many therapists and, as for me, I didn't see them often enough—a perfect marriage of contrasts. She wrote that the therapists might be having a bad effect:

> *Think there is no structure to counseling; it is not putting structure into my work life leading up to my stress – did I lose part of who I am I feel like I've gotten needier and even though show it more without moving forward.*

She always thought she was most focused when she got her divorce, concentrated on graduate school, worked at Biosearch, took the year off to see Asia, and during our initial year in the mountains of Virginia.

The song by Florence and the Machine, "Shake It Out," really describes where Margo and I were with this depression:

> I can never leave the past behind
> I can see no way. I can see no way.
> I'm always dragging that horse around.
> And our love is pastured such a mournful sound
> So I like to keep my issues strong.
> But it's always darkest before the dawn.

Yep, Margo was always dragging that old horse, depression, around.

Walking Through the Broken Beginnings

I suppose the real problems began not in Minnesota or Virginia but in the mountainous state of Colorado where we were headed to visit our daughter Karla (one of my children from my first marriage). Beyond what happened in Colorado were Margo's genetic ties to her mother.

While still in Minneapolis, Margo had gotten over Stage 1 breast cancer, which required trips for twenty-two straight days for radiology under a Mr. Coffee-looking machine—I even have a picture of a smiling Margo standing next to it—and a knee replacement and subsequent infection and cure. It was mere child's play given what we would be facing in the future. We had cast all the old stuff behind and we could both still walk pretty well. Though we had been totally enjoying our rugged surroundings in Virginia and I had gotten over my burns, it was time for a change of pace. Woods, mountains, hiking, and visiting—we were looking forward to it all. It was the first time we had flown to see Karla. From Denver, we were then going to drive on to Utah, through Monument Valley, and on to Arizona to visit two nephews who worked for the Forest Service fighting fires, designing parks, and building hiking trails. Our hope was to see lots of blue sky, a blazing orange sun, and serpentine hiking trails. And once we arrived in each new locale, we would start out our new day with a family tradition—a walk.

Margo was not a tennis star or a basketball heroine or Olympic pole vaulter, but this lady could walk and walk fast with her thirty-six-inch stride. During her Asian adventures she would go off on ten-mile walks just to get a feel for the land. Margo took walking seriously and even had a vanity license plate that read WALKMOR. She calculated that if a person went to the grocery store two hundred times a year and parked at the far end of the parking lot, at the end of that year they would have walked forty miles. Now that's a way to stay fit instead of trying to find a parking space at the very front, which is what most people do. When shopping centers are designed in the U.S. they are done with the thought no shopper is willing to walk more than five hundred feet without getting back into the car.

My courting of Margo was defined by the many fun if not exhausting walks we took. In New York City one evening we walked to Columbus Circle from Grand Central Station (stopping in many bars along the way) and back; in San Francisco we walked to and then across the

Golden Gate Bridge (beyond noisy) and back from the Embarcadero; in Chicago, up and down the entire "Gold Coast" along Michigan Avenue; in Indiana, through the Hoosier State Forest and back. Once, in St. Paul, Minnesota, we walked so far along the Mississippi River that when we got back we were so tired we lamented that we'd left the car at the far end of the parking lot. Of course, in Minneapolis we circumnavigated Lake Calhoun, Lake Harriet, and Lake of the Isles many times.

We did all this in spite of the fact that the definition of walking is pretty ungainly. Rebecca Solnit in her book *Wanderlust: A History of Walking* put it in practical terms. "Human walking is a unique activity during which the body, step by step, teeters on the edge of catastrophe. Man's bipedal mode of walking seems potentially catastrophic because only the rhythmic forward movement of first one leg and then the other keeps him from falling on his face." She also notes that "walking is an act of resistance to the other mainstream." Solnit writes that there are three prerequisites for taking a walk for pleasure: one must have free time, a place to go, and a body unhindered by illness, injury, or social restraints.

Geoff Nicholson, another British writer (are they the only ones who walk?) who broke his arm while walking, wrote in his book *The Lost Art of Walking*: "The older you get the bigger a deal it is to fall down. When you're age five you can hit the deck, skin your knees, bleed profusely and be up and playing again in five minutes. The older falling person is much more vulnerable. She's less supple, less accustomed to the experience. She feels more pain, embarrassment and humiliation."

Margo learned the hard way. The Rockies are rugged, with lots of dangerous trails. You have to be careful, and two days into the trip she tripped, fell all wrong, and broke her hip. The irony is that we were walking not in the mountains, but two blocks from where we were staying in the fancy, sedate Cherry Creek neighborhood where our daughter lived. Margo was totally focused on gazing at all the fancy renovated houses that morning and not on where she was walking. She tripped on the curb and fell onto the hard concrete. She landed right on her hip. She was in much pain and knew right away it was bad. My daughter and I tried to get Margo and her long legs into our car to take her back to the house. We didn't yet know how serious the fall was and got Margo half way into the car before we stopped—she was in torturous pain.

We then gave up trying to move her and called an ambulance. It came in a couple of exasperating minutes. Her face was ashen and contorted with pain. They comforted her with soothing words and then sedated her with two shots of morphine before they attempted to move her. Sirens blazing, we took her to Rose Medical Centre in town and found a surgeon to patch up her hip. This fellow was one of those dashing surgeons, full of himself, with boundless energy. He also tended to the Denver Nuggets basketball team and the Colorado Avalanche hockey team. The surgery was performed at the Rose Medical Center which is one of the newer hospitals in Denver. Margo ended up getting a semi-hip replacement, but the surgeon put the femur in at a slight angle which caused significant problems later on.

The surgeon's glorious bio says: "Actively involved in innovative medical research on sports-related injuries; results widely published in a variety of professional journals; lectures extensively, nationally and internationally on the subject." I think the lesson here is you might go for the guy who writes less and practices medicine more.

After the operation Margo wrote the doctor a nasty letter stating that his surgery had led to multiple complications. Below is that letter, sent on November 24, 2004. (You have to read between the lines to appreciate her anger.):

This is Margo Freivalds. I feel compelled to share events subsequent to the April 24 emergency semi-hip replacement you gave me. You might remember my case; I was in Denver on vacation from Lexington, Virginia. The surgery was the day after the Nuggets defeated my hometown team, the Timberwolves. At the time I expressed my concern regarding potential post-surgical infection based on my history. Unfortunately, my concern was valid. On May 28th I was hospitalized on an emergency basis for an infection in that hip. I had a white cell count of 35,000 upon aspiration of the synovial fluid and masses of pus were found in opening the incisions. The ball was replaced and I was sent home a week later on six weeks of Vancomycin.

The second fact you might recall is that the x-ray of my hip and then of my femur at my follow up visit with you on May 3rd revealed a shadow at the base of the prosthesis stem and that the stem came very close to the edge of the femur. I was warned, by my orthopedic surgeon at UVA, that in fact made the femur more vulnerable to breakage should I fall. Well on August 3 the worst fear materialized. I fell, the femur broke at the base of the prosthesis, and I had to be helicoptered to UVA 60 miles away.

I was released from the rehab facility at the end of August 6th after six weeks of IV antibiotics. I have completed that course with no complications and now have two-plus more months of non-weight bearing status on that left leg and a year or more on oral antibiotics.

Fortunately, I am otherwise healthy and have a great husband for emotional and physical support.

Sincerely yours,
Margo Freivalds

Translation: the prosthesis that you put in me was not sanitary and it was placed at a bad angle.

Margo was to recuperate in the hospital for a week. After spending one day with a fuss bucket woman who was always sorting her clothes, Margo demanded that she have a separate room. We decided I should still go on by myself and visit my nephews. I drove to see them and saw beautiful views and stars at night while Margo was looking up at the water-stained tiles in the hospital room.

This is what she wrote about Denver:

4/24/02
Fell in Denver 4/25. Emergency semi-hip replacement by Dr. Traina @ Rose Medical. 3 ½ days in hospital, Tues. – Sat. @Spalding Rehab. Did OK – moved along into therapy.

I had lain looking at similar tiles just the year before and with nothing else to do I counted about 4,000 perforations in each one of the ceiling tiles—just in case you ever wondered how many there were. Margo told me she did cry a fair bit while I was visiting my nephews.

When I got back she could leave the hospital, but needed to hang out for a few more days in Denver. There was a smoothie kiosk in the hospital parking lot and I brought her a couple several times a day. A bright and bushy-tailed friend from Margo's past came over, all chipper and healthy. She just came from playing tennis or some other like sport. We were both so jealous of her cheery good health. While Margo's fall was the first of many she would endure, she would outlive her friend by quite a few years, as her friend would be dead of a mysterious illness within the year. Life really has no permanence, no right or wrong. Death can creep up at any moment and we started thinking about that. I started thinking about how to be both a caregiver and a husband—a set of tasks that I quickly discovered was more demanding than I thought.

Returning home turned out to be a challenge. We had flown to Denver, first leaving Roanoke on a tiny regional plane and leaving our car there, and then flying to Charlotte, North Carolina, and then directly to Denver. The smaller regional jets fly out of Roanoke, but it's no big uncomfortable deal since you're flying to a larger airport with larger planes in less than an hour. There is no way we could do that on the return flight.

Margo's leg was in a stiff brace and couldn't bend. So I first inquired about an air ambulance. It was US$14,000 to go from Denver to Roanoke. I called a billionaire rich friend, the guy I would eventually do the book on, but he did not offer up his plane—"We're busy." Yeah, sure. We then called for first-class airfare from Denver to Charlotte on Continental and the reservation person apologized for the cost, US$2,000 each—"We'll take it." So that's how we got home. In Charlotte, we rented a car to drive to Roanoke (a scenic 200 miles) to pick up our car.

At home it was spring, with purple, yellow, and red flowers blooming everywhere and Margo itching to go outside and garden. But that was not to be. Her day consisted of reading and recuperating! The surgeon advised her not put weight on her left leg for six months—toe touching they called it. Walkers and wheelchairs will provide the mobility. So what was a typical "recovery day" like for Margo? She wrote this some two months after the fall in Denver. It breaks my heart to read this because she was making such progress. All this progress, though, would be put at risk in a couple of months. Could a, would a, should a. But these were glorious recovery days. To wit:

June 8-13, 2004

Nothing too remarkable. Was able to be up and about desk, out in garden and even painted for a couple of hours on Thursday for 2/3 of each day. Then slept two hours or so.

Emotional state shaky part of most days – yesterday (Sunday) was quiet listless even though I planted for four hours outside! Food is not very interesting to me – people are saying I have lost a significant amount of weight – but its only 10 pounds since the accident I had gotten to 170 prior to that. Friday I went to Staunton to Milmont Green House. Nice to get out but very exhausting.

Things really perked up after Margo started seeing Dr. Thomas E. Brown, a well-dressed, youngish orthopedist in Charlottesville. His offices are right next door to the Health South Rehab Center where I had recovered from my burns and where Margo would go after her next fall. But he sounded perfect with special expertise in adult reconstruction primary and revision hip anthroplasty, femur fracture repair et al.

June 16, 2004

Finally met Dr. Brown and Angie (his nurse). He has no plans for further surgery on my leg! And agrees that these infections are not the result of Bad Luck! My body definitely at risk for some reason. He has a definite presurgical antibiotic regimen + does research in area of infections.

Wow – I feel like I have been reborn ever since meeting with Dr. Brown. The relief from being told no more surgery has been terrific! We spent three hours @ Glen Maury Fiddler Fest (Fiddlers' Convention) – I walked for an hour around the campground listening to 'jam sessions.'

We would make an excited yearly pilgrimage to this fun event. Fiddle Fests abound in southwestern Virginia, but the one in nearby Buena Vista had a totally different tenor than anything to be found in over-educated Lexington. The town's sign reads: "Welcome to Buena Vista: 6002 citizens and three old grouches." It's home to Southern Virginia University (the Brigham Young of the East thus a Mormon school) and in a reversal of what most college bars do, some in Bewna stopped serving alcohol so as to attract Mormon students who do not drink.

Though Fiddle Fest was only one of many such festivals held annually in rural Virginia, it took place in mid-June when it was fairly warm, and Bluegrass fans from all over the country would show up to listen or to strut their sounds on various instruments, only some of which I recognized. To wit, I knew what a fiddle was (a violin that plays different tunes—that's it), but I didn't know there was blues fiddling, Cajun fiddling, world-beat fiddling, zydeco-style fiddling, folk dance fiddling. I also learned that all banjos are not created equal, as there were competitions for claw hammer banjos as well as a bluegrass banjo. And then we had the dulcimer (autoharp) and Dobro (steel guitar) and old-time and blue-grass mandolins. Pete Seeger's brother came and played the guitar and autoharp.

Besides the music, there were scrumptious foods: grilled hamburgers and hotdogs gooey with mustard, ketchup, and onions. Nothing could taste better and be messier—everyone who came to these had ketchup or mustard stains on their clothes. Margo and I would tap each other and point to each other's mouths to let us know to clean off the stains. Very few types from Lexington were present which seemed hundreds of cultural miles away.

Margo and I would say we were from Mt. Atlas which was the real name of our "neighborhood" even though we seemed to be the only people who lived there in amongst the trees. Margo was wall-to-wall smiling, being outside and listening to this gorgeous music and the sights and sounds of real people. Ralph Lauren need not apply.

Sunday I spent 3 hrs in am and 3 hrs in pm pulling weeds from screen porch steps! A bit stiff today, but happy I could move my butt along and accomplish as much! Today John and I walked the big circle trail. Another big event – and I drove to therapy.

I know if we were really true yuppies we would talk about our last trip to Paris, meeting with the Pope, and how much we like our new Bentley, but these were such glorious times after that horrific fall, and all the more poignant in retrospect, considering what was about to happen.

The entire time we lived in Virginia, our grandson Josh would make the trip from Minneapolis (1,200 miles away) to stay with us for at least a couple of weeks each summer. We saw no reason to cancel this summer's trip because of Margo's fall—we would make it work one way or another. Josh's mother and father were quite dysfunctional. How dysfunctional? My eldest daughter can have custody of Joshua as long as she lives with my first wife who in essence is raising Joshua. So Margo and I thought we could provide some normalcy (did I really say normalcy?) and fun during his visits.

Either his mother or a friend would fly Joshua down, and when he got older, he would fly as an unaccompanied minor. Inevitably when his stay was through, we would drive back, usually taking two and a half days and visiting lots of train museums along the way.

At Hickory Ridge there was always swimming in the pool, kayaking on the Maury River, bike riding, hanging out with some neighbor kids, playing baseball and shooting off my rifles, and just being in nature. Oh yeah, and visiting every electric train shop within fifty miles. Yep, we did all that.

Josh was now eight and into trains. The electric trains we set up together eventually turned the garage into a giant train table: five sets of trains actually running at the same time. The layout was based on a coal mining town Margo and I had visited south of Lexington—Pocahontas, population 441—which had been a center of coal mining a hundred years ago, and at that time was one of the richest towns in the U.S.

On the trip to Pocahontas, in July of 2006, we kept driving and ended up in another coal mining town—Hazard, Kentucky. We were just walking around when a middle-aged man in jeans and a white T-shirt approached us and asked: "Are you tourists?"

"Well yes," I responded. Margo and I smiled at each other with a look that asked, "What's this all about?...are we aliens from Mars, terrorists from Somalia?"

"We don't get many of you tourists around here. You have to go see the mayor," he almost commanded.

I never found out who this guy was, but off we went to city hall in Hazard, Kentucky. Why not? According to its website, "Hazard has a population of 5,000 and is located in the Appalachian coalfields of eastern Kentucky." At city hall I met P.T. Gorman, the town's short, stubby, and energetic mayor. (Margo was sore so she stayed in the car.)

The mayor was so thrilled by our presence that Margo was commissioned an honorary citizen of Hazard and given the title "Duchess of Hazard" and I became a "Duke of Hazard." We both got nice proclamations to put on the wall. A TV show called *Dukes of Hazard* had become very popular (now in syndication) and while filmed entirely in Hollywood, California, it represented the Hazard, Kentucky, we found ourselves in. The show dealt with two rough-and-tumble guys always getting in trouble with the bumbling sheriff.

We were even given a key to the city. When visitors to our house saw those proclamations on the wall, they were impressed. "What did you do to earn those?" we would be asked. Heck, we never got this treatment when went to New York!

So that was yet another reason why coal trains played such a prominent role in our train layouts. Well, Josh thought the layout was so neat that he suggested we put up billboards on nearby I-81 and have people come up and pay to see it.

But Josh was demanding, sometimes spoiled, and always a handful, so with Margo recovering from the Denver fall, we looked to take some day-trips to get away and to give her some needed peace and quiet. On that fateful day, we chose to go to the Cass Scenic Railroad about a hundred miles away in the most remote and unforgiving part of West Virginia. The brochure drooled of old-time trains: "The loud gruff of the stack, the clanking of gears and pistons, the furious steam of the whistle at the crossings and the ever present clickety clack of the rails will indeed make you feel as if you have been transported back in time."

Preparing for our departure frightened me, for now I had become the neurotic Mother Hen. This would be the first time since we returned from Denver that I would leave Margo alone. She kept reassuring me she would be safe. But over and over I told Margo: "Stay upstairs—DO NOT GO DOWNSTAIRS. You're getting well; don't risk anything."

We left early that morning for the two-hour drive and would be back in the late afternoon, but I kept worrying. It was like one of the admonitions you hear in a melodramatic horror movie: "Don't go downstairs!" Read, do art, watch mindless sitcom TV, sleep, enjoy solitude, internet your friends, just "Don't go downstairs!" I must have said it ten times until Margo felt I was harassing her. Being who she is, she didn't want a husband bossing her around, and even if I was also the caregiver, she still saw me occasionally as her overbearing husband who had to be defied every once in a while to keep her self respect. If a doctor has written out "Do not attempt stairs," she would have followed the dictate to the letter. But the message coming from me was sometimes optional.

The words she used on her "fall chart" tell it all:

- *I have to reach the phone*
- *Excruciating pain*
- *Land at bottom of stairs*
- *What do I do?*
- *At times I felt desperate – how anyone would find me*
- *Horrendous pain*

- *Scared*
- *Delirious I was sure I was going to be able to get up*
- *Realization I had done the big no-no*

Later Margo wrote this.

> *Suddenly I was unable to get up to walk away from the site of my fall. Falling was not a new experience for me as I have plenty of experiences tripping on my own feet or over some root, rock, etc. And I had always been able to get up, ground myself, and then take off. This time I couldn't even move. What a horrible feeling. I was devastated and in great pain.*
>
> *Life really turned nasty when I found myself at the bottom of the stairs on the floor. This time I was all alone – no Jani to comfort me and to get me help. The pain was horrendous; I couldn't move and I knew I had broken my femur.*

After all this I was really angry and full of guilt. I was angry at myself for going to the Cass Scenic Railroad, for if I'd stayed home this never would have happened. I was also angry at Margo for doing what I told her not to. After I cleared my pipes of frustration and anger, I then dug down and said, "Where do I (we) go from here?" Like Florence and the Machine say, "It's always darkest before the dawn." But the fall unleashed a chaos that Margo was never able to recover from.

After the fall, Margo was flown to UVA Medical Center by helicopter—the same one I was flown in earlier as a result of my burns. After her fall, she had to crawl some agonizing fifty feet before she could get to a phone to call 911. When they saw how bad the break was they knew she had to go to UVA and they called the helicopter.

It landed on the flat land surrounding the Virginia Horse Center which was halfway between Lexington and us. After this I thought of getting a wind sock to put on our property so helicopters could land near our house. It made for an interesting story, but we had accumulated too many by now—my burns and Margo's previous fall. We didn't need an encore.

During her stay at Health South Margo was in therapy from August 12 to August 31, 2004—nineteen days in the very hottest part of summer. Patients, including Margo, received lots of exercise as they make you immediately fend for yourself. For example, you have to reach for

239

your pills and water when the nurse brings it instead of having her put it in your hand and up to your lips—little stuff like that to get you back into gear.

I visited Margo every day she was in the facility, as she did while I was housed in the same facility convalescing from my burns. I would usually come in early afternoon.

John came at noon and stayed until 2:30 – that seemed to work best – better than late afternoon when I am tired. It was fun having him at therapy also. What a sweetie – then Sundays he would bring Emma and a picnic lunch – what a refreshing interlude.

I would tell the nurses to leave us alone and we would snuggle in bed and, yes, even managed a way to make love. On weekends, I would bring Emma and a picnic lunch and we would go to the far end of the parking lot and sit in the shade and talk about life's up and downs.

And, yes, we the sensuous couple would pet in the car.

"This is great therapy," Margo said to me.

"But not covered by our insurance," I responded.

We would both chuckle.

Tears would come to both our eyes when I had to leave and make that lonely sixty-mile drive home to a dark house. Goodness, I did that trip thirty-eight times (nineteen round trips – 2, 280 miles or thereabouts). I played mental tricks to make the ride go faster; I divided the trip into three parts. I always kept in mind Margo did the same for me when I was hospitalized. Again, too weird.

Reading through Margo's diaries I came across this passage. She wrote it when she got back from Charlottesville after visiting me in the same hospital. Her words reflect exactly how I felt in August 2004 as I drove home from the hospital. The parentheses are mine.

I feel overwhelmed with being responsible for John (Margo), *lines of communications, house, yards, pool, bills, Emma, cars, John's business* (Margo's enterprises). *I miss him* (her) *as part of my life badly and it takes so much energy to be with him* (her) *– to be positive; to listen and try to understand; to see him* (her) *so weak – even tho he* (she) *is doing so well! "*

So I did the only thing I could—I drank Myer's rum and diet Pepsi until I fell asleep.

Our medical drama was only just beginning! Many of the staff there remembered my name and asked: "Margo, are you related to John Freivalds?" I mean really, the same helicopter rescued us, and then we ended up in the same therapy hospital with the same staff taking care of us, and then later we ended up with the same surgeons and nurses. Too weird.

241

It was amazing how our medical paths intertwined into this symbiotic relationship. We were truly joined at Margo's bad hip. The year 2004 turned out to be a bummer as Margo had spent eight months of it in a wheelchair, crutches, and using a walker due to her falls.

In therapy Margo started to think about it all. Dr. Saleh was now her surgeon at UVA Charlottesville, sixty miles away. He had just come from Minneapolis and knew Margo's previous Minneapolis surgeons. Margo was now glued together with nuts, bolts, rods, screws, and whatever Dr. Saleh could find.

The biggest lesson from this is patience. I can't put any weight on my left leg for three months and that's just the way it has to be even if everyone around me can walk on two feet – I cannot... It continues to be very sobering that I am not going to be mobile for six months. It will be the middle of winter. But I so want to be able to garden, walk, hike and bike again. So I must find the strength to do what I need to do. And how can Jani really deal with this – to have his life also put on hold for so long! ...Am going to make up a card to keep in view those list activities that give me a life when the black hole appears.

- *Dixie Chicks or Pointer Sisters*
- *Draw or paint*
- *Solitaire*
- *Scrabble*

Before leaving the hospital, Margo had a final check-up. Her physician, Dr. Tranna, gave her some bad news—they had found some osteomyletis. Yuk. I looked it up in the *Mayo Family Health Book*: "Osteomyletis is a bone infection caused by bacteria. The infectious organism may be acquired by a wound, fracture or other injury and carried to the bone by the blood. It can lead to destruction of bone and surrounding tissue…in some instances surgery may be necessary to remove the infected tissue." Margo's admission and discharge diagnosis appears below:

In and Out of Therapy
(8/12/04 – 8/31/04)
Admission Diagnoses

1. Gait abnormality and impaired activities of daily living, status post open reduction/internal fixation and antibiotic spacers of

the left periprosthetic femur fracture.
2. Postoperative acute blood loss anemia.
3. Osteopenia.
4. Anxiety/depression.
5. Left hip pain, controlled.

DISCHARGE DIAGNOSES

1. Gait abnormality and impaired activities of daily living, status post open reduction/internal fixation and antibiotic spacers of the left periprosthetic femur fracture.
2. Postoperative acute blood loss anemia.
3. Wound hematoma.
4. Chronic osteomyelitis of the left hip.
5. Osteopenia.
6. Anxiety/depression.
7. Left hip pain, controlled.
8. Tinea crusis.
9. Calf pain, resolved.

HISTORY OF PRESENT ILLNESS

This patient is a fifty-nine-year-old who sustained a hip fracture in April 2004 and is status post a unipolar prosthesis for this. This was complicated by a joint space infection with Enterococcus faecalis, which grew from both the joint fluid culture and a deep wound culture. The patient received irrigation, debridement and 6 weeks of intravenous antibiotic for this. However, the original stem remained in place. Unfortunately, the patient fell down the stairs and sustained a left periprosthetic femur fracture on August 3rd. She was admitted to the University of Virginia, and is now status post ORIF and placement of antibiotic spacers.

We got everything squared away—enough said—and headed home. Then came the procedure which really tested our resolve. Margo was to take an antibiotic called Vancomycin (affectionately called Vanco) at home.

Vanco is a glycopeptides antibiotic used in the prophylaxis and treatment of infections caused by Gram positive bacteria. Translation: if Vanco can't kill it, nothing can. Margo had such a bad time with infections they needed an antibiotic on steroids to make sure it killed all the life-threatening bacteria that would not let wounds heal. This would be an ongoing problem for Margo. The cause of this condition is unclear but its effects ever so apparent. In any event we became amateur pharmacologists and came to know more about drugs than most people. Margo started keeping a detailed medical diary because this was spinning out of control. The onslaught of pills would eventually claim me as a victim as well.

Here's the Vanco schedule: 6 a.m., 9 a.m., 12 noon, 6 p.m., 9 p.m. and midnight. And to do this for six weeks. We calculated that in these six weeks (42 days) Margo spent 10½ whole days doing nothing but taking antibiotics; it took a long time for the drip to run out, set up the next IVs, and make sure that they were always flowing properly. The Vanco came in a big bowl thing that we kept in the fridge and then had to hook it up to a pic line in Margo's arm. We waited until it was done and then disconnected it before putting in another on. It was mutual misery and neither one of us slept well. but Margo's pain pills did give her a pain-free buzz.

Fuck, shit, damn!

So how could just doing a home IV take so long? Were Margo and I just spastic wimps? Here are the instructions Margo wrote down to explain the procedure for dispensing the drug. I think we earned nursing degrees to go with the pharmacologist degrees we had already earned.

Antibiotic instructions
1. Flush pipe line with saline (5cc)
2. Take cap off saline
3. Take cap off needle
4. Insert needle into needleless syringe, inject saline into tube
5. Swipe oil /port white with alcohol
6. Hook saline syringe onto port and push 5 cc; in-save syringe for post dosing

Drug mixing
1. Fold bag in half to burst membrane between fluid and powder
2. Milk bag so that fluid is going down into powder container
3. Keep milking and shaking until all powder has been dissolved
4. Make sure tubing is not empty (if it is, run fluid into line – to remove air bubble

5. Close clamp
6. Insert tubing into bag
7. Wipe port with alcohol
8. Hook IV tubing into white port
9. Open line
10. Count drips (15 min) – is rate wanted
11. Close clamp on tubing
12. Really flush with heparin
13. Unhook flush with saline
14. Close port tubing

Be very cautious in *all* movements – use walker to get into bathroom

Margo was walking but couldn't put weight on her bad leg, and we started using the extra-sized wheelchair a lot. And through it all we still found ways to snuggle and make love. Margo mused:

The IVs are a pain in the butt, brace is not so bad. I'm up for about 1/3 of the day. I hop around the staircase at least twice a day and then do the exercise. I get to bathroom via walker and also kitchen and then sit in wheelchair.

After my burn incident, I started to write and give talks on avoiding burns and bad incidents. It was my stupidity, ego, and inattention that made the "accident" possible. After the burns, I went into rehab at Health South in Charlottesville and in my "class" of twenty trauma patients was an industrial safety engineer.

"The choices we make are the chances we take." Those are the words he said and they will resonate in my brain for the rest of my life: "The choices we make are the chances we take." I will never forget them.

Never.

He said you have to look at everything as a risk, figure out the upside and downside of doing something, and then do it. But most people don't think like that. Americans are doers—they just go out and do it. I didn't evaluate any risk before I blew myself up. The NIKE motto "Just do it" isn't helpful. It should be, "Think about doing it, and then do it." Unfortunately, there is even a website (www.break.com) which glorifies mindless recklessness. Here are the grim statistics: every sixteen minutes in the U.S. there is a fatal home accident and every four seconds a disabling injury. In total, eight million disabling accidents occur in the U.S. every year.

One day my daughter Karla, now the energetic TV producer, called to say she was going to do a shoot in Louisville, Kentucky (400 miles away), and would we like to come and watch. We said, "Sure we'll go." So we packed up the wheelchair and the Vanco in an ice chest and drove to Louisville to meet her. We got there, ate lunch the next day with Karla, and then, with Margo in a wheelchair, went for a "stroll" along the Ohio River. We stopped by a tree to ponder and hung Margo's IV from a branch. We laughed and cried at the same time. Life had now become a process by which we learned to continually adapt. The free and easy days of just getting up and going somewhere were a distant memory. We now had to plan things out.

One day, now driving, she mused:

> As I drove yesterday I remembered how I used to act when a single man was in my presence – always trying to flirt – and then trying to find ways to see this man – run into him and fantasizing about a relationship with him. Since I have been with John I have hidden that part of me – I keep saying I can /could live on my own again and be perfectly happy yet that may not be so true after all. Yes I liked the idea of doing what and when I liked but having a real partner is what I wanted all my life.
>
> Now – I have had that for 12 years. How fortunate I really am to have found John. We do have a partnership with very similar goals.
>
> How would I have coped with my medical surgical problems without him? His help has been in all forms psychological, physical, etc. We're both ready to enjoy some average time – all year and longer. That puts some pressure on me not to fall or do anything to harm myself physically. Also it means that I seriously have to exercise and increase my strength and flexibility.

But more challenges were to come, and come, and come. It took four months to get over the hip fall in Denver and the subsequent infection. Margo was occasionally tutoring and was figuring out how to get around. We even went shopping for antiques and again used our adaptive behavior to its utmost. We went to an Asian antique shop in the funky part of Charlottesville and asked at the store if they had other pieces we could look at. We wanted a chest for our living room. "Yep," the knowledgeable and very well dressed owner said, "but we have to go to the warehouse." After a short drive to an old and musty building perched on a hill, we went inside, looked around and the owner said "Let's go upstairs."

"Margo can't do stairs," I said.

At that moment, we both saw a big black conveyor belt, slightly worn along the edges, that went to the second floor. We looked at each other and came to the same conclusion: she would sit on the conveyor belt (maybe at a thirty-degree angle) which would take her upstairs. We tried it and it worked. We went up and found a nice antique Chinese chest which now sits in my living room. I wish Margo were here to enjoy it with me and the endless retelling of how we got it.

Rather than sit and mope—"woe is us"—we started to do things.

Margo wanted to travel to Baltimore so we went to visit our friends Art and Narelle Krieger. He is one of that subculture that manages hotels on five-year contracts. I met him when he undertook the management of the Radisson Daugava in Latvia where 3,000 people applied for 300 jobs. In Baltimore he never knew if anyone would show up for work. He then went on to manage hotels in St. Paul, Baltimore, and several in China.

We drove to Baltimore from Virginia and Margo stayed with them as I drove off to see clients. Narelle later wrote this about Margo's visit.

"Margo arrived in Baltimore on two crutches. I think at that time she had gone through the rigors of breast cancer, knee surgery, hip surgery and was on her second bout of knee surgery as one of her knees has become infected and the whole operation had to be redone as well as clearing the infection. I was alarmed at Margo's appearance as she looked tired and drained. I welcomed her with open arms and ushered her into our bird nest of an apartment high over the roof tops of downtown Baltimore. I made her some chamomile tea and suggested she lay down for a few hours and she willingly agreed. So unlike the Margo I remembered.

After a long nap Margo emerged from the bedroom flushed and rosy cheeked from her long nap. Night had descended and I offered her a glass of wine before dinner. We sat together sipping the wine and caught up on all our news and planned our next day together. To my surprise Margo wanted to go to a certain shopping center. I explained that I did not have an American driver's license and was also terrified of driving in Baltimore. At the time, I was suffering anxiety brought on

247

through a low thyroid function. Not to mention my ignorance of the city. No problem says Margo. I will drive! I was concerned because she was on crutches and she assured me that she was capable of driving our big old barn of a Cadillac car as she called it. Her assurance did little to relieve my anxiety.

The next morning Margo looked refreshed, she hobbled to the car, opened the back door of the car, threw her crutches onto the back seat, clambered into the front driver's seat, threw the car in gear and we were away. We discovered once we got going that we did not have a map in the car or a GPS. My anxiety was at an all time high and we got hopelessly lost and we drove for hours, Thelma and Louise style, laughing, chatting and swapping stories as we passed country side that I had never seen previously.

We finally lunched at a little wharf-side cafe somewhere on the outskirts of Baltimore mid-afternoon. After lunch we bought ice cream cones and sat on the wharf in the sunshine dangling our feet in the water like two little girls. As the sun began its descent, Margo struggled to her feet, grappling with her blessed crutches and stated that we had to find our way back home. After many wrong turns, asking of directions and laughter, we eventually got back to the hotel. Upon arrival Margo put the car in park and said, "I am glad that is over!" and laughed again. Me too! I exclaimed and felt relief at being stationary. I was pleased we never made it to a shopping mall. I discovered more about my friend, her courage, her wit, her sense of the ridiculous and most of all her humor."

One day it occurred to me that as our train layout in the garage had gotten bigger, the space available for Margo's art had gotten smaller and smaller—in fact, maybe down to ten square feet. I said to Margo, "Let's build you a real studio." Boy, did that make her happy – and focused.

On our many trips back and forth to Charlottesville we remembered going by a number of places that sold ready-to-use cabins, roughly twelve by twenty feet in size. We went to a strip part of Highway 11 which runs along I-81 and bought a cabin with picture windows all round.

We then hired a tradesman to put in a level gravel pad to set the cabin on. When the cabin was finally delivered, it was carried on the back of this neat truck. It all worked on the basis of hydraulics, and the crane the truck had attached to it was able to put the cabin down to within a half inch of where we wanted it.

Once the cabin was in place, there was lots of do: wire the cabin, build an old-style southern porch on which to drink good scotch and watch sunsets, buy a gas fireplace, put down a floor, get furniture, and put in insulation. We both felt alive. When the work was complete, we had a wonderful dedication party and Margo started to use the studio to draw. It also served as a wonderful place for her to spend some desperately needed time alone. We even put in a fire pit so she could look at a glowing fire at night when by herself.

Then Margo wrote me a poem alluding to a song we'd planned to include in our wedding ceremony—"If I Were a Carpenter." (It was never played at the wedding, but that's another story.) In any event, Margo wrote me this poem and gave me a sculpture of a hammer as we were building her studio.

Remember our wedding
When the song to be sung was
About a hammer
We never heard it
Yet you are my carpenter
Building our life together
On this mountaintop we love and celebrate our life
My soul mate, my playmate
And now with a hammer
In hand, we build together
A studio with a view
Which I do cherish
So to honor you and your
Skills, I give you this
Sculpture to hang
Upon your wall in celebration
Of our thirteen years
And to remind you
That I love my carpenter
My man with a hammer
Together with our
Skills we have built a life of

Joy, friends, family, dogs
And though I am a sleepy moody wife, I am
A very happy mookster
With Love, the M

Long ago we realized that we had to keep moving, moving, moving to keep happy and not sit and lament with endless "could a, would a, should a." One day I saw Margo reading a newsletter from Cheap Joe's, an art supply store in Boone, North Carolina. Margo could paint but wanted to paint more, and now with the studio she was ready to go.

She had been taking art classes at a place called Beverly Studios in nearby Staunton, Virginia, thirty miles away, but to do that she would have to climb this long flight of steep stairs. Even going up on her butt backwards would be hard. We now had to think of how we would get into buildings and would have to call ahead and ask: Is there a ramp, elevator, handicapped bathrooms? A whole new world faced us, the world of the handicapped.

When Beverly Studios turned out to be physically inhospitable to Margo, it was time for Plan B. I said let's take a week-long class at Cheap Joe's. She couldn't believe I'd said that. I would take her to class and then I would read, write, or whatever, and be the ever-vigilant Mother for the rest of the day. As Cheap Joe Miller advertised: "Cheap Joe's Art Workshops: The most fun you'll ever have working." The workshops had names like "Watercolor: Simple Fast and Focused," "Controlling Moisture and Color," and not to be forgotten, "Adventures in Acrylic and Negative Painting." It was 227 beautiful mountain driving miles away in Boone, North Carolina, so not a long drive at all.

10/19/04

Arrived on Sunday afternoon. Enjoyed the ride through SW Virginia and North Carolina Mountains. Many Christmas trees being grown all around...The Cheap Joe's workshop conducted by Taylor Kim is great! The first day was fun but I didn't get very far...but the second day was great. I let go to do two paintings of flowers. Then I did an abstract of a wild flower working on brush strokes and colors. The 1ˢᵗ flower was loved by all and really is dynamite. I was quite mesmerized by it when looking at it from a distance. The class is full of fun enjoyable people. All are doing well – most have been painting

250

for a while. Joe, owner of Cheap Joe's, is delightful as is entire staff – it was a good decision to come for this. It's inspirational. ...Jani and I are doing well overall – just a few bumps. I'm going to class in wheelchair and wearing a brace all day. Painting takes my mind away from the brace.

She had this quote hanging over her desk which was her "painting philosophy" and was written by an artist named Joyce Hifler.

"Painting a picture is the same as living a life. Some of us only get the outline sketched while others find the time and desire to mix beautiful colors and brush them on canvas. Color is used sparingly on some canvases, others are somber and dark with little or no highlights. But those who use cheerful colors, cardinal reds, sunflower yellows, and all shades of purple and lilac, show us that life does not have to be ordinary... We have been given the general sketch but it is left to us to fill in the colors, harmonizing and blending until we get the right tones. Each of us is a painter and each has the charge to make life a work of art."

On the last day of class the irony of irony happened. Margo did not get hurt but one of the students did and ended up in the hospital. There is little flat land around the Cheap Joe's building. It sits up on a ridge with steep drop-offs on both sides of the building.

On the last day the students wanted to take pictures of each other. One guy had everyone lined up and he kept backing up to get a better picture. Then he realized—too late, of course—that there was no ridge left to stand on and he stumbled backwards into the rocky gully behind him. An ambulance was called to take him to the hospital. My friend's admonition once again resonated in my head: "The choices you make are the chances you take."

It's darkest before the dawn. I never would have thought that after Margo's last fall we again could be celebrating life.

12/1/04

The last month of 2004! Won't be too sad to leave this year behind. Certainly, there have been positive gains during the year.

My painting has taken off and I've done three paintings I am particularly proud of: the Wyoming open prairie, the big flower and the foothills with purple flowers in the foreground. And again I am not embarrassed but grateful for the opportunity. More swimmers this year; seedlings planted; maintenance of gardens, swimming for me, etc. This AM our lovemaking was hot!

Once the studio was in place and the excellent course at Cheap Joe's completed, she was off to the races.

Something else that greatly influenced her artistic sensibility occurred when we travelled to New Orleans. I had to give a speech in the Big Easy and insisted Margo come with me. After I gave a boring speech about the perils of biotechnology, Margo and I met a Latvian friend of mine (probably the only Latvian in New Orleans) who also happened to be the founder and director of the New Orleans Institute of Art. He has the impossible name of Auskelis Ozols. It probably helped to have an exotic name in the staid fine-culture-starved environment of New Orleans. His name meant "neck tie oak" in Latvian (if that makes any sense), but at the art institute he taught classes and had firm opinions about art. Margo listened more than attentively while he talked one evening as we roamed the Garden District. I was a mere tourist while Margo was beginning to immerse herself in the art scene.

He gave Margo two fun little books to read by the noted writer Tom Wolfe—*From Bauhaus to Our House* and *The Painted Word*—both critical of the current art scene. In writing this book I thumbed through them and came across these words which Margo had underlined:

From *From Bauhaus to our House*: "Every child goes to school in a building that looks like a duplicating parts wholesale distribution warehouse. Not even the school commissioners who approved the plans can figure out how it happened.

From *The Painted Word*: "A painting should compel the viewer to see it for what it is; ascertain arrangement of colors and form on canvas."

Little did Margo know when see got these two books that she would be moving shortly to Lexington, Virginia, where Tom Wolfe got his BA degree from Washington & Lee University. Life indeed is a tight circle.

But back to the narrative.

To get our heads and hearts in order, we went to see every sort of doctor and surgeon. Margo kept going to her shrink to help her process all that was happening. We regularly worked out at Augusta Medical Center (AMC) and she worked in her studio. But pain would appear as would weariness about her body and yes, me, I was overbearing yet I was over afraid. *"Annus Horribilis,"* that was how Queen Elizabeth II described 1992, a particularly horrible year for the royal family. Well 2004 was our "*Annus Horribilis Maximus*" with two nasty falls, breaks, pain, and anxiety—2005 was to be better. Early that year Margo took off on her own for three days at Twin Falls Park in West Virginia. The state is unique in that it maintains beautiful, state-run parks and resorts. Margo went there to relax, paint, and get away from me. I drove her and picked her up. This is what she wrote about her stay at Twin Falls.

> *3/30/05*
> *Glorious morning and end of three great days at Twin Falls resort. It's warm and sunny this a.m. I walked for 35 minutes yesterday around the campgrounds and did my exercises, then I sketched and painted yesterday which I thoroughly enjoyed.*
> *Last year is over. I'm on the road again – strengthening… I'm very happy to be doing what I am doing, considering I was hospitalized with an infection in my hip a year ago next week. Whenever I think about what I really experienced this past year, I'm blown away! Pretty traumatic.*

A new factor entered our life this year—one Kayla Finlay who we mentioned earlier.

Margo needed someone to spill her guts to and I was not attuned to that, nor were many of her friends. Frankly, I was a pain in the butt to Margo, constantly fearful of another fall, and still in guilt about the last one. And being an injured duck in a pond of healthy ducks didn't work as many of the "friends" Margo thought she had made in Virginia just didn't come around, call, or invite her.

> *I'd love to have someone other than John hold me and let me sob for an hour or whatever it would take to get all of those pent up feelings out. It wouldn't be a feel sorry for myself acknowledgement of the shit I've been through. When John brings up I put on my 'oh it's not so bad' face and attitude not allowing myself to feel the fear, anxiety, and hurt I have had. I distance myself from it to cope.*

Kayla turned out to be that person.

Margo knew something about faith healing and spirituality. Some years ago when we lived in Minneapolis, she visited a friend by herself out west. Her friend turned out to be in my class at Georgetown when I went there, but had gone off to study nursing and then healing. She now lives in San Diego and has given herself the following title on LinkedIn:

Dr. Liana Carbon, Shamanic and Energy Medicine Healer, Author, Spiritual Director. She is a certified master Practitioner in Energy Medicine and Luminous Healing through the Four Winds Society, A Visionary Healer, Shamanic Coach, Author, Teacher and Spiritual Director. She is an Ordained Minister and Earth Steward, a founding member of the Society of Shamanic Practitioners, a member of the World Association of Holistic Shamans and a member of the Royal College of Alternative Medicine.

And all this to go along with a PhD from the University of Kansas, a MA from the University of Louisville, and a BS from Georgetown. Liana came to visit Margo before she met Kayla and after Margo had gone to visit "Hogan" in New Mexico. Consequently, Margo was well versed in alternative medicine. Me? I just take ibuprofen from Walgreen's when I get a headache.

So she would go have a "healin." First, Kayla would place her hands by Margo's ears and then concentric and release energy. Whatever it was, it soothed Margo, who was having continual hip and knee problems—pain and lack of energy.

About the healing I could feel the energy moving around my body as she moved her hands. I felt very relaxed and a little bit light headed still now at 9 AM so something happened. I felt like maybe I walked better.

Kayla's healing business was not as formal then as it is now. This is what she wrote on her web page (www.kylafinlay.com):

"She is simply a woman friend and compassionate human being who is gifted with the ability to tap into the Divine source of all healing and channels it with the Divine Intelligence that resides within each and every one of us in order to initiate optimal health and vibrant living."

Her big things are the private sessions that Margo and she had at the studio. These are settings where people who have been told by the western medical world that there is NO hope or cure for their disease can come with an open mind/soul to discover and access the amazing ability of the body to heal. There is always HOPE!

Strange, isn't it, that self doubt or "woe is me" didn't enter into our

254

lives when we were constantly battling this or that medical issue, but now that we had a welcome break and started to feel a little at ease, Kayla continued to come up the mountain to 'heal.'

France in Our Future

Through all this I wanted to stay relevant and I was more than aware it was Margo's resources that were keeping us financially afloat. I needed to do something with my mind. We were constantly picking and bickering at each other, me more than Margo. The flow of visitors from out of town and out of the country had slowed to a trickle as we were uncertain about our physical and emotional shape from day-to-day.

Thus I sent out letters, edited by Margo, offering to do marketing communications (fancy words for public relations) for firms. I usually would have an intern or two on the mountain to help me. In response to our many mailings, I got two responses—one from a newsletter publisher in DC and another from a language-service provider in France that wanted to increase its U.S. business.

Well, wouldn't you know it, a firm in France responded and said they wanted to meet with me. I remember going out to our porch and telling Margo I just spoke with a guy in France who wants to do business with me. He's paying for my flight to France. I asked her if she would like to go too. So less than a year after her first fall in Denver and six months after her second, we are off to France. Margo was in heaven.

The firm was WH&P and run by a tall, charming, handsome, quadrilingual guy (German, French, English, and Italian) by the name of Gunther Höser, probably in his mid-forties. *"I could go for him,"* Margo confided to me afterwards. His firm was the largest translation firm in France and he wanted more exposure in the U.S. market. He was located in Sophia Antiopolis Technology Park which is the Silicon Valley of France.

Much of the park falls within the commune of Valbonne. The concept behind the park was to bring people together from different intellectual horizons and have them meet, which would bring added value and generate innovation. We both eagerly boned up on where we were going and thought how neat it was that a French firm in the middle of that intellectual environment would call us here all alone on top of a mountain and invite us to visit and give them ideas.

Not far from the French Alps (you could see their snow-covered peaks in the distance) was the Cote d'Azur. Margo just about flipped out for painters such as Matisse, Picasso, Chagall, and Monet who all came to the French Rivera to paint. She decided just to come and observe, not paint.

This was an opportunity I couldn't pass up. I have been managing well walking a fair bit and then sleeping a fair bit. There's no way I could go at this like I did in Riga five years before and I'm certainly not ready for mountain hikes. I'm very happy to be doing what I am considering I was hospitalized with an infection in my hip one year ago next week. Whenever I think about what I really experienced this past year, I'm blown away.

Our flights here to Nice were uneventful. Turned out to be a blessing to request wheelchair. An attendant and a chair met us at each flight (Roanoke-Cincinnati, Cincinnati-Paris, and Paris-Nice) and whisked us on to the next. In Paris we bypassed customs and lines and didn't have to figure out Charles DeGaulle Airport which seemed like a giant maze.

5/23/05

We're on our way home after one, if not the best, vacations in our married life. Getting out of Lexington was the biggest problem – I finally told John if we had anymore stupid arguments / picking at each other I would turn around and come home.

We were to stay at an 18th century restored provincial house with 16 rooms. The brochure said this: Five minutes from the international technology park of Sophia Antiopolis the Hotel les Armoires is ideally located in the medieval village of Valbonne with over 20 restaurants nearby. Surrounded by more than 15 golf course and 15 minutes from Cannes and 20 minutes from Nice International Airport Cote d Azur.

Sunday when we arrived the staff at Hotel les Armoires fixed us up with Heinekens, toast, cheese and fruit cocktail when we couldn't find anything to eat in town. We ate up in the breakfast room on the top floor with the lifted ceiling. Valbonne is a wonderful charming village so happy we stayed here rather than in Nice or Cannes.

Most evenings we had a couple of beers or wine on the village square with everyone – lots of young children playing while parents socialized – very charming. I walked around village a lot each a.m. and the two of us would do same in evening.

Mon. I had lunch in restaurant next door – entrecote w béarnaise sauce and wonderful au gratin potatoes (lots of garlic) oh and they served tapenade and French bread as appetizer!

Then we went up to fresh produce shop at the upper parking lot and we got Jani a sizeable piece of quiche (I was still full from lunch) – Beautiful fruit! Ripe pears had red fingernail polish on stem! Strawberries smelled scrumptious. I took long afternoon nap Mon. – Wed., but also slept marvelously at night.

Wed. we took bus to Cannes where we spent a couple of hours watching folks at film festival. Would have been fun to go at night to see costumes – but just not our style.

I went to office for afternoon. I sat in square and sketched a little. Each p.m. we drank our 12-year-old Dewer's – very rich and smooth.

Found we couldn't get just ice cream at a place that is open for meals <u>only</u> – had to go to "bar" where meals, snacks and beverages are sold all day.

Stores close from noon to 2:30 or 3 and then again at 7/7:30.

Thurs. a wonderful drive, lunch and visit with Günter and Colette. They live out and up further from Valbonne in village of Tourette de Loup – their home has much in common with ours.

Fri. J and I drove up to Gorges du Loup. Saw snow capped Alps, marvelous wild flowers, fresh mountain air – beautiful day! Just fun to be out – and alive.

I had Denny, the hotel manager, make us dinner reservations at Cour La Soleil as I really wanted a nice dinner and knew J would suggest bread and cheese (I wanted a <u>real</u> meal). Turned out he actually enjoyed it – the ambiance of eating wonderful food outside on narrow walk – back off a square. Spectacular love making.

Had fun time buying tablecloth and Provincial bowls from Marie – Kiwi married to Frenchman with two young daughters. She's a cutey! Also bought wooden and metal rooster and a fun shawl for me.

Oh yes – Fri. was market day. They started setting up at 6 a.m. – so NOISY but fun to participate in.

Sat. train to Paris on TGV (high-speed train) – We got to Nice RR station with no problem and an hour to spare. TGV train was very comfortable and <u>smooth</u>. We enjoyed French countryside – surprised to have mountains nearby for half of trip. Hotel Concorde St.

Lazare, a five star with a gorgeous lobby and a view of the Eiffel Tower from our room. It was beautiful! Our ambling on Sat. p.m. with Barb Boldt was frustrating but OK. She seems to be in her element. John left us about 4 p.m. She and I finally got to Champs Elysee – taking multiple rests along the way and stopping for tea and a custard.

Sun. a.m. John and I took cab to Notre Dame and walked around for four hours! I was EXHAUSTED by the time we got a cab back to hotel! However, our wandering was perfect – best was coffee and crepe suzette at "5 Corners" on left bank. People watching at its best! Very energizing. Then a tour of Paris at night to see Paris with all its lights. Perfect ending to a perfect trip.

Oh – and the very best part is that J loves his new client WH&P & Günter is <u>fun</u> to work with! What more could one ask for?

We did exactly as we had planned on this trip – and I feel very good with all of our (my) decisions – walking in museums had no appeal to me due to legs – I wanted to 'experience' France and that's what we did! I am so HAPPY!

And just like Margo did on her Asia trip, she wrote down what we bought and who we bought it for.

French Purchases
- *Tablecloth*
- *Six bowls*
- *Vase for us*
- *Vase for Jean & P*
- *Cricket vase for porch*
- *Rooster*
- *Two T-shirts – Gourdon*
- *Two books*
- *Globe – Maija*
- *Candy*
- *Scarf*
- *Plant pot*
- *Three posters*

Did we really bring all that stuff back? We sure did! I must share a funny story that goes with one of the three posters I bought on the Left Bank. The Left Bank of the River Seine in Paris is an intellectual buffet. Mimes are there advertising who knows what, used bookstores, kiosks abound, and then you have people selling unique and culturally diverse posters. I have brought many of them back to the U.S. with me over the years (you can order some by going to www.jfamarkets.com).

I learned that the three most popular posters were Joe Camel (a camel smoking cigarettes), Che Guevara in tie die and one of Vladimir Lenin. For those of you who are history-challenged, Vladimir Lenin was a Russian revolutionary who brought communism to Russia, which became the Soviet Union and now is Russia again. In any event, his image is well known in Europe and is on that poster I saw on the Left Bank. The pictured is decked with his white image, bald head and a copy of the communist newspaper *Pravda* (truth in Russian), being held firmly in his right hand. The background is scarlet red. That would be interesting enough, but in the upper left hand corner we have a perfectly proportioned and correctly colored McDonald's arches with the word under it that reads: McShit. My take away from that poster was that both communism and capitalism stink.

In any event, I bought the poster and made copies of it when we got back. I sent one to my investment banker friend Paul Rogers in Concord, Massachusetts, birthplace of the American Revolution.

He loved the poster and showed it to his fifteen-year-old daughter. He asked her:

"Do you know who this is?"

"No," she answers.

"Lenin," he responded.

"John?" she came back.

So there you go: How quickly people disappear into history. Thus one reason I wrote this memoir is so that Margo would be more than some lonely, forgotten tombstone.

Back to the Mountain

After we got back from France, I had to slow Margo down before she overdid it. We did a lot of bickering during this time—I was anxious to get more professional work and Margo was just trying to keep her head above water.

259

John called to my attention the fact I was always on the go when I was home. I had no energy for him much less myself. I quickly realized he was correct. I hated to stop my free clinic efforts (getting 300-pound women to lose weight) and the Goddess worship in Lynchburg.

Margo took up Sudoku and went into it big time, which calmed her considerably. Then it all came together one June day:

Another roller coaster period with today being at the very top. The best lovemaking in months. Jani was cute, gentle, handsome, calm. Nice – I was able to focus and even now I feel a bit of trembling and excitement.

Although the trip was fine, we came back to the same medical problems we had before. Pain in the hip and the left knee was going bad. Margo went to see one doctor about the hip and all we got was, "Give it time." Plus she was really starting to miss her family more and more.

Early in 2006, a couple of months after our trip to France, Margo said, *"I want to go to Guatemala."* Immediately, I voted, "No," but her niece, Annie, and husband were there doing volunteer work and she wanted to see them there. I voted against it because every day was a crapshoot with Margo. Would she or wouldn't she be in horrific pain? She was bored with my family as they made her feel she was *"just an appendage that wrote checks."*

Although still walking with a cane, Margo set off by herself to Guatemala, Central America. I was scared shitless, but Margo was not going to be stopped. I offered to go with her but she flatly said, "No." This was a trip she wanted to make by herself.

This should have been a warning sign: whenever Margo was starting to feel strong, she felt she had to be on the move. She wanted to do this by herself and the trip was in the offing to go to Antigua, Guatemala, where her niece and husband were living. Antigua is a city of 60,000 set off in the central highlands of Guatemala. It's surrounded by three volcanoes, full of baroque Spanish architecture, known for its elaborate religious celebrations, and full of gringos from the United States looking for culture. With a great deal of apprehension, I took her to the airport in Roanoke and saw her off.

This is what she penned, starting in September 20, 2006:

Guatemala

Well, I made it with mixed feelings – every day the same wave – happiness to desperation tears – one minute I might have relief from pain and mere movement is painful – plus it makes me tire easily.

I can't say that I find Guatemala particularly exciting or wonderful. The plusses are friendly people and colorful native clothing that we saw outside Antigua; lush greenery and mountain sides; colorful fronts of many buildings. But Antigua feels so far like a city with its life behind walls or big wooden doors. That seems bizarre and unwelcoming to me.

So here are my observations:
- *Open sewers huge potholes*
- *Cobblestone streets*
- *Slanted walks*
- *Cracked walls*
- *Reds, yellows, blues, greens*
- *Patterns next to patterns* (ed. note – someone's been taking art classes!)
- *Gringos everywhere*
- *Where is the real Guatemala?*

Sadness that I can't move as once I did. Disappointed over difficulty of moving to see and enjoy. Pain in shopping decreases interest more. Feeling shy and unstimulated. How disappointing it is. Yet there are joys of connecting with Annie and Jeff. How gentle and supportive can two people be and that was my major goal. Perhaps I'll be able to establish a common Antigua /Lexington coffee connection to help coffee farmers of Antigua. That would be a reward.

Last day in Guatemala. Travel day home. Sad to leave. A clear sunny day but couldn't see volcanoes. Once on plane (upgraded to first class) I felt so tired like I hadn't slept last night. So I took a marvelous nap after lunch (tasteless chix in tomato sauce over rainbow pasta – bread and butter and apple caramel cheesecake was wonderful).

Margo, forever the nutritionist!

Upon returning to Hickory Ridge from Guatemala, her knee was just about shot and her hip was acting up. The pain was great, the depression was building and living together became a challenge for both of us. Every day was a rollercoaster of emotion for both Margo and I. I was on the edge; she was in pain. I wake early; she wakes up late. Something

261

was wrong: but what?

We decided to go see Dr. Tom Nelson who did Margo's first knee surgery in Minneapolis. During our consultation, he recommended Margo have a total hip replacement as well as a total knee replacement at the same time.

After all her health issues and chronic pain, Margo had reached a point in her life when she could finally ask for help:

> *I always thought I should figure everything out on my own and if I were to ask for help that would be a sign of incompetence – somehow I missed out on the lesson to ask for help. Now Jani has been trying to drill that idea in my head for 10 years. Actually I needed to work for someone like John on my first job or somewhere along the line.*

The best year in our married lives was probably 2006. We had overcome serious burns, falls, hospitalizations, and we enjoyed ourselves on top of the mountain. Our Christmas letter that year expresses that joy.

Holiday Greetings to all our friends and family this December of 2006 from John and Margo Freivalds. Our year was blessed with many highlights, including

The best Jana Diena (Latvian Summer Solstice Celebration) ever with a bonfire to beat all bonfires and a thunderstorm which quickly dissipated bringing a perfect coolish summer evening for our 70 guests (including 10 Latvians from Latvia & one U.S. Congressman) to enjoy.

Spectacular driving trip through New England at the peak of leaf color.

John went to Latvia to claim ownership of land he inherited from his mother in Jurmala, Latvia's well-known seaside resort town, and to visit Latvian friends.

In September Margo had a wonderful visit with her niece Annie and husband Jeff in Antigua. Guatemala, attended Miss Annie's third grade classes and pounded a few nails at Common Hope, a non-profit much like Habitat for Humanity, which happens to be based in St. Paul, MN.

Identifying the site, finding a prefab building and finishing it for a 10 x 14 studio for Margo (where she can get away from adoring John by locking the door!). It is charming (has a picture window, sleeping loft, propane fireplace, and wraparound covered porch 150 feet from the house. It feels like being far away-she is in heaven!

A fun several weeks with grandson Joshua who just reached his first "double-digit" birthday. Swimming, trains, computer games, gathering wood, hanging out in a WVA state park and horseback riding at Margo's cousin Mick's in WI were amongst the highlights of our time with Josh.

Daughter Maija and her boyfriend Billy flew Josh out to VA. That was a special treat as it was Maija's first visit to the mountain. They were taken, as all guests are, to a down-home country store, Gertie's, for a fabulous breakfast.

Discovery of several Iowa gems: Hotel Pattee in Perry, a beautifully restored, five star historic hotel (now up for sale as they only charged $150/night), the Majarashi University in Fairfield, IA, and the first truck stop to be built on Highway 20 between I-35 and Waterloo.

Becoming the Duke and Duchess of Hazard (KY) by proclamation of the mayor. We were his first visitors in 15 years-so he also gave us a bronze key to the city!

Waking up every morning to a new view of the sunrise and mountains and the reverse in the evening; always being amazed and thankful for our home and life in VA, our family and friends and the fabulous books we find to read helping us to better understand this world.

As always, 887 Reid Road, Lexington, VA 24450. Come visit anytime!

14

the hip parade

Blessings do not come in pairs
Misfortunes never come singly.

– Chinese proverb

*W*e finally got through the physical breaks and the subsequent emotional turmoil from the falls, and now we needed to deal with Margo's hip replacement and increasingly chronic bum left knee. Considering the severity of all that had happened to her, Margo showed her true colors: she was recovering from the falls, yet started art classes, traveled to France and Montreal, and went to Guatemala by herself; we built and outfitted an art studio, went to Washington, DC for a couple of embassy parties, and returned to Minneapolis several times to be with her ailing dad (as if Margo herself wasn't ailing). We put on our best St. John's Day summer festival ever, with a U.S. congressman and many diplomats in attendance, bought a "new" 1967 turquoise Mustang convertible to go zooming around the countryside, and went to many lectures as long as there was a safe way to get in and hear them, Margo learned to get around and garden on her butt, and graciously entertained the steady stream of guests who came to visit. Oh, yes, and she was also constantly painting.

I behaved reasonably well. We snuggled every morning, sometimes introducing wonderful verbal fantasies, and I told Margo repeatedly: "All this hip and knee stuff is as much my issue as it is yours; we are in this together."

During this time, she projected a persona, at least publically, that showed her capacity to handle the challenges before her. I came to the conclusion that one should not say "this" is bad or good, it just "is." If you say something is too "good," then you really feel bad when something "bad" happens. So living I learned is about how things "are" without making a qualitative judgment. Ying and yang just go together.

I know all this medical BS and jargon is boring (as it is to me), but we learned quite a few lessons as things unfolded. I suggest that you save this book somewhere so when the time comes for you to have replacements—and it will my friend—you can dig it out and learn from it.

For those of you who have already experienced those painful replacements, you know what I'm talking about. In fact, I only came to really *know* how much frustration, pain, and discomfort Margo was in after I had my right knee replaced a few months after her death. I delayed getting it done because we both could not be immobile at once—someone had to look after and care for Margo. My right leg got so bad that due to the searing pain that coursed through my back and into the other leg, I could only walk about fifty feet, and I wobbled back and forth like a penguin every step of the way.

The day after my US$37,000 surgery at the Mayo Clinic, the leg hurt like hell and it felt like I had a concrete block attached to my hip. I asked myself, "Why the fuck did I do this?" It took sixty—yes, sixty—trips to the therapist before I began to function somewhat normally, and after six weeks I still didn't have enough strength in my right leg to push the accelerator down in the car. Sometimes, the pain was so bad and so deep late at night that I wanted to take a sharp knife and plunge it deep into my leg in the hopes that I could reach the pain and make it stop. Enough of my surgery; let's get back to Margo.

To help get her mind off the pain which would range from excruciating and horrendous to mild, Margo took up, as I mentioned earlier, Sudoku, which she would now play wherever she could. I had never seen her deeper in thought—it became a form of meditation. *The Washington Post's* Sudoku was best.

> *Midnight. Feel like I've been in an Indian trance of some kind while I play Sudoku, some numbers I feel have a power: 6 hostile; 7 friendly, gentle; 4 powerful; 1 just the ever present.*

The next best thing for meditation was Emma, our then five-year-old lab mutt. Margo was a sucker for puppies and whenever she felt bad about something, she went to the pound and picked one out. During our house owning years, we had three: Coco, Sammy, and Emma.

A website called *Dog Play* notes that dogs can play a role in "animal assisted therapy" and they don't cost US$90 an hour and up, like many therapists do these days. "Dogs offer entertainment and make people feel less depressed, a welcome distraction from pain and infirmity. People often talk to dogs and share with them their thoughts and memories. Stroking a dog can reduce a person's blood pressure and petting encourages use of hands and arm and stretching and turning." And where else can you find such unqualified love? Yep, dogs are good therapy and we quickly got used to dog hair and chewed slippers all over the place.

Coco, a black lab, was our first dog and we got her in Minneapolis. We gave her that name because she was a dark color, and, boy, could she run. We did not like to chain dogs to a pole, and since we had four acres and lived in a quiet neighborhood, we felt that we could let Coco roam. She tolerated Margo and me and would come home when she darn well felt like it. But when she did come home, we loved to play ball with her on the floor. We would nudge a rubber ball along the floor to her and she would use her nose to send the ball back to us. She was not all that cuddly and at night would be happy to sleep under the bed.

One day we let her out to do her thing and she didn't come back for a while. Then I saw her coming, dragging her hind feet. She had been hit by a car driven by our drunken neighbor.

We got her patched up and hoped for the best. Margo left on a business trip to Florida for a couple of days and called the night she arrived. She wanted to stay home with the injured dog but the reason was not good enough for corporate America.

"How's Coco?" she asked apprehensively.

"She's gone," I said with a lump in my throat. I heard a mourning wail and then lots of sobs. A member of our family had died. The collision with the car had perforated her colon and Coco died of septic poisoning. The hardest part was watching Coco die more each day. She just laid on her mat and looked at me with her gorgeous eyes as if to ask, "Can't you do something?" We had her cremated and scattered her ashes in our woods.

A few weeks later we returned to the pound where we'd gotten Coco and Margo found a calm black lab in a litter with a lot of active siblings. We took her home and gave her the name of Emma. Why I don't know. Emma was not a runner, but a cuddler and I think she developed a closer bond with Margo than with me. Yep, I did get jealous. Dogs can understand two hundred words and Emma obediently responded to all of our commands, intonations, shrugs, raised eyebrows, eye rolls, and hand signals; she never strayed from the house, always wanted to jump in Margo's lap whenever she could, and slept at the edge of the bed. Whenever Margo was feeling down she would gently pat Emma. And Emma sensing whatever space was next to Margo, would jump up and calm would prevail. We got Emma in Minneapolis, took her by car to Lexington, Virginia, later to Dubuque, Iowa, and then back to Minneapolis. She's now with a family in Denver. After Margo died, I didn't want to keep Emma. She knew of her, and my, loss.

In her whole life with Margo and me, Emma never had a leash on. Metaphorically she represented Margo who never would allow anyone to put a leash on her either. Born free. The only leash that Margo had was her own fears, but other than that she was free as the wind. When we went to the mountains of southwestern Virginia it was heaven for all concerned.

We walked our 3 ½ mile gravel drive down to the main road to get the mail with Emma running through the woods catching up with us periodically.

When Margo could no longer do the walk, we would let Emma out at the bottom of the hill and she would run up alongside the car. Virginia, those woods, Emma running, they all represented freedom, and Margo and I just soaked that freedom in. Emma would bark furiously at night at a passing herd of deer or an occasional raccoon or skunk that hunkered through, but we eventually got to the point where we slept through that. We had our grandson at times, but the stories we liked to tell our many visitors were not of him, but of Emma, Margo's constant and loyal chum and emotional guardian.

Squirrels abounded in our woods and they would approach the bird feeder hoping to clamber up one of the posts, jump onto the feeder and then eat the food we had laid out for the cardinals, blue jays, finches, and the occasional oriole. Emma would amble up to the screen door, see them, bark and they would scatter. At times, we would open the screen door and let her chase the squirrels that would always clamber up a tree just an inch beyond the reach of Emma's strong jaws. I knew one day a squirrel would come, turn the wrong way, and give Emma that extra second she needed to catch it.

Then one day, Margo and I and her constant companion, Emma, were standing looking at the mountain views when a lonesome squirrel bounded onto the deck. Emma's ears perked up and we opened the screen door and said, "Go get 'em."

It only took three seconds. One second for Emma to reach the squirrel, which turned the wrong way, a second for Emma to grab the squirrel by the neck and shake it to death, and a third for Emma to come jaunting back to us to continue our sightseeing. She looked up at us gloating as if to say, "Got 'em!"

"Wow," exclaimed Margo, *"that was quite a quickie!"*

The left hip wasn't working, and to make it worse, Margo's left knee was shot as well; balancing was becoming more and more of a challenge. She decided we should go see Thomas Nelson, the surgeon who had originally operated on her knee, and to see if he would replace both the left knee and the hip at the same time. We had become experts on recoveries from surgery by now and Margo reasoned: *"Let's have both done at the same time and only have one recovery."*

Her health was fine and her strength was a back from the falls—OK, sort of—so off we went to see Nelson in Minneapolis. At that moment we learned just how booked orthopedists are around the country. America's real threat is not radical Islam; rather it's bad knees and hips. It's not like you can walk in and get a surgery scheduled for next week.

Lyra Spratt Manning, a friend who lives in another beautiful place, Boise, Idaho, came to visit (she actually came to visit us several times):

"I got to know Margo one weekend when I interviewed for a job that was not to be, but was invited to visit Margo and John at their hilltop dream home in Virginia. A perfect place that seemed to heal my damaged ego. Driving up the winding uphill path to their home I found a smiling Margo sitting in a wheelchair. I was surprised, but soon was told of the trials she had endured. But what was so amazing was that she did not dwell on these "little medical emergencies" as she called them, dismissing them out of hand to talk about her world, her dog, her grandchild and her life in Virginia… we talked about local politics, her love for her home and garden and books. She talked about the importance of finding joy with what you have, not what you wished for – or thought you should have in life."

Margo wrote this on February 18, 2007, of a surgery that was going to take place in May:

Tom Nelson in Mpls. has agreed to put a socket in my left hip and replace the miserable left knee on May 10, 2007. God I hope it makes a difference that my pelvic stress fracture has healed. I am now buzzing around in a wheelchair and taking Vico 2-500 mg every four hours. Neurotin for sciatic pain.

John is wonderful but I have days/weeks where I'd just totally veg. Food and cooking is pretty uninteresting to me.

It's interesting to follow some of this "is" day thoughts from Margo, as we awaited the first surgery. Basically, on those with little or no pain she was able to look forward, and on those days with lots of pain she thought backwards.

Sunday, March 23, 2007
An amazing five days these have been. Last Wednesday I felt the best and most alert that I have felt I have been in six months. My pain has come under control, my emotional health returned far more positive. I feel like I am really climbing out of this quagmire. It's a long, long journey. I have goals for the first time in ages:
- *Get strong enough to actually swim laps again with real strokes*
- *Get in a few lessons on swimming to improve technique and help me on my crawl kick*
- *Go on Liana's spiritual trip to Peru*
- *Be able to hike a mile at least*
- *Be able to pick up fallen branches in the woods*
- *Walk to lower level of house to help John with ease (where I had my office)*
- *Develop and work on a plan to spend substantial time drawing paintings; go to 'the Natural way of drawing'*

But then in a few days with more pain we start to look back.

March 6, 2007
Ending the day in a very melancholy way – dreaming and thinking re why I have never connected with people in a group – small or a large one. I'm always a loner. Think of all the scout camps, sales meetings; manager meetings; internship book club here; newcomers, etc.

Today's answer is that I have never had a passion or anything I've really gotten really interested to learn about – starting with clothes as a teenager or college student casual clothes as an adult, music or movies or movie stars, etc.

Now I love books, gardening but I seldom remember enuf to talk about it. Books I can do better than ever before but I really don't remember detail from a book I've read.

Before I met John cooking was as close as I got but he squashed that because he said I got too stressed out about it. So now I really have little interest. I collect recipes thinking it might inspire me but so far no luck.

Then the question of how was I able to be successful enough to live this life we've lived for the past ten years?"

And then the sun shone, the pain abated, and no more thinking of the past.

March 25, 2007

Wow! Beautiful 75 degree days much is happening in the woods and gardens. Jill (our oldest daughter) *helped me rake the rock garden on Friday and today it is really alive. Five hawks circling. One flew through the woods by the studio while we were on the evening porch. It's like a positive omen passed through…Slept in the studio last night – figured out the 'bed' arrangement. Thank God for my studio.*

Each day was an adventure as the beautiful weather and chirping birds inspired her, yet the looming surgery made us more apprehensive. Margo had to deal with the pain which sometimes required two Darvons. We stumbled on some good books about God, though we came to believe, along with some of those writers like Richard Dawkins, author of *The God Delusion,* that there wasn't one. Why all this suffering? Pray all you want, but you are not God. You are your health's project manager. We filled a three-ring binder with names and phone numbers of physicians, their all-important assistants and nurses, the drugs we were taking, the places to go or call to get them, and insurance information. It was on-the-job training for Medical Management 101. We had no section for divine guidance, but we probably needed one.

In addition to us merely praying, Margo took to meditation and different types of healers. Having the studio enabled her to have people come to give her healing and to get away from an increasingly uptight me. What I missed the most was those little things that Margo used to do; make coffee the night before, do the bills particularly the medicals, the laundry, empty the trash baskets, fold laundry after I brought it in, go grocery shopping, and distribute all our pills in the morning. Actually from this point forward I did the grocery shopping.

I was fried. Yuk. I had gone to one therapist in nearby Staunton in the same office complex as Margo's psychiatrist, but I didn't like him. He was originally from New York and very demeaning, like a Marine drill sergeant. He treated me like a mental cripple which was not what I needed at that point. I wanted to hear, "What's up with you?" and be given the freedom to talk. Instead, "I got it; you're a jerk." Maybe this is therapy New York style. I always wondered what was worse—watching the love of your life suffer with pain and you not being able to do anything about it or being the one in pain.

The four-and-a-half-hour surgery finally happened at the modern Abbott Northwestern Hospital in downtown Minneapolis and we recuperated at the guest apartment at St. Therese retirement residence where Margo's dad lived. It was in Hopkins, a first-ring suburb of Minneapolis where Margo grew up, known for its old time Main Street with little shops. There were no Big Box shopping centers. It was home.

St. Therese from the outside was pleasant enough, surrounded by lots of green space, walking trails, a lake with a fountain, plots where residents could grow their own vegetables.

All this coming back and forth from Virginia was expensive and to stay at the guest apartment for two weeks was only a minimal cost compared to US$100 plus a night at a hotel. The unfortunate thing was that the apartment was dark, smelled old, stale, and had two beds that had stained mattresses, and creaky, rusted-out box springs that were way too low for Margo. But like the old saying goes, "You get what you pay for."

I wanted to leave right away and go to a hotel with better beds—and smells—but Margo didn't want to upset her dad, who thought it was neat that we were staying in the same building with him. How could we tell him that the place where he lived smelled? So we adapted. I built the couch up in the living room with pillows and cushions (Margo called this her Polish bed) so Margo could easily butt her way up to the bed. I threw the mattresses on the floor and slept on them without the creaky, sagging box springs. The apartment looked like a bunch of refugees from Central Asia had moved in.

Yes, those were lovely times.

Finally we couldn't stand it at St. Therese anymore. Neither of us was getting any sleep on the improvised beds. We decided to spend the last week at a nearby Hampton Inn. Wow! Bright and cheery, recently renovated, high wonderful beds, a nice non-sickly smell to the place, and a huge handicapped room that had raised toilets, et al.—this place was Shangri-La in comparison. Many of Margo's friends came to see her here and their presence cheered her up quite a bit. Unfortunately, these same friends were the ones who didn't want to share their views on Margo's life experiences after she died. The absence of their voices made this book that much harder to write.

Since this was a planned trip to a hospital, unlike the previous ones, we had plenty of time to tell (commiserate with) our friends and relatives about what was going on. They responded with cards and letters that I mounted on a collage we kept in the room with us.

Some of the messages:

THERE'S NO SPEED LIMIT ON THE ROAD TO RECOVERY

TOUGH TIMES NEVER LAST...TOUGH PEOPLE DO

I'M PRAYING AS HARD AS I CAN

And one I already mentioned: Perhaps I cannot control the winds, but I can adjust my sails.

After all this, we drove back to Virginia to try to heal. It was nice to leave the hustle and bustle of the Twin Cities to go back to our mountain top. The trip back must have been uneventful for I can remember nothing about it nor did Margo scribble anything down. We had driven back and forth to Minneapolis so many times over five years that all those 1,200 mile, two-and-a-half-day Interstate highway trips (I-94 to I-39 to I-74 to I-57 to I-64 to exit 55 in Virginia), seemed to meld together. The traveling goal was to avoid Chicago and Indianapolis congestion at all costs and hit Louisville, Kentucky, at a non-rush hour time. We always seemed to stop at the Holiday Inn Express in Evansville, Indiana (700 miles from Minneapolis and 500 miles from our mountaintop in Lexington) not far from where Margo used to live in her condo beside the Ohio River. We couldn't wait to get to Mt. Sterling, Kentucky, where you saw the Appalachian Mountains for the first time while heading east on I-64. Seeing the mountains always soothed us. It saddened us going the other way as we wondered when we would be back.

Once home, Margo got a "healer" named Claudia to come to her studio. She was overjoyed with Claudia's presence. It was only when I dug into the steamer chest that I learned of Claudia's existence, as we never met. Margo spent a lot of alone time in the studio which was a hundred yards from the house. She had her cell phone and could call friends, paint, and make appointments. I would always bring her some lunch (Whopper Juniors from Burger King were a favorite). If she was still there in the evening, I would bring some Dewar's scotch or a Gordon's gin and tonic and we would watch the sun go down while sitting on the porch I built. Margo was proud of the sign she put up when we finished the studio, "No Boys Allowed," and I respected her right to be alone.

6/20/2007

The beginning of a real healing happened with the arrival of Claudia – 63 years old, happy, hi-energy, positive, enthusiastic, has a Master of Fine Arts degree, teaches painting to kids, teaches Montessori, does Reiki – which is what she gave me today.

For you Reiki-challenged readers, Reiki is a Japanese technique for stress reduction and relaxation that also promotes healing. It is done by a "laying on of hands" and is based, I am told, on the idea that an unseen "life force energy flows through us and is what causes us to be alive." If one's "life force energy is low, then we are more likely to get sick or feel stress, and if it is high, we are more capable of being happy and healthy." Linguist that I am, I looked up the origin of the word Reiki. It is a composite of two Japanese words, "Rei" which means "God's wisdom or the Higher Power" and "Ki" which is life force energy. So Reiki is actually "spiritually guided life force energy."

Fascinating – when she started at my head I felt light-headed, at top of shoulders I was chilled, on my upper chest very warm and soothing, stomach – coolish, pubic – coolish, thighs – a bit warm, knees – right warm, left no, calves ok.

She said she feels strong and energy from me as well as very creative and that I have been leaning towards this healing stuff. She says she will introduce me to her group. This feels like it will be a wonderful friendship. I'm to visualize a golden, yellow, orange orb at my lower abdomen, bright red at my legs, lapis blue at knees and green on my hip sides. She encouraged me to make an altar, and put out my paintings from the workshop. This is the most hopeful I have felt since the knee surgery.

A succession of friends came: Joann Greenwall from Minneapolis, Ginger Cubelis from Indianapolis, Jeri Johnson from Wausau, Wisconsin, Jean Kelly from New York City, and Liana Carbon from San Diego. These were friends from Margo's past well before we met. The ones I had the most chemistry with were Jeri and Liana who went to Georgetown the same years I did, though we didn't know each other then. Both had no compunctions about me writing this book.

Margo's nephew and his wife, Heidi, who helped us move to Virginia, came as well. But an ongoing source of tension was that my daughters did not come very often, particularly Karla with whom Margo eventually developed a bond. Of course the heartache of her not coming always coincided with whatever personal pain Margo was going through.

During this time, Margo's knee wound did not heal properly and her hip was not right. The last surgery didn't resolve the problem. We went back to see Dr. Saleh, the surgeon who fixed Margo up after the fall, to get his opinion and to see if he had any suggestions to help ailing Margo.

"I'm not going to help you," was his response.

His ego would not allow him to operate on Margo for she had gone back to Minneapolis to get her knee and hip operated on, and he simply said, "Go back to Nelson; let him fix this mess." So in effect, we were thrown out of his office. Once we got back to the car, we sat and thought for a while. "What now?" We weren't crying or sad, at least I wasn't; it was just another hoop to jump though.

We were at a loss. "Fuck, shit, damn!" We didn't want to go back to Minneapolis to see Nelson; we were thrown out of Saleh's office in Charlottesville. So what to do? What credible orthopedic surgeon could we get to see—and fast? The answer rested in Ned Hooper, a friend and an orthopedist who specialized in hands and performed the surgery on me (ulnar nerve transposition) after my burn accident. Did Hooper know anyone?

Indeed he did—Dr. William Jiranek, a medical school classmate in Richmond, and he would make a call to get us in right away. So we trudged off to Richmond, which was 120 miles away, and really the beginning of the Deep South. It was, after all, the capitol of the Confederacy during the Civil War and a very busy place, if not totally overrun by traffic. The twang we heard in Lexington was replaced by an identifiable southern accent. It was hot and flat and a place where you saw cotton being grown. We grew sad when we could no longer see the mountains.

By this time we had traded in the four-door Nissan Maxima sedan for a Ford Freestyle SUV which we could configure so that Margo could lay down totally flat in the back. The vehicle also had a "well" in back to put the wheelchair in. I was really building up my pecs and forearms with all the wheelchair lifting I was doing. Every time we went to a new doctor, Margo spent time calling the hospitals of previous surgeries to urgently send x-rays ASAP. This was a full time job to get everything sent to Jiranek. Margo wrote this the day before we left for Richmond: *"Tomorrow we go to Richmond. I so hope Jiranek can be helpful and give me real guidance. I just want out of the pain!!"*

Mamma Mia Santa Maria, what a résumé! Where to begin? This from his website—special expertise: hip surgery, hip surgery replacement, Chairman Dept. of Orthopedic Surgery St. Mary's Hospital, consultant *Review Journal of Orthopedic Research*, Associate Professor Commonwealth University School of Medicine, etc. etc. His office was across from the beautifully landscaped and walkable Stony Creek Fashion Mall. It is the most upscale mall in Richmond and was surrounded by the most exclusive neighborhoods. We were exclusively miserable in having to go to another doctor, so we fit right in!

The mall was an interesting experience for us, as we had come from shopping-deprived Lexington where our shopping experience was limited to a Walmart. We got to our appointment early and haltingly walked through the pedestrian-friendly mall. It was not like most shopping centers where the stores face an immense parking lot. Here the shops faced an inward winding pedestrian-friendly walkway.

We would see a lot of this area over the next six months. Fashion Park advertises itself as a "beautiful blend of Southern charm and local architectural features." One blogger wrote, "Like no other as far as I'm concerned…it's a treat to go there – not an annoyance like other malls."

After each of our many Jiranek visits, we would treat ourselves to lunch or dinner at one of the cool restaurants like Bro Tuscan Grille (authentic Italian specialties) or Fleming's Fine Steakhouse (prime beef) or P.F. Chang's China Bistro (Chinese, what else?). On our first visit there we bought a heated, vibrating car seat at Brookstone, the fancy gadget store. You plug it into the car's power outlet and it gives you a heated butt-back massage in the car—another addition to our warehouse of apparatus.

So before our first visit, we rambled through the mall until it was time to see the doctor. After a brief wait, we were ushered into an examination room. Then the door opened and a cheerful man in a white frock came in.

"I heard you've had some troubles," were Jiranek's first words to us. Tears welled up in both our eyes as we looked at each other. He was fiftyish, slim, and had a Southern grace and charm about him with just a bit of a Southern accent. He exuded confidence with none of the pomposity and indifference, if not disdain, we got from Saleh, who I really wanted to punch out. Excuse my French.

For some reason that wonderfully illustrated classic children's book *Are You My Mother?* came to mind. In it a baby chick is born and the mother flies off to find food. He does not understand where his mother is and goes off to find her. In it he asks a kitten, a hen, a dog, a cow, a man, a boat, a junk car, even a steam shovel, "Are you my mother?" They all say no. I wanted to change the words and have them say to each of the surgeons Margo and I have met so far, "Are you the surgeon who can finally fix my sweetie's hip?" Alas, they all metaphorically answered "no," and as it turned out, Jiranek didn't have the answer either. But we didn't know it at the time.

So he did an inventory on Margo and saw that there was no infection of either the hip or the knee (good), the hip needed to be fixed with some additional strengthening akin to chicken wire (good), but the knee wound hadn't yet healed up (bad), and Margo had been experiencing bone loss in her pelvis (bad). He would not operate on the hip until the knee wound was healed (bad and good).

He sent us off to see a wound care doctor, one of the few specialists we hadn't seen at St. Mary's Hospital, a pleasant wooded place located right by Monument Avenue in Richmond. This avenue, now in the

Historic Register, has thirteen monuments placed in the middle of it, mostly dedicated to Confederate heroes (Robert E. Lee, Stonewall Jackson, etc.). At St. Mary's we met a nice female doctor, Emily Standish, who set Margo up with a wound suction pump which would help the knee heal quicker. She set up a daily regimen for Margo to follow. We were to check in with her and Dr. Jiranek at a later date. We then went back to Lexington. When we saw our mountains again, we felt better.

Oh goody! Now for sure our house and refrigerator looked like a medical supply warehouse: antibiotics, pain meds, anti-depression pills, crutches, wheelchairs, enough gauze to outfit any number of mummies, walkers, and now a wound suction pump. Instead of giving a tour of our gardens to visitors, I now felt I should show them how all our medical paraphernalia worked. It was too much. Since the wound hadn't healed, Margo could not go swimming. I, nevertheless, kept the pool in immaculate condition for our friends. I had no interest to swim by myself.

In fact, our reasons for moving to the top of the mountains had largely disappeared, except for the solitude. Solitude was what Margo wanted, but I could only live in a place that I could maintain. My Latvian heritage wouldn't allow it. Like my mother, I couldn't look at dead tree limbs. Everything had to be "tidy, tidy." I didn't want to hire people to do it—I wanted to be part of the land. In many ways our lives revolved around medical appointments—not the seasons to which our land was subject and which I could not turn off. My nerves were fried!

July 19, 2007
This weekend John announced we need to move. He is so overwhelmed physically and emotionally. Hickory Ridge is too much when he needs to pay so much attention to me.

He's also pissed at Reid (our farmer whose land our road runs through) *for no acknowledgement of our road maintenance efforts or cleaning up after ice storm in February. John feels he's at the breaking point which I think I pretty well understand. But I'm finding a deep sadness in me to leave our ideal home and land. I love it so MUCH! And then I'm at the beginning of a few fine friendships that have taken five years to develop.*

Although it was a surprise announcement to Margo, the plan had been brewing inside of me for a long time. I didn't want to mention it before so as not to add more worry to an overwrought Margo, but I was emotionally and physically falling apart.

In fact, I started thinking about moving right after Margo's second fall. What sense did it make to live in an isolated house with tons of stairs that lead to the outside and down to the pool, and a slope that led to her studio, set on a steep ridge, three-quarters of a mile from the main road—gravel at that. I was fearful of another fall and, in fact, she fell twice in the garden and never told me about it. She told a friend:

> I fell twice in a week in my garden landing somewhat on my hip. I did nothing – neither was a bad fall. This happened because I was tired and in hurry. I had hip pain and thought it would go away. A month later I had x-rays and told nothing was wrong and the pain would go away. Well both statements were wrong. I later learned that the femur head had been knocked loose and was digging into the socket.

Margo did not understand that she could do little to nothing for a long, long time and that staying at Hickory Ridge with all its gardens to tend was just too much temptation for her. "Weeds just don't wait."

As I mentioned earlier, the February ice storm was scary, especially since it occurred right after her surgery. The thought of Margo being trapped alone, if such a storm where to occur without me there, was too much for me to bear. Equally discouraging was my run-in with Reid Mackey after one of his lumber trucks forced Margo to drive backwards down the mountain. This caused Margo such pain as she had just had surgery and was also coping with two compressed vertebrae in her back.

After chewing Reid out and venting big time, we went back up the mountain and lay down in our comfortable king bed. I cuddled in Margo's strong arms that night and I told her I just couldn't take it anymore. "I've got to get you well and fuck this place, fuck Reid Mackey, fuck everything else." We fell asleep hiding from the bitter truth that faced us. Margo wrote in her diary on August 4th:

> Life is feeling very crazy here. John is over the top in control 'you don't understand how much stress I'm under, I want out of here.'

But a month later Margo was pretty resigned to the reality of our situation.

September 4, 2007

A life of health turns to one of surgeries and pain; how to cope with a total change of life activity. No more hiking, not even walks to energize and be fit. Swimming has disappeared into an open wound; taunting me always at the sparkling aqua pool. Volunteering also vanished away.

It's amazing how one's thinking changes once a decision has been made to leave a place. Those things you previously felt you had to obsess about, like fixing, cleaning up, and organizing around the house, no longer matter. So it was with us. Nothing remained but to call Lucy Turner, the agent we bought the house from, and put it back up for sale. One factor which I didn't mention in my list of reasons why I wanted to move was that we were still in the real estate boom and by selling at this time we would probably make US$150,000—not bad for a five-year investment.

We assumed that given the nature of Hickory Ridge, once we put our property up for sale it wouldn't be sold until after Margo's surgery which would be in December, three months way.

We first thought about staying in Lexington and looked around everywhere, but everything we saw we compared to Hickory Ridge. There simply was no comparison. We came to the conclusion that since we had moved here for Hickory Ridge and not just for Lexington, there was no point in staying in an ordinary house in Lexington when we could find an "ordinary" just about anywhere. Further, our families lived so far away and our doctor were 120 miles away—an ordinary house in Lexington just wouldn't do.

We did not want to go back to Minneapolis as the sudden change from our isolated woods existence to urban congestion would be too much of a shock. Besides, Margo didn't want to be around my ex-wife whom she felt was constantly intruding in our lives. Nevertheless, we agreed we wanted a house. Margo wanted a house where she could have a separate office with a door she could close. We were not going to go back to a multi-story condo like the one in which we started out our marriage.

We thought about it and finally agreed that our new dwelling had to have some natural beauty and be close to, but not in, the Twin Cities. Margo loved her condo on the Ohio and we began thinking of river towns—someplace where there might be barges. After all, we were Midwesterners, not Southerners, and the twang was beginning to weigh on me; the Midwest had no mountains but it did have the beautiful, sensuous Mississippi. Yes, the Mississippi, but where? Hudson, Prescott, Red Wing, Winona, La Crosse, Prairie du Chien? We were partial to Minnesota and Wisconsin (the great north woods) and river towns had a certain panache to them. But Iowa? In Minnesota Iowa was the butt of many jokes. Years later after finally moving to Iowa, I was eating in a fancy restaurant with my daughter in Minneapolis and the waitress overheard that I was from out of town. She asked:

"Where are you from?"

"Iowa," I responded

"I'm so sorry," she said.

Her snide remark was nothing compared to what Steven Bloom wrote about Iowa during the 2011 Republican primary campaign in the *Atlantic* magazine. Iowa was one of the first states to have a presidential primary and was in the news every day. He wrote:

"Considering the state's enormous political significance, I thought this would be a good time to explain a little about Iowa. On the state's eastern edge lies the Mississippi dotted with town with splendid names like Keokok, Tollesboro, Fruitland, Muscatine, Montpelier, Sabula, Davenport, Dubuque and Guttenberg. Each was once a booming city on the swollen banks of the river that long ago opened up Middle America. Not much travels along the muddy and polluted Mississippi these days except rust bucket barges of grain and an occasional kayaker circumnavigating garbage, beer cans and assorted debris. Those who stay in Iowa are often the elderly waiting to die, those too timid (or lacking in education) to peer around the corner for better opportunities, an assortment of waste toads and meth addicts with pale skin and rotted teeth or quixotically believe, like little Orphan Annie, that 'the sun will come out tomorrow'."

So who cares what people think about Iowa and its river towns? Consequently, we added Iowa river towns to the list—Clinton, Davenport. Margo and I remembered driving through Dubuque—the bluffs and how wide the river was—and I said, "OK, on the way back I'll stop in Dubuque and see what that's about."

These were not happy times. Our friends Peter and Jean said I was manic and depressed, if not downright abusive. They were right. Margo was continually in pain and I was continually uptight, angry, and unreasonable, and I always felt on the verge of a heart attack. My blood pressure went through the roof one day reading 170 over 110!

Josh, my grandson, was with us for the summer again. After his stay, I drove him back to Minnesota. He was constantly drinking sodas and I, consequently, had to stop constantly so he could go to the bathroom. He had grown out of the cuddly little grandson stage and was now a preadolescent with a mind of his own. He was less and less interested in the train hobby that we had shared in his younger years—a hobby that I, by the way, continue to enjoy to this day. He was now into paint ball, XBOX 360, Legos and Chicken McNuggets, which I detested. He was overprotected and spoiled by my ex-wife with whom he lives most of the time. A good kid, nonetheless, but that was his reality. Margo was glad we both were gone.

> *John is on his way to Minneapolis with Josh. We need this break but I somehow need to make some fun. I was going to go to Charlottesville but I can't manage that, even a drive through the mountains.*

Our Growing Drug Culture

Margo tried to deal with her clinical depression two ways: first, with psychiatric drugs and then later with faith healers of one sort or another. Even though there were side effects we struggled to control, the entire outside world pretty much saw Margo's big wraparound wall-to-wall smile and thought she was just fine. Regardless of how miserable she felt inside, she felt it was her job to keep those around her as happy as possible.

One side-effect from all the drugs was the almost lethal overdose of Seroquel Margo once mistakenly gave me. Every morning she would be the friendly family pharmacist in doling out the day's drugs. I took some for my high blood pressure and GI issues while Margo took a bunch for pain and the recurring depression. She would take Seroquel at night to reduce her pain and help her sleep. She would wake up quiet and groggy when she took them. Drug distribution was easier to manage when we were at home and everything was always in the same place; it was much harder to keep track of the drugs when we were on the road. The chart on the next page shows how intense the drug regimen was for her (us).

A Day in the Life of Margo's Drug Schedule

Drugs taken/Days taken	6/2/04	6/3/04	6/4/04	6/5/04	6/6/04	6/7/04	6/8/04	6/9/04	6/10/04	6/11/04
Wellbutrin 150 x 3										
2 a.m.	✓	✓	✓	✓	✓	✓	✓	✓	✓	✓
1 p.m.	✓		✓		✓	✓	✓	✓		
Prozac 1x/d 4 x 20 mg	✓	✓	✓	✓	✓	✓	✓	✓	✓	✓
Amphetamine 3 x 30 mg										
8 a.m.	✓	✓	✓	✓	✓	✓	✓	✓	✓	✓
12 noon	✓		✓	✓	✓	✓	✓	✓	✓	✓
5 p.m.						✓	✓	✓		
Tamoxifen 2 x 10 mg										
a.m.	✓	✓	✓	✓	✓	✓	✓	✓	✓	✓
p.m.	✓		✓			✓	✓	✓	✓	
Celebrex 1-2 x 200 mg	✓	✓	✓	✓		✓	✓		✓	✓
Rifampin 3 x 300	✓	✓	✓	✓	✓	✓	✓	✓	✓	✓
Vanconycin 2 x 1250 mg										
8:15 a.m.	✓	✓	✓	✓	✓	✓	✓	✓	✓	✓
8-9 p.m.	✓	✓	✓	✓	✓	✓	✓	✓		
Ferrous Sulfate 2 x 325 mg										
a.m.	✓	✓	✓	✓		✓	✓	✓	✓	✓
p.m.		✓			✓	✓	✓			
Vitamin C 2 x 500 mg										
a.m.	✓	✓				✓	✓	✓	✓	✓
p.m.	✓	✓	✓			✓	✓	✓		
MG	✓	✓	✓			✓	✓	✓		

One of our greatest frights involving our drugs occurred when we were on our way to Denver to visit our middle daughter. We decided to drive along the winding U.S. Highway 20, the longest in the U.S. by the way, to see the back roads of America. One could see the topography changing from row crop agriculture (corn and more corn) to grass pastures and rolling treeless hills. We would joke about buying a long-abandoned diner along the way and going into business—it would be a great business since no one would come and it would be a stress free.

At Sioux City we crossed the wide Missouri. Just up a couple of miles north was South Dakota where the very-well-off lived, protected by many tax shelters. Across the river was Nebraska where many Bosnians and Hispanics lived and worked in the many pungent meat packing plants. We drove all day from Dubuque across Iowa (300 miles) and spent the night on the Nebraska side of the Missouri in Nebraska City.

I had been here before while researching a book, but hadn't spent much time here. Tyson and Morell had huge packing plants in the vicinity. The focus of their operations was to take all the fat trimmings from the many plants, congeal them into sixty-pound blocks, and then ship them to fast food outlets and companies that supplied ground beef to grocery stores around the country. The fat trimmings, now affectionately called "pink slime," would be added to pure hamburger meat— cholesterol anyone? When you buy a fast food hamburger, you're really buying a beef patty that's half ground beef and half fat trimmings that most likely come from odiferous Sioux City. (Hamburgers with lean meat aren't quite so bad.) The company that produces these "textured meat trimmings" as they like to call them, sued Diane Sawyer and ABC for disparaging remarks that caused their business to suffer. When you're there, you do feel like you're far away from civilization, some place in the middle of nowhere. In fact, a bar in Sioux City advertises "The best country music from the middle of nowhere."

Since I was writing a book about the world's largest cattle feeder who once lived in Sioux City, we wanted to drive around the tired and run down town in the morning just to look around before heading out to Denver. Among other notables who had once lived in Sioux City was George Koval, Soviet atomic spy and the only Soviet agent to infiltrate the Manhattan project which built the first U.S. atomic bomb. That's about it for famous people from Sioux City.

There were many bridges and freeways, all named after this or that politician who found the money to build the structure. They crossed back and forth and forth and back over the bends in the Missouri, so you never really knew what state you were in.

During the morning everything seemed fine. I was just a little groggy when I awoke up, but strong coffee took care of that. We had crossed to the Nebraska side and anticipated a nice day together driving out west. So we dealt out our morning pills and drove over the bridge across the swollen Missouri into Sioux City. Everything seemed fine and we were looking to having a nice day together. Then as we crossed into the leafy, hilly outskirts of the city, an overwhelming drowsiness hit me like a huge tidal wave. Whoa doggies!! I had become sleepy while driving at other times, but this was very unusual and was occurring way too early. I rationalized it as not having slept well the night before. Margo snored by the way.

I pulled over on a side street and told Margo I needed to close my eyes for a minute. Since it was a weekday, I realized that the gray parking meter needed money. I went out and dropped some coins into the meter and got back into the car. As I hit the seat, the lights went out and I crashed!

I knew that this sleep was deep but didn't know *how* deep until Margo started to talk to me. *"Are you OK?"* she asked. I tried to answer, but though my brain said talk, I couldn't. *"Are you OK?"* She put her hand on me and I then realized I had been sweating profusely. It was a very cold sweat. She said, *"You're not OK."*

I then realized I was trapped inside my body. I heard Margo do and say things but I couldn't respond. I heard her call 911 to get an ambulance, but Margo didn't know where we were—some side street in Sioux City, Iowa. She described to the 911 operator what she saw out the bug-stained windshield and she hoped the ambulance could find us. She told me she stood outside the car and vigorously waved when she saw the ambulance driving back and forth in the distance. Finally, they saw her waving. I was chalk white and fading fast. They immediately gave me oxygen.

I didn't know what was happening to me—a stroke, a heart attack, or maybe I was cashing in my chips? I rationalized I had had a good life, said, "Well, this is it," and wondered how Margo would cope with a bad hip on crutches.

Then I was unconscious.

The next thing I knew I was in an emergency room and had a graying, bearded, forty-something doctor with a weary and haggard look on his face say, "Can you hear me?" I heard him read out my signs 110 over 80 to a nurse so I couldn't have had a heart attack or stroke as my blood pressure was normal. I heard the usual chatter of other patients in the emergency room, some moans and calls for water. Only faded-stained curtains separated one patient from another.

I saw Margo next to me. She was smiling and had her comforting soft hand on my head. Yuk, I then realized I had peed in my pants and was uncomfortably wet. As of yet, they hadn't put a hospital gown on me.

I was coming around. The doctor came again and then he asked, "Do you know where you are?"

I thought back to all the bridges crossing back and forth, in and out of Sioux City, Nebraska City, and Dakota City, and responded, "I don't have a clue where I am." Margo got it and we both laughed hysterically and all that tension started to flow out of us. The doctor looked puzzled —why are these guys laughing so hard?

The doctor told me he didn't know what was wrong but that they were running a bunch of tests. As I started to wake up, I started to think more clearly. "When have I ever felt like this before?' I thought. I remembered it was once when I took Benadryl for the first time: I took two whole pills which sent me to gaga land. Now if I have to take it, I just take a third of one pill which chases away the allergy or itching. Seroquel is much more powerful. I asked Margo could she have slipped me some of her Seroquel by mistake. She thought and nodded, yes. Houston, we have solved the problem.

After the Seroquel incident, I was too emotionally wiped out to drive to Denver to see Karla and I told Margo so. She was a bit disappointed. But then her eyes lit up, and she said, *"Let's go to Wyoming instead!"*

So after a near fatal drug overdose, Margo mentally rebounded, got me excited, and off we went—not home, but to Wyoming. Ride 'em cowboy. Remember that's where we had our ad hoc honeymoon. Our goal was Caspar, Wyoming, which was 500 miles away. We knew we couldn't make it there in a day, so as we drove through Nebraska's beautiful bluff country around Chadron and then into Wyoming, we decided to stop at a little rough and tumble, windswept, and quite dusty town called Lusk, Wyoming. It is on the border with Nebraska. Margo was in heaven, for along the way we had to stop and wouldn't you know it, three surprisingly well-dressed cowboys were moving a herd of cattle across the road. This was always a good omen for us and it had happened every time we had been in Wyoming.

The motel we stayed in was called the Covered Wagon. It was comfortable, but no Mana Lani like on our honeymoon—yet it was better than the dives Margo stayed in while she was in India.

Lusk was one of those paint-fading Western towns that had never seen good times in the olden days or now. It was in the high plains of Wyoming; the Little Big Horn Mountains were not yet in sight. We wanted to sip wine and I went to the local bar (the only one in town). I bought the only bottle they had—I forgot to ask the vintage and *Wine and Spirits* rating. There was one restaurant, mostly a pizza take-out, and I got what they called a pizza and went back to our room. When I arrived Margo was engrossed in some mindless sitcom on TV. It was convenient, for it was one of those old-time motels where you could drive right up to the door. We drank the wine, laughed off the drug overdose, and fell asleep in each other's arms. When we woke up in the morning, we made super-duper love.

Ah, back to normal.

The Known and the Unknown

As I reflect upon our time together, I think the speed with which we moved from cold and frigid Minnesota to the warm, humid, and always spring-like mountains of Southwest Virginia may have been a contributing factor to Margo's health problems. I also think it may have had something to do with Margo's mother's medical history—she, too, was inflicted with severe osteoarthritis.

Margo wrote in her diary that she didn't want to tell any male suitor about her mother's medical history for fear it would scare them anyway. She believed it was genetic and it most likely was. So deep down I think Margo knew that major health/bone issues would eventually appear. I also think she wanted to experience as much of life as she could before the inevitable. That thought struck me as I was reading a book called *Sugar Barons*. It detailed the life of the young, rapacious sugar barons in the Caribbean in the 1700s who lunged forward to do as much as they could before retiring back to England "while they still had their mental and physical health—their 'constitutions'—in one piece." Perhaps another reason for the Asian adventure, at least in Margo's mind, may have been that she knew that such a trip would not have been possible just ten years later.

Regardless, she may not have had control over her degenerative health problems, but she certainly could have avoided her falls; she could have reduced their probability by being more cautious and less of a risk-taker. Her wonderful experiences while she explored Asia and climbed mountains and glaciers were forever seared into her being and she truly believed she could go on doing those types of activities forever. Intellectually reckless she remained to the very end.

14

mississippi and the mayo

The Mississippi River towns are clean, well built,
pleasing to the eye and charming to the spirit.
The Mississippi is reposeful as a dreamland,
nothing worldly about it... nothing to hang a
fret or worry upon.

– Mark Twain

*I*t's probably a good thing that our last memories of living in Virginia were a bad "is." We had long ago moved out of our resort-like dream house in the mountains surrounded by flower gardens, deep private forests, and spectacular views, and for the last several months had been living in two-star hotels with badly faded and slightly leaning art work which was haphazardly nailed to the walls. Even with medical insurance, our co-pays were through the roof. So five-star hotels were out of the question, although when you think about it Eggs Benedict is nothing more than a high-class Egg McMuffin with "Bernice" sauce, as they pronounce it in rural Virginia.

I never did figure out how much all this hotelling cost in Virginia, but it must have been a ton. The emotional toll was even greater. We were totally fried emotionally from what we had gone through in the last year. I am getting tired even thinking about it.

Our first hotel, the one in Richmond, had a great scenic view of the rundown K-Mart across the street. We stayed in that hotel after Margo's last surgery. In her My Life Margo wrote: *"We spent three weeks over Christmas and New Year's alone in a motel in Richmond – an ugly city with horrendous traffic. I was always in pain. John tried hard to bring me things that would make me happy but I was not to be cheered except when he had the hotel staff come in the room and sing me 'Happy Birthday'."*

Those twenty-one days were in some ways like the movie *Ground Hog Day* in which Bill Murray wakes up each day to find that it's just like the last one. I would wake up at 5:30 a.m., too early for "breakfast" at the hotel, and go to the nearby convenience store. Then I would get a large cup of coffee (black), buy the *Washington Post* and *NY Times*, and take them back to the room. I would read each from front to back and then tear out that day's Sudoku to give to Margo when she woke up: "Good morning, sweetie, here are the two Sudokus."

She would groggily accept them, as she was still in a drug haze from the night before. By this time, the hotel would be serving breakfast and I would get Margo some cereal and juice and pick up a copy of *USA Today*. I would read that from front to back (or was it back to front, I can't remember) and hand Margo the *USA Today* Sudoku. About an hour after that, I would put the paper down and literally have no recall of what I had just read. I must have read something for my hands were covered with black newsprint ink. I would go wash them.

Then I had three whole papers to throw away—the *Post*, the *Times*, and *USA Today*. I never once thought about buying the Richmond paper for I felt like an alien and didn't care a hoot about local news. I would then turn on our laptop and just look at CNN.com and ESPN. com all day.

I was brain dead.

The hotel had tiny trash baskets so I went across the street one day and bought some big black trash bags from the beyond-messy Kmart. Then, when Margo had gotten rid of her drug haze, we would walk down the hall a bit with her clutching her walker, and wait for the daily therapist and home nurse to come change her bandages. Oh, such fun we had. We did not snuggle, not once in those twenty-one days in medical captivity.

So the next day, and the day after, and the day after that we did the same thing—over and over again.

Since you asked, the big stories in December 2007 were:

- Prime minister of Pakistan was assassinated
- New England Patriots become the first team since the NFL expanded its regular season to sixteen games to go undefeated during that span
- A tiger escaped from the San Francisco zoo and ate three people

That's it.

After Richmond, Margo and Emma stayed at Hunt's Ridge in Lexington. She basically moved from one dreary hotel to another. It was dark, with no view, cheap, but they did have a nice staff. They really did take good care of both Margo and Emma. Margo had a housemaid with very bad teeth (or should I say "sort of greenish tooth" as most of the others were gone) and we paid her extra to walk Emma. She was such a nice lady but it pained Margo to look at her. The dark room was pretty full of stuff that the movers didn't take to our new place in Dubuque; we had arranged for UPS to start shipping them to Dubuque where a neighbor would put them into the new house. Margo did have our Lexington friends come visit her every day and take her out to different places. *Menos Mal*, that's a phrase in Spanish I often use meaning less bad; or in our new lexicon a really good/bad "is"; or as I learned later in my Buddhism class, we were in *Magga*, the middle path out of hostility as in *Dukka* getting away from negative feelings.

Meanwhile, I moved us into to our new, bright, airy, and beyond spacious digs—only two years old—at 8671 Kemp Court, Dubuque, Iowa 52003. (You probably can still get a picture description of it by Googling that address.) It had 1.3 acres backing onto Catfish Creek which meant Emma had plenty of room to run and even go swimming when it was warm. The woods along the creek enabled her to chase squirrels, one of her favorite stay-in-shape activities. Once Emma learned where the property line was on both sides, she did not wander off and knew where she should do her business. I'm sorry I could never be one of those people who has their dog on a leash and holds a plastic bag of warm poop. I envisioned myself as a James Bond-type guy and I never saw Bond holding a bag of poop—much less warm. Emma liked to prance in the snow so she was more than happy when we arrived in snow-covered Dubuque where few houses have front porches. Unlike Southerners, people here were more introspective.

I was busy unpacking some five hundred boxes. They were all marked and the movers knew exactly where to put them. I spent my time hanging up Margo's beautiful clothes, putting away her gorgeous jewelry, getting a bank account, changing our car insurance, getting an Iowa driver's license and license plates, opening up a client number at the Walgreen's where we would become their best customers, subscribing to the local newspaper (the *Telegraph Herald* which has a neat editor, Brian Cooper, with whom we would later become friends), and stocking our huge pantry with food from the Hy-Vee, a real cool grocery store ten minutes away. I may have overdone it, as I still have a case of tuna fish that I bought in Iowa here with me in Minnesota. Is that legal?

Then to surprise Margo when she arrived at her new home, I bought the fanciest bed cover and softest sheets I could find. I also purchased a new washer and dryer and finally joined the YMCA. I went to the local Unitarian church for the first time and learned there was one other Latvian in town.

"You mean you moved to Dubuque just because you wanted to, with no family or job connection?" is what one startled woman at the church asked me on Sunday in disbelief.

"Well yes," I said.

She didn't know that Dubuque was not to be our retirement home but rather our "interregnum." You learn words like this at Georgetown.

Interregnum: a lapse or pause in a continuous series
Synonyms: discontinuity, hiatus, interim, interlude, gap,
 intermission, interruption, interstice, interval
Antonyms: continuation, continuum
[Source: Merriam-Webster Dictionary]

I couldn't be a snoot and say to her and others, "No, we are really just here for our *Interregnum.*"

We knew we would eventually move back to Minneapolis (five hours away—300 miles), but we were not emotionally ready to do that yet and the house prices there at that moment were forbidding. In fact, as I write this, I am helping one daughter get out from her underwater mortgage which she got at about that time.

We would say our place "was close enough to go to Minneapolis on weekends, but too far away to run errands." Having sold our place at top dollar in Virginia, we needed to find some other place in which to live quickly. It wasn't quite like our moving to the Shenandoah Valley, but it was another adventure, which Margo and I were always game for. We thought we might live here five years (sixty months) but, in the end, it ended up being thirty-three months. So I did fudge things a little bit as all our stationary had inscribed "On the Mississippi" on it before the street address. But, in fact, we were five minutes away from the river and, besides, that's what Catfish Creek flowed into. So technically we were on a tributary to the river. I think I missed my calling as a spin doctor in the Washington, DC, political game. When asked where I lived by people around the country, I said "on the river," not Dubuque. In reality, there were top business people who worked in Dubuque but lived across the river in East Dubuque, Illinois. Many of them lived there just so they could say they lived in Illinois which doesn't sound as hokey as Iowa. Regardless, Iowa is not all hokey; parts are, but if you go to West Des Moines it's like Silicon Valley. I don't think Iowa will ever get rid of its negative image.

Then one day a neighbor came over, introduced himself and asked: "You ever going to run out of boxes to throw away?"

I thought that was a funny way to make an introduction. I would have said, "Hi, I'm John and I live across the street and welcome to the neighborhood." OK, I get it—from now on I will go up to people and ask: "Are you ever going to run out of macaroni and cheese?"

Another neighbor brought over Dubuque's signature dish—a "turkey dressing sandwich." Talk about soggy, and spread out on shapeless white bread, no less. It was the last time I had one. If you ever travel through Dubuque, I would pass by the opportunity to have a turkey dressing sandwich and the T-shirt heralding it.

Full of enthusiasm, I busied myself trying to figure out who would be where in our new house. Margo would have the whole upstairs while I would exile myself to the walkout ground floor. The living room had a huge cherrywood mantle over a gas fireplace and built-in bookcases on each side, with a tremendous flat-screen TV in the middle. Remember, in Virginia we just had rabbit ears and watched only what atmospheric conditions would allow. Here, while Margo was recovering, we needed some home entertainment. At first we thought of getting rid of the TV and putting up our favorite painting of the Virginia Mountains, but in the end we decided to watch some TV as the house had cable—something new for us. Over those thirty-three months, I must have watched *The Godfather, Goodfellas,* and *The Fugitive* many dozens of times for the TV stations were always playing them it seemed, and I never got bored watching them. In fact, I watched the same scene so many times from *The Godfather*—the one where Clemenza is teaching Michael how to make spaghetti sauce—that I know the recipe by heart.

After the Direcway cable guy set us up, I had him hook up all the stereo equipment in the bookcase for US$70. It was well worth it; I never would have figured out how to do it myself.

Just off the great room was Margo's office. It used to be a little girl's room with a multi-pastel colored ceiling fan and sort of mauve walls; it was funky and we decided to leave it that way. From out her window, we could see a neighbor's ponderous brick house and then a weathered red barn and hills in the distance. I hooked up her little waterfall so she could always hear the soothing sound of running water. We eventually outfitted this room with a new corner desk and bookcase combo. In her office, Margo would finally be able to enjoy the smell of incense and the relaxing sight of candles.

We turned the workout room downstairs, which had a padded rubber floor, into an art studio because it got lots of light. We bought an orange four-wheel-drive Kubota side-by-side tractor to take her down to the studio so she wouldn't have to do stairs. We put a hydraulic plow on it which was the envy of our neighbors. They all had John Deere-converted lawn tractors that couldn't handle the really big snows. The steamer chest full of the material that made this book possible fit perfectly under what was once our dining room table, but was now to become a work table full of paint brushes, paints, pencils, and drawing paper.

Could a, would a, should a. I wish I had the time to read all those diaries then, so I could have asked Margo what *this* was about, tell me more about *that*, and what were you thinking of when *that* happened. But now I ask and ponder those questions by myself, alone.

The whole house was painted in a variety of soft earth tones—very soothing. Margo would have the upstairs master bedroom to herself and her clothes would be in the huge walk-in closet beside that most spacious bedroom. A TV was set up on a dresser in front of her for the times she didn't want to come into the great room. Some spectacular, some ordinary, but always welcomed snuggling was enjoyed in that room by the two of us. I would have the little bedroom downstairs with a full bath next to it as well as the home office. The house had intercoms, but we would send each other emails or call each other on our cell phones. I had a landline for the house put in and one for the fax—we still got fax orders for our posters. We were wired, baby!

There was a huge family room downstairs with a fireplace, a bedroom, and a home office. The previous owner worked at home selling something, and this downstairs office had a huge walk-in storage room where the Russian army could have hung out. The previous owner had built-in shelves with labels to indicate where paper, address labels, scotch tape, and other items would go. This woman was an anal retentive neatnik.

But the *pièce de résistance* was the huge storage area off the downstairs family room. In Virginia, and earlier in Golden Valley, I had to stick all my trains into spaces meant for other purposes—a bedroom or a garage. Here I could stick them in the beautiful huge 20x20-foot room and close the door so it wouldn't interfere with what might be going on outside. Later, I would paint the walls a sky blue and then put in murals of green mountains and plunging waterfalls. We would carpet the floor to muffle the sounds of my trains. The first electric trains I had were in Washington, DC, and I played with them in a dark basement with a dirt floor. I was selling posters and I made a rack to store the several thousand I still had that were in flat, wide cardboard containers. This was in a 15x10-foot part of the storage room. Perfect. All the trappings and hobbies of my past life could be tucked away. We had never experienced that before.

Margo also had a great upstairs kitchen to putz around in. It had an island, a breakfast nook, and a pantry so big you could sleep in it, which I did one night to prove a point—what point was that? From the kitchen you looked out onto a huge living and dining room, a humongous bedroom, a spa bath, and shower. The shower didn't have a door—just a wall—and there was beautiful tile everywhere; the previous owner was in the tile business.

All-in-all, Margo had four times the room to roam around in her motorized wheelchair or easily walk with her walker. I had put in one ramp from the kitchen to our three-car garage to make that transition manageable.

I do remember one drive to Dubuque. It was in the dead of winter but the weather was mild and everything green until we got to Davenport. It's one of the Quad Cities (along with Moline, Bettendorf, and Rock Island) that are all clustered around a bend of the Mississippi. At that point, the green disappeared and patches of snow became visible.

This continued for sixty miles until we reached the city, which was encased and totally covered with it.

Welcome to the Midwest in January!

Some thirty miles south of Dubuque you notice that the church steeples look all the same. We have entered hyper-Catholic country and all of the churches have the same black and gray steeples, as if they were made from the same blueprints. Germans and the Irish were the first settlers of Dubuque and they brought their Catholicism with them. In addition to the many churches, there are a number of abbeys and monasteries, now hardly occupied, and they all seem to be located on high ground with terrific views of the Mississippi. Many people in Dubuque were very low-spirited and lacked confidence in themselves (the woe is me syndrome) and I wonder to what extent this prevailing attitude had something to do with the heavy mantle of the Catholic Church. You know all of your rewards will come in the afterlife so play it cool for now.

Our house was not in the city of Dubuque per se, but in the county which was good because once we got settled we would have bonfires in the back of our land (still too big to call a yard) which were prohibited in the city proper. Before we came here I asked my French friend, Lionel Mellet, how a Frenchman would pronounce "Dubuque." He told me an American speaker could not pronounce it correctly because it had a sound not found in American English. Phonetically it is pronounced Dew–boo-ka, and you say it almost with one's lips puckered. For the most part, locals would say "Da Buick" almost harshly.

It turns out that a Frenchman named Julien Dubuque came here in 1785. Believe it or not, he had to receive permission from both the Spanish government who ran things then and the local Fox tribe, to mine lead. In fact, the biggest lead digs are now encased in a regional park not far from our house. It is called the Mines of Spain.

So here's a quick visual tour: lots of hills, woods—but not nearly as tall as the ones in Virginia—windy roads, the Mississippi River Museum which is worth seeing, a rail line to take you up a bluff which is the shortest and steepest railroad in existence, and two casinos. One is the more upscale, Diamond Jo, and the other down scale, Mystique, a former greyhound race track. How down scale? Well, in a display case in the lobby they had a couple of prizes you could win by being a frequent gambler: a crock pot and an electric tooth brush. Diamond Jo has the best restaurant in town called the Wood Fire Grill and a French-speaking Moroccan waiter who knows his stuff and doesn't cringe when you try out your French on him. Margo took French in college and would whip it out on occasion.

When we arrived, smoking had just been banned in bars and restaurants in Iowa, but not in casinos; they were too big of a moneymaker and the people who smoked were the gamblers.

N'est-ce pas?

In the summer, there are steamboat tours down to an artsy-crafty town, Bellevue (more French), twenty miles downstream, and there is always eagle-watching on the bluffs—winter is actually best. The eagles hang out at the edge of open water and then grab a fish when they see one. There might be fifty eagles and they are each exactly ten feet apart. What social order!

The town had changed when IBM arrived with 1,200 data-processing jobs and occupied offices in a renovated department store called The Rostick. An attempt at an upscale restaurant called Mana Java was put in on the ground floor and is ongoing. OK, I tried their eggs Benedict and got a sunny-side-up egg on wheat toast. And, of course, they have turkey dressing sandwiches on the menu!

There are four colleges in town, each with sports teams. I never got to see any of them play. There is a minor league hockey team, the Fighting Saints, but I never got to go to one of their games either. However, Dubuque became the home of the national Dock Dog Championships and I did get to that. OM, are you dock-dog challenged? Dogs run off a diving board and then try to grab a round rope in their teeth before flopping into a tank. The distance the dogs have to jump keeps increasing, and the winner is the dog who is able to grab the furthest ring of rope. Very exciting, but I did not buy a T-shirt celebrating the national Dock Dog Championships.

That's about it—no real traffic, one shopping mall which is the only place to go for a safe walk in the winter, lots of people in sweatshirts either for Iowa State or the University of Iowa, and many semi-tanned woman who go to tanning parlors. Margo always wondered why the women went to these parlors—the tans looked so unnatural. There is also something called Dubuque-styled hair. What does it look like, you say? You'll know it when you see it.

So what did Margo think about all this?

2/5/2008

All right, the beginning of new journal in a new home in Dubuque, Iowa. It feels a bit weird to realize we really did make this move in the midst of my health problems.

I remain overwhelmed – my body aches all over, I'm concerned re my hip – it hurts at the seat and in the folds of my leg meeting my body. I don't know if it's normal or not. It's easy for me to get down about it. I'm so stiff and achy and find it hard to make myself do exercises – I feel like it won't matter in the end – how shameful when I've always felt in being in shape, I even have moments of thinking to eat as much and whatever I want just to get fat.

And then there's the breast cancer stuff. I'm freaked that I might need a mastectomy – can't even imagine the healing process I could face.

When Margo and I finally got to our house there was a lot to do. None of the paintings or art work had been put up; her closet had her clothes, but not in order and boxes were strewn about. We ignored all that and did what we knew how to do: we started calling hospitals and doctors to learn who had the best cancer treatment. We had brought Margo to Iowa, but we also brought that stupid cancerous tumor in her breast. I got a big notebook with dividers and we were off. It was a bad "is" to be doing this, but it was glorious to see Margo getting information and calling people. She was determined, in charge, and empowered. I just stood by in awe and watched her bring every network she knew into play. There was no self-doubt at all. Whenever self-doubt crept in, guess what? Snuggling time!

My first task upon arriving here was to find a surgeon at a major medical center. This was a priority as we had had a problem with this in the past. We filled up Margo's book with names of potential surgeons. We first drove to the University of Wisconsin Cancer Center to check them out. It was -26 degrees when we left to go there—the center was a bone-chilling ninety miles away. Margo had also gotten names for the University of Iowa in Iowa City some eighty-two miles away. We left for there two weeks later after a major snowstorm. The number of cars and trucks in the ditches was incredible. We stopped counting at sixty-two.

Both of these hospitals were superior in their parking, treatment of people, food service, physical layout, and in the systems they had in place than either UVA in Charlottesville or at VCU in Richmond. The facilities in Richmond, to my mind, resembled a third world hospital with a Soviet Union-style attitude—doctors first, then staff and, last, the patients. In VCU, patients were considered an intrusion as opposed to the reason that the hospital existed. We were pleased to have moved here if for no other reason than to be so close to good care and we hadn't even been to the Mayo Clinic yet.

The University of Iowa seemed to have the best recommendations (even better than the Mayo Clinic) and that's where we decided to have the lumpectomy done.

Finally in April it was taken care of but my hip was not right.

Contrary to conventional wisdom, you don't need a recommendation from the President of the United States to go to the Mayo Clinic. We went there fourteen times in the thirty-three months we lived in Iowa. In fact, the Mayo Clinic treats over 150,000 patients every year, although the city in which it's located, (Rochester, Minnesota) has only 107,000 residents. It is probably the only town these days that doesn't shudder at the sight of Arabs in traditional dress, as the Saudi royal families and other top people from the Middle East come here for treatment. They often arrive a little more ostensibly than we did—in chartered 747s.

A couple of months before our grand entrance two 747s landed at Rochester's airport. One plane was full of people who were scheduled to see a variety of doctors while the other plane was to carry back stuff.

The prices at the various shops in Rochester are very high as the Saudis and rich Arabs aren't budget shoppers. On more than one occasion the Saudis have asked the Apache Mall in town to close early so they could shop in peace. Of course, the Mayo Clinic has an international center where thick aromatic Turkish coffee is served and a number of Arabic-language newspapers are available.

OK, Jiranek in Virginia did know the head of Orthopedics at Mayo, Dr. Daniel J. Berry, and he was the first guy we saw. Of course we drove there after a humongous snowstorm, but smartly followed a snowplow most of the way.

I was fortunate or unfortunate, depending on your point of view, to spend a lot of time in the Mayo. Margo underwent some intricate surgery to fix her bum hip, and as a result, I saw just about every nook and cranny in the clinic, including the emergency room. Mayo is a US$7 billion dollar a year operation and is world renowned for its exceptional medical services. While in discussions with our insurance provider, I discovered the Mayo is no more expensive than any other medical center. After observing the operations at the Mayo, I decided to record my observations in a syndicated article that appeared in a number of newspapers around the country. To wit:

- **Patients do come first**. This is how the Mayo distinguishes itself. Other medical centers may come close to rivaling it in technical expertise, but they can't come close to its humane treatment of patients. From the time you arrive at the Mayo, you have armies of people who simply care. They don't chew gum at their desks; they want to help you get out of the car; they want you to arrive at your appointment on time and will help you get to your appointment on time. There are no throw-away jobs; everyone acts, talks, and dresses professionally and wants to be there. When you are in the Mayo, you know you are in a different place.

  While all Mayo facilities are soothing, they are also informative. In the ER waiting room at St. Mary's Hospital is an electronic "scoreboard" which graphically shows which examination rooms are full, what doctors are where, how many people are waiting, what their average wait time has been, and where you are in the queue—unless it's a life and death emergency.

- **Practice team medicine.** Mayo has an intricate computer networking system began in 1969 which enables each physician to easily communicate with others to figure out how to solve a particular problem. Nurses from Dubuque commute to Mayo to be part of this mentality—and earn better wages than are available locally. It was two surgeons in two different specialties who eventually got Margo's hip fixed.

- **Values matter.** The Mayo Clinic could not have started in any place but the Midwest. People are hired at Mayo not just for the skills they possess but because of the values they hold—values that are found in this part of the country.

In any event, our mood changed for the better after arriving at the Mayo. Margo's hip had moved and she would need more surgery. This was not necessarily good news, but we finally felt confidence in the medical center where the surgery would be performed. Egad, Margo had had three hip surgeries and none of them worked. This first visit was followed by thirteen more to Mayo until we became part of the woodwork. At the Mayo, we felt we were in good hands and this gave us hope.

16

2008 was great and 2009 was just fine

Yea, I'm thankful for the chance to breathe
For the chance to feel the earth beneath my feet
For the chance to laugh, and the chance to cry
Yeah, gratitude is a friend of mine

– John Smith, "Down a Gravel Road"©

*W*riting this memoir is wearisome because I am writing about a loss —I lost a chum, the love of my life. Oh, come through the door, Mookie, and rub my shoulders like you always did while I sit at this desk and type away. Writing the last four chapters was more than wearisome because they all deal with falls, surgeries, more surgeries, indifferent medical care, and still more surgeries, packing up and moving from our mountain home and leaving our dreams behind, and of course the pain and mental anguish we went through. "You guys are so strong," people we met would say. Bullshit! We were coming apart at our emotional seams. I was still a mess. I was now more than a husband; I was also a harried caregiver: the difference was that a patient would pay more attention to a caregiver who wasn't also a husband. It was ever so hard.

When we finally got back to Dubuque after our first encouraging visit to the Mayo Clinic, we found ourselves almost relaxed, and really for the first time in years, I mean really, medically hopeful. We decided to have some fun: we planted, decorated, painted, swam, meditated, shopped until we dropped, met new friends, volunteered, partied, took up snuggling again, played trains, explored, wrote, thought, listened to music. We did all this even though Margo was still chugging along in a wheelchair and walker.

Then one day in spring she wrote:

> *Whew! No metastasis or signs of bone cancer PET/CT scans. Almost hard to believe after all this time in air. Jani is extremely relieved – poor guy. He was having us sell the house and travel the world one last time and that's what I would have wanted to do also. I'm stunned…Now I hope I can gather myself together and get excited re life and him and us. We need some fun; travels, biking, kayaking, art shows. And I need to find a passion – get going on calling these art centers for medically and physically challenged.*

She still had to go to radiation every day for a while at a nearby hospital and regularly visit the cancer clinic—Margo used the term *"boob zapping!"* We would combine those visits with exploring Dubuque's hilly neighborhoods.

The roads around Dubuque followed the many ridgelines in the area as well as the huge bluff drop-off to the wide Mississippi. Since it was only a short five-minute drive from where we lived to the mighty Mississippi, we frequently went to the riverside as it always cheered us up. We would get even more excited if there were huge, throbbing barge tows going up and down the river. There were railroad tracks—one on either side of the river—and you could always hear the hundred-car trains rumbling up and down. The river was alive with power both on and off shore, the town bustled with this commerce and the bluffs alongside were full of dive-bombing bald eagles.

> *April 15, 2008*
> *Amazingly – I look better, have a little less hip pain, radiation is o.k., have birds; house finch, yellow finch eating from birdfeeders and robins are all about. Yesterday it felt like 55 degrees, sunny, and blue skies! We drove along the river in town – watched a couple of boats go by and then had fun watching a dog training class. Have been investigating adult trike – at least I could go biking – will be strange to be on three wheeler.*

Margo's goal now was nothing more than to be able to walk with a cane. No more thoughts of climbing Fox Glacier or of fearlessly darting up Angel's Landing in Utah or even going downstairs when you weren't supposed to. There was no looking back and saying,

"I used to be so healthy." She decided to make the most of what she had. Margo immediately started touting up the benefits in the following chart.

Pluses and Minuses of Leaving Virginia for Dubuque, IA

Pluses

Chicago for a few days is doable
Visitors though lately not many
See Mick and Chris regularly (Margo's cousin)
Able to see family regularly and easily in Minneapolis
Have friends nearby
Closer to the West for vacationing
Probably lower cost of living
Closer to Ginger (best friend)
Kayaking is easier
Good/better biking

Minuses

Lose access to DC and those friends
Lose bluegrass music and folk music scene
Moving out just as female friends becoming solid
Lose the spectacular scenery
Lose great dog sitters

Margo's Iowa diaries were written in a notebook with flowers and hummingbirds flitting about on the cover and were inscribed with the words:

Believe • Imagine • Dream
This journal is meant to serve as an inspiration format for personal growth revelation and development

And a bunch of inspirational days went into this book.

May 11, 2008
Rejuvenation day! How wonderful. I slept soundly until 8:45. Jani suggested that I stay home from church and that sounded like very good idea. So I read the paper in bed all a.m. – he brought miniature cream puffs from church. We made love and had an afternoon nap.
It's evident I have not nourished my body well at all this year. Food

wise I have been awful, too much junk food, not enough fruits and vegetables, let my weight creep up too high. The meditation is a good step, now some simple yoga, alternating with swimming. I ordered my tricycle on Friday.

I have gratitude today for:
- *a nice phone call from daughter*
- *lots of interesting books to read*
- *painting supplies which I used today*
- *a husband who can 'read' my energy and support me when I need it*
- *a wonderful chum in Emma*

And speaking of spirit, we are Unitarians which is a Buddhist-like spiritual sect. Its followers are accepting, and we found a church of some forty members in Dubuque. There is no dogma attached to it, the ministers don't wear elaborate robes, nor do they have ponderous rituals or magical incantations, and no one tries to recruit members. Detractors of Unitarians don't believe it is a "church" at all—too "squishy-wishy" one person told me.

At the beginning of the service you light a chalice, give thanks and recognize people in need. I don't know anybody in the congregation who drove a pickup truck which seemed to be *de rigueur* in most other parts of Dubuque. There is always lots of upbeat music, not ponderous like "A Mighty Fortress is Our God" but uplifting, and a sermon about something spiritual and relevant—never any allusions to sheep and shepherds in the Holy Land. On a typical Sunday one might see maybe twenty-five people in the church; on special occasions it would be 'packed' with maybe fifty. A soft-spoken minister named Kent Mayfield came every month from Dodgeville, Wisconsin—sort of near where the famous architect Frank Lloyd Wright was from—to conduct a service. He was the fellow who presided over Margo's life celebration in both Dubuque and Minneapolis after she died. I was too wiped out to have one in Virginia as well although I was encouraged to do so.

When Kent wasn't there, members of the church would lead the service. Margo and I took on the responsibility a couple of times. I talked about being an immigrant and the prejudice, if not hate, being thrown at immigrants today. I am here in the United States because of the Displaced Persons Act of 1946. The president signed it into law under protest for it allowed us Latvians and other Baltics in, but did not allow

Catholics or Jews into the U.S. after World War II. Prejudice against immigrants seems to be an American rite of passage in spite of all the talk about a "melting pot."

In any event, we were welcomed to the neighborhood. I remember one woman, who later became president of the congregation, said we added a "spark to the life of the church." Such a nice thing to say since we felt we had the life taken out of us by the blessed mess and hip parade we had been through. This church then became a centerpiece of our lives in Dubuque and we made many new friends there. Margo put a lot of her creative energies to work and eventually became a member of the board, delegate to many Unitarian gatherings, and ultimately the finance director.

Of her work Cindy Weise, the president of the congregation, wrote:

"My thoughts of Margo always reflect on her leadership abilities. She would just look at me, the board, whomever, and say, 'Just get on with it. Life's too short.' She kept a meeting going. She wasn't one to mince her words. Margo spoke her mind, said her piece, and moved forward with a project or task. Margo was a 'lead or get out of the way' type of gal. You see, Unitarians often take time making decisions...but there always comes a point when I look up at everyone around the table...and say, 'Let's just get on with it.' You know, 'Life's too short'!"

Boy, you got that right. Frank Potter, one of the keystones to the church, gave another spin about our arrival:

"When you two came to the Dubuque Fellowship you made such a nice impression. Here were two worldly people from Virginia who wanted to be close to their children in Minneapolis but not too close to interfere. Margo was such a classy, handsome, and personal lady that had to use a crutch for failed hip replacements. John was a big sentimental oaf who wondered how he got so lucky to get her. They made a great pair."

"Big sentimental oaf!" and I had this James Bond image of myself!

One problem with the church, however, was that it lacked a handicap access. The church is an old white former Baptist structure at 16th and Iowa Streets at the edge of Dubuque's historic district. In one direction, there were spacious old homes being restored, while in the other there were pawnshops and ramshackle apartment houses. The entrance was marked by some cement steps leading to a small landing with a rickety, treacherous handrail on one side and then two double doors. Margo was doing toe touch with a walker when not in a wheelchair, and I didn't want to risk lifting her up out of her wheelchair or placing her back in it. Carrying her up or down the stairs was out of the question. She really got pissed at me at times for being so overprotective, but we couldn't risk another fall, and Margo the adventurer was at times oblivious to danger.

What to do? Go to Plan B. There was a little parsonage next door that had no steps. The congregation decided we could have a service inside the parsonage so Margo could get in. The parsonage was small and the congregation barely fit, but it worked. However, some in the congregation thought, "Why did we do all this work on the church (the inside *was* beautiful) and here we are having services in the parsonage?"

As a result, the parsonage service experiment ended quickly. Then we went to Plan C. Our new house had a huge great room with an eighteen-foot ceiling and windows that looked out at the countryside. Why not have services there? So that's what we did, and it worked out beautifully. Twice. Then her mobility started coming back and we could gingerly go to church. The access issue did not disappear, though. I'll let Frank Potter speak about Plan D—the building of a ramp at the church:

"There was an obstacle for both to participate and that was the most basic one – Margo could not safely negotiate steps into the building. I was thinking that the cost might be US$10,000. I think it was soon after at another announcement time the president said the estimate the Board received was US$30,000 and the Board decided to accept the bid and ask for donations from the Fellowship. The president also announced that someone, later determined to be the Freivalds, had offered to match gifts. It is a beautiful ramp on the west side of the building. A bronze plaque with Margo's name has been made and was being installed next to the ramp.

The greatest tragedy was that Margo did not get to use the ramp more and we did not get more time with her. She got sideswiped by a brief bout with cancer when she was focused on her chronic orthopedic problems."

The plaque on the ramp to that church is the only permanent visual reminder on earth that Margo Mogush Freivalds lived, as she was cremated and I scattered her ashes in the Boundary Waters Canoe Area of Northern Minnesota.

In addition to becoming an active participant in the church, she also purposefully set out to expand her social network soon after arriving in Dubuque. Margo shifted into socialization gear almost immediately and very quickly met Mary Ellyn, a vibrant eighty-year-old woman, always well dressed and coiffed, who had recently lost her husband. She lived in a funky house in a gracious bluff area of Dubuque and ran a funky antique shop in a slowly developing artistic area. I'd like to live to be eighty and be called funky by someone. Mary Ellyn told me she plunged deeply into antiques as a way to get over the grief of her husband's death. I thought she mentioned his name too much but I find myself doing the same thing with Margo's name now, which more than irks some of the female companions I have been seeing. One even asked, "Can't you just forget about her?" Well, I wish I could.

Mary Ellyn saw Margo as a flower and put it this way to me one day:

"Though I am not an artist, I have mused about painting a very large bouquet of all of the beautiful souls I have known and representing them as the flowers I see them as. Immediately a flower popped into my mind, that of Margo, standing in a field…tall…straight, as a single, lone sunflower. That is how I see Margo. Her feet standing firm in the ripening grain that almost reached her hips, and though the wind blew lightly, she stood unbending, facing into it with the amazing, radiant warm smile that was always a part of her and stayed with her through our last visit. That is the Margo I knew and will always remember."

We too hit it off immediately as she told me of some of her travels which included Kashgar in far eastern China near Kazakhstan where I had been. What a treat to discover someone who had been to Kashgar where Margo and I had talked about going; this neat old center point of the Old Silk Road across Asia. Trade on the Silk Road was a big factor in the development of the great civilizations of China, Egypt, Persia, Arabia, and Ancient Rome. Camels were the beasts of burden in those days which are probably why I collect camel figures and figurines. Imagine talking about those places with a knowledgeable person while living deep in mid-America.

Another project was planning and then helping Mary Ellyn with a big silent auction project. The church always needed money whether for ramps, to fix leaking roofs or flooded basements, or just to pay the hydro bill. A silent auction was one way of doing this. Mary Ellyn and Margo came up with the idea to sell seats at a 4th of July dinner at Mary Ellyn's bluff house. It was from here that you got a splendid view of the fireworks set off down by the river bank. That brought in about US$1,000 dollars and then Margo, ever the dietitian, and Mary Ellyn figured out a very fancy dinner to serve.

It had been a long time since Margo had a bosom buddy like Mary Ellen and they began to spend a lot of time together. Margo was also more aware of her appearance and paid more attention to it, which was just fine with me. All this activity was good for her. For in truth, I was overbearing and she needed to get away from me sometimes. Nevertheless, I was scared shitless about another fall. Together they came up with the idea to have an art exhibit at the church for people with disabilities. This idea drew her back into expressing herself artistically again and we decided to put a window in what used to be a workout room at our new house.

The workout room now became Margo's studio. It was a perfect location because it jutted out from the house and had huge windows on all sides. We took her huge old dining room table and made it into her work table, and built pull-out shelves filled to the brim with brushes, pencils, paints, and photographs of landscapes. *Could a, would a, should a.* I am now taking art classes and wish I would have taken them with Margo. She left lots of paintings and I have framed many of them. They now serve as wonderful gifts to friends and family. Margo was too modest and unfortunately didn't sign many of them. I would just love to sit around with her now and talk about analytical cubism and other obtuse art-related subjects.

Of her new-found zeal for art, she wrote:

I am feeling the urge/self push to paint finally. However what do I want to paint/what style?

- *I am now starting with a clean, new palette – first in two years!*
- *Now going to read some palette magazine stuff and practice something.*

I'm spending afternoons in my lovely studio. Have spent an hour drawing fingers. My hand looks the best so far but proportions and shapes are still off.

And then she noted this one day while sitting in her studio.

A big 'a ha' happened to me today recently when I sat down to paint. I picked up several paintings I did earlier in the summer. They were all dark and a bit dreary. I reworked them to warmth and cheeriness.

And if that wasn't good enough, then this:

Prayers of gratitude for no organ dysfunction; no excruciating pain, loving and thoughtful husband, real friend and support with Mary Ellyn and winter started to be over.

Margo and I could never leave the land we lived in well enough alone so we called Wagner's Nursery, the best place in town, and asked them to develop a landscape plan for our property. The plan was made in color, no less. We landscaped one side of the house and put in a waterfall with 800 gallons of circulating water. It wasn't Niagara Falls but it sounded and looked very nice and even had a light shining behind the falling water. At night it was magical; we could hear it out the bedroom window. And, yes, we could hear coyotes howling at each other almost every night too.

As for our neighbors, it's not that they were different, so much as that Margo and I were. We were asked one evening by one neighbor next door to come over and play some cards. Margo and I both played lousy Bridge so we went over thinking it would be Bridge or maybe Poker. It wasn't Bridge or Poker but a rural thing called Euchre (you-ker). Margo and I both had master's degrees and all we could do was hopelessly look at each other. I looked it up on *Wikipedia* later, but at the time it was well neigh unintelligible to Margo and me, sitting with another couple at a card table. Phrases like cross boarding, stealing the kitty, cut throat, dud four, dead set, were flying fast and furious and all Margo and I could do was laugh—at ourselves. The couple across the card table from us kept shaking their heads in disbelief at our incompetence in playing this card game. The TV was on, as it often was in many Iowa households, but no one was watching—strange. We passed on the turkey-dressing sandwiches being offered. When we finally got home, the Glenlivet double malt scotch tasted mighty fine and we laughed our silly heads off at our lack of Euchre skills.

Then I was asked to watch a pro football game by another neighbor on his BIG screen TV. We basically sat around, watched whatever game was on (wearing whatever football jersey that happened to be around) with four other people and drank beer, and then drank more beer, and still more beer, and then ate nachos covered with warm Cheez Whiz. I tried to be humorous and say that at my high school we invented high-brow words and cheers for football. For a better defense we would yell "repel them, repel them, make them relinquish the ball" and a fumble we would term an "ellipsoidal imperfection." No one laughed.

After those two efforts we weren't invited back for any more neighborhood events, although people did come over for the bonfires we had, which were spectacular, and also to "borrow" logs for their own smaller fire pits.

Years ago I wrote a book called *Grain Trade* and in it I wrote a chapter about my Peace Corps years and the fact you were lucky if you could change even one person's life. Well, Margo and I were lucky. We were able to positively change the life of a neighbor's son. Noah Herber was fourteen when we met him and right away we knew he was different. Not only was he polite to us, but he wanted to know about the world we came from, what was outside the city limits of Dubuque. He started out mowing grass for us after he finished mowing his own. He then slowly became a valued *aide de camp* doing all sorts of things. We ended up paying him a "retainer." He got interested in guitar playing and I gave him an old one to use. He learned it quickly and before long Margo would greet his always-smiling face at our door and he would say, "Does John want to jam?" "Sweet Home Alabama" by Lynyrd Skynyrd and "Copperhead Road" by Steve Earle were the songs we liked to play.

What made him such a joy was that he was the glue of all the neighborhood kids. He would make a football field or a baseball field depending on the season, and one time he made a WWW wrestling ring as he liked that sport, not to mention building an elaborate tree house in the woods by our creek. The previous owners of our house wouldn't let him do that for it was considered "unsightly." Then, like a coach, he would organize the games. I liked what he was doing so much I called the editor of the local paper and they did a story with the headline, "Keeping Up with the Anti-Video Game Kid."

In the picture book Margo made for me she wrote:

*And then there's your guitar buddy who has brought joy. So much
joy that the Telegraph Herald did his story – thanks to you.*

Noah was also an entrepreneur in babysitting and doing chores up
and down the neighborhood. I let him use the Kubota one winter to set
up a snowplowing business. All the John Deere lawnmower guys had
plows as well, but this was the real deal and could get driveways done
in a tenth of the time. In addition to being a great kid and wonderful
neighbor, he knew the value of money. We were very proud to learn he
saved most of the money he earned. With our support and guidance,
Noah was well prepared to confront both the educational and occupa-
tional challenges he would confront in the very near future. He was dear
both to Margo and to me.

Our love of nature and woods never waned even when we were in
Dubuque. To that end, we decided to plant a number of trees on our
property. This led one neighbor to come over and ask: "Are you putting in a forest?" These were mature trees from a place called Instant
Shade in nearby Platteville, Wisconsin, and not saplings that you would
get at Home Depot and Lowe's. In Dubuque one can expect pines to
grow a foot a year, while in Virginia the loblolly pines we planted grew
three feet a year. We put birdfeeders out, and to our delight, had hundreds of birds visit us every day. The fat robins were the first to arrive
in the spring, and then migrating warblers, goldfinches (the state bird
of Iowa), thrushes, orioles, red-winged blackbirds, cardinals, and the
bully blue jays. The most strange and wonderful were the hummingbirds which would frantically helicopter around the sugar water that
Margo laid out on the back porch/deck.

Since I am a Latvian, we had to have a decent woodpile. In Latvian
folklore, fire chases away the long nights, as Latvia is on the same lati-
tude as the middle of Hudson's Bay (58 degrees north) where nights are
long and days are short most of the year. In that tradition, we built a big
fire pit; not some small metal thing to burn wood in like so many of the
neighbors had—I mean a serious fire pit. Part of our dinner ritual, especially when friends were over, was to sit by a huge fire and sip cognac.
Yep, we were effete snobs.

The culmination of all this was something called *Jana Diena*,
St. John's Day, or in pagan terms—celebrating the summer solstice.
June 21st is the longest day of the year and the ancient Latvians, who

were pagans, celebrated this important day. As mentioned earlier, we celebrated the date every year when we lived on Hickory Ridge in Virginia. On this day, homemade brews would be drunk, men named John would wear oak-leaved crowns, and women would wear tiaras made of daisies which were in bloom that time of year. Epic songs called *Ligo* would be sung and huge bonfires made to make the day even longer. Young men and women would then jump across the fire in leaps of joy. I even drove to Chicago (183 miles away) where an ethnic liquor store had stocks of Latvian beer, real black bread rye, and sardines which I brought back and served at our *Jana Diena*. But having a big fire was the key and thank goodness we lived in the county of Dubuque, and not the city itself, for we could have as big a fire as we wanted.

In addition to art, Margo's interest in music continued to grow. She not only played the piano at home but also became very interested in seeing touring musicians. Yippee, normalcy for a change. She relied on an advertising tabloid called *Dubuque 360* which covered the local entertainment scene and discovered a musician named John Smith.

The words to his song "Gravel Road" are the epigram to this chapter. Upon hearing him, we immediately fell in love with his music. We bought his CDs and would regularly check out where he would be playing next (www.johnsmith music.com). He lives in a beautiful Wisconsin river town called Trempealeau where Margo and I once considered living. He is a slight man with a fetching, lilting voice and sings lyrics like those below:

> And there ain't no place that I'd rather be
> Than sharing the gifts that were given to me
> Share my loss and share my gain
> Share my joy and share my pain

Margo wanted to build a church fundraiser around him. He would charge US$800 for a night's performance and we would use the church as a place to play and bring in a new crowd of people. Alas, we never got around to doing that given all the stuff that was to fall upon us.

Since Margo loved classical music, we went to hear the Dubuque Symphony and actually bought season box-seat tickets for the 2010-2011 seasons, which Margo did not live to attend. I gave the tickets away to our German neighbors, Hendrik and Uhli Shultz. Stuff like this was featured in 2010-2011 season:

"Dvorak's Seventh Symphony is well known and considered by many to be his finest, but several of his pieces in this program will be played by the orchestra for the first time including British composer Coleridge-Taylor's dance rhapsody 'The Bamboul,' American composer Gottschalk's 'Grande Taranell for piano and orchestra' and Mexican composer Marquez's 'Damson No. 2'."

Class!

While in Virginia, Margo had enjoyed going to the university to audit classes, but her physical condition didn't allow that here. Instead, we got our mental stimulation from the Dubuque Area Council on Foreign Relations [DACFR]. They would meet every month at the country club, host a dinner, and invite a speaker in to talk about a foreign relations issue. I even spoke once about Latvia and NATO, but the audience was very small—everyone was into the Middle East and terrorism.

Through DACFR Margo got involved, still using a walker, with helping the illegal immigrants who were seized and then held in limbo after the biggest immigration raid in U.S. history in Postville, Iowa, about fifty miles north of Dubuque.

DACFR hosted a professor from the University of Arizona to speak on his special field of study—Cross-Border Migrations. He was very interested in learning more about the U.S. Immigration and Customs Enforcement (ICE) raid on the Agriprocessor's kosher meat-processing plant at Postville, Iowa, and I suggested that if he could come to Dubuque a day early, I would arrange a visit to Postville.

As soon as Margo learned of this, she asked if she could go with us. Needless to say, I was delighted to take her, but I was also somewhat surprised because she was still recovering from a round of surgeries. Margo, of course, was not about to let this opportunity pass her by, which was entirely characteristic of her.

We drove the fifty miles to Postville, a small community in the picturesque hills of northeast Iowa. This corner of Iowa was settled in the 1800s by Norwegian and Swedish immigrants, and until the Agriprocessor's plant was purchased by new owners and converted to a kosher processing facility, the population had been composed almost entirely of the descendents of northern European Lutherans and Catholics. Following the change in ownership, a number of Hasidic Jewish families moved to Postville, as well as several hundred Latino workers who were hired to work on the production lines.

At the local church we met with Reverend Paul Ouderkirk and several of his staff. Margo was intensely interested in the human cost of the raid. The ICE agents were extremely zealous in carrying out their mission, which resulted in children being taken out of school rooms, mothers being incarcerated while their suckling babies remained unattended at home, and so on.

When Margo asked Rev. Ouderkirk why the raid took place in such an out-of-the-way place as Postville, his answer illuminated several things for us. He pointed out that Postville is far from America's political and media centers, a location where ICE might carry out their mission without publicity or public outcry.

Agriprocessors was in Postville for similar reasons. In Postville they were able to circumvent U.S. immigration and labor laws because they were isolated and because the plant was so important to the local economy. In this way, the Postville raid was a "perfect storm" and the churches and the community were left to pick up the pieces as best they could.

Margo offered to help financially and I suspect she did more than that as time went on. She was a remarkable woman with deep feelings not only for those she knew personally.

Margo jumped into DACFR with both feet and through it met the Tullys—Tom and Joan. Tom was a cherubic and cheerful guy who was once mayor of Dubuque. He set up DACFR, once lived in DC, worked for the Pentagon, and was a man of the world. He and I became instant friends as did Margo with Joan who was into very, very fancy handicrafts. I finally had an intellectual chum. To top it off, Tom's brother and his wife lived in Abington, Virginia, which was just 100 miles south of where we were in Lexington. When his brother came to visit, we would sit around and reminisce about the Shenandoah Valley. Finally, Tom fell in love with my train layouts and decided to do one of his own, but on the HO or smaller scale as he lived in a condo. Later we developed further ties that would bind us even closer together.

We were really feeling our oats, out exploring our environs continually, and now even contemplated getting a real country place as a retreat. For while we could see farms and woods from where we lived, immediately around us it was much more manicured and we could always hear those John Deere riding mowers cutting grass. What a waste of time. You fertilize the grass, increase the nasty run off, the grass grows faster, and then you cut it and put it in bags. You don't even want the clippings to blemish your lawn. I know I am an immigrant and we soon will have politicians campaigning for office to learn someone's stand on lawn mowing. Yuk, so we started looking for a weekend getaway somewhere not too far away.

Years before we even moved to Virginia we had briefly explored the Kickapoo River Valley, a 126-mile tributary of the Wisconsin River, which in turn flows into the Mississippi. Kickapoo is an Algonquin word meaning "one who goes here and then there." It's a fitting name as the river is very crooked, frequently doubling back on itself. And along the river, Wildcat Mountain State Park and the Kickapoo Valley Reserve form a continuous protected area. That's where we started to look.

After driving around for a while and looking at nondescript acreage, we found something we liked—seventeen acres of land which had a huge old tobacco farm (yep, they used to grow a lot of tobacco here before spelt moved in) and a huge half-built pioneer cabin at the edge of a huge cliff. It looked like something straight out of *Little House on the Prairie*. Eight acres were open fields and the rest were woods; silence and tranquility were all around. You half-expected Henry David Thoreau to come out of the woods and start preaching to you.

It was near the unincorporated township of Rockton, home of the Rockton Bar which offers "the almost famous BBQ chicken." And it proclaims that its establishment is smoke-free "except when the chickens are cooking."

We liked it and decided to come back hauling our 4x4 Kubota so Margo could see the property better. First we checked out the distance; it was 97.4 miles to Dubuque, which meant almost two hours of driving. When we came back with the Kubota one warm day, we drove up to the cabin in which you could fit a small house, and just sat and pondered with the sun warming our faces. It was gorgeous, but then we looked at and examined our bodies and how they were when we first moved to Virginia and how they were now after the burns and all the falls and all the surgeries. Worse yet, even if we built out the cabin, there was nothing around but the Rockton Bar—Margo needed a place to swim, not eat BBQ chicken. And given our schedules, it would be two years at least before we could have lived there comfortably. Margo was through with backpacking and my Peace Corps years were long behind me. Now all we wanted was down covers and hot tubs. You could sum it all up in a Christmas book Margo put together for me celebrating our life in Dubuque with a picture of the tobacco barn and the pioneer cabin. It began:

The thought of a place in the woods to which we could retreat to the woods.

The caption under the cabin photo read:

"Could we finish this old cabin?"

The caption under the barn photo read:

"Or could we sleep in the old tobacco barn?
I don't think so."

So that was us exploring the northeast. What other directions did we explore? Just about every direction imaginable, but nothing really caught our eye until we went straight east one day and stumbled across Eagle Ridge Resort (www.eagleridgeresort.com) in Galena, Illinois, about thirty miles away on U.S. Highway 20, which is the longest U.S. highway, stretching from Maine to Oregon. Galena is a picturesque town with lots of shops squeezed together along a main street with every kind of restaurant and potpourri store. It follows the pattern of Mystic, Connecticut; Williamsburg, Virginia; Sausalito and Carmel, California; and Santa Fe, New Mexico—just quaint. It was a total change of pace and culture from Dubuque. The resort is made up of people who made their money in Chicago and retired in Eagle Ridge to a lifestyle of golf and quiet. The resort and the territories around it are a matched pair and the entire housing and building décor match. It was the Switzerland of Illinois for it was near the highest point of that state, 1,260 feet above sea level.

The place totally soothed us and thus began a long relationship, with us buying a 900-square-foot cottage in the adjacent wooded and serene Galena Territories. Margo really enjoyed the resort when she needed to get away. She went there first by herself. This is how she described it:

Wow, I'm in the midst of my retreat at Eagle Ridge. It's yucky out-
side but wonderful inside. I had a marvelous facial, nail and Swedish
massage. Muscles were relaxed on my left side but two hours later

*tightness is back. I focused on healing my bones during it all as well
as cleansing steam. Jani and I decided that this place is so nice that at
least one of us will come weekly to swim, steam, workout, etc.*

She made a list of goals from the retreat:

Goals for this retreat
1. *Quietness – rest from conversation*
2. *Body treatments*
3. *Draw*
4. *Meditate of "bones healing"*
5. *Developing my own meditation*
6. *Some swimming*
7. *Eating – lose a pound*

She then wrote down in detail what she ate each of the three days she
was there. To wit on one day she had a liquid protein drink, hi pro bar,
large apple, eight oz. prime rib sandwich, chips, fried onions and three
glasses of skim milk.

It was a perfect time.

*My retreat is almost over; I'll be going home to the intensity of liv-
ing with Jani. He deserves and wants more attention. He requires
more concentration than comes naturally to me. He's often so intense
– but I love him and married him so I have to make him #1 before me.
He's the only one who is really concerned and worrying about me. And
I know when I am in pain I am not very nice.*

After this, we became members of the resort for just about the same
price as belonging to the YMCA in Dubuque. The only difference being
we had to drive thirty miles to get here. But given our constant driving
to get anywhere in Virginia, this was no big deal. The Y in Dubuque
wasn't a pleasant place. It was old and really needed to be bulldozed and
built anew. Margo hurt herself coming out of their pool:

*The pain in my hip has gotten significantly worse since I got out of
the pool this past Monday. I went into the large pool (John was not
present) where the steps are quite apart – too far for me but I climbed
out without difficulty apparently disrupting my hip and causing pain.
SHIT! SHIT! SHIT! It even hurts lying down. Feels much like it did
in October 2006 upon return from Guatemala.*

Duh, we never felt refreshed after working out there like we did in Galena. This of course added to our image of effete snobs, for in truth the people in the Territories hardly ever came to Dubuque—then maybe only to gamble in the casinos. I never met anyone in the resort who lived in Dubuque, save us.

We did make a really big east trip when we drove to Indianapolis for Margo's best friend Ginger's wedding. Margo and Ginger were buddies dating back to her Mead Johnson days in Evansville. And after a year of living alone, she met a nice man and they were off to the races.

Wonderful weekend in Indy. Jani was a jewel and even seemed to enjoy himself. Got to see Ginger and so happy to meet Norm. Often it's a surprise to meet spouses but he is definitely in love with her.

We were crawling out of our skins with joy on these trips for we were enjoying the normalcy other people just take for granted.

Our exploration of the area surrounding Dubuque included areas south. As one travels along the widening river, neat towns like Bellevue and Sabula begin to appear, hugging its shore. Bellevue was twenty miles away, but a wonderful drive and a place that had the wonderful Mississippi Ridge Kennels where Emma often stayed when we went galloping around the globe. In fact, whenever we took her, she would walk in the door and then go straight to the back to her pen. She knew the deal and was comfortable staying there.

Bellevue had a lock and dam where we would watch the tow barges slide through; I have a wonderful framed picture of one hanging in my kitchen. A rich guy bought a whole waterfront block and put in a first-class restaurant, coffee shop, and art gallery with a fully-stocked wine cellar in the lower level. Class! In the summer, we would always buy BBQ chicken and beef ribs from a vendor who sold things out of his truck. We enjoyed watching the Ski Bellevue, an old-fashioned water ski performance, you know—fifteen water-skiers being pulled along with girls on the guys' shoulders in a pyramid formation waving American flags. Yep, it was Americana through and through, and we loved it. It was normal and something was always going on there. It was a place we would always take our few visitors as the view was magnificent due to the river's width.

One of the visitors was funky and off the wall Ben Sargent and his squeeze. Ben is a wiry vegetarian who I met when I worked in the localization business, the arcane art of making computers work in other languages. He was visiting Cargill in Minneapolis and was willing to come to Dubuque if I picked him up, which I happily did. He didn't eat meat and promised to prepare vegetarian meals for us the whole weekend. So we got barbecued tofu and morel mushrooms, but no spelt.

Margo and I had to take him to Bellevue which he loved and then on to Sabula, twenty miles further south. If Bellevue fashioned itself as a bed and breakfast destination, Sabula was bed and beer. It's Iowa's only island town situated smack dab in the middle of the river, right where the scenic Mississippi stops—there are no more bluffs with spectacular views.

In fact, when Margo and I and Ben and the squeeze pulled into Sabula, we ended up in a darkened VFW beer hall. The 50ish bartender was standing outside and when she saw a car full of yuppies (we drove down in the Mustang convertible), she motioned us to come on in. She had tended bar everywhere from Colorado to Florida and now found herself trapped in Sabula, Iowa, a tale of woe, most certainly. "Want another beer?" Now I had gotten to be a good beer drinker and we had a rip roaring good time. I even snatched a sign of an upcoming event which really points out what Sabula, Iowa, is all about. It read:

IRON HORSE SABULA IOWA
Bike & Music FESTIVAL
Boston • Jimmy Van Zandt
Ultimate Fighting
TT Motorcycle Racing
MUD BOGS
$600 WET T SHIRT CONTEST
LABOR DAY WEEKEND
thehorserally.com

To tell the truth, when Ben and his vegetarian cuisine left, Margo and I went out and had the greasiest hamburgers we could find.

Let's see, we now have gone northwest to the Kickapoo River Valley and straight east to Galena and south to Sabula, so let's go due west. I always said that Dubuque is separated from the rest of Iowa by a cornfield, and once you get to Dyersville, about twenty miles east (where the movie *Field of Dreams* was filmed and home of the National Farm Toy

Museum, don't you know) you're in corn country. I wrote for *Successful Farming* magazine and we headed east one day to visit the editor in Des Moines (216 miles) and then went on to Minneapolis to see Margo's dad, who was not in a good way. As we drove along that bright spring day, Margo and I would engage in a mock question-and-answer ditty. I would ask:

"What's in front of you?"

"Corn," was the answer.

"What's in back of you?"

"Corn."

"What's to the left of you?"

"Corn."

"What's to the right of you?"

"Corn."

Iowa is all about corn, and since so many of you out there are urban, here's a quick and dirty on corn. Iowa produces 20 percent of U.S. corn (known as maize in most other countries) and 40 percent of it goes into ethanol now. The corn lobby is all powerful and the early Iowa political primaries are the reason. To get the votes, politicians promise everything to corn farmers, i.e., crop subsidies and subsidies for ethanol and subsidies for subsidies. Corn farmers are wrapped up in subsidies and the ethanol subsidy is one of the most absurd. Ethanol doesn't make economic sense because you spend more energy to make it than you get out of it when you burn it as fuel. The guide the corn industry prints states that "corn is produced on every continent of the world except Antarctica"—now aren't you glad you learned that.

We saw Loren Kruse, the editor of *Successful Farming*, and also a fellow who grows Christmas trees on the side, and we asked him if there was anything really neat nearby. Without hesitation he said, "The Hotel Pattee in Perry, Iowa."

If the plaque to celebrate Margo's life and generosity at our church is a monument to her life, then the Hotel Pattee is a monument to Roberta Green Ahmanson and a neat one at that. Although she is a controversial person due to her beliefs, she nonetheless put US$20 million to restore an old hotel in an otherwise scruffy farm town. She wanted to bring life back to the town and the restoration would be part of that. We hadn't really seen anything like it. The hotel is forty miles from Des

320

Moines, Iowa's capital, and is surrounded by cornfields. With the forty themed rooms and uniformed staff (with bellmen wearing top hats), it proclaims itself as "one of the finest boutique hotels in the world" (www.hotelpattee.com), and it blew Margo away. She would come back many times just to be surrounded by so much coolness.

Words cannot do justice to the interior of the hotel's rooms, each of which is richly decorated following a specific theme. These were Margo's favorite five rooms and she stayed in each and every one of them:

- Southeast Asia Room. In the 1970s and 80s immigrants from Laos, Vietnam, Cambodia, and other Southeast Asian countries made their way to Iowa. This room was for them.

- RAGBRAI/BRR Room. People travel every summer to take part in the Des Moines Register's Annual Greta Bike Ride Across Iowa (RAGBRAI) and in the winter they bundle up for the Bike Ride to Rippey (BRR). Grab your bike, helmet and enjoy.

- Russian Room. In the 1950s Nikita Khrushchev made a controversial visit to Iowa and rode through Perry on his way to a see a modern farm where corn, of course, was grown. Today Iowa is a sister state to Stavropol.

- African Room. Decorated with designs from regions such as Sudan, Somalia, and Zimbabwe, this room draws on the cultures of some of Iowa's most recent immigrants.

- Chinese Room. In the late nineteenth century, immigrants came to build the railroads across the American West. Men came from China and some settled in Perry. This room now remembers them.

It was a real joy to stay here. The hotel also has a bowling alley and a sumptuous sauna and steam room. In fact, it had the third best steam room I have come across: first is the Jewish Community Centre in Minneapolis, second the University Club in Washington, DC, and the third in Perry, Iowa!

After Perry we headed north, and although one should never be grateful in the face of death, Margo was grateful we lived in nearby Iowa when her father was dying in Minneapolis. Being so close, she had a chance to be with him quite a bit. We wondered how we would have been able to handle things, such as her father's illness, if we were still living in Virginia. There is always a reason for things and I suppose our move back to the Midwest was a perfect example.

Dad got out of the hospital and he's in much better shape than I expected. Everyone is relieved that I came.

I brought order to medical scene and joined forces with Shirley (her dad's companion) to agree to begin throwing out and getting rid of stuff. Tonight was my real drive – started thru albums, bathroom cupboards. Threw away towels, Mom's douche bag, cologne, make up stuff, 20-year-old bottles of lotion and first aid stuff – it had rusted on the shelf of Dad's bathroom. Then I threw out some knick knacks – anyway 10-12 bags of stuff.

He was then moved into a hospice room at a nursing home and I got to see what a hospice setting was for the first time. Her dad was miserable and in pain for he had been suffering not only from shingles—a very painful skin rash related to the chicken pox virus—but from congestive heart problems. He had been having trouble breathing for six months. The doctors suggested open heart surgery to fix his heart, but at age eighty-seven it is a surgery you never recover from.

Margo and I were in the room when a nice nurse came in one day and asked: "Is there anything you want, Mr. Mogush?"

"Yes," he said, "I want to die."

So on July 23, 2008, Margo penned this:

Dad died 20 days ago on 7/3/2008. Tonight I'm missing home, missing checking on him and having a parent to care about. I'm aimless, in pain, not too interested in anything and just go to woods.

His funeral service was a celebration like I tried to make Margo's when she died. All the living presidents of Cargill came and his great grandson Benjamin was running around in short pants. People talked about old times—no tears, just fondness.

We went back to Iowa and Margo, remembering her advice to her father about an unnecessary operation, thought about the need for another one for her hip—number four! The hip had moved since the last time we went to Mayo and another operation was necessary. Thus:

I want some reassurance from Dr. Berry that he thinks he has a good chance of making a difference. I am somewhat going crazy waiting for him to call. Since I have raised the question within myself about the worthiness of the surgery, I have put myself in limbo. I would so love to have it over, the pain gone, and be able to do normal things without getting so tired.

We ended up taking many more trips back and forth to the Mayo Clinic and Margo underwent more tests until finally on September 19, 2008, she wrote down this bit of news:

Last day of week at Mayo. Surgery postponed until 12/16 but an itsy bitsy chance this week's test will show cause of slow healing. The other good news – being hooked up to an endocrinologist, Dr Kearns, who will monitor osteoporosis and start me back on power infusion or injection to rebuild bones. Plus I like her a lot.

This week is noteworthy as it's the first time in two years that I have been able to be alone out of town and to shop as I wanted.

Wow, have I shopped. It's shocking how much I've spent but I am finally treating myself for all the misery I have endured. It's been fun.

It couldn't get any better than this.

When she got home, Margo put on her new duds for me. They were smashing and of course that led her and me to snuggling. Going into Christmas 2008 was eventful, as we learned. Margo's surgery was now going to be on January 7, 2009. The surgery had been delayed many times as Dr. Berry continued seeking advice from many colleagues as to the best approach to take—something that hadn't been done before. They basically were going to attach the hip to her pelvis: part of the operation would be performed by Dr. Berry and part by a pelvic surgeon.

She then pondered about Christmas:

What is Christmas? We're told it's about joy and giving. But giving gets confused with how much to spend, fairness to kids. Traditions need to be celebrated. Winter solstice, excitement that more light is coming. Candles burn, fires roar. Lighting up our home. Special food and song. Yule logs are pulled into the warmth. Fir trees are decorated. Signs of spring. Our happiness that spring is on its way.

We talked about some of the miserable Christmases we'd had. Margo mentioned being alone in India one year and I brought up the miserable time in Richmond staying at a motel. We spent Christmas 2008 this way:

Our Christmas Eve was a bit magical – watching Mormon Tabernacles Choir, a little wine and piragi, a Latvian goodie, and opened gifts. Jani loved his metal camel (really), his coal car and the framing of a Panamanian mola. Yeas! I love the velour jacket, then the fun Studio 57 Teddy bear factory and the replica of Frank Lloyd Wright's farm in Spring Green – I backed it up to one of my mountain paintings. It's the right size, cool.

Then right after Christmas Kent Mayfield gave what Margo and I thought was his best service. Margo put it this way:

Kent's service was very inspiring/thoughtful and touched home – we all have darkness and it's OK to share it – it's OK to occasionally mope about it. My surgery is going to be a success – allowing me to have more mobility and walk with just a cane.

Margo was one of these unlucky individuals who had a birthday (December 30) right after Christmas, but that made me work doubly hard to recognize the importance of her birth and how much she meant to everyone she touched. On this birthday, her sixty-forth, she was as happy as a five-year-old. But do we really ever grow up from being a five-year-old?

Happy 2008

OUTSTANDING BIRTHDAY

Surprise, surprise flowers came from Minnesota – from your 'friends in Dubuque' or Dubuque friend. Mary Ellyn apparently knows and is sworn to secrecy. I'm now down to Kent – but whoever it's wonderful. Birthday email from Art and Narelle in China, birthday card from Liana who called!! Calls from friends, sorority sisters and everyone in family. Fun gifts from Jani and a perfect poem.

I'm telling everyone that the surgery (just a week away) is going to succeed and that I will be walking without pain in 3 months and only with a cane. Mary Ellyn and I can go on shopping excursions, explorations, etc. Jani and I can plan and execute trip to New Zealand and Australia next fall.

Forever young!
All-in-all, 2008 was a great year.

Last Best Hope

We are at Victoria's Restaurant in Rochester, Minnesota, just down the street from the Mayo Clinic. It's January 6, 2009, and tomorrow Margo will have her fourth hip surgery. Even though Margo's mortality was not staring us in the face, we were pretty much wiped out.

It was, however, for our close friend, Tom Tully, who started DACFR and who had joined us that night at Victoria's with his wife Joan and their two children. Tom had mesothelioma and his operation was the next day as well. What a coincidence that these two people from Dubuque would undergo life-enhancing surgeries in the same clinic on the same day. In any event, mesothelioma is a rare cancer of the lining of the lung. It may develop twenty or even forty years or more after exposure to asbestos fibers. Tom pushed papers all his life and was mystified that he would come down with this, but then he remembered as a teenager he worked in the family lumberyard in the days when he would sell asbestos insulation. That is where it started. He couldn't believe it.

So Tom was there to have one lung removed to give him a little longer to live. That was that. As the Mayo Clinic family health handbook says, "There's no treatment to reverse the effect of the disorder."

But that night, at least, was full of profound joy for all of us. We ate, no, we stuffed ourselves; there were no doggie bags. We drank many bottles of wine, laughed, cried, hugged, tears of joy, of sorrow and, yes, hope. We must have stayed there for more than three hours talking about our lives and why we still dreamed. We told the waitress what was up and she told the people around us for we were loud and they lifted their glasses. One guy even sent over a bottle of wine. I have never been at a dinner table where a tighter bond existed. At midnight the food and drink stopped as neither Tom nor Margo could have any more.

Margo had an eight-hour surgery the next day. Dr. Berry cleared his schedule in case of more complications and the pelvic surgeon—I never did get his name—was to spend three hours connecting the hip to the pelvis.

As Margo was rolled into her rather big room at the Mayo Methodist Hospital right after her surgery, she got a big surprise. Three of her sorority sisters came to spend the night with her. When Margo groggily realized what was going on, tears flowed from my sweetie and then a flood of tears from her sisters. Margo had all sorts of tubes going in and out of her swollen body.

Fast forward three months after rehab, swimming, and careful toe touching. Hand in hand, Margo and I are going to church up the handicapped ramp that was dedicated to her. Even though we hadn't been for a while, Margo walked in wearing a big brace (hidden under a flowing dress) and walking with a cane. Everyone, and I mean everyone—there must have been a mass of twenty-five people—stopped yakking when they saw us and then, as if cued by a conductor, broke out in joyous clapping.

The surgery worked, now what?

Both Margo and I were so damn tired of being held hostage by her ill health that normality, a word we both hated, was, oh, so welcomed! Margo was driving once again, but had to wear a big clunky brace from hip to toe. We had to strap her in every morning as if she were a race car driver. She swam three times a week at the Eagle Ridge Resort in Galena and also started talking more regularly to pal Kayla. Margo was looking forward to the possibility of Kayla coming to give a bunch of healing seminars in Iowa. As for me, I signed a contract to write a biography of America's largest cattleman who fed one million head of cattle a year. He supplied Walmart with all its beef; he was the fellow who sued Oprah Winfrey over a TV show she did over ten years ago defaming meat—but more of that later, in my next book.

To my surprise, Margo was also sneakily preparing something for my 65th birthday which is on March 12. In case you want to know, 65 is really not as big a deal as 40 or 50, but it officially marks one as a senior. As such, it gets you social security and Medicare.

When I woke up on my 65th birthday, I got some nice snuggles and little gifts (can't remember what they were). You would think that a 64-year-old woman who has had two breast cancer surgeries, several knee operations, cataract surgery, was wearing a hearing aid, four hip replacements and encumbered by a hip brace and walking with a cane would not have much of a libido.

Wrong.

So among the many presents I got that morning, the only one I can remember was a letter—which I still cherish. It said:

Jani, my love,

It's so fitting that your 65th birthday is full of love and lovemaking which of course entails fantasies-so-so ... followed by falling asleep all tangled together (and four pages of tangles were included).

That and the morning snuggle would have been enough, but then in the afternoon when I was watching the five o'clock news there was a knock at the door. I thought it was some local kid selling raffles for some cause. Margo was in the kitchen doing something. "I'll get it!" I yelled. I opened the door and couldn't believe my eyes. It was my three daughters and grandson and they all yelled, "Happy Birthday." I was really dumfounded. Big hugs all the way around. They came in and Margo joined us in one big group hug. I remember Maija unfolded a big sign that read Happy Birthday and hung it up. Then Margo told me we were having a party in my honor and the two women who cook at the Black Horse Inn would be bringing dinner and that a whole bunch of my friends from Dubuque would be coming over to celebrate. Had I not been barefoot, all this would have knocked my socks off.

Even with all the hassles, 2009 turned out to be just fine. I'll let the words Margo wrote in our December 2009 Christmas letter sum up our thoughts on the year:

Hard to believe it but we have been in Dubuque two years. We con-tinue to be happy with our decision to move to NE Iowa as the terrain is much to our liking being quiet, hilly and woodsy. Plus the Missis-sippi's always a joy to see... A highlight of the year was our purchase of a 900-square-foot townhouse (we call our cottage) in Galena, Illinois, woods and hilly territory. It's 40 minutes from home with a whole dif-ferent feel to it which is helped by a wood-burning fireplace. There is a lake (we have kayaks), walking/bike trails, in and outdoor pools and four golf courses. With two bedrooms and a queen-sized sofa there is lots of sleeping space for friends and relatives – all of you – whom we hope will visit one of these days?

As for Margo, the short and sweet of it all is that she again faced two surgeries. The first, as I mentioned, was in January and it was a huge success as her pain was gone for the first time in three years. It was a complex eight-hour surgery, but her Mayo Clinic surgeon managed to secure her socket to her pelvis where it has stayed attached all year.

However, she experienced seven hip dislocations in five months, and, as you shall see, these dislocations were becoming rather tiresome. As a consequence, surgery number two became necessary on November 4th. At this point we hoped we were finished with this hip thing, as it was taking a horrible toll on both of us.

17

dislocation nation

*If you can't pin it or cast it,
then screw it!*

– Anonymous Orthopedic Surgeon,
Memorable Medical Quotations

*A*fter her big hip surgery in early 2009, Margo was given a laundry list of her medical condition from a clinical care nurse at the Mayo Clinic. Quoting from a February 2009 memo, the laundry list included:

- Revision of failed left hip arthoplasty
- No postoperative complications other than postopanemia…She has been wearing her hip abductor brace at all times except for bathing. She is to maintain non-weight bearing status on her lower left extremity at all times with walker until advised by Dr. Berry.
- Postoperative anemia
- Received five units of RBCs during her hospital stay (hemoglobin now stable).
- Osteoporosis
- Failed biophosnates due to multiple spontaneous pelvic fractures… Currently managed with Forteo injections, calcium and Vitamin D.
- Depression anxiety
- Her mood remained stable on Wellbutin SR, Effexor, Xanax, and Seroquel.
- Esophagitis
- Epigastric pain is well controlled with daily Prilosec.
- Borderline hypertension

- Her blood pressures remained stable and no anti-hypertension drugs needed.
- Constipation
- Initially need Dulcolax suppositories… Bowels have been moving regularly with Colace and Senna.
- Right rib fracture
- Spontaneous fracture of right rib one week before her hip surgery. Pain was managed with Tylenol Oxycodone and rest.
- Skin blisters/breakdown from IV site/tape burns
- Left arm has several blisters and open areas from tape burns and skin break down from IV site infiltration that were treated with Xeroform dressings twice daily.

She passed all the constitutional reviews, needed two quarts of oil and windshield washer fluid added, and brakes adjusted, but otherwise she was okay, and the nurse concluded:

"No further therapy was recommended until she is able to have weight bearing. She has all assistive devices at home including a reacher, sock aid, dressing stick, and a long shoe horn. Husband will be helping with housekeeping, laundry, shopping and transportation. Patient ready to learn, patient expressed understanding of the content."

In her Life Story, Margo penned this:

So far so good. Time will tell. I try to be optimistic and succeed most of the time.

After all we had learned about medicine from these trips to the hospital, we felt confident about our future. After my birthday on March 12th we were on a roll. I was writing the biography *(Feathers Are My Enemy)* about a big shot cattleman, and Margo was zipping around on her own doing volunteer work, painting, figuring out our church's finances, and going to help her friend set up all sorts of wellness seminars. We were driving three times a week to the Galena resort to go swimming. We had many snuggles, enjoyed almost every morning, and we fawned over a patch of sky we saw out our bedroom window that we called our "blue triangle." Every morning we thanked our lucky stars for being able to see "blue triangle," for moments of solace and calm, and for our deep love for one another. We invited people over to the house for dinner and we in turn were invited to their houses. We saw new movies and we stayed home to watch old movies. Our day-to-day living experiences would never get us into *People* magazine or invited to the White House, but man did it feel good!

Then one bright day that spring Margo wrote:

This must be the fullest day I have had in a <u>long</u> time. Lovemaking, eggs a la Jani, paint Adirondack chairs hot pink, blue and bright yellow, 1 hr. nap, 3 hr. computer class, 30 min. walk thru nature center by the Mississippi, saw big turtle and an oriole; made a nice dinner, tilapia, basmati rice with peas with a bit of cumin; more bird watching, sauerkraut making, kitchen clean up! Phew! It's 9:30 p.m.

Then on April 23, 2009, Margo's hip dislocated. Before the year drew to an end, her hip would dislocate six more times. One learned journal put it this way: "Technically speaking there are a number of reasons for dislocations after a total hip anthroplasty (THA) including obvious mal-positioning of the components, inadequate tissue tension, work-out of loose sockets and implantation in each of disabled patients. The various prosthetic designs and surgical procedures may occur as a result of two or more suboptimal conditions working together." So there, Margo's hip was suboptimal! She lamented:

What did I do to deserve all this shit, coping surviving all these health issues?

The hip popped out seven times and I was with Margo for three of them. One happened when she went off to a weekend Unitarian leadership conference in Beloit, Wisconsin, ninety-three miles away. I said no to her going, but you know how far that got me. A second dislocation occurred while Margo was just sitting in a chair at home. A neighbor was kind enough to take her to the hospital. With each dislocation, there was minimal pain, "only" the emotional trauma of "Oh, my God, when will all this crap end." Each time she went to the hospital, the doctors were able to set it right almost immediately. Each dislocation occurred when she was not wearing her brace—she often mentioned that the brace was very uncomfortable to wear. I guess the absence of the brace was a contributing factor to each dislocation.

We of course called the Mayo Clinic right away and they reiterated some of the rules of recovery from a hip operation (pay attention now for it might happen to you) which were simple yet complicated. At the same time, we posted notices all around the house.

- Avoid combinations of movement. Do not sit with your legs crossed because in that position you both bend your hip and bring your hip across your body
- Do not sit on low chairs, beds or toilets
- Do not lean forward while you are sitting down or as you sit down or stand up
- Do not bend over more than 90 degrees

And on and on. I couldn't keep it straight. Dr. Berry at Mayo said dislocations are not unusual and that Margo should "baby" the hip. Although these dislocations were worrisome, they were not considered emergency situations.

During this time, Margo's thoughts were deep and focused:

Intention to heal; intention to paint and to explore art. Intention to never dislocate hip again or fall. My body and soul are healing. I have to continue to create sacred spaces for myself; now I need to spend time in my studio – the home of my soul and spirit.

In spite of Margo's best intentions, the hip kept dislocating, and although it was an emotional downer, they weren't that painful. Margo and I had every confidence in the ability of emergency room staff to fix her hip each and every time it dislocated.

The first of the more "memorable" dislocations occurred in Galena. Think about how awful that sounds. Imagine sitting around with friends over dinner and saying, "Let's discuss your memorable dislocations, not vacations, not movies, not restaurants, but how your bones came out of their sockets." Everyone wanted to invite us to their parties?

The first in Galena was when we were going to close the deal on buying our cottage in the Galena Territories, our yuppie retreat away from working class Dubuque. We were going back and forth so much as we went swimming at least three times a week, we thought wouldn't it be nice to have a place nearby to crash in after the swim. Or just to spend a weekend contemplating. And it offered the possibility of safe alone time for Margo.

So we bought a small cottage. Margo and I were doing the final go-through of the house with our realtor as we wanted the owners to do certain things before we signed the papers. Margo sort of sat on a kitchen counter and was talking when she sighed out loud, *"My hip is*

332

dislocating." It just sort of slipped out of the socket. We gently laid her down on the floor.

Previously, at home, we could get her into a car rather quickly and then zip off to the emergency room. This time the car was too far away. We ended up calling 911. Eleven volunteer firemen—yep eleven, I counted them—and an ambulance came. It must have been a slow day for disasters. One guy knew what he was doing, got Margo settled, put her on an IV drip, and then they scooted her off to the Midwest Medical Center in Galena, maybe a ten-minute ride away.

I followed the ambulance and watched them wheel her into the emergency room. The emergency room doctor was this charming woman born in Vietnam who was barely five feet tall. She got Margo settled, gave her a mild sedative and then told me what she was going to do.

She would have to climb up on the bed, raise Margo's leg and then, with the aid of a nurse, put pressure on the hip to slide it into the socket. It was quite a sight to see this tiny woman, standing on the bed, raise Margo's legs which seemed as tall as her, slide the hip in until she heard a "click." She had obviously done this before.

I can't really remember if that was dislocation number two or three. In any event, I remember the last one, which happened at home just after Margo and I had taken Emma around the trails in the Kubota. As we got back to the house, the hip slipped out of the socket again— Margo wasn't wearing the brace. I got the Jeep and drove it right up alongside and we were able to get Margo into the front seat. We were then off to the hospital.

She was not in a lot of pain, just bewilderment, and once we approached Dubuque I asked, "Which hospital should we go to?" We had been to the two Dubuque hospitals before and since hip dislocations aren't critical injuries, there was always a wait. We knew the triage drill.

Margo said, *"Let's go to Galena, the time before was OK, as there is usually no one watching."*

So we drove twenty miles south to get to the Midwest Medical Center. As we approached the hospital, we saw an ambulance with its siren going and lights flashing pull in front us to get to the emergency room. The back doors opened and I could see the harried paramedics applying electric shock paddles to an overweight middle-aged man who was white as a sheet. By their feverish activity, I knew that was serious stuff and by the look on the paramedic's face I sensed the man wasn't going to make it.

He didn't.

They rushed him into the emergency room and we followed some of them after I got a wheelchair for Margo. I saw there was no longer any feverish activity around that man who lay in the next bed over, some fifteen feet from where Margo was put. He had died.

It was a surrealistic scene. My dear wife laying on the bed waiting for her hip to be placed back in its socket, and just a couple of feet over a corpse which just seconds before was a living human being surrounded by a hubbub of activity as many caring individuals tried to keep him alive. Now he was just a lifeless cadaver.

After the man died, the emergency room doctor—not the Vietnamese woman we had seen before—had gone out to talk to the family members who were streaming in, to inform them that he didn't make it.

From what I overheard, he had been watching TV and all of a sudden had the heart attack. They called 911 and the ambulance was first going to take him to a Dubuque hospital, but then realized he wasn't going to make it. They stopped in Galena hoping he could be saved.

This was my second premonition of death. The first had been when I was in the hospice with Margo's dad and he told the nurse all he wanted to do was die. All the same, we still felt that death wasn't in our immediate future.

Then a guy from a funeral home who was chewing gum appeared at the hospital. He brought a body bag and a gurney. The nurse helped him put the body into the bag, zip it up and then without any ceremony he was off. "Death be not proud," a poet once wrote. The contrast between the energy and group activity expended to try to save the man's life and the lonesome indifference and matter-of-factness of the people attending and removing the lifeless body struck me both then, and now, years later, as I write this.

The emergency room doctor had to fill out some paperwork. He came back to us with a sense of relief and said, "Okay, lady, what do we have here?" Then I noticed this doctor was huge—6'6" and maybe 250 pounds—whereas the Vietnamese doctor was 5' feet and maybe 120 pounds dripping wet.

"I don't know if I can do this," he said. The duty nurse reminded him that the tiny Vietnamese doctor had clambered onto the bed and with her help had gotten the hip back in. "You're huge, you can do it," the experienced nurse told him. And so he did.

After this last dislocation, we called Mayo and told them the hip had been "babied" enough. Dislocations were now coming days apart and we needed to fix it. Immediately. Comprende! Two days later we were back to the Mayo Clinic for another consultation. As a consequence, Margo would have surgery a month later, during which they would lengthen the stem, put in screws, and change the angle of prosthesis. Dr. Berry did say this was the last best hope, for we had just about done everything we could with the hip, and Margo was all metal and screws and wires. Oh yeah, those screws that were put in – they were no ordinary screws you get at Home Depot, as they cost US$125 a piece. The surgery was successful, and we later received a wonderful letter from Dr. Berry, Margo's surgeon at Mayo, on May 22, 2009:

"Two weeks from now if you are doing well and putting full weight on the walker, you may gradually start making the transition from the walker to the cane."

Wow, Margo was never so happy to be able to walk with a cane!

Energy Healing and Sacred Space Workshops

One may think it a coincidence, another fate, and a third sly manipulation, but whatever one wishes to call it, Margo's faith healer friend, Kayla Finlay, resumed communication with her. Kayla wanted to put on a series of workshops in both Illinois and Iowa with Margo's help called "Energy Healing and Sacred Space Workshops." In the midst of all the dislocations, Kayla Finlay came to Dubuque to see if she could get people to attend the workshops so she could make some money. She in turn had been dislocated from Lexington, Virginia, to Yardley, Pennsylvania.

Kayla, if you remember, worked in an International Food Store in Lexington, Virginia, a thousand miles and seemingly years away. The store didn't make it, so she started a restaurant called the Patisserie which suffered the same fate. Now she had given up on the food business and was going to try the healing and wellness business. Margo had received healing sessions from her in Virginia and benefitted; Kayla also benefitted, for Margo invested US$10,000 in her business, and now, when she was in Iowa, she was looking for more money—US$7,000 to be exact.

I voted not to give it to her. My vote didn't count for much, though. Margo vetoed it, as was her right, and she gave Kayla the US$7,000.

DO NOT GO DOWNSTAIRS!

Kayla arrived in Dubuque in a beat-up station wagon full of papers and her disheveled self, but so what. Margo wrote this: *"This week with Kayla is wonderful."*

Kayla gave a seminar each day and these were the topics:

Traveling Light – On the road and in life
Soul Restoration – Rediscover and restore your spirit
Right Livelihood – Your True Career Path
Shifting Suddenly Single into Consciously Single
Divine Source Healing – Discover your ability to heal yourself
    and others
Creating and Holding Sacred Space – Create a direct path to the
    sacred space within yourself, accessible in an instant…
    wherever you are and in light of whatever is happening
    around you

I really don't know how successful the workshops were financially, but emotionally Margo had found a kindred sportive spirit, something that she much needed. By the way, Kayla stayed with us the entire time she was in Dubuque.

Margo helped Kayla design and distribute flyers at our church and all around town. Kayla packaged herself as a "nationally recognized energy healer, intuitive, and life coach for over fifteen years. Has offered her services to clients in hospitals, in their homes and in her offices in Lexington, Virginia and Yardley, PA."

After one of the Sacred Space sessions, Margo wrote:

I am going to sleep in my studio and draw and paint that are my passion and I will cherish my space. I'm excited. More at ease, more natural smiles, more confident that I am doing the right thing and am more grounded.

For once Margo didn't think about her hip. Kayla's visit enlivened Margo. Little did she know that the relationship would grow deeper roots once that writing project of mine on the world's largest cattleman got underway.

18

labyrinth

Life was not a valuable gift but death was. Life was a fever-dream made up of joys embittered by sorrows, pleasure poisoned by pain; a dream that was a nightmare confusion of spasmodic and fleeting delights, ecstasies, exultations, happiness's and despairs-the heaviest curse devisable by divine ingenuity; but death was sweet, death was gentle, death was kind; death healed the bruised spirit and the broken heart and gave them rest and forgetfulness; death was man's best friend when man could endure life no longer, death came and set him free.

– Mark Twain

Labyrinth: an intricate combination or paths or passages in which it is difficult to find one's way or to reach an exit.

*T*hat's what Margo and I felt like we were in constantly. When would the surgeries, the pain, and all the discomfort end? Oh, Lordy, make it end. In spite of it all, we decided to add a pleasurable touch to our endless wandering by making up a "bucket list" of the things we wanted to do in a given year.

For many years now, Margo and I would start the year by telling each other the things we wanted to see while we bided out our time in beyond-staid Dubuque, Iowa. Although we didn't know then how close to death we were, we knew that we would not live forever—we decided we just had to go and do it, whatever it might be. So our list for the year

2010 included: going back to Panama where I had been in the Peace Corps and where Manuel Noriega had me thrown in jail; taking a car trip across the Canadian prairies to Banff, the Canadian Rockies, and Lake Louise; a solo trip to Minneapolis for Margo to visit her friends and family; and a trip back to Lexington, Virginia, to attend a wedding and visit all the friends we'd made there. We did three out of the four before the cancer ended Margo's life, but, hey, three out of four is a lot better that most people get in life.

It was a really strange year because there was really no normalcy in our lives—none whatsoever. Every day was a unique event to be determined and defined by how Margo was feeling. How swollen was her hip? How woozy was she from the many drugs she had taken the night before? What time of day was she able to get out of bed as a result? I was always up at 5:30 a.m. and would have to ramble around the house for hours alone until Margo awoke. It was over the top frustrating to me and, unfortunately, I showed it too many times. Many entries like this appeared in her diary during 2010.

> *End of last week was pretty bad – I was and really still am on the verge of tears – depression is here as Jani says I was strange all weekend and I'm sure I was as I'm feeling ½ present and ½ floating away. Pain was horrific on Friday – John finally got me to go for a convertible ride to Bellevue (20 miles south of Dubuque on the Mississippi). When we got home I went straight bed – focused on being in the here and now…isolation, lonely, unloved except by John, blah, who cares, what difference does it make because my body is never going to feel good; uninterested in anything or in myself.*

Bucket List Item # 1: Panama

"How do you say ice bag in Spanish?" Margo asked the bilingual and quite pleasant and vibrant cabdriver in Panama City, Panama, in June of 2010.

"Ice bag," was what he replied.

Margo and I cracked up with laughter. We were at the end of our two-week trip to Panama where I had served in the Peace Corps some forty years before. On our way back from the cool mountains 200 miles away from hot, humid, and super-congested Panama City, Margo's hip started to hurt and was swollen. We needed to get the ice to calm it down. We had driven all over the country, including the border with

Costa Rica where I lived many years ago in the little town of Rio Sereno, population maybe 200.

"A trip of a lifetime" is how Margo described it in her diary.

Today is 3/24 on this trip of a lifetime and I am going to write for the first time. At the moment I am having lunch at the Miraflores locks watching two gigantic ships go thru each – wow! Being at the locks makes one more interested in transiting the canal though not likely to happen.

Jani is at Peace Corps office across the road sharing his experiences as a volunteer with them. They all had heard of the couple who was jailed by Noriega so he is having a spectacular time. This is true wherever he goes and with whomever he meets. He's making our taxi driver happy with his chatter – stories, experiences, history, commentary. In fact on Sunday our driver was an older guy and Jani and he got into talking Panamanian Spanish slang. They said "goodbye you asshole." Both were falling over with laughter.

We arrived very auspiciously in Panama City one night on Continental Airlines from Houston. Sweltering and humid, I always called Panama City a three-shower-a-day city as its oppressiveness caused you to sweat all the time. It was a great place if you wanted to lose weight. We flew first class from Minneapolis to Houston to accommodate Margo's swollen and at times painful hip. Upon landing in the beyond-chaotic Panama City airport, Tocumen, we asked for and got Margo a wheelchair and were immediately adopted by a cheerful, effervescent chatterbox named Enrique who was wearing a Continental Airlines shirt. He ended up being our concierge, cab driver, tour guide, and general handyman throughout our time in Panama City.

Enrique pushed Margo through customs along with a former Secretary of Agriculture who had just gotten back from the Cleveland clinic after some surgery. Weird, for he was dealing with a condition that had too much bone growth while Margo didn't have enough. I could not believe how Enrique was able to push both wheelchairs at the same time and straight through customs without much effort. Our fellow passengers waited in long sweltering lines to get their passports stamped, while Enrique pushed us out to his car past customs and then went back to get our baggage. I was worried we were being taken but eased up when I sensed his sincerity. He drove us to the venerable El Panama Hotel; he was even more of a yakker than me, if that's possible.

It's hard to imagine a more convoluted place than Panama City. Car horns are always blowing and one-way streets, full of rushing cars, always seemed to lead you in a direction you didn't want to go. The El Panama Hotel, which years ago was the cat's meow in town, was now a little tattered from all those days in the sweltering sun. The rooms were huge and opened up onto a corridor open to the outdoors. It had an immense sinewy pool with one of those pool bars you swim up to. The *rabiblancos*, white bloods, rich Panamanians, still frequented this hotel, and at breakfast you always saw a parade of well-dressed men and women with rings the size of boulders coming in to eat. I loved hearing Panamanian Spanish which is quick and slangy and "s" is always dropped at the end of words.

After two days of decompressing from the trip, we got our air-conditioned rental SUV, a far cry from the rickety buses I used to take across the country when I was in the Peace Corps. We then hired a cab to show us the way out of the city and then we were off to the Costa Rican border and the mountains where I had lived—and had been arrested and jailed, and then driven to Panama City under armed guard.

As we drove the 200-odd miles to David (pronounced Dah-Vid not David), I told Margo the full story about how my ex-wife and I were taken away by Manuel Noriega. Here is the short version. When we left for the mountains, I told Margo that Noriega was just one of the two most important people in this affair. Noriega was a memory and in jail, but Alvaro Pittí was still alive and well and the fellow who saved me from Noriega. When the troubles started in Panama in 1968, there were five people who declared themselves president and two at the same time. I told my best friend and store owner Alvaro Pitti to call the U.S. Embassy in Costa Rica and to ask them if the U.S. military could come and take me away. He did this at considerable risk to himself.

I lived in the farthest part west of Panama hard on the Costa Rican border. In fact, half the town I lived in was in Costa Rica—and that half was earth years ahead of the Panamanian section in development and political sophistication. The Panamanian part had no roads, just tracks; it did not have electricity or any of the amenities of modern life. You learned to depend on yourself and you learned what you were truly made of. While it was over 90 degrees in the flatlands, it was always 20 degrees cooler in the mountains. Strangely, it was one of the happiest times of my life.

The military overthrew an elected president who had been in office for just eleven days. In the mountains where I lived, most of the populace was for the ousted president and an insurrection began. It was centered in another small coffee-growing town, Santa Clara, about two hours away by horseback from where Tom Campagna, another volunteer, lived.

As a naïve and hence fearless volunteer, I had frequently traveled to Santa Clara on horseback to visit Tom, not thinking what people in Rio Sereno, many retired military types, would think. So when a military patrol led by Noriega came into town, a local *sapo*, literally frog, but one who squeals, told the patrol I had been to Santa Clara.

My first wife and I were on our way to Alvaro Pitti's store when the military stopped us. We must have appeared out of place to them. Why would two Americans who have everything live out in the middle of nowhere? They must have thought we were doing something bad or illegal. Noriega confronted me.

"Were you in Santa Clara?"

"Yes," I said.

"You must come with us for there will be an investigation." I complied for I learned many years ago that you don't argue with a man wearing four hand grenades.

We were taken away. They marched us out of town to where a military truck picked us up two days later. We were driven to Davis where finally a CIA guy came and got us out of jail. He accompanied us to Panama City with an armed guard; we were released and then asked to leave the country. While being marched out of town, Richard Koster in his book, *In the Time of Tyrants Panama 1968-1990,* described the scene as follows:

"Noriega. Noriega. His name told all through the time of tyrants. His first mission after the coup, a day or so after, was to take a squad up the region called Rio Sereno and bring down a couple of U.S. Peace Corps Volunteers, Susan and John Freivalds, who the Guardia thought might be helping the guerrileros. The Freivalds then in their 20s remember the trip. It took two days to go 20 miles for the roads were washed out. En route Lieutenant Noriega requisitioned a horse and let Mrs. Freivalds ride it. But the gesture was less gentlemanly than it appears. He had her carry the squad's automatic rifle and wear a Green Guardia cap. If there were snipers around, she'd draw their fire."

There was no sniper about when Margo and I finally drove up to Sereno. What a mind-blowing experience that was. The town now had roads, electricity, and running water. Alvaro gave me a big hug and a Cheshire cat grin when we met. We had prepared a photo book for Alvaro with lots of pictures he had never seen and newspaper clippings from the American and Panama Press; the latter ran headlines like "Cuerpos de Paz Conspiraba Contra LaJunta" (i.e., Peace Corps Conspires Against the Junta). When I first showed the headline to Margo, she said, *"I guess that means you can't run for political office."*

Alavaro was a kind host and he introduced us as people who wanted to buy land. Hot stuff! He proudly showed us his ranches and the white Brahma cattle that were munching on the tall pangola grass. Margo found the ranches and the cattle fascinating; we both loved the smell of the pangola grass. Alvaro, who spoke very little English, couldn't pronounce "Margo" very well and dubbed her "Margaret Thatcher" instead.

Whenever we went to a new ranch, the cattle would recognize him, and when he shouted, "Venga!" (come) they would amble over the fence hoping that Alavaro had some corn or salt to give them. Margo got into the Venga act as well. When we got back to Iowa, I changed the plates on Margo's car to Venga in honor of that trip and kept the tradition going even when I moved to Minnesota.

Margo and I had harbored the idea of going into the Peace Corps when we retired and had visited a couple of retired volunteers. But the creature comforts of civilization got to us and we decided we didn't want to spend two years riding on rickety buses again and sleeping on bad beds. We had both been there (Margo on her Asia trip) and done that (me in the Peace Corps where two diagonal ropes and a mattress passed for a bed and box springs).

Bucket List Item #2: Moose Jaw and Mountains

The flat, expansive, and windblown prairies, be they in the U.S. or Canada, have always fascinated me—less so Margo, but she granted me this indulgence to drive across Canada and even stop in Moose Jaw, Saskatchewan, where I always wanted to go. It was late April when we headed out.

> *...drove 6M mile through Saskatchewan, Alberta, Banff and Lake Louise, across the Canadian Rockies, Sandpoint, Idaho where we stayed in our friend's lovely Schweitzer Mt. condo, drove the length of Idaho, fun meeting with our friend in Boise, great mandolin and guitar playing and then across Wyoming, South Dakota and Minnesota...All along I have struggled with falling asleep and horrific pain – John and I slept together well, I didn't snore but horrible leg pain, hot baths, healing pads, ice.*

That's all Margo wrote about our almost-three-week journey in early May 2010. Margo was preoccupied with pain during our Canadian venture as well as afterwards when she wrote about it.

Despite the pain, we both enjoyed the calmness of Canada and getting away from the noise, if not paranoia, of American politics and materialism. What she didn't mention was Moose Jaw is really a neat place. I did feel a little like the time we were in Hazard, Kentucky, where we were the only tourists; there were not too many Grey Line tours that stopped in Moose Jaw either. The highlight of Moose Jaw was The Temple Gardens Mineral Spa Resort. Don't know where Moose Jaw or Saskatchewan is? Not to worry, neither do many Canadians.

Saskatchewan is a fertile (wheat, canola, and beans—lots of beans) prairie province that touches the northern borders of North Dakota and Montana. Moose Jaw is a city of 35,000 which is more or less 700 miles north of Denver, Colorado. Like many cities in the middle of nowhere, it was dying; businesses closed their doors, young people left, and some people had lost hope.

But one young entrepreneur, Debbie Thorn, was intrigued by the fact that the Cree Indian name for Moose Jaw, *Moscatani-Gaw,* meant "a warm place by the river." The fact that the city sat on top of some geothermal springs had been reinforced years earlier in the hunt for natural gas. Deb Thorn—whom we met during our visit—not only wanted to

343

reopen the well, but to build a world-class destination spa around it. She got a thousand Moose Javians (yep, that's what they call themselves) to buy shares of US$1 a piece (minimum 500) to build the spa. It opened its door in 1996, was an immediate success, and now has a four-star designation like the Greenbrier. It offers things like a "moor mud anti-stress facial for US$60." Busting at the seams with demand from stressed out business types and seniors like us with creaking joints, it underwent a huge expansion. The gymnasium-sized warm springs mineral pool now acts like a town park where locals come and sit on underwater benches to shoot the breeze.

Moose Jaw was okay, but Margo only got excited when we got to the Canadian Rockies and Banff. This was always a goal of hers and we finally did it. We stayed at the Chateau at Lake Louise. Views of the turquoise lake and the jagged mountains enlivened her, but she was always a little somber, for she never knew when the pain and discomfort would reappear.

The indoor pool was simply gorgeous at the Chateau and they had a steam room with eucalyptus-scented steam coming in. There was an awful flight of stairs to go down to get to it; this was too hard for Margo to handle. So I went to the concierge, actually at the Chateau they had three. I handed him US$20 and said, "Let's figure out a way to get my wife down to the pool without stairs."

I wish I could have given somebody US$20 to get us out of the medical labyrinth we were in, but the US$20 got us through the labyrinth of the Chateau's innards and to the pool with ONE step for Margo to navigate. The concierge commanded a wheelchair and got us on it. We took the maid's elevator to a subbasement through a laundry room, prep kitchen, past the boilers, out into the parking lot behind the chateau, and to a door that led into the pool. Once you opened the door, Voilà, the pool was one tiny step away. We both luxuriated in having solved this labyrinth and we both smelled like eucalyptus for days.

After luxuriating at the Chateau for a couple of days, we headed back to the U.S.A. via Standpoint and Boise, Idaho, but first drove through the backside of the Canadian Rockies which are sharp and jagged. Margo's heart leaped with joy.

And we had to laugh when we reached the paranoia of the United

States once again. We crossed the border at a little town in Idaho. The customs agent took my passport and looked at it. It said I was born in Latvia.

He looked at me sternly and asked, "Why were you born in Latvia?"

You can't make that kind of stuff up.

Bucket List Item #3: Minneapolis Alone

The year so far was one of dichotomies. On the one hand, we were constantly fighting with all the health issues; on the other, we had experienced two wonderful trips. Margo sensed I was cracking under the constant pressure of being her caregiver. We needed relief from each other.

She wanted to drive up and do a week in Minneapolis by herself and I urged her not to do that six-hour drive as it would be too hard—it was hard on me and I was relatively healthy. I suggested that I drive her there and back and that her friends and family could drive her around or she could take a cab. This gave me some sense of security even though I was reluctant to let her go alone.

> *Fortunately I had a wonderful time in Minneapolis. The complete high was disrupted by my fall Friday evening as I got out of a taxi at the hotel. I had stood up and somehow tripped on my feet and before I knew it I was falling backwards – tried to turn so my right side took the big hit and the back of my head – had a big lump which by morning and the help of ice disappeared. Of course I was beside myself. So upset that I did it and so concerned about my falling (it has happened too many times). My brother and sister-in-law came over for a while to calm me and to check on me. I waited until John had picked me up in LaCrosse to tell him. All week I was very clear about how weak I am and how much I really, really need to listen to him.*

This all happened a month before Margo's death. Right about that time, we received an invitation to attend the wedding of our Virginia helper, CJ. We were getting ourselves mentally ready to go but Margo's body would not cooperate. She was not gaining any more strength and the hip kept swelling even with constant wrapping.

Every day was more of a challenge, but we thought it would eventually pass. A funny whistle sound began to appear in Margo's breathing and she had next to no appetite, but was gaining weight—mostly water we assumed. We decided to call the Mayo Clinic and get it checked out. Margo's last diary entry was on August 27, 2010. It read:

What is wrong with me that I don't stop falling? It's like I have a death wish — I hate myself for it...I must use my walker.

19

end of the line

Well it's all right, if you live the life you
please
Well it's all right even if the sun don't shine
Well it's all right, we're going to the end of
the line

– Traveling Wilburys, "End of the Line"©

So we made an appointment with the lymphedema unit at the clinic, where a wonderful woman, Sara Richardson, had taken care of us before, to see what was up. On the day we left, thirteen days before Margo's death, she drove the car as far as LaCrosse, Wisconsin, about half way to Rochester, Minnesota, where she couldn't keep her eyes open any more. She wanted to keep driving but I could see she was fading and said, "Let me drive." After I got behind the wheel she promptly fell asleep.

We had planned to make this a day trip—just go up, find out what was wrong, get some prescriptions and better wraps, and be home that evening. She did mention a shortness of breath.

"You look just awful," said Sara at the lymphedema clinic when we got there. She had dealt with Margo before and at that time made a remarked about how *well* Margo was doing. This time Margo got no such kudos. Sara said, "There is something else going on. We have to find out."

It was a Friday, but Sara got us in to see an internist who scheduled a battery of tests and then wanted to see us the next Monday. Something was going on, but he didn't know what. Even then we didn't suspect cancer for Margo's mammogram, etc. were all clear. A letter was even sent to us dated September 15th from the Mayo Clinic which said, "We have reviewed your previous mammograms and compared them to your most recent mammogram here. We are pleased to inform you that the results are negative for cancer."

After the session with the internist, we had every test done known to man, from chest x-rays to the extraction of every type of liquid in her body. The first x-rays were not encouraging. They revealed nodules in Margo's lungs that were taking away her breathing capacity. They were sure to be found cancerous—not some strange fungus.

We had no extra clothes or anything with us and I decided to drive back and get them. Margo was exceedingly weak and I couldn't leave her in the hotel alone. I asked her brother to come and stay with her for a night at the hotel while I went to get our things.

The internist was worried about Margo. She had labored breathing and he told me not to hesitate calling 911 if it got worse before he could see her again on Monday. Her brother came over and spent the night with her, and wouldn't you know it, he called me and asked what to do when Margo was having a hard time. "Call 911," I said.

I headed back to Dubuque and while there I penned this note to Margo's friends and family.

"You would think that with five hip operations, two knee replacements, seven hip dislocations, and two breast cancers…there would be no further medical issues for the rest of her life. Not so lucky.

Just got back from Mayo where a mysterious chest cancer popped up. Some nodules were discovered and we will have the final test results shortly and we will see the oncologist when I get back. Margo was out of sorts last week even though a local doctor did a check up on her and said everything was OK even though she had a huge water build up and no appetite and was very weak.

In any event, all major cancers were ruled out: ovarian, bone, liver, etc. I am worn out from taking her to get tested for this and that. How do you know you are emotionally worn out? When you try to use your car keys as the TV remote.

Margo was very anxious (duh) and she had been given oxy so she is in a narcotic buzz till the appointments start again. What would be nice is if you could send a card with good wishes so that when she gets home she will have a pile of mail that is not bills.

p.s. Thank you for letting me vent!"

While I was gone, Margo's breathing did get labored and her brother did call 911 and she was taken to the emergency room at St. Mary's Hospital. The oxygen revived her. I came immediately back to Rochester.

She stabilized in a couple of days and was moved back into the general population, but still on oxygen. Then the bad news. When the oncologist came with full test results, we were informed she had cancer and that it was what they call pleomorphic sarcoma. It had spread everywhere and it was fatal. She could live a couple of months with chemo, but the chemo would be horrendous as it is nothing more than poisoning your body to kill the cancer cells.

Imagine the shock we were in from just going to Mayo for a check-up and a couple of days later being told that the game is over.

It was Margo's call. She decided she wanted to die in peace. She did not want to pursue the exotic treatment, which promised to be agonizing but would provide no quality time. With the decision made, she got on the phone to her best friends and family and they all said they would be in Rochester as soon as possible. I pretty much went into shock and felt completely numb.

My daughter Maija set up a Caring Bridge site (www.caringbridge. org/visit/margof) much like the one I had ten years before when I was burned and people could send get well messages and I could provide updates.

After Margo had called everyone, armies of family and friends descended on the hospital. And when her sorority sisters showed up, she let out a big whoop like she did when we got married. With the arrival of her best friend Ginger, she found some peace and the decision to go to a hospice was formed. I was pretty much a useless basket case by now, as everything that had happened in the last couple of years descended on me. I just remember blankly staring at walls.

Kids appeared in the form of her nieces and nephews—children who jumped into bed with her—and her friend Kayla of Thelma and Louise fame came. It was rather overwhelming. Ginger became a drill sergeant and started to do a triage on who could and could not come to see Margo as the poor girl was becoming exhausted by all the visitors.

Then a miraculous thing happened; one day Margo woke up and felt totally fine. She had an appetite, joked, and had strength in her voice. It appeared as if she was totally well and completely free of any

349

narcotic buzz. It was kind of spooky in a way and the social worker at Mayo said she had seen this happen before where the body just decides to have one perfect day before succumbing to all the ills that have overtaken it.

Then a hospice near Minneapolis was picked and we found an ambulance to take her there. Ginger would go with her in the ambulance. Margo not only wanted to be surrounded by friends and family when she died, but by three things: her dog Emma, her racing bike that she had acquired years ago, and the beautiful Chinese screen that adorned our living room. I was to go get them and bring them to the hospice. The oncologist didn't say how much longer Margo had to live after she left the hospital, but we had hoped for a couple of weeks. So I set out for Dubuque (two and a half hours away) and Margo was taken to the Twin Cities (ninety minutes away). My goal was to spend the night at home and be back in Minneapolis by noon the next day.

Soon

Our church had been apprised of all the events that had transpired. That night when I arrived back home I found they had arranged a potluck at our house for me so I wouldn't be lonely and hungry. It was very nice to be surrounded by people who cared for me.

It was around 8:30 that night when Margo's friend Kayla called and said Margo was fading fast and for me to head back NOW. She got Margo on the phone and all I heard from my wife's weak voice was, *"Soon."* Those were the last words Margo ever spoke to me.

It's 8:30 p.m., I am totally frazzled and it's a six-hour drive to Minneapolis. What to do? I was going to do it anyway, but I interrupted everyone and said, "I need a volunteer to drive me to Minneapolis tonight. Margo's going to die tonight!"

Frank Potter, an educator and rather wordy speaker at our church, said he would do it. We stopped by his house and picked up some things and off we went with Frank driving. I was in a semi-catatonic state and couldn't drive; he ended up driving the whole way. We got there in about five hours and it was around 1:30 a.m. when we got in. Kayla, Ginger, and my daughter Maija were there. I went into the room where Margo lay breathing heavily, the last throes of life were leaving her body. I sat down beside her and placed my head on her arm and squeezed her hand and whispered to her. She squeezed my hand back and I felt good; she knew that I had made it back. She died at around 5:30 that morning.

I was looking at her face the moment she died and saw all the wrinkles disappear from it. There was this angelic glow as all the agonies and pain left her body. Maija took a picture of her death mask but still hasn't shown it to me.

I was in shock. Maija took me to the car and drove me to the hotel. The staff at the hotel knew what had happened and nodded in silence as I was led to my room. Maija helped me undress and put me to bed and a flood of tears and numbness came over me as I eventually fell asleep.

I started writing this book in earnest some time in the late spring of 2011 and finished these last words on Easter Sunday 2012. A resurrection of sorts. I now have accepted Margo's death and have found people who won't deny me her memory and who enjoy hearing of the joy we shared in our lives. I can now listen to love songs on the radio and not cry, and have decorated the house with her paintings, not as a tearful but as a joyous reminder of the life we led, and gosh still are leading together. I have found joy and love with new people and new perspectives on so many things.

That old beat-up brown steamer trunk full of her diaries and full of her hopes for the future still sits in the corner. I have pored over every word in them in order to write this book.

It is perhaps fitting that I should end this book with the very same words we used to start Margo's Celebration of Life in both Dubuque and Minneapolis. Attributed to Mark Twain, these words in so many ways embody the spirit of my dear, dear, Margo:

Twenty years from now you will be more disappointed by the things you didn't do than the ones you did do. So throw away your bowlines. Sail away from the safe harbor. Catch the trade winds in your sails. Explore. Dream. Discover.

John Freivalds
Easter Sunday
April 8, 2012

epilogue

A famous person who lost a wife and a son in a car crash said it best. "Trust me. There will come a day when a reminder of her will come about, but instead of a tear in your eye, there will be a smile on your face when you think back." The book I ended up writing was one means of dealing with it and finding that out for myself.

- **Grief.** "Keen mental suffering and distress over affliction or loss; sharp sorrow, painful regret." This is what the dictionary says but grief doesn't have to consume your life if you realize and do some simple things like I did.

- **Realize that coping was a religion**. Given Margo's fragile bone structure that led to many falls, and all the things I did to cope with it, I now recognize her condition had become my religion, which I practiced for the thirty-three months we lived in Dubuque and even some of the time we had in Virginia. So when she died my whole life changed from the daily devotional to the religion of pain and coping—to a big void. I not only missed Margo's intellectual and physical company, but was left with being by myself. So what to do?

- **Reach out and tell someone**. I didn't hide under the bed and weep and drink (at least not all of the time), but told everyone what had happened, and lo and behold, help came coming in—from unlikely sources. Clayton Yeutter was once the head of the Republican Party and Ronald Reagan's Secretary of Agriculture and later special trade representative. You know, one of those heartless Republicans. He gave me the best advice. His wife died abruptly at age sixty-two and he learned some lessons.

352

- **Grieve. Don't hide your emotion and try to be strong.** There is no right or wrong way. I went to a couple of seminars for grieving people and hooray found out I was "normal."

- **Don't make any major decisions.** Don't go out and move to Hawaii or marry the first woman you see.

I actually met a young woman who said it will be at least two years before you can be somewhat normal again. I didn't believe her and thought my mind and emotions could just get an app for grief.

But she was right, though it took some painful if not pitiful attempts at relationships to realize that. In addition to a motley if not sordid collection of internet dates and bar flies and flirts, I did encounter some interesting people. One steamy if not tumultuous eight-month relationship was with a beautiful, rich, urbane, extremely intelligent, religious zealot, who looked at me as a project rather than a companion. And in the end she wanted to snuggle closer to God and not to me. I told my witty neighbor about this and she quipped, "John, all men fantasize about threesomes, but this is one you didn't count on."

Then there was the gentle if not fawning ex farm wife who wanted to do nothing more than cook and clean for me. I found a winner who alas wasn't that interested in me, but was a kind and gentle athletic biking companion who sent me the nicest messages. In the end I lucked out in meeting a beautiful, energetic, and street-smart businesswoman who knew how to build and run restaurants and be totally honest. She will be a friend for life.

But the best way to find someone who matches perfectly, one who really fits, is to have the patience that Margo had.

I have three marvelous daughters and I asked them to describe how I have dealt with grief. Here's what Karla said:

"It's been nuts – especially the dating. In the first few months after she died I bought him a T-shirt that said 'No Soliciting' just to remind him in a fun way that it was too early. But then the time became right. Of course he doesn't want to be alone and deserves to be happy with someone, but he's still looking for Margo in a wife in every woman he meets. How could he not? Everybody gets compared to her every trait – from looks to intelligence, grace, elegance, spirit, even handling conflict within the relationship."

"He is struggling to find his new identity and place in the world. Sometimes it's like swinging from tree to tree trying to grasp onto something that will stick. It can be very hard to see him struggling for balance, and the one person who could put it all back together is gone. I think that's the hardest part of death. It's the worst irony.

The one person you want to talk to the most about your loss is the person who caused it and therefore is gone."

Maija, my youngest, chimed in with this:

"Watching my dad go through the many stages of grief over the past two years has been devasting, frustrating and fascinating-all at the same time. Observing the evolution as he's slowly climbed out of the depths of grief confirms that the heart and mind are truly connected – that if one gets out of balance, it can throw everything off.

He's used this time to explore who he truly is, since his identity as a husband was so abruptly stolen from him. Whether it is an artist, a student of religion, an athlete, a craftsman, traveler or an author, my dad is paving a path that will guide him for the rest of his life and is working to discover what really matters to him."

So What Have I Learned?

- We are arrogant when we say that some people died before their time as we can't be a judge of that. We can, however, rejoice in every moment we shared with that person, and if you are a writer like me, document it.

many thanks

I didn't realize how many people had helped me write this book about a kind, tall, and gentle enterprising woman from Hopkins, Minnesota, U.S.A. But Margo was one of those people we encounter in our lives who touched everyone she met, so this list is quite extensive and indeed worldly. The people below helped with providing snippets as well as truckloads of information and giving wonderful editing comments. I spent a lot of money on postage, FedEx and phone calls.

I had to use a lot of creativity and persistence to get all the facts. The best FedEx story came from Gray Packer who Margo hung around with in New Zealand. He had some neat photos I wanted but the photo reproduction studio he usually went to was destroyed by an earthquake. I sent him a FedEx pack to send them back to me and I got them duplicated here and then FedExed them back. And I got hold of Rida Ali, one of Margo's bosses in Evansville, Indiana, who was in Cairo in the midst of their Arab spring. And then I tracked down someone Margo met in Thailand by running newspaper ads in Mississippi by hiring Gladys Briely, private investigator, in Mississippi to find him in Gulfport. And I had to be pushy. Many people who knew and enjoyed Margo had moved on with their lives and didn't want to be reminded of her death. I was sometimes perceived as grieving too long but as my friend Tom Veblen wrote: "Nothing in the world can take the place of persistence… not talent, education, genuine persistence and determination alone are omnipotent." So I hope my prose lives up to the persistence I have shown.

Let us begin.

New Zealand: Gray Packer; **Australia:** David Cranna, Art and Narelle Krieger; **Thailand:** Mitch David, Stephen de Forest, Sally Duke.

New Jersey: Joan Newman and the gals at Hydromer, Jean Kelly;

Indiana: Ginger Cubelis, Christine Helfrich, Luis de la Cruz, Dr. Rida Ali, Kim Carpenter, David Gray, Win Hamilton.

Minnesota: Barbara Kalina, Karen Lundgren, LaVonne Lutz, Anne Mogush, Sue Barker, Liana Carbon, Pat Cicardelli, Mick and Kris Ellis, Jan Kruse, Mary Beth Frischmeyer, Lynne Hardey, Phyllis Haman, Meg and Joe Hillan, Bob and Barb Hill, Janet Keysser, John Thompson, Jean Robbins, JoAnn Wiggington, Ann Zietlow, JoEllen Finch, Heidi Mogush, Johnny Mogush, Paul Mogush, Jeff and Annie Mason, Patty Belois, Jane Iwan, Laurel Sandberg, JoAnn Greenwall, Kori Petersson.

Virginia: Lou Hodges, Lucy Turner, Hensons, CJ Goad, Peter and Jean Sils, John Murphy, Susan Bushnell, Ned and Kelly Hooper, Susan Racinet, Vic and Nancy Schiller, Micheal Hoffman, James Dickovick, Jeff Kosky, Stephanie Hoddie, Susan Racinet, Kayla Finlay, Jeff Pufahl.

Iowa: Mary Ellyn Jensen, Laura Schlegel, Charlie Sisler, Mirdza Berzins, Jeanne Harrington, Herbers especially Noah, John Luckstead, Kent Mayfield, Cindy Weise, Dick Landis, Joan Tully.

Then of course we have all those people who helped me after Margo's death and these include:

Frank Potter, my daughters Karla, Maija and Jill, Clayton Yeutter, Diane Mitchell, Barbara Boldt, Jeri Johnson, Daryll Natz, Brian Cooper, Natalie Deutmeyer, Donna Parrish and the nonlinear crew at Multilingual.

Daria Kuligana, Uldis and Ilze Salenieks, Ellen Belot Roggemann, Sara Schiffler, George and Ann Spanos, John and Nancy Pielmeir, Joe Kress, Paul Schnabel, Peter Cers, Hendrik and Uhli Schultz, Gale Belk, Bill Mott.

Jack and Yunhae Martinson, Ben Sargent, Harald Frederiksen, Larry Baill, Joshua Rubo, Susan Freivalds, Jim DeWall, George Foulkes, Abby Garard, Peter Blair, Elaine Jablonski, Paul and Rosa Rogers, Gladys Brierly, Justin Loxley.

Bill and Johnsie Price, Tom Campagna, Alvaro Pitti, Andy and Randi Steinfeldt, Billy Hogan, Ryan Kelley, Peggy Nessler, Ulrich Henes, Marcel Didier, Yvonne La Pinotiere, Stephanie McKenna, Wendy Eckman, Rebecca Ryskamp.

Mary Bentley, Carla Ferrell, Donald Gallehr, Aaron Higgins, Dana X. Marshall, Gloria Norton, Mike Sayre, Roger and Sherri Schiffler,

Anita and Gary Schmied, Tom and Linda Veblen, Brian and Jennifer Havlovick, Linda Ford Kelley.

Jeff and Greg Brink, Bill Gladstone, Kenneth Kales, Gene Leman, Smith Yewell, Brett Lawrence, Paul Miller, Tom Martinson, Loren Kruse, Auseklis Ozols, Daina Racinska.

Judd Frost, Warren Lester, Lee Egerstrom, Peggy Sands Orchowski, Lee Bernet, Lee Zimmerman, Ausma Giga, Jane Kloss, Lisa Andrusyszyn, Jeanne Mahoney, Briana Biggs, Marsha Freeman, Don Colpits, Ruth Ann Holetz.

Allen Olson, Dina Blumenfield, Carl Katz, Liz Vanderlinde, Steve Dupor, Bill Hinchberger, Gary Mach, Skaidrite Stolcera, Jon Loxley, Melinda Colwell, Noelle Stoyles, Lindsay Freise, Luke Stevens-Royer, Sharon Recker, Doug Harwood.

James Crumpler, Kathy Kessler, Bert and Sharon Schwartz, Doug Wagner, William E. Hogan II, Chuck Carlson, Geneva Benoit, Rory Cowan, Karl Altan, Rina Zhang, Gavin Grimes, Larry Kaufer.

Gone but not forgotten are Jim Ferro, Jeffrey Norton, Kip Codrington and Andrea Pampinini.

Mayo Clinic: Dr. William Berry, Sara Richardson, Christine McNamara.

In Memoriam: Mimi Freivalds and John Mogush whose generous legacy made our lives so much better.

Finally to these guys who lent their skills to make the book happen: Lory Strom, Javan Kienzle, Michael Kunka, Karen Lafferty and my chum Linda Ford Kelley.

appendix:
the legend of thelma and louise –
new england style

*I feel really awake. I don't recall
ever feeling this awake. You know?
Everything looks different now. You
feel like that? You feel like you got
something to live for now?*

– Lines spoken by Thelma in the
movie *Thelma and Louise*

So what does this legendary duo have to do with my writing a book about the world's largest cattleman? Please let me explain, but first, *Thelma and Louise*. This was a 1991 film starring Susan Sarandon (Louise) as a waitress and Geena Davis (Thelma) as a housewife who leave their lives of quiet desperation and go off to see the world, mostly the Western U.S., in their 1966 Thunderbird (the Lexus Coupe of its day). The Thelma and Louise legend was reincarnated by Margo and Kayla when they met up in New Jersey and headed off for a girls' only tour of New England in 2009 while husband, John, clunks away on a book about Paul Engler while sitting in his yacht off the New Jersey shore.

OK, Paul Engler. The short version is that he is probably the world's single largest cattle feeder who feeds one million head of cattle a year—enough to supply Walmart with all its beef needs. Blah, Blah. According to Engler he got interested in having a book written about himself when another Texas billionaire, T. Boone Pickens, asked Paul:

"When are you going to write your book?" Pickens had written several.

"I can't write, but I know who can," was Paul's response. I had met Engler in Iran of all places in 1970—and stayed in touch, sent him all the books I had written, many articles, and thus the old adage strikes through, "Share of mind is share of market."(My next book will be about Engler and the cattle business so stay tuned and read all about that meeting in Iran.)

From Margo's perspective it was a good project for my suffering ego, but for her not as good, as I got very hyper doing it. It was a tough project, for Engler wanted a family-style book of memories (tell 'em about how good Aunt Nellie's potato salad was), and yet wanted it to be commercially recognized, which meant talking about his suit against Oprah Winfrey. By the way, the suit made Dr. Phil famous as he was her "spiritual advisor" during the trials in Amarillo just as Kayla had become for the trials for Margo. To speed things along, Engler finally agreed to be interviewed by me alone. We tried to do it in Amarillo but that didn't work as there were too many distractions.

So we agreed to meet on his gleaming ninety-two-foot yacht, the *Yoli*, off the New Jersey seashore in a town called Forked River in late August. Fork River is eighty-three miles south of New York City. The captain "parked" it there for the hurricane season. I asked, "Can I bring Margo along?" and he said, 'Yea." We would sit and talk, pontificate, smoke cigars, and the hope would be that Margo would read and look at the ocean. I was continually talking to Engler's sister and told her about Margo's hip brace, and when Engler heard about it, she was un-invited. "The circular staircases would be too tough for her to navigate," he said. And that was that.

What would Plan B be? Margo would still drive out to New Jersey with me, but meet her chum Kayla who would come down from Yardley, Pennsylvania, not too far away. I would go "sailing" with Engler for a week and we would all meet up again in another little port town called Brielle, fifteen miles up the coast. It would be just like sailing around the Caribbean, only New Jersey style.

We arrived the day before Engler did, and in spite of his admonitions about Margo sleeping on his yacht with the hip brace, she did, as did Kayla. The captain of the yacht did not know about the admonitions and was happy to have us for company.

Thus began the legend of Thelma and Louise. The big difference being that Margo would be Thelma and Kayla would be Louise. A whole series of emails followed their trip which ended on September 24, 2009, and pretty much continued until Margo died, almost exactly a year later. Margo wrote:

> *The end of Kayla's and my Thelma and Louise trip thru New England. Live with intent and integrity. Love with abandonment. Live on the edge as if each day is your last. Honor your friends and family.*

And she wrote Kayla:

> *We had a wonderful trip home. We were pleasantly surprised with the turnpikes as they have vastly improved since the last time either one of us had traveled them. PA was simply gorgeous — more color than many places. I wore my new stylish outfit yesterday which John loved and made me feel young and more normal than ever in the past few years!*

Memos from Margo to Kayla (Louise)

DATE	MEMO CONTENTS
10/27/09	I just got the word that surgery is on for next Wed., the 4th. We'll head to Rochester Mon. afternoon to be ready for presurgical tests and meeting with Dr. Berry. It's great they were able to get it scheduled so quickly, but he did not want to have any more episodes. So lots of healing energy is requested!
10/29/09	I am feeling in a good place re: surgery. I learned from the surgery scheduler for Dr. Berry, with whom I have had a number of conversations over two years, that he has left the entire day for me in case he should need it, but in talking with the seemingly very competent resident, if there are not any surprises it should be a pretty straight surgery requiring four or fewer hours. Yea! It is nice though that they are prepared for not so good. I am confident this will be a piece of cake with a rapid recovery. I asked Dr. Jones was he a resident or fellow. When he said "resident," I told him I was very pleased and impressed with his manner and kindness and that he "should have a very successful career." I'm sure he thought

who is this woman? But for residents he is at the top in my experience in terms of communication and compassion – which I told him as well.

Kathy Chambers spent Tues. night with me as J was in Chicago to be present at Paul's induction into the great Meat Hall of Fame—which was a five-hour ordeal.

12/14/09 We, of course, had our history making blizzard last week. John and Noah had a marvelous time plowing people out and Emma loves running and leaping in the snow. I had some smiles watching her from the kitchen window.

John gave the talk on Sun. at church re: his experience with burns and our motto of: the choices you make, the chances you take. Unfortunately I had a terrible night of pain and bad sleep so we decided it was best if I stayed home. I was sorry to miss hearing him, but he received lots of hugs and love back. And bless him he went again to the therapist last week for more insight on his "anger" outbursts. He really listens and pays attention. And, of course, fortunately he likes the therapist who has told him he needs to be seeing/doing things with people other than me. Which is true, but then there is me who can't do much without him being involved. Oh ugh—my hip/thigh and even lower leg are giving me some pain, particularly if I have been up and about too much. I am afraid to say anything to anyone but you as I don't want to go to Mayo before 1/7 and maybe it is psychosomatic.

12/31/09 All is well here. Emma is loving the frigid weather and even I am enjoying taking her out to run on the Kubota. The colder it is, the faster she runs it seems. It certainly shows how much energy is wasted all the time she is sleeping.

The holidays have been and are a non-event for us. Tonight we're having shrimp cocktail in front of the downstairs fire and playing Scrabble. I will bring in the New Year from my studio futon! Then Fri. we'll go to the cottage for a couple of days.

Follow up at Mayo at the end of the week.

John invited a young couple he had met a church a

few weeks ago over for dinner on Sat. and has invited several others for this Friday. It is the extent of our holiday entertaining.

01/09/10 Thursday I was freed from my brace and walker and can walk on both legs with a cane and I can swim and soak in the tub!!! John thought he was having knee replacement surgery this spring, but we all agreed that it was not necessary at this point. They removed 50 cc or so of liquid from his knee and gave him a cortisone shot and he feels great! Yea!

01/19/10 Overall all is well here. John, of course, continues to be a challenge, obviously some times more than others. This a.m. I am feeling irritable about him, just for small things. Plus it has been overcast for a few days and my therapist had a medical emergency this a.m. so had to cancel my appointment. Pooh! I did, though, have quite a fun time with Kathy Chambers yesterday. We had lunch at her daughter's restaurant where her parents were also lunching. Her mom is great! I really, really like her and her dad is an interesting character. We ended having a good ten minutes of belly laughs over her father and his need to plan everything in the family, way in advance (Kathy has nine siblings!). Then we proceeded to Los Aztecas for two margaritas. The most "girl fun" I have had since being with you.

I am finding my body is being much slower than previously in healing. My thigh is still quite swollen, which affects my walking—I guess some is because my thighs overlap or something like that. I have swum three times so far and loving it.

01/21/10 Oh yes, the business of living with someone after a significant period of time, I think, no matter what their issues are is an extremely difficult thing for those who have decided to finally take care of ourselves.

I have enough trouble with John's desire to decide things that in my "provincial" thinking he "shouldn't" / I don't want him to. Decorating the house/cottage is one of those. He is really hot on that and thinks about things faster than I do and then he has to do it NOW—not tomorrow or next week

If John dies before me, I would never consider living with another man and maybe not with another woman. I was quite happy making my very own decisions and running my life my way. And yes, I am feeling a bit irritated or agitated about my sweetie. The book stuff is so intense I will be happy to never hear Paul Engler's name again or anything about cattle feeding. Fortunately he landed two interns from U W Lacrosse (3½ hours away). They both have been here for a couple of days at different times. J gets energized by these young folks and they take some of the burden of putsy stuff off both of us. Best, they are somebody for J to talk to about it all.

Overall we are fine but I'd love to take another little trip alone, but I need to be stronger before he would consider letting me go (I sometimes feel like I am in captivity). Because I know my strength and pain level, I don't argue about it currently.

One other point on the BOOK is that J received a call from one of the thirty literary agents he wrote to who is very interested in taking it on and thinks it could be BIG. Now we just have to get Paul to go along.

02/01/10   John and I have finally booked a trip to Panama for 3/20-31. He was in the Peace Corps there and we have talked for years about going. So, since I am doing well—getting stronger by the day as I walk and swim regularly—we decided that this is the time to do it. We are both looking forward to it very much!

I started some private yoga lessons this evening and wow is it going to be good as it is stretching parts of my body that really need it and will help in the general strengthening.

We head to Iowa City tomorrow for six-month mammogram and visit with surgical oncologist—pretty much routine, though they stare at my films a long time as there are calcifications they're watching.

03/07/10   I am having more and more wonderful days (still some not so good, but none horrible). My thigh remains the same—double the size of the other.

There is actually a hematoma or seroma the length of my thigh! So far no fluid seems to have been reabsorbed into my body. The problem it creates is a really weird looking left side from both front and back and incredible pain some nights interfering with sleep. But last night there was none (controlled by drugs) and I think helped by a really good water workout yesterday. I walk with a cane or stick and only on occasion with the walker. So I am getting stronger day by day. I realize though that Panama will probably be a challenge walking wise, but I am reminding myself that at least I will be there seeing and doing a lot more interesting things than I am here in Dubuque.

I finally signed up this week to be a mentor to two girls at our inner city grade school where ME mentors two. And today at church we had the most wonderful service ever, though ME almost walked out—pretty interesting. I won't go into that now. But the subject was how two women in our congregation came to find out what their "ministry" or I say "mission in life." They ended by asking people to come forward and share that theirs is—I couldn't get up because I was sobbing so—one of them mentioned how lonely she had been growing up and what she was doing about that now.

It was like a wind blowing in over my head saying, "Margo, go out there and befriend children who are in need of a friend." You know I have been searching for what I should put my energies towards and today it was clear it is children. So once I get back I will explore other things I might do for/with kids.

John is working away on the book. Paul fired him about a month ago because he changed his mind on what kind of book he wanted—now it's a family history! Well, first there is not much good to write about and we think he just was getting nervous about the whole deal and second John has no interest in writing such a book. So they mutually agreed that John would go on to write a biography of Paul without any more input from Paul. So it will be solely "by John." This came about a week after John got a call from Bill Gladstone, an agent who has worked with T. Boone Pickens and other interesting people who I can't recall at the moment. And he just published a most interesting book, though ME again was bored I guess with it because it is fiction dealing with 12/21/12. In any case John and I were fascinated.

Anyway he said he wanted to represent John and Paul. We were so excited. No comment came from Paul! Perhaps he realized this could actually turn out to be a published book. But who knows. J feels huge relief as I guess all he was getting from P was negative comments/criticisms of how he was approaching things and what he was writing about. So we're happy. Then a couple weeks later J received a call from a Wiley editor expressing interest in the book!

04/07/10   It was interesting being in Panama. I felt totally divorced and uninterested in Dubuque or even life here. I feel like I live in space, some place unconnected to anything and hardly anybody. Fortunately John really likes it here and I just try not to think about it. Maybe one day it will feel like home (don't say anything to Mary Ellyn about these comments).

Panama was over the top! Everything went smoothly. John's worrying was controlled some by meeting great taxi drivers who either were our tour guide or led us out of or into the city, which does not have street signs and many streets are one way and you don't know it until you are about to turn, plus, of course, traffic is very heavy. Plus we flew first class (the only way I could have handled the long flights and had wheelchairs to take us through customs and to luggage—a great help). It was hot and steamy, which I sort of enjoyed. The people and scenery were magnificent and it was terrific to finally be in the little town of Rio Serena where J was in the Peace Corps forty years ago and to imagine getting there on rocky, muddy roads. J is writing a blog which I will share, which will tell the fun stories of our adventures. He really did not think we would pull this trip off; his worrying self apparently thought I would fall or dislocate the hip or some such tragedy would occur so he is thrilled as am I. A trip of a lifetime.

Yesterday I met and spent time with my second and third grade girls who I am mentoring until the end of the year and probably into next. They are very sweet and bright young ladies—so I am thrilled with that. Tomorrow I am committing to spending the day painting! I have put it off and put it off long enough. It gave me great joy when I did it in VA so it is time to rekindle that.

Spring is mostly here—the grass is green, green and we have daffodils blooming. I will be getting my bike out soon; surgeon said no kayaking (boo—but I understand as he reminded me that there probably can never be another surgery on my hip!). And gardening, he prefers I stand and cultivate and have someone else do the ground work, though he said I could bend forward from a chair to do some. No sitting on the ground and pulling myself up, which surprised me. So I am not thrilled with his ideas, but he's the expert, right??

John is good. He took a total holiday from the book, which I had requested, so he'll slowly move back into it. His agent has not yet landed a publisher. His best friend and one I love is dying of mesothelioma—he'd been in remission for the last six months, but it has returned with a vengeance. It's so sad as he is a very lively, bright guy and we both will miss him greatly, but it is the first real friend J has had in years so it is doubly sad.

05/10/10   As for me, overall I am very good, though I have some weeks where I do not feel quite right and so don't have the motivation to seek people out or obviously think about them (ME as major example). Last week I suffered severe pain at night in my thigh, knee and calf keeping me from good sleep and then I had GI probs plus I was working on updating John's directory using my new computer with Windows 7 which is taking some time to acclimate to. Blah, blah, blah. The last couple of days that side has swollen more and the hip itself has been aching—my dream would be that my surgeon was here in town so I could easily consult with him.

07/14/10   I will write more tomorrow. All is overall good; I just continue to have issues to deal with and last night I realized that I am sitting in a low level depression and need to find a good psychiatrist to help me with medications. There is lots to share.

08/18/10   Fortunately I had a wonderful time in Minneapolis. The complete high was disrupted by my fall Friday evening as I got out of a taxi at the hotel. I had stood up and somehow tripped on my feet and before I knew it I was falling backwards—tried to turn so my right side took the big hit and the back of my head—had a big lump which by morning and the help of ice disappeared. Of course I was beside myself. So upset that I did it and so concerned about my falling (it has happened too many times). My brother and sister-in-law came over for a while to calm me and to check on me. I waited until John had picked me up in LaCrosse to tell him. All week I was very clear about how weak I am and how much I really, really need to listen to him.

We received a surprise invitation to the wedding of CJ, our former high school male helper in Lexington, for September 25. John immediately said let's go—I was amazed and thrilled. So we will go to Lexington for four days or so. Maybe it'll be when you are in Crozet?

Since returning home on Saturday and falling again in my bedroom I have felt pretty miserable – not sleeping except when I am in a chair, having minimal energy – but I had my first real PT appointment yesterday and will have 3/week for a while. I am so terribly weak so I am hopeful this will help.

I hope we can talk soon—no energy for emailing. John asked me this p.m. if I would stay at the cottage for at least a week as he is feeling extremely stressed out by my unstableness, tiredness, etc. I am so glad he asked me as I have been very worried about him having to cope with me. So out we both go tomorrow. He will stay for two nights and then leave me out there. It will be good.

08/23/10   It would be a blessing if you called. We are one hour behind you. I have PT from 11-12 today and then doctor at 2:30.

08/24/10   Well I am a day late in my responses to you. I apologize but these days I am not at my computer much so this is my first time on since yesterday a.m. My schedule for the rest of the week is:

Rest of today I am free and available all day and evening.

Tomorrow I am off to swim and to PT, back by 1 and home the rest of the day.

Thursday—free all day until 5:30 when I hopefully will be off to meet with some of my church group.

Friday—gone most of the day.

Saturday and Sunday—I have no plans.

I am lying low to heal—I am going to get a TENS unit this week to see if that will eliminate or reduce pain. So far the doc can't detect any reason for my other concerns. I have little if any energy to be with people.

I am on to looking for hotel in Lexington—if John and I decide to do our two-room deal you could then bed down with me for a night, depending on schedules.

08/25/10   Today has been one of my better days of late. Actually slept very soundly for six hours in my chair—really the only way I seem to be able to get comfortable enough to fall asleep. I actually got up about 7:30 (a rare occurrence for me). And today I came home from PT with a TENS apparatus and hope that it will provide some relief more regularly as last night was due to 10 mg of oxytocin.

08/26/10   I am SO excited that we will be able to get together that week—I am crying thinking about it. There are some miracles and I believe this is one. I so need to be amongst friends like you. Hopefully we can give each other some loving energy and laughs.

I received a TENS unit yesterday so have been trying to find thigh tissue that is not scar tissue so that there is some conductivity. I have found, not surprisingly, that my thigh has lots and lots of scar tissue.